ISSUES IN KARTVELIAN STUDIES

Edited by

Tamar Makharoblidze

Ilia State University, Georgia

Series in Language and Linguistics

VERNON PRESS

In the Americas:
Vernon Press
1000 N West Street, Suite 1200,
Wilmington, Delaware 19801
United States

In the rest of the world:
Vernon Press
C/Sancti Espiritu 17,
Malaga, 29006
Spain

Series in Language and Linguistics

Library of Congress Control Number: 2022939749

ISBN: 978-1-64889-475-6

Cover design by George Bagrationi. Grunge background image designed by aopsan / Freepik.

Table of Contents

Maria Polinsky
University of Maryland College Park

Nancy Clarke
Amazon AWS AI

Michaela Socolof
McGill University

Svetlana Berikashvili
Georg-August University of Göttingen; Ilia State University

Irina Lobzhanidze
Ilia State University

Yidian She
Université Paul Valéry Montpellier

Léa Nash
Université Paris 8/CNRS, France

Tamar Makharoblidze
Ilia State University, Georgia

Ekaterine Nanitashvili
Ilia State University, Georgia; Georg-August University of Göttingen, Germany

List of Figures and Tables

Figures

Tables

Introduction

Georgia is a part of the Caucasus region, located at the intersection of Eastern Europe and Western Asia. It is bounded to the west by the Black Sea, to the north and east by Russia, to the south by Turkey and Armenia, and to the southeast by Azerbaijan. Georgia covers a territory of 69,700 square kilometers (26,911 sq mi), and its approximate population is about 3.716 million.

Georgia is a motherland of Iberian or Kartvelian languages: Georgian, Svan, Megrelian and Laz. This is a language family indigenous to the South Caucasus and spoken primarily in Georgia. In addition, the Georgian sign language is a natural language of Deaf and Hard of Hearing people in Georgia. The language disintegration scheme below shows this process:

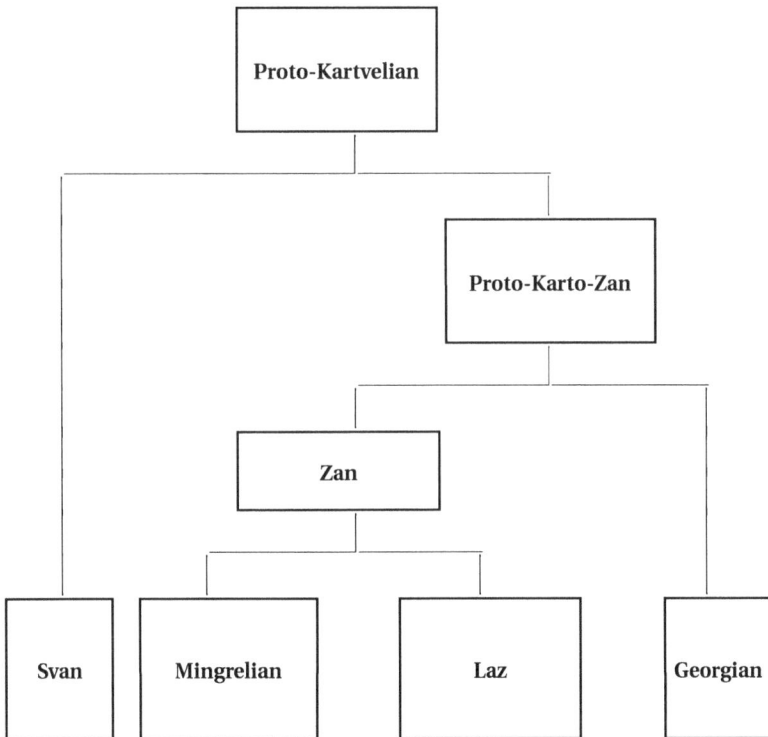

The Kartvelian Studies has a pretty long history covering all fields of humanitarian sciences – linguistics, history, religion and culture. This volume offers the works of the best scholars of Kartvelian studies of the recent period. This is a fairly diverse collection, which is mostly devoted to a wide range of linguistic works, such as descriptive studies of the Kartvelian languages and the Georgian sign language along with some theoretical contribution, dialectology, lexicography, psycholinguistics and computational linguistics, as well as history, ethnography, religion and educational issues. These articles are not only the best studies of Kartvelology, but they also clearly show the contribution of Kartvelology to world science.

This is the first volume of its kind in English, and I hope that the reader will learn a lot about Kartvelian studies and enjoy this book.

Editor
Professor Tamar Makharoblidze
School of Arts and Sciences
Ilia State University
Tbilisi. Georgia.
tamar.makharoblidze@iliauni.edu.ge

Linguistics:
Kartvelian Languages

Chapter 1

Hints at Georgian Dialect History:
A Study in Miniature

Jean Leo Leonard

Paul Valéry University Montpellier 3, France

Abstract

This study proposes a set of hypotheses on the formation of the Georgian Dialect Network (GDN) from the standpoint of *Language Dynamics* and *Complex Systems Theory*, through a *model* articulated on ten fundamental notions from General Dialectology: (L1: *L* standing for *Layer*) *The Dialect Split Layer* (DSL), (L2) *The Buffer Zone Effect* (BZE); (L3) *Variable Bleeding* (VB), i.e., *Relative Chronology* (Scalar Change); (L4) *The Feature Pool Effect*; (L5) *Emerging Isolates* (EI) or singleton or dendrographic outliers; (L6) *The Center-Periphery Effect* (CPE), i.e., the Bartolian centre/periphery intercourse; (L7) *Phonolexical Endemic Patterns* (PLEP); (L8) *Word Geography* (WG), i.e., lexical diffusion; (L9) *Local Semantic Shifts* (LSS); (L10) *External Factors* (EF). A database of 243 cognates compiled from classical sources referenced in Georgian dialectology allowed quantitative tests for dialect clustering using *Gabmap* (i.e., Levenshtein algorithm), with particular attention to *Hierarchical Clustering, Difference Maps, Multiscalar Dimension Plots*, and *Weighed Average + Group Average Probability* clouds). It results from this first endeavour in Dialect Dynamics applied to the GDN a certain number of orientations for future research in Georgian dialectology and sociophonetics, in particular on the properties of type L1-4 and L5-6 of this diasystemic topology, which highlight some deep patterns of organization. These prospects could turn out to be heuristic, and could help to lay the groundwork for a dialectometry applied to the GDN, in partnership with current projects, such as the *Georgian Dialect Corpus*. Further research should focus, e.g., on L7-10, in order to explore more superficial levels of diffusional trends.

Keywords: Language Dynamics, Levenshtein algorithm, computational Dialectology, Dialectology, Georgia, Georgian, Dialects, Caucasus

***

1.1. Introduction

Anyone familiar with the historiography of dialectology will have noticed the title of this chapter is a tribute to Sarah Gudschinsky's seminal paper (1958) on the history of a Mesoamerican language –Mazatec. Moreover, I also have a debt with another impressive piece of scholarship on a similar topic, yet applied in this case to the Caucasus and a region located in north-eastern Georgia: Johanna Nichols' article (2004) on « The Origin of the Chechen and Ingush: A Study in Alpine Linguistic and Ethnic Geography ». These contributions made a decisive step forward in their respective fields: on the one hand, designing an elegant model for the description of geolinguistic dynamics from both internal and external factors, on the other hand, applying Victor Murra's concept of the Vertical Archipelago (Murra, 1956, 1985) to the Caucasus, which makes it possible to embrace a vast number of phenomena of population dynamics, settlements and interactions in space and time within a unified ecological framework. A third source of inspiration also triggered the tentative approach I will present here on Georgian dialect history and dynamics: Alexei Kassian's endeavor (2015) to test algorithmic complexity on Lezgian languages (North Caucasus). Kassian tests a wide array of quantitative methods (distance-based, as StralingNJ, NJ, UPGMA versus character-based, as Bayesian MCMC, UPM) to match the available "standard classification" or "received taxonomy" of Lezgian languages, obtained through qualitative analysis of cognates (in other terms: through isoglosses, i.e., types and trivial characters). Kassian's approach reminds of the Popperian falsificationist methodology, which entails that scientific knowledge makes steps ahead, through the plausibility of hypothesis or results to be confirmed or denied by further evidence or alternative methods (Popper, 1934, 1963). Results of any scientific inquiry are not given once and for all: they should be designed so as to yield fruitful response to validity testing, and to falsificatory procedures (here, in sections 3.1-3, confronting the output of Figure 1.1 in section 2).

I will refer to *Gudschinsky's Model of Dialect Dynamics*[1] as GMDD, whose premises are sketched in (1). In terms of general systemics, L1-3 (L stands for *Layer*) are ascending variables, i.e., competing to enhance the dialect network inner diversity, and giving its external shape (*emergence*). L4 and L7 entail *flows of information* and models (structural patterns, paradigms). L5 is typically a generative parameter, either local or regional. L6 can be defined as a strongly dynamic parameter of self-organization (*autopoesis*), which modifies the spatial structure and the thread of the dialect network – as an anamorphosis distorting physical space, to give shape to the topology of the network. L8

---

[1] *Dialect Dynamics* is a component of *Language Dynamics*, intended here as in Heinsalu et al. (2020).

is typically extensive and diffusional (*centrifugal flow of information*), whereas L9 is typically intensive and structurally introverted (*centripetal self-organization*). L10 should be accounted for as a model of more or less compelling external pressure (political power and the conditioning of social agentivity and interactivity between speakers).

(1)   The GMDD applied to the Georgian Dialect Network (GDN):
        L = (geolinguistic or areal) Layer.

L1: The Dialect Split Layer (DSL). This level of analysis accounts for the main divisions of a dialect network, such as West *versus* Center and East in the "Standard Classification" of Georgian dialects (SCGD). This major level of division involves e.g., sound changes akin to the "Neogrammarian Laws" (Machavariani, 1965; Gamkrelidze, 2005), such as the famous hissing-hushing obstruent division (Asatiani, 2008) or the /a/ vs. /o/ opposition between Georgian and Zan at Kartvelian level, but also within the Georgian Dialect Network (GDN). The geolinguistic contrast between varieties preserving modal and glottalized uvulars, such as / q, q ʼ / also works to some extent as a L1 variable, though allophonic variation is fairly high in current speech and may vary according to idiolects and sources, resulting in some subsequent blurring from a synchronic standpoint.

L2: the Buffer Zone Effect (BZE). Once main dialect divisions appear in a common language as a result of DSL variables, a trend to areal overlapping generally occurs as a by-product of social interaction, contextual or free variation between neighboring dialects. At a higher level, the Central area in the GDN stands as a buffer zone between East and West of the domain.

L3: Variable Bleeding (VB). A DSL (i.e., L1, above) entails subsequent complexification or simplification of the sound law or structural change at stake –relative chronology generally accounts for the intricacy and the hierarchization of this process. This trend may also feed the latter one (BZE), or focus on one or both divisions, enhancing further splits and differentiation, at sub-dialect levels (the north-eastern area in the East and the Gurian area in the South-West provide good examples of this trend).

L4: **The Feature Pool[2] Effect, First Grade (FPE I)**: structural polymorphism, especially systemic trends to a certain probability of contextual or free variation.

---

[2] A *Feature pool* can be defined as a complex set of variants available for the same function, more or less freely available to speakers of a dialect network, as in a Creole continuum, or mingled together in mixed varieties. Diversity of free variants in competition blurs dialect frontiers, and makes up a *pool* –or a *pond*– of variation quite different from the "traditional dialect/sociolect" settings (Mufwene, 2001, 2013).

L5: **Emerging Isolates (EI)**, as the rise of single dialects[3], out of local rules and idiosyncratic trends (as *bVr* > *brV* metathesis in the South-Western dialect, see *bevri* 'much' –item 1, Table 1.2 below). The labiopalatalisation of front vowels in Ingilian for items 1 'much,' 3 'mill' and 7 'side' in Table 1.2 (Grg *bevri* INGIL[4] *bövrü*; Grg *ciskvili* INGIL *cückül*; Grg *gverdi* INGIL *görd*) gives further examples, for a singleton variety, out of contact with Azeri Turkish, due to typological areal convergence).

L6: **The Center-Periphery Effect (CPE)**, or the *Bartolian effect* (Bartoli, 1945), which predicts the high probability of centrifugal *versus* centripetal phenomena of diffusion in any geolinguistic space. According to this trend, central innovations expand in space and time, yet being hindered or blocked by retentions at the periphery. Dialect zones located in compartimentalized highlands, such as the North East PSH, MOX, MTIU/GUD and TUSH, or located in areas far from the main centers of diffusion of leading town dialects, or whose populations have migrated abroad (INGIL, FEREY) tend to belong to these so-called 'lateral zones.' The CPE is cyclical: it may work at macrolevel (the whole GDN) or at regional levels (e.g., H&L IMR, and to some extend L-GUR behave as centrifugal, leading dialects interacting with surrounding sub-dialects, as LCHK or ADJA). The main center of gravity of the GDN indeed lays around the KAR dialect in the central part of the country, in strong historical interaction with the KAXET dialect, in the East.

L7: **Phonolexical Endemic Patterns (PLEP)** could be called *The Feature Pool Effect, second Grade* (FPE II). In this case, the diversity of morphophonological rules of surface realizations, at what can be called phonolexical level, blurs variation patterns, as item 8 'come' aorist 3Sg, in Table 1.2: GRG *movida*; XEV *mavi*; PSH *moida*; MOX *movida*; MTIU *moida*; RACH *mevida*; H-IMR *mevida*; L-IMR *mouda*; IMRX *mojda*; GUR *mevida*. Too many micro-scale interactions occur in the syllabic template between adjacent onsets and nuclei, out of homorganic contact of -*ov*- in the stem, with redundant [Labial] feature for *o* and *v*, making geolinguistic patterns undecidable. Most of these microtrends do not make up a clear-cut regular sound law, resulting in another type of dialectical feature pool.

L8: **Word Geography (WG)**, or lexical diffusion. Items may not be comparable cognates either because of different structural choices in the inherited lexicon and/or semantic shifts (as *testa* versus *capo, cabeza, chef* in Romance

---

[3] The term 'isolate' here points at any dialect variety which strongly differs to some extent from average variation within the Georgian Dialect Continuum. By no means we intend a 'phylogenetic isolate', here.

[4] Abbreviations for Georgian dialect varieties are given in Table 1.1 below.

languages for 'head'), or out of complex processes of derivation, blurring the calculability of cognates in the word list (at least for automated dialectometry).

L9: **Local Semantic Shifts** (**LSS**): not handled here; nevertheless, some of these items may still be used for comparison at phonological level, in our data processing.

L10: **External Factors (EF)**: history, geography and geopolitics, competing native or foreign hegemony and superimposed contact languages, etc. In this respect, one could argue that from the standpoint of Braudelian "Long Duration," the main division between Kartvelian languages (Svan and Zan in the West, Georgian in the Central and Eastern part of contemporary Georgia) reminds the geopolitic contrast, in ancient times, between the kingdom of Colchis versus the Kingdom of Iberia in Western and Central-Eastern Georgian –with Argveti as a former "buffer zone." Later on, the same division within the GDN still holds, with a strong influence of foreign hegemonies (Turkey in the West, Persia in the East). Although this is a fascinating issue, I will avoid handling it here, but I hope the diversity of interpretations which flows from the various dialectometric topologies I will highlight can be used by more acknowledged specialists –historians and geographers–, as the title of this paper suggests: *hints* at Georgian dialect history.'

In section 2, I will first describe the structure of the data used in this chapter. I will present the canonical classification of Georgian dialects, as a compass to make our way into the maze of the Georgian dialect network. I will provide samples of the data (Tables 1.2-4), and give an account of the processing of the totality of the database, before testing results on the basis of smaller sets of cognates. I will therefore survey three subsets of data, corresponding to a bunch of phonological variables. First, the hissing-hushing fricatives and affricates, as a prototypical DSL (Dialect Split Layer) variable; second, the uvular stops and ejectives, as a false DSL and a genuine polymorphic and unstable variable (FPE); third, the labialized stops (Cv), which will provide evidence of the Bartolian dynamic field (CPE), and highlight some trends of the FPE and EI – to some extent. Then, I will close the chapter by establishing a link between what General Dialectology may provide to a specific field of research as Kartvelian studies, and how, in turn, Kartvelian studies may enrich considerably General Dialectology.

1.2. Data Processing: The Standard Taxonomy of Georgian Dialects vs. Alternative Topologies

I will use a database compiled by Hélène Gérardin (Inalco, Paris) in 2018, within the framework of the IDEX EMERGENCE project LaDyCa (*Language Dynamics in the Caucasus*), a *Complexity Theory* and *Language Dynamics* project carried out at Sorbonne University in 2017-18 (Léonard, 2019, 2017), and two sets of dialectometric results: from Flore Picard's quantitative processing of 243 cognates on *Gabmap* and *Gephi* (Picard et al., 2018). Table 1.1 shows the SCGD (thus, the standard dialect network taxonomy of Georgian dialects) according to Gigineishvili, Topuria, and K'avtaradze (1961)[5]. Table 1.2.1 provides a sample of the LaDyCa 2018 database by Hélène Gérardin (Inalco). Abbreviations used in this chapter to refer to the 22 dialect varieties surveyed are given in Table 1.1, within brackets (IMR, GUR, KAR, etc.).

Table 1.1. The Gigineishvili, Topuria, and K'avtaradze (1961) Georgian dialect classification

West		East		
Northwest dialects	**Southwest dialects**	**Central dialects**	**Northeast dialects**	**Eastern dialects**
Imeretian (Imeruli, იმერული) [IMR]	Gurian (Guruli, გურული) [GUR]	Kartlian (Kartluri, ქართლური) [KAR]	Mokhevian (Mokheuri, მოხეური) [MOX]	Kakhetian (Kakhuri, კახური) [KAXET]
Lechkhumian (Lečkhumuri, ლეჩხუმური) [LCHX]	Adjarian (Ačaruli, აჭარული) [ADJA]	Meskhian (Meskhuri, მესხური) [MESH]	Mtiuletian-Gudamaqrian (Mtiulur-Gudamaqruli, მთიულურ-გუდამაყრული) [MTIU] [GUD]	Tianetian (Tianeturi, თიანეთური)
Rachan (Račuli, რაჭული) [RACH]	Imerkhevian (Imerkheuli, იმერხეული) [Turkey, Imerkhevi] [IMRX]	Javakhian (Javakhuri, ჯავახური)	Khevsurian (Khevsuruli, ხევსურული) [XEV]	Ingiloan (Ingilouri, ინგილოური) [NW Azerbaijan] [INGIL]
	Taoan[6] [TAO]		Pshavian (Phšauri, ფშაური) [PSH]	Fereydanian (Phereidnuli, ფერეიდნული) [Iran] [FEREY]
			Tushetian (Tušuri, თუშური) [TUSH]	

Source: https://en.wikipedia.org/wiki/Georgian_dialects[7] (modified)

---

[5] NB : also quoted in quoted in a reference paper, such as (Tuite, 1989:5).

[6] Not mentioned in the source of Table 1.1, but documented in our database. See Chokharadze et al. 2018 about the social history of this south-western variety, mostly spoken in Eastern Turkey.

[7] See map Online on https://commons.wikimedia.org/wiki/File:Georgian_dialects.svg.

One of the technical problems arising from this kind of second-hand compilation of dialectical cognates from a complex set of written sources (see Appendix 2 for a sample) lays in the empty cells (filled with a low bar – in the tables). A first data processing has therefore been achieved according to a cascade model, computing dyads of each variety compared to the whole corpus separately, in order to thereafter unify the results in a single matrix (see Appendix 1).

Table 1.2. A sample of the LaDyCa database, by Hélène Gérardin (Inalco)

	1	2	3	4	5	6	7	8
	'much'	'we'	'mill'	'horse'	'one'	'wolf'	'side'	'come' AOR3Sg
GRG	*bevri*	*čven*	*ciskvili*	*cxeni*	*erti*	*mgeli*	*gverdi*	*movida*
XEV	*bevr*	*čven*	*ciskvili*	*cxeni*	*erti*	*mgeli*	*gverdi*	*mavi*
PSH	*bevri*	*čven*	*ciskvili*	*cxeni*	*erti*	*mgeli*	*gverdi*	*moida*
MOX	*bevri*	*čon*	*ciskwili*	*sxeni*	*erti*		*gördi*	*movida*
MTIU	*bevri*	*čon*	*cviskvili*	*cxeni*	*erti*	*mgeli*	*gordi*	*moida*
GUD	___	*čven*	*cviskvili*	*cxeni*	*erti*	___	___	___
TUSH	___	___	___	*cxenĭ*	*ertĭ*	*geli*	*gverdĭ*	*moid*
KAR	*bevri*	*čwen*	*ciskvili*	*cxeni*	*erti*	*geli*	*gwerdi*	*moida*
KAXET	*bewri*	*čwen*	*ciskvili*	*cxeni*	*erti*	*mgeli*	*gverdi*	*moida*
KIZIQ	*bewri*	*čwen*	*ciskvili*	*cxeni*	*erti*	*mgeli*	*gverdi*	*moida*
FEREY	*bevri*	*čön*	*ciskili*	*cxeni*	*erti*	*geli*	*gerdi*	*moida*
INGIL	*bövrü*	*čon*	*cückül*	*cxen*	*er*	*gel*	*görd*	___
MESH	*bevri*	*čön*	*ciksvili*	*cxeni*	*jerti*	*ngeli*	*gördi*	___
RACH	*bevri*	*čven*	*ciskvili*	*cxeni*	*erti*	*geli*	*gverdi*	*mevida*
H-IMR	*brevi*	*čwen*	*ciskvili*	*cxeni*	*jerti*	*geli*	*gverdi*	*mevida*
L-IMR	*brevi*	*čwen*	*ciskvili*	*cxeni*	*jerti*	*geli*	*gverdi*	*mouda*
LCHX	*brevli*	*čvene*	___	___	___	*geli*	*gverdi*	___
ADJA	*bewri*	*čven*	*cxeli*	*cxvari*	*ʔēti*	___	___	___
TAO	*bewri*	*čwen*	*ciskwili*	___	*ēti*	*geli*	___	___
IMRX	*bewri*	*čwen*	*ciskwili*	*cxeni*	___	*geli*	*gwerdi*	*mojda*
H-GUR	*bewri*	*čwen*	*ciskpili*	*cxeni*	*eti*	*geli*	*gverdi*	*mevida*
L-GUR	*breuli*	*čwen*	*ciskpili*	*cxeni*	*eti*	*geli*	*gverdi*	*mevida*

The LaDyCa Georgian Dialect Database provides the following set of results (figure 1.1), for the whole set of cognates (n = 243). I suggest some basic tenets for reading the Gabmap[8] figures, as in Kassian (*op. cit.*): first, distinguish between a

---

[8] Gabmap is a free software for dialectometry using the Levenshtein algorithm, or "editing distance", (Levenshtein 1966) hosted by CLARIN (v. Http://portal.clarin.nl). See

core-area or a core-cluster *versus* its outlier(s); second: apply cyclically this technique to the inner structure of each set of clades; third, point at putative Gudschinsky's Model (the GMDD), as a tentative orientation for further potential research, especially from the standpoint of EF (External Factors: L10) –although I will remain cautious in this respect. For instance, the dendrogram in Fig. 1.1a is based on Ward's Method (hierarchical clustering). I deliberately decided to generate five clades at each step of the computation, no more, in order to match the standard taxonomy for the GDN, as exposed in Table 1.1.

Figure 1.1. The LaDyCa Georgian Dialect Database: 243 cognates

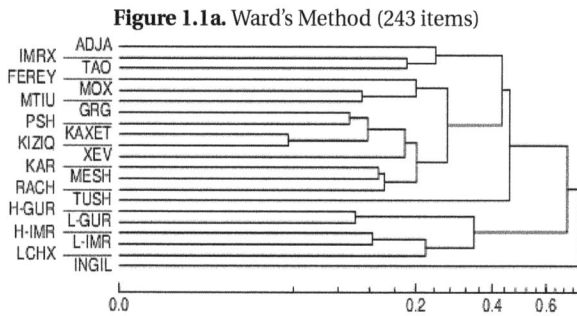

Figure 1.1a. Ward's Method (243 items)

Figure 1.1b. Statistical distribution of differences

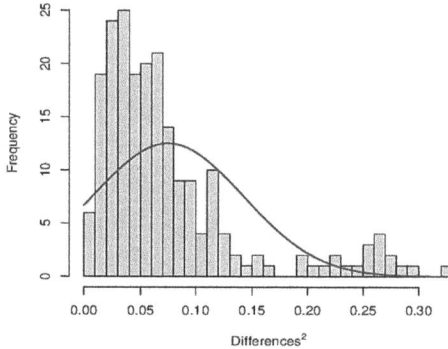

Leinonen et al. (2016), accessible at https://www.sciencedirect.com/science/article/pii/S0024384115000315.

Figure 1.1c. Multidimensional scaling (r = 0,88)

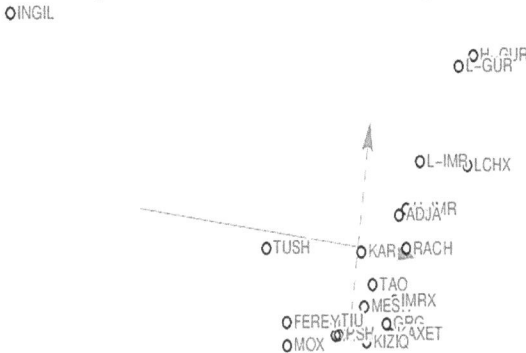

Figure 1.1d. Probabilistic dendrogram (Weighed average + Group Average; limit 60%, noise: 0,2)

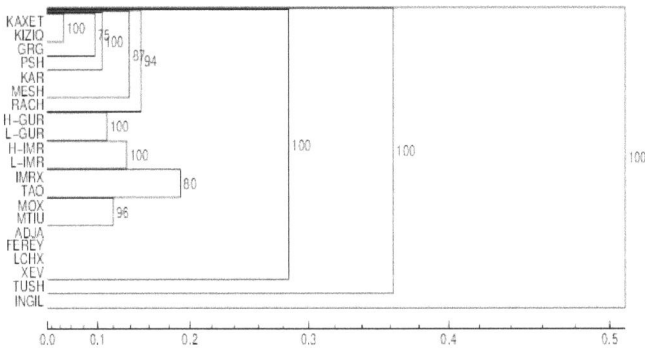

At first sight, a massive core stands in the upper part of the tree, from FEREY to RACH, including most of Eastern and Central varieties of the GDN. Three peripheral southwestern varieties make up its outlier, which can be explained as an obvious expression of Bartolian CPE. The whole complex has TUSH, a typical isolate (EI) belonging to the eastern complex, as a peripheral outlier. Now, the core of western Georgian appears clearly as a competing center of innovations, with GUR on the one hand, and IMR on the second hand. LCHX happens to play the same role as an outlier to this group as TUSH did for the core-cluster of Central-Eastern Georgian (as a kernel group), associated to the distant south-western periphery. Now, if we apply GMDD –our geolinguistic modelling of the output of our Gabmap testing– to each set of clades, the central-eastern core shows up with an intricate and massive topology, which suggests this area has been evolving toward a Feature Pool (L4: FPE I), rather than a confederation of clear-cut distinct dialects –whereas the Western segment of the GDN seems to have split into a twofold network: on the one hand, a recessive, peripheral zone, associated to the central-eastern complex, on the other hand, a fairly innovative, consistent and compact central-western confederation of dialects, including IMR/LCHK and GUR (cf. L6: CPE). The remainder, INGIL, at the periphery of the whole GDN, should be considered as a singleton, embedded in a strong field of interference with Azeri abroad. Both core areas emerge as competitors, with satellite isolates as outliers of their clades: respectively TUSH (which has undergone intense contact with Tova-Tush, a Nakh-Daghestanian language) and INGIL (intense contact with a Turkish language: Azeri) –here, languages in contact as an EF (external Factor) goes without saying.

The subsequent figures 1.1b-d provide more information about the statistical structure of the sample (Fig. 1.1b) and the probability of the inner structure of the topology (Fig. 1.1d). In short, the former shows that the sample has a strong negative skewness (tail to the left: smaller or rather simplex differences occur more frequently than complex, heterogeneous differences); the latter reveals interesting patterns, as the IMRX/TAO cluster in the center of the diagram, which matches more optimally the standard taxonomy (i.e., SCGD) than in Figure 1.1 dendrogram. Figure 1.1c strikingly confirms the trend of the bulk of central-eastern dialects to make up rather a Feature Pool (L6: Feature Pool I) than a clear-cut segment of the dialect network with competing components. The lower arrow points to this trend, while the upper one confirms the GDN unfolds as a dialect network proper (instead of a Feature Pool), as we proceed to the West: first to ADJA, then to IMR, and ultimately to GUR. The position of INGIL at the opposite side of the scale, to the left, confirms its status as an emerging isolate (EI) – out of exogenous contact, as already mentioned. Fig. 1.1d has the advantage of summing up two alternative computing techniques (Group Average and Weighed Average), making discrete blocks more salient within the dendrographic inner structure. I will therefore systematically use these four representations of data: hierarchical clustering, statistical distribution of differences, MDS plot and probabilistic dendrogram.

In other words, what this set of data shows does not basically contradict the standard taxonomy, as it opposes the Western part and the Central-Eastern part of the GDN. Nevertheless, it blurs the inner frontiers and subdivisions, and it splits the Western area in two. It therefore fulfills its promises: quantitative methods are more designed to enrich and challenge qualitative methods than to match them straightforwardly. One expects heuristic values –*hints*– from their results, instead of a faithful picture of what was already available for public knowledge and enlightenment. The GMDD provides inspiring insights into diasystemic trends evolving or having evolved at different stages of the history of the GDN, from the initial putative DSL (the major dialect split) to the Bartolian CPE, through the emergence of competing dialects (IMR/IMRX and GUR) and emerging isolates (TUSH, INGIL).

1.3. Testing Non-Intersecting Subsets of Data

Another important consequence of the GMDD method lays in its heuristic properties: the ten layers (L1-10) may be used as a compass to select subsets of variables, and check to what extent they match with conventional taxonomies. The product of this confrontation always turns out to be heuristic.

1.3.1. Hissing-Hushing Obstruents

Table 1.3 shows six out of the eight cognates processed for results in Figure 1.2a-d (to which items 2 'we' and 3 'mill' add up, from Table 1.2 above)[9]. As diagrams in Figure 1.2 suggest, with *Gabmap* small samples can provide fairly relevant and encouraging results. Nevertheless, fricatives and affricates are not the only variables here: they mingle with other characters, such as vowel tension (lax *ĭ* in TUSH), with a palatal expansion *-j* (approximant) or *-i* (vocoid) of the nucleus for items 13 'brother' GRG *ʒma* vs. TUSH *ʒmaj* and 14 'other' with velarized fricatives: GRG *sxva* vs. TUSH *cxvaj*, L-IMR *sxwai* and GUR *sxwai*, endemically. But at this stage of the sampling, I deem necessary not to skip off this fine grain of variation.

The output is striking, as compared to the former set of dendrograms, obtained from a comparatively huge amount of data. The dendrogram in Figure 1.2a matches considerably more the standard taxonomy (i.e., SCGD) for the Georgian Dialect Network than the previous one: two well-balanced cores are now competing: a western complex (with GUR and IMR/LECHX as a kernel block, and ADJA, IMRX and TAO as a satellite, according to Bartolian CPE) versus a Central-North-Easter core, in which GRG and KAR are properly embedded, while TUSH shows up, again, in the periphery as an outlier. The outlier cluster federates mostly eastern varieties, with a northwestern core (XEV, MTIU/GUD, MOX) as opposed to two peripheral satellites: MESH in the westernmost southeastern stripe of the territory on the one hand, and INGIL on the other hand. This clustering points more at a default condensation of statistically asymmetric objects than to any close kinship. One should not forget that genealogy is but a by-product of automated language classification than a proper phylogenetic tool, as e.g., the cladistic method applied to biological entities may be. Above all, what quantitative dialectology produces is *statistical taxonomies* –which can eventually be interpreted from a genealogical standpoint.

---

[9] Nevertheless, even with such a small sample, the data overview yields the following proportions: 22 varieties/objects, 176 instances, 925 characters (among which 29 unique characters), 886 tokens (among which 30 unique tokens). With any automated endeavour, even small may turn out big…

Table 1.3. Hissing-Hushing obstruents sample from the LaDyCa database

	9	10	11	12	13	14
	'shadow'	'back'	'straight'	'cross'	'brother'	'other'
GRG	*črdili*	*zurgi*	*ṣcori*	*žvari*	*ʒma*	*sxva*
XEV	*čdili*	*zurgi*	*ṣcori*	*žvari*	*ʒma*	*sxo*
PSH	—	—	*ṣcori*	* žvari*	*ʒma*	*sxva*
MOX	—	*zurgi*	*ṣcori*	*žori*	*ʒma*	*cxo*
MTIU	*čirdili*	*zurgi*	*ṣcori*	*žori*	*ʒma*	*sxo*
GUD	*čirdili*	—	—	*žori*	—	*sxo*
TUSH	*čdilĭ*	*zurgĭ*	*ṣcorĭ*	*žvarĭ*	*ʒmaj*	*cxvaj*
KAR	*čdili*	*zurgi*	—	—	—	*sxwa*
KAXET	*črdili*	*zurgi*	*ṣcore*	*žvari*	*ʒma*	*sxwa*
KIZIQ	*črdili*	*zurgi*	*ṣcore*	*žvari*	*ʒma*	*sxwa*
FEREY	—	*zurgi*	*̣cori*	—	*ʒma*	*sxo*
INGIL	—	—	*̣coor*	*žor*	*zmaj*	—
MESH	*čyrdili*	*zurgi*	—	—	*ʒma*	*sxua*
RACH	—	*zurgi*	*̣cori*	*žvari*	*ʒma*	*sxva*
H-IMR	*štili*	*zrugi*	*ṣtori*	*žvari*	*ʒmai*	*sxva*
L-IMR	*štili*	*zrugi*	*sori*	*žvari*	*ʒmai*	*sxwai*
LCHX	*štili*	—	*x̣cori*	*žvari*	*ʒma*	—
ADJA	*čidili*	*ʒrugi*	*ṣtori*	*žvari*	*ʒma*	*sxwa*
TAO	*čirdili*	—	—	—	*zma*	*sxwa*
IMRX	—	*zrugi*	*ṣcori*	*žwari*	*zmai*	*sxwa*
H-GUR	*čtili*	*ʒrugi*		*žwari*	*ʒmai*	*sxwai*
L-GUR	*čtili*	*zrugi*	*ṣtori*	*žwari*	*ʒmai*	*sxwai*

Figure 1.2. Hissing vs. Hushing obstruents: a sample from the LaDyCa database

Figure 1.2a. Ward's method, Eight cognates

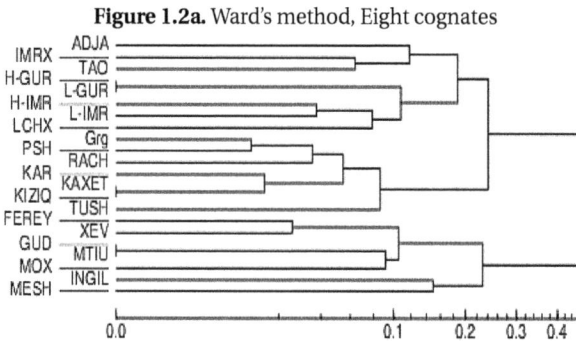

Figure 1.2b. Statistical distribution of differences

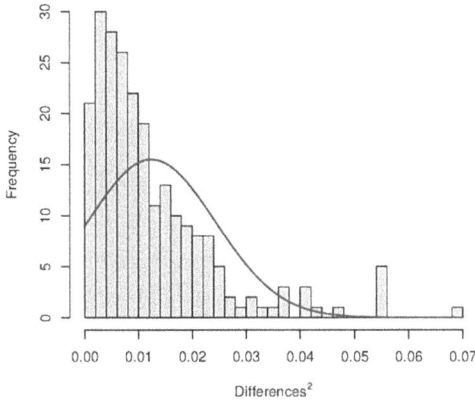

Figure 1.2c. Multidimensional scaling (r = 0,92)

Figure 1.2d. Probabilistic dendrogram (Weighed average + Group Average; limit & as previously)

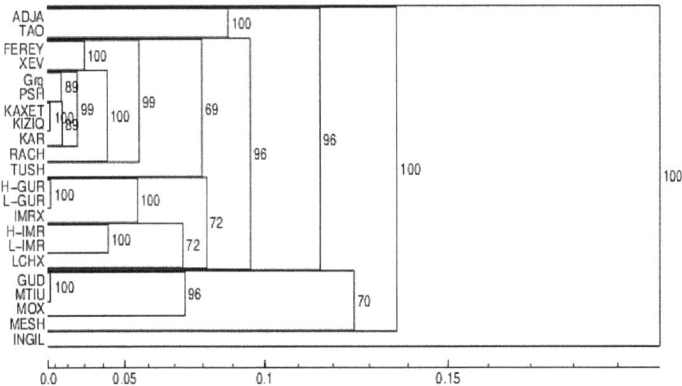

However, the topologies of the various diagrams in Figure 1.2a-d differ substantially from the previous ones in Figure 1.1a-d. The statistical distribution (Figure 1.2b) is fairly similar, with negative skewness and similar threshold of complexity, so that this small sample of hissing and hushing obstruents can be considered as a fractal of the whole database. Instead, the Muldidimensional Scaling Plot shows up as far more diffuse than in the previous figure, and most of the objects (i.e., varieties) tend to be more or less equidistant. Sections, separated by the two arrows (statistical vectors), are clear-cut, and the major central-eastern dialects, as KAR, KAXET and of course Georgian (GRG) stand as the center of gravity. In Figure 1.2d, the same impression of consistency and distinct blocs is confirmed, and probabilistic estimations range very high, except for the most peripheral varieties (index 70). A low index of 69 also points at some fuzziness at the root of the central block, though – confirming the FPE for this complex, innovative and expanding area, at the very core of the GDN.

Therefore, the hissing-hushing obstruents variable might deserve indeed the status of variables of the DSL-type at GDN level, as they have already proven to be decisive at a much higher degree of phylogenetic taxonomy, for Kartvelian languages. Nevertheless, the effect is somewhat smoothed by other factors, like VB (Variable Bleeding), in labialized contexts as for items 2, 4 (in Table 1.1), 12 and 14 (in Table 1.2), and a strong Bartolian CPE, which has strengthened the central-eastern variants all over the GDN along time. Nevertheless, some noise entered in the processing of the variable, as other variables (such as the endemic -i stem extensions, vowel laxity, etc.) were not skipped off, in order to cling to "real," raw data. In the next set of results, I will make sure this noise does not interfere, in order to test its effect on the ouptut.

1.3.2. The Uvular Stops Variable

Uvular stops, simplex and ejective (as in GRG *cq̇ali* 'water,' XEV *q̇orci* 'meat' vs. GRG *xorci*) also range among the dialectically relevant variables to analyze. The next set of results mostly concerns uvular onsets, in strong position, free from all other variables.

Figure 1.3. Uvular stops, simplex and ejective[10]. Results from *Gabmap*

Figure 1.3a. Ward's Method, 5 clusters

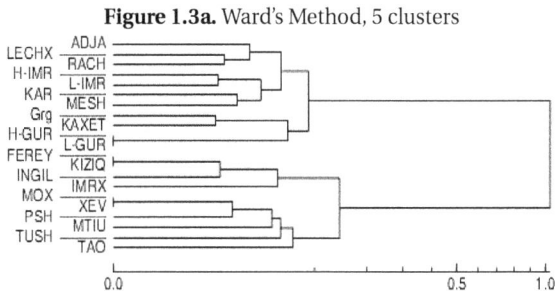

Figure 1.3b. Difference map

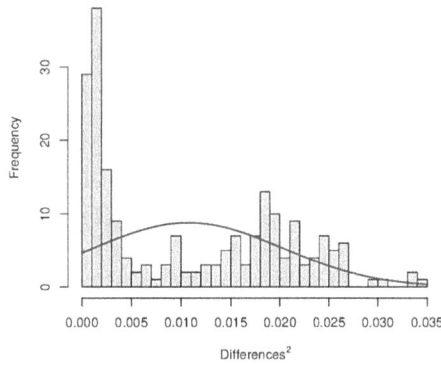

Figure 1.3c. MDS plot (r = 0,98)

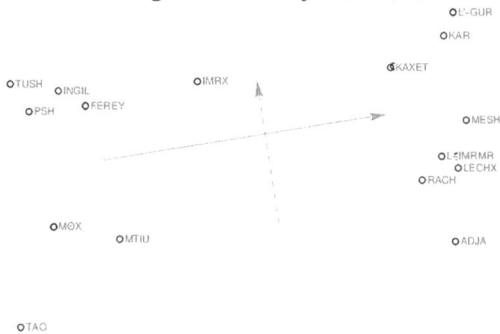

---

[10] Size of the sample: 21 varieties, 10 cognates/items, 210 instances, 1068 characters (23 unique), 1025 tokens (24 unique).

Figure 1.3d. Probabilistic dendrogram

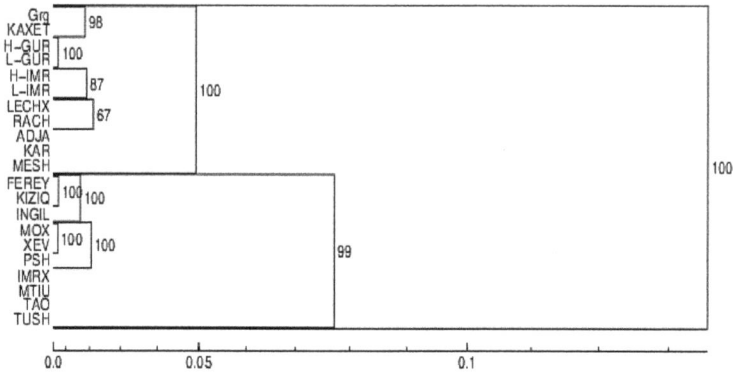

This topology is nevertheless rather fuzzy, although patterns are clear-cut (see Figure 1.3c: a much scattered MDS plot, with no center of gravity, and bundles of more or less equidistant objects). The East-Center vs. West division is blurred (KAR is included in the Westen cluster; Grg and KAXET mingle with GUR, in the upper clade of Figure 1.3a). The core of the diasystem is missing here, as in the MDS plot. The lower clade in Figure 1.3c does capture indeed the "easternness" of the diaspora varieties of FEREY (in Iran) and INGIL (in Azerbaijan), for the first time in our dendrographic survey, associating them with KIZIQ, but the fact these varieties can cluster here with a south-western subdialect as IMRX is embarrassing. Moreover: the fact that KIZIQ is separated from KAXET, in two different major clades, is simply a serious flaw. The lower clade is a trifle (but not much) better: the clustering of all north-eastern varieties in the kernel of the clade is good news –with TUSH as a satellite in this microtopology, as it could be expected. But the fact that this kernel clusters with such a far distant southwestern variety as TAO sounds like bad news, even if it shows up here as a default excentric object. In short, not much can be saved from this experiment of trying to get the purest of an allegedly heuristic variable – the uvular stops –, and of suppressing the "noise" induced by the occurrence of other variables in the subset of data. In fact, anyone familiar with uvular stops (and uvular ejectives) in the world's languages could have suspected this result. The explosive phase in these phonological segments is so prone to allophonic variation that one should better not bet too much on them for diasystemic taxonomy.[11]

---

[11] See http://aldelim.org/ and in particular http://dalima.aldelim.org/ for Easten Mayan languages. We also noticed much allophonic variation between the plosive and the fricative realization of uvular stops and ejectives in Totonaco-Tepehua doing fieldwork in 2015 in the state of Puebla, Mexico.

Therefore, the characterization of the uvular stop and ejective variable can by no means pretend to qualify as a DSL variable (a major split variable). It doesn't fit the FPE (the Feature Pool), nor the Bartolian CPE; it is partially conditioned by VB (contextual variation, relative chronology), and the nice clustering of the north-eastern varieties in the lower clade of Figure 1.3a suggests that, at best, it can be involved in the EI layer of emerging isolates (or subdialects).

1.3.3. The Labialized Stops Variable

I will further handle another phonological variable which I would place at the crossroad between the efficient and heuristic hissing-hushing variable and the uvular plosive and ejective: labialized stops (the Cv- variable),[12] as in Table 1.4.

Table 1.4. A sample of the Cv- variable, from the LaDyCa database

	15	16	17	18
	'still, yet'	'child, son of'	'you' 2Pl	'eye'
GRG	ḳidev	švili	tkven	tvali
XEV	ḳide	švili	tkven	tvali
PSH	ḳiden	švili	tkven	tvali
MOX	ḳidav	švili	tkwen	toli
MTIU	ḳidan	švili	tkven	twäli
GUD	ḳidav(a)	___	tkven	toli
TUSH	ḳiden	___	___	tvalĭ
KAR	ḳide	švili	___	___
KAXET	ḳidena	šwili	tkwen	twali
KIZIQ	ḳidena	šwili	tkwen	twali
FEREY	ḳide	švili	ken	toli
INGIL	ḳedem	šül	tkön	tol
MESH	ḳide	šüli	kten	tvali
RACH	ḳidomec	švili	tkven	tvali
H-IMR	ḳide	švili	tkven	twali
L-IMR	ḳido	švili	tkven	twali
LCHX	ḳidom	švili	tkvene	twali
ADJA	ḳido	___	___	twali
TAO	ḳide	šwili	tkwen	___
IMRX	ḳido	šwili	tkwen	twali
H-GUR	ḳido	___	tkven	tvali
L-GUR	ḳidom	___	tkven	twali

This phenomenology is interesting from several prospects. Although it does not qualify as congruent with the standard taxonomy of Georgian dialects on several decisive points (in the upper clade, western ADJA and GUR mingle

---

[12] Data processed: 22 varieties, 10 cognates, 220 instances, 1124 characters (29 unique), 1104 tokens (29 unique).

aberrantly with eastern varieties such as KAXET and KIZIQ), many details of the inner structure of the topology in Figure 1.4a provide interesting cues about the general, or perhaps even the deep structure of the GDN.

Figure 1.4. Labialized stops in the LaDyCa database: a sample. Results from Gabmap

Figure 1.4a. Ward's Method

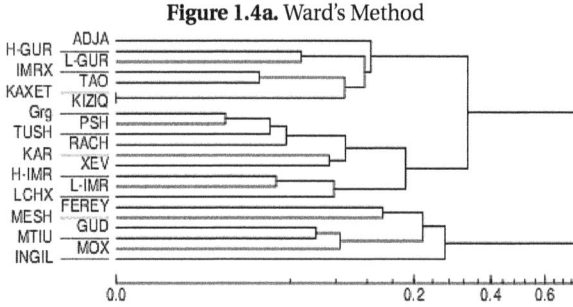

Figure 1.4b. Difference map

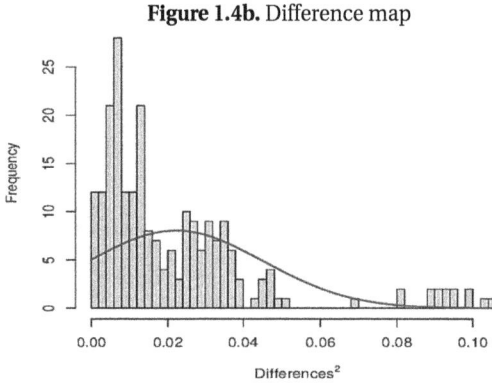

Figure 1.4c. MDS plot

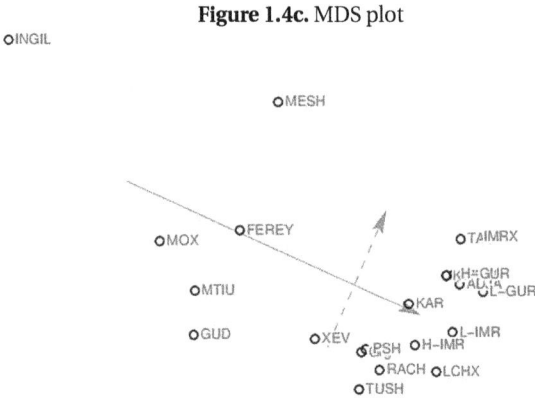

Figure 1.4d. Probabilistic dendrogram (ibidem)

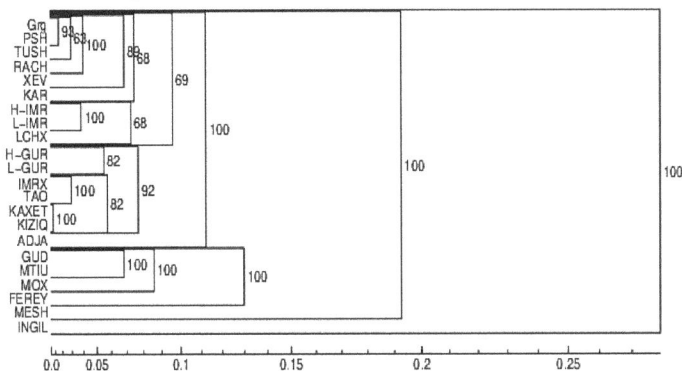

First, there is a solid core in this topology: the central clade, which associates the central (GRG, KAR) and the north-eastern varieties (TUSH, PSH, XEV, with the addition of RACH in the West, according to a northern highland continuity dynamic[13]) as a core, on the one hand, and the IMR/LCHX dialect complex in the North-West on the other hand. This is very consistent, and it points clearly at the kernel, or the nucleus of the DSL (the major division between C/E and W), and at the Bartolian dynamics –both areal cores having been or being leaders in their geographic realm. Second, the clade in the lower part of the dendrogram points at two patterns: on the one hand, a default clustering of peripheral eastern dialects (FEREY, MESH, INGIL), on the other hand, a split of the north-eastern bundle of varieties, since MTIU/GUD and MOX) join them in this clade –i.e., the westernmost complex out of this compact bundle. Now, remember we saw the same split in the previous topology (uvular stops, previous section). We could think this was due to the erratic behavior of the sample. We see it may not be so. These facts, as the mingling of RACH with the easternmost varieties of the north-eastern complex in the northern highlands might hint to some kind of a former "cordillera" dialectical continuity, which somehow was striving to emerge at some moment of history, but collapsed thereafter. Third, if the chain MTIU/GUD-MOX in the center of the lower clade can be seen as a core area, then the FEREY and MESH subclade qualifies as a first concentric circle of default aggregation, whereas INGIL comes next, in a second circle of distant, although plausible convergence. INGIL is no more a satellite disconnected from the rest of the GDN: its structural ties with the eastern complex surface clearly for the first time. Although this set of results

---

[13] I would even use the term, in this case, of a kind of "cordillera effect", as the variable follows here the Transcaucasion mountain ridge.

might seem arguable because of some mingling between East and West, it does bring new and interesting cues about the inner structure of the GDN.

Moreover, the distribution of differences in Figure 4b differs from the previous one: it shows less negative skewness and of what looks more like a Gaussian curve than in the previous difference maps. The MDS plot points at an FPE trend, with most varieties condensating in a pole, at the right of the plot, while KAR stands not far from the center of gravity, as could be expected. What strikingly emerges from this picture is a kind of central-western configuration this time, instead of the canonical central-eastern confederation. Escaping from this cloud, the "northern cordillera" and the easternmost peripheral varieties raise to less crowded areas of the plot: to the left for MOX and MTIU/GUD, and far above, as far as MESH and INGIL are concerned.

The main conclusions we can draw from section 3 read as follows, in (2)

(2) Trends in the GDN according to the GMDD

(2a) Although the GDN started with a bunch of structural variables inherited from the various phases of the Kartvelian split, it has long undergone a process of bipolarization between the core of the Western block (IMR/LECHX, and GUR as a first circle periphery) and the core of the Central-Eastern bloc (mostly KAR). Each of these cores developed fairly strong Bartolian CPE.

(2b) The BZE (Buffer Zone Effect) in the center (involving the north-eastern complex, in strong interaction with KAR) undergoes a strong FPE I (Feature Pool) with eastern Georgian (KAXET/KIZIQ).

(2c) At the periphery of these competing cores, two major trends arise: either EI (emerging isolates) from the second or third Bartolian circle (CPE), as PSH, TUSH in the north-eastern zone, or ADJA, IMRX in the West, out of VB (variable bleeding) and PLEP (Phonolexical Endemic Patterns) on the one hand, or straightforward singleton dialects out of language contact beyond the frontiers of the two former geopolitical hegemonies (Turkey and Persia), on the other hand.

(2d) Differences have been eroded by the powerful influence of the literary language, although the complex shape of the geolinguistic landscape has to some extent preserved retentive trends, as in the Greater Caucasian highlands, from RACH to TUSH, or in the valleys where ADJA is spoken. Some varieties as MESH or TAO have emerged from intricate processes of settlement and resettlement, and are embedded in contact with exogenous languages, such as Armenian for the former, Turkish for the latter. All these peripheral zones show greater idiosyncrasy, oscillating between the CPE and the EI. Consequently, they are preserved from the FPE (Feature Pole Effect) or from the BZE (Buffer Zone Effect).

(2e) Due to phonological and morphological complexity of Kartvelian languages, VB (Variable Bleeding, or Relative Chronology) and PLEP (Phonolexical Endemic Patterns) should be carefully sequenced and controlled in any quantitative attempt to measure distance or similarity in the GDN. These two effects contribute to the blurring of deep evolutive trends in the GDN (as in Figure 1.1, with 243 cognates). In processing phonological variables, we tried to avoid this bias. This selective approach gave encouraging results, though partial and, of course, provisional.

(2f) In the future, we can prognose the GDN will intensify a monopolar Bartolian Dynamic Field (CPE), with GRG on the lead. Yet, competing core or first-circle peripheries as GUR may still flourish to some extent. Most second or third circle varieties will either fade away under this assimilation process by Standard Georgian, or will survive in their foreign community surroundings, although some, as TAO, are now highly endangered (Chokharadze et al., *op. cit.*).

Therefore, an urgent task is to observe these processes of dialect assimilation or resilience and transformation, and to document as many oral and written texts as possible (as *The Corpus of Georgian Dialects*-project already does, see Beridze et al. 2009). Moreover, particular attention should be given to oral history of interactions between dialects, within the framework of the South Caucasian Vertical archipelago (Nichols, op. cit.) and its fractal components (e.g., the North-Eastern complex in relation to KAR; ADJA inner complexity, in relation to TAO and to IMRX, as in Chokharadze et al. ibidem).

1.4. Conclusion and Prospects

What did this survey of a 243 cognates database of Georgian teach us that we did not already know about a well-known topic? First, that standard taxonomies should not be taken as definite knowledge and unquestionable authority: most of their power lays instead in their refutability and falsifiability. Through the process of challenging the canonical picture of a dialect network with statistical tools, we can grasp otherwise unattainable cues on the complex inner structure of the diasystem. Second, by challenging the qualitative picture of the dialect network, quantitative methods also face a challenge. The filiation of emerging isolates (EI) such as INGIL or FREREY is not easily captured by quantitative methods, whereas it is more easily established by philological and qualitative tools (isoglosses). Yet, it depends on how we calibrate samples of data. In turn, the quantitative approach may enhance deep patterns which could hardly be seen with qualitative tools, as the "northern cordillera effect." Second, quantitative tools are designed for calculation and taxonomy building –a noble, but yet trivial task, epistemologically. We need more, for the sake of General Dialectology. Quantitative tools, as computational dialectology, are all the more powerful if they are rooted in linguistic theories, such as Gudschinsky's Model (the GMDD). From this standpoint, the GDN continues ancient trends which have been decisive in the Kartvelian linguistic stock, as the hissing-hushing correlation, which points at the DSL. From the Western *versus* Eastern split, a complex buffer zone (the BZE, or Buffer Zone Effect) has emerged, associating the Kartlian-Meshkhian area (KAR and MESH), in the midlands, with the North-eastern area, in the north-western highlands (MOX, MTIU/GUD, XEV, PSH, TUSH). This interaction of the Vertical Archipelago type (Nichols, 2008) has weakened a plausible former Transcaucasian highland continuum, from TUSH to RACH. Eastern and central dialects mingled conspicuously through time, so that the eastern dialect complex has constantly been expanding (with transborder outliers as INGIL and FEREY) and recessing (being incorporated by KAR, or developing into MESH, migrating towards the South-West). This constant diastole and systole movement often happened under the pression of foreign hegemonies, especially the Persian hegemony, to the East (EF), and gave shape to a dense Feature Pool (FPE). However, the GDN has also evolved according to a Bartolian dynamic field (CPM), opposing two main innovative dialects: KAR vs. IMR. In turn, Western peripheral dialects, especially GUR, followed more or less the trends expanding from the North-West (from IMR), and could even overdo them (causing VB entropy). From the South-West, the trend was rather to peripheral idiosyncratic innovation (EI), and to diastole, heading westward, leading to the emergence of innovative varieties such as ADJA, IMRX and TAO.

The overall shape of the GDN is rather unified, as the difference maps suggest, and the low differences one can find in the matrix of data in Appendix 1.1-2. Standard Georgian, as a powerful and prestigious dialect, with a long-time written tradition, and outstanding tools for diffusion (among which a very original and practical alphabet and spelling), has been unifying the dialect network for a very long period already. Yet, underneath, a rich array of fine-grained variation still lingers and provides many hints at history and at original patterns in the phonology, the grammar and the lexicon of this most valuable language –Georgian.

References

Asatiani, Rusudan. 2008. "Directions of Diachronic Developments of the Kartvelian Languages." *44th International Congress on Medieval Studies, University of Kentucky*, available Online: https://www.ayk.gov.tr/wp-content/uploads/2015/01/ASATIANI-Rusudan-DIRECTIONS-OF-DIACHRONIC-DEVELOPMENTS-OF-THE-KARTVELIAN-LANGUAGES.pdf.

Bartoli, Matteo. 1945. *Saggi di linguistica spaziale*. Turin: Rosenberg and Sellier.

Beridze, Marine, and David Nadaraia. 2009. "The Corpus of Georgian Dialects." *Proceedings of the NLP, Corpus Linguistics, Corpus Based Grammar Research. Fifth International Conference Smolenice:* 25–35, *Jazykovedný ústav Ľ. Štúra SAV*, Bratislava, Slovakia.

Chokharadze, Malkhaz, Shota Rodinadze, and Natia Abashidze. 2018. "The Taoan Dialect of Georgian Language and Linguistic Space of Collective Memory in the Chorokhi Basin." *Journal of Arts and Humanities*, 07 (10): 65-72.

Gamkrelidze, Tamaz. 2005. "Reconstruction of proto-language and its chronological levels." *Perspektiva*-XXI, VI, Tbilisi, ena da kultura: 84-87.

Gigineishvili, Ivane, Varlam Topuria, and Ivane Kavtaradze. 1961. *kartuli dialekt'ologia I* [Georgian dialectology, I], Tbilisi, TSUG.

Gudschinsky, Sarah. 1958. "Mazatec dialect history: A Study in Miniature." *Language* 34: 469-481.

Heinsalu, Els, Marco Patriarca, and Jean Léo Léonard. 2020. *Languages in Space and Time. Models and Methods from Complex Systems Theory.* Cambridge: Cambridge University Press.

Kassian, Alexei. 2015. "Towards a formal genealogical classification of the Lezgian languages (North Caucasus): testing various phylogenetic methods on lexical data." *PLoS ONE* 10(2): e0116950. doi:10.1371/journal.pone.0116950.

Leonard, Jean Léo. 2019. "Méthodes pour l'analyse et la documentation des langues et des dialectes kartvèles, à la lumière de la Théorie des Dynamiques Langagières / Théorie de la Complexité." Mikadze, Manana et al. 2019. *The Fifth International Scientific Conference Language and Culture*, Kutaisi, Akaki Tsereteli State University: 625-650.

—. 2017, "Le projet LaDyCa (*Language Dynamics in the Caucasus*, IDEX Emergence 2017-18) : avancées et résultats." Tbilisi, ILIAUNI, *Kadmos* 9 : 42-77.

Leinonen, Therese, Çağrı Çöltekin, and John Nerbonne. 2016. "Using Gabmap." *Lingua* 178: 71-83.

Levenshtein, Vladimir. 1966. "Binary Codes Capable of Correcting Deletions, Insertions, and Reversals." *Soviet Physics – Doklady*, 10 (8): 707-710.

Machavariani, Givi. 1965. *Proto-kartvelian consonants system.* Tbilisi: TSU press.

Mufwene, Salikoko. 2013. "*Complexity perspectives on language, communication, and society.*" Massip-Bonet, Àngels and Albert Bastardas-Boada (eds.), 2013. *Complexity Perspectives on Language, Communication and Society*, Springer: 197-218.

—. 2001. *The Ecology of Language Evolution.* Cambridge: Cambridge University Press.

Murra, John Victor. 1956. *The Economic Organization of the Inca State*, Ph.D. diss., Department of Anthropology, University of Chicago.

—. 1985. "El Archipielago Vertical Revisited." *Andean Ecology and Civilization*, edited by Shozo Masuda, Izumi Shimada and Craig Morris, 3 (13), Tokyo, University of Tokyo Press.

Nichols, Johanna. 2004. "The Origin of the Chechen and Ingush: A Study in Alpine Linguistic and Ethnic Geography." *Anthropological Linguistics*, 46 (2): 129-155.

Picard, Flore, Hélène Gérardin, and Jean Léo Léonard. 2018. "A report on the LaDyCaproject (*Language Dynamics in the Caucasus*, IDEX Emergence,

2917-18)."International Workshop *Methods in theoretical and empirical dialectology, talk at Methods for Endangered Kartvelian varieties documentation and Analysis according to Language Dynamics Theory, II,* 23th of February 2018, Ilia State University, Tbilisi.

Popper, Karl. 1934. *Logic der Forschung.* Wien: Springer.

—. 1963. *Conjectures and refutations.* London: Routledge.

Tuite, Kevin. 1989. "The geography of Georgian *q'e.*" Aronson, Howard (ed.) *The Non-Slavic Languages of the USSR: Linguistic Studies,* Chicago Linguistics Society: 283-302.

Appendix 1.1. Levenshtein Distance, According to the LaDyCa Database (Compiled by Hélène Gérardin, 2018): 244 Items.

	GRG	XEV	PSH	MOX	MTIU	TUSH	KAR	KAXET	KIZIQ	FEREY	INGIL
GRG		0,12	0,09	0,14	0,12	0,30	0,12	0,078	0,09	0,18	0,51
XEV	0,12		0,13	0,18	0,16	0,26	0,19	0,16	0,14	0,19	0,48
PSH	0,09	0,13		0,14	0,11	0,28	0,14	0,10	0,08	0,17	0,47
MOX	0,14	0,18	0,14		0,10	0,35	0,19	0,17	0,16	0,17	0,44
MTIU	0,12	0,16	0,11	0,10		0,33	0,17	0,12	0,11	0,18	0,45
TUSH	0,30	0,26	0,28	0,35	0,33		0,33	0,33	0,30	0,33	0,47
KAR	0,12	0,19	0,14	0,19	0,17	0,33		0,09	0,11	0,17	0,46
KAXET	0,07	0,16	0,10	0,17	0,12	0,33	0,09		0,03	0,18	0,52
KIZIQ	0,09	0,14	0,08	0,16	0,11	0,30	0,11	0,03		0,17	0,50
FEREY	0,18	0,19	0,17	0,17	0,18	0,33	0,17	0,18	0,17		0,43
INGIL	0,51	0,48	0,47	0,44	0,45	0,47	0,46	0,52	0,50	0,43	
MESH	0,10	0,18	0,13	0,19	0,16	0,33	0,13	0,11	0,14	0,18	0,49
RACH	0,11	0,20	0,15	0,22	0,18	0,33	0,14	0,14	0,15	0,20	0,51
H-IMR	0,16	0,22	0,17	0,25	0,21	0,33	0,17	0,19	0,20	0,23	0,50
L-IMR	0,19	0,24	0,21	0,25	0,23	0,35	0,19	0,20	0,21	0,25	0,50
LCHX	0,25	0,26	0,26	0,31	0,29	0,38	0,23	0,25	0,25	0,33	0,56
ADJA	0,22	0,27	0,24	0,31	0,27	0,37	0,24	0,20	0,22	0,26	0,51
TAO	0,23	0,23	0,25	0,281	0,26	0,39	0,23	0,22	0,20	0,26	0,51
IMRX	0,17	0,20	0,16	0,21	0,18	0,32	0,16	0,16	0,14	0,22	0,52
H-GUR	0,26	0,32	0,31	0,36	0,30	0,40	0,24	0,27	0,29	0,35	0,54
L-GUR	0,25	0,30	0,30	0,34	0,30	0,39	0,24	0,27	0,28	0,33	0,53

Appendix 1.2. Levenshtein Distance, According to the LaDyCa Database (Compiled by Hélène Gérardin, 2018): 244 Items.

GRG	MESH	RACH	H-IMR	L-IMR	LCHX	ADJA	TAO	IMRX	H-GUR	L-GUR
XEV	0,10	0,11	0,16	0,19	0,25	0,22	0,23	0,17	0,26	0,25
PSH	0,18	0,20	0,22	0,24	0,26	0,27	0,23	0,20	0,32	0,30
MOX	0,13	0,15	0,17	0,21	0,26	0,24	0,25	0,16	0,31	0,30
MTIU	0,19	0,22	0,25	0,25	0,31	0,31	0,28	0,21	0,36	0,34
TUSH	0,16	0,18	0,21	0,23	0,29	0,27	0,26	0,18	0,30	0,30
KAR	0,33	0,33	0,33	0,35	0,38	0,37	0,39	0,32	0,40	0,39
KAXET	0,13	0,14	0,17	0,19	0,23	0,24	0,23	0,16	0,24	0,24

KIZIQ	0,11	0,14	0,19	0,20	0,25	0,20	0,22	0,16	0,27	0,27
FEREY	0,14	0,15	0,20	0,21	0,25	0,22	0,20	0,14	0,29	0,28
INGIL	0,18	0,20	0,23	0,25	0,33	0,26	0,26	0,22	0,35	0,33
MESH	0,49	0,51	0,50	0,50	0,56	0,51	0,51	0,52	0,54	0,53
RACH		0,13	0,17	0,20	0,27	0,26	0,28	0,21	0,28	0,28
H-IMR	0,13		0,14	0,16	0,19	0,22	0,27	0,20	0,23	0,24
L-IMR	0,17	0,14		0,12	0,21	0,25	0,27	0,22	0,22	0,23
LCHX	0,20	0,16	0,12		0,17	0,24	0,28	0,21	0,19	0,19
ADJA	0,27	0,19	0,21	0,17		0,24	0,35	0,25	0,24	0,26
TAO	0,26	0,22	0,25	0,24	0,24		0,23	0,22	0,28	0,29
IMRX	0,28	0,27	0,27	0,28	0,35	0,23		0,18	0,30	0,32
H-GUR	0,21	0,20	0,22	0,21	0,25	0,22	0,18		0,27	0,27
L-GUR	0,28	0,23	0,22	0,19	0,24	0,28	0,30	0,27		0,10
GRG	0,28	0,24	0,23	0,19	0,26	0,29	0,32	0,27	0,10	

A sample of the sources for the cognate list by Hélène Gérardin (2018), a random list.

Jorbenadze Besarion, *kartuli dialekt'ologia*, I 1989 and II 1998.

Gigineishvili Ivane, Topuria Varlam, Kavtaradze Ivane, *kartuli dialekt'ologia*, Tbilisi, 1961.

Rogava, G. *kartvelur enata ist'oriuli ponet'ik'is sak'itxebi*, mecniereba, Tbilisi, 1984.

Gigineishvili B., "zogi kartveluri sit'q'va-pormis rek'onst'rukciisatvis," in *et'imologiuri dziebani*, VI, mecniereba, Tbilisi, 1997.

Zviadauri N., "naxur-daghest'nur enata leksik'a kartuli enis mtis dialekt'ebshi," in *et'imologiuri dziebani*, VI, mecniereba, Tbilisi, 1997.

K'ak'itadze K'. "leksisk'uri dziebani (manch'k'vala)," in *et'imologiuri dziebani*, VI, mecniereba, Tbilisi, 1997.

Mach'avariani Gigi, *saerto-kartveluri k'onsonant'uri sist'ema*, TSU press, Tbilisi, 1965.

Uturgaidze Tedo, *kartuli enis mtis k'ilota zogi tavisebureba*, mecniereba, Tbilisi, 1966.

Topuria Varlam, "kartvelur enata dialekt'ebis monacemta mnishvneloba enis ist'oriisa da zogadi enatmecnierebisatvis," *in macne* II, Tbilisi, 1965, p. 179-183.

Rogava, G. "decesiur-harmoniul k'omp'leksta sist'emisa da ist'oriisatvis kartvelur enebshi," *in macne* II, Tbilisi, 1965, p. 184-191.

Schmidt Karl, "Problemy geneticheskoj i tipologicheskoj rekonstrukcii kavkazskix jazykov," *in Voprosy jazykoznanija*, IV, août 1972, nauka, Moscou 1972, p. 14-25.

Gigineishvili B., "Sravnitel'naja rekonstrukcija i vopros o variabel'nosti v jazyke-osnove," *in Voprosy jazykoznanija*, IV, août 1972, nauka, Moscou 1972, p. 48-52.

K'art'ozia Guram, "Sibilant'ta shesat'q'visobis darghvevata axsnisatvis kartvelur enebshi," *in Enisa da lit'erat'uris seria*, 2, Tbilisi, 1984, p. 130-144.

Topuria Varlam, "dialekty kartvel'skix jazykov i voprosy obshego jazykoznanija," *VII mezhdunarodnyj kongress antropologicheskix i ètnograficheskix nauk*, nauka, Moscou, 1964.

Chuxua Merab, *kartvelur ena-k'ilota shedarebiti leksik'oni, Ibero-Caucasica*, Tbilisi, 2000-2003.

Topuria Varlam, "Nekotorye voprosy sravnitel'noj fonetiki kartvel'skix jazykov," *XXV mezhdunarodnyj kongress vostokovedov, izdatel'stvo vostochnoj literatury*, Moscou, 1960.

Topuria Varlam, "ponet'ik'uri dak'virvebani kartvelur enebshi," *Tbilisis universitetis moambe*, X, Tbilisi, 1930.

Klimov Georgij, "K tipologicheskoj xarakteristike kartvel'skix jazykov (s sopostavlenii s drugimi iberijsko-kavkazskimi jazykami)," *XXV mezhdunarodnyj kongress vostokovedov, izdatel'stvo vostochnoj literatury*, Moscou, 1960.

Mikiashvili Otar, *Kartuli enis dialekt'ebis urtiertsherevisa da int'ereperenciis sak'itxebi,* TSU Press, Tbilisi, 1986.

K'iziria A., Kavtaradze I., Ch'abashvili M., Uturgaidze Teo, *K'itxvari kartuli dialekt'ologiuri at'lasis masalisatvis,* mecniereba, Tbilisi, 1984.

Ziziguri šota, *Ziebani kartuli dialekt'ologiidan, samecniero-metoduri k'abinet'is gamomcembloba,* Tbilisi, 1954.

Khelaia Aleksandre, *samk'urnalo leksik'oni,* 2010.

Klimov Georgij, *Etimologicheskij slovar' kartvelskix jazykov.*

Sarjevaladze *etimologiuri leksik'oni…* and various monographs for each of the varieties studied in this paper.

Chapter 2

Lexicography in Georgia

Tinatin Margalitadze

Ilia State University, Georgia

Giorgi Meladze

Ilia State University, Georgia

Abstract

Georgian lexicography faces major transformation in the modern era. It should develop into an interdisciplinary branch of knowledge incorporating many components, including corpus linguistics, as well as natural language processing (NLP) methods and theories.

The paper discusses major events in the history of the Georgian lexicography. History of lexicography, and, generally, history of a language are deeply interwoven with the history of a nation. This is also true of the Georgian lexicography which is discussed in the paper against the backdrop of some landmarks in the history of Georgia.

The paper analyses some lexicographic works of the early period, the ground-breaking explanatory dictionary of Sulkhan-Saba Orbeliani and his lexicographic principles. The paper looks at the nineteenth century, which witnessed a dramatic change in the political situation in Georgia, its incorporation in the Russian Empire, which resulted in the production of only Russian-Georgian dictionaries. The twentieth century was marked by the publication of many dictionaries: explanatory, bilingual, terminological, etc., although the majority of bilingual dictionaries were still Russian-Georgian. The instances of the compilation of bilingual European-Georgian type dictionaries were mostly individual initiatives of specialists of foreign languages who strived to fill the existing gaps and to meet the growing demand of the Georgian society for the study of foreign languages.

The paper discusses the development of digital lexicography in Georgia, hampered by the troubled history of the country throughout the twentieth century: the Soviet occupation and the domination of the communist ideology which regarded cybernetics as "pseudoscience" for a long time; the collapse of the Soviet Union, when due to the ensuing political turmoil and civil war, Georgia was thrown into chaos for more than a decade. As a consequence, the full-scale history of digital lexicography in Georgia begins only in the twenty-first century.

Keywords: Georgian lexicography; Sulkhan-Saba Orbeliani; bilingual dictionaries of Georgian; history of Georgian lexicography; digital lexicography

***

2.1. Introduction

In 2020, The Centre for Lexicography and Language Technologies was established at Ilia State University.[1] The Statute of the Centre states its objectives: to support the development of the Georgian lexicography into an interdisciplinary branch of knowledge; to promote the effective introduction of corpus-based and NLP methods and theories into Georgian lexicographic practice; to support the complete digitalization of the Georgian language, its integration into international digital translation products and programs which should ensure retaining by Georgian its applied value and function in every branch or sphere of modern social, cultural or scientific activities in the country.

The objectives thus stated clearly identify the problems which face lexicography in modern Georgia. The way of the Georgian lexicography to its present-day challenges was long and difficult. Below, we will try to briefly outline the major landmarks in its history.

2.2. Early Period

Literary and lexicographic activities developed almost simultaneously in Georgia. Early conversion of the country into Christianity in the beginning of the fourth century gave impetus to the translation of books of the Old and New Testament into Georgian. Like the European lexicographic tradition, the first stage of the Georgian lexicography was characterized by the compilation of glosses, marginal notes and explanations added to manuscripts. In the Middle Ages, being familiar with the Greco-Byzantine tradition of appending glossaries to the books of ancient authors, Georgian scholars and translators started to introduce this tradition into the Georgian lexicography. For example, Eprem Mtsire (XI cent.), an outstanding Georgian scholar and translator, appended his translation of Psalms with a minor glossary, which is regarded to be one of the first explanatory dictionaries in Georgian (Shanidze, 1968; Tvaltvadze, 2009).

---

[1] It was established by the team of the "Lexicographic Centre", which has 25-year-long history of implementing numerous bilingual lexicographic and corpus-based projects in Georgia.

2.3. Sulkhan-Saba Orbeliani

Sulkhan-Saba Orbeliani (1658 – 1725) is a Georgian writer, lexicographer, diplomat and public figure. He created the *Georgian Dictionary*, so-called *Sitqvis Kona*, which is the first complete explanatory dictionary of the Georgian language [SSO]. He worked on his dictionary for 40 years and produced its three revised versions. As far as Saba formulated the principles for the composition of his dictionary by the end of the seventeenth century, his ground-breaking work should be regarded as a creation belonging to this very period (Ghlonti 1983: 38 - 76).

In the foreword to his Dictionary, Sulkhan-Saba Orbeliani writes that Georgians had previously had a dictionary, which they subsequently lost and this, in his words, resulted in the corruption of their mother tongue [SSO]. Unfortunately, there is no precise information as to when this dictionary was composed, or what principles it was based upon.

Saba's dictionary contains over 16 600 words (according to his autographic dictionaries) and is interesting from many points of view. Saba analysed 140 sources for his dictionary, which included both original and translated works: books of the Old and the New Testament, hagiography, i.e., the lives of saints, *The Knight in the Panther's Skin* by Shota Rustaveli, *Amiran-Darejaniani* by Moses of Khoni, Georgian folk epic *Rostomiani*, a popular medieval Georgian medical handbook *Karabadin* by Zaza Panaskerteli-Tsitsishvili, etc. Every word included in the dictionary is attested in literary sources and is supplied with the information on these sources.

The study of lexical meanings of words is based on the analysis of contexts, which are, as noted above, in many cases cited. One of the achievements of Saba's dictionary is his treatment of polysemy. He singles out polysemous meanings of words and often indicates their sources as well. Saba's *Georgian Dictionary* includes definitions of anthroponyms (person's names) and toponyms (place names), which fact imparts to it a certain encyclopaedic character. In his dictionary, Saba uses conventional symbols. Celestial bodies (the Sun, the Moon, stars), birds and animals, fishes and insects are marked in the dictionary with special symbols, which roughly correspond to subject labels in modern dictionaries. The dictionary also uses a special symbol (0) to designate words of foreign origin.

Especially noteworthy is Saba's lexicographic principle of including synonyms or related words of a headword in a dictionary entry. Synonyms and related words are defined in an entry in order to show even the slightest differences between them. For example, in the entry for წვიმა (tsvima) *'rain'* the lexicographer included and defined the following related words: თქორი (tkori) *'drizzle'* is rain which is fine and difficult for men to see; თქეში (tkeshi) – is thicker than *'tkori;'*

ფრუტი (prut'i) is *'tkeshi'* that is misty; ჟღმურტლი (zhghmurt'li) is rain that is heavier than *'prut'i'* and more misty; ღლოფო (ghlopo) – means the rain that is heavy and darkening and torrential; ქარიშხალი (karishkhali) *'(rain)storm'* is heavy rain with wind; შხაპი (shkhapi) is sudden and rapid rain; and the phenomenon when tree leaves laden with raindrops after downpour begin to drip, is called ლეშხი (leshkhi) or ჟვავი (zhvavi).

As can be seen from the above-cited example, the entry for **rain** comprises different types of rain: fine and difficult for men to see, or heavy, or misty, or windy etc. Definition of each related word in the entry includes the hyperonym, which, in this particular entry is *rain*: "rain which is fine and difficult for men to see," "rain that is heavy and darkening and torrential," "is sudden and rapid rain," "heavy rain with wind," etc. and differential semantic components. This principle is implemented throughout the *Georgian Dictionary* and reminds of the tradition of Aristotelian philosophy, which is known as a definition *'per genus proximum et differentias specificas,'* i.e., by stating the superordinate class to which something belongs, together with the specific characteristics that differentiate it from the other members of the class. By using the above described lexicographic principle, Sulkhan-Saba Orbeliani managed to document hundreds of unique concepts lexicalized in the Georgian language of his time, which were lost in the following centuries and are no longer present in the lexical stock of the modern Georgian language (Margalitadze 2022).

Sitqvis Kona is an explanatory dictionary in the first place; however, along with Georgian explanations it includes also Italian, Armenian and Turkish equivalents of Georgian headwords in Georgian transliterations. Some words have all three equivalents, some – two, while others have only one.

Georgian Dictionary by Sulkhan-Saba Orbeliani is a landmark lexicographic work of the seventeenth century, whose importance reaches far beyond the limits of specifically Georgian lexicography. Saba's *Sitqvis Kona* laid foundation for the Georgian scholarly lexicography and brought it to the level of European and Asian lexicography of that time.

Saba's dictionary became as popular as *The Knight in the Panther's Skin* by the great Georgian mediaeval poet Shota Rustaveli. As a result, up to 150 surviving manuscripts of the dictionary have come down to our times, which were copied in the eighteenth century and in the first half of the nineteenth century. *Georgian Dictionary* was first printed only in 1884, some 160 years after its author's death.

2.4. Georgian Bilingual Dictionaries of the Seventeenth-Eighteenth Centuries

2.4.1. Georgian Bilingual Dictionaries of the Seventeenth-Eighteenth Centuries with Oriental Languages

Despite the country's predominantly Western political and cultural orientation, which found its most evident expression in the early conversion of Georgia to Christianity (in preference to Zoroastrianism and, later, to Islam), our country, due to its geographical disposition, had to inevitably deal with Eastern civilizations and nations as well. Cultural, economic, diplomatic and political relations (although not always peaceful) with neighbouring countries, such as Persia (Iran), Turkey and others, logically led to the necessity to adequately study and understand Persian, Turkish, Arabic and other Eastern languages. As a result of this, the Georgian bilingual lexicography with Oriental languages (with Georgian alternately appearing both as a target and source language) has a long-standing tradition in the history of Georgia's cultural life. Among various lexicographic endeavours, most notable are: *Georgian-Arabic-Persian Dictionary* by Parsadan Gorgijanidze and Lexicographic works of King Vakhtang VI of Kartli.

Parsadan Gorgijanidze was a prominent political figure, historian and lexicographer of the seventeenth century (1626 – 1711). He spent many years at the court of Shah Abbas II of Persia. He also held the office of the prefect of Ispahan, the then capital of the Safavid Iran. Gorgijanidze had converted to Islam and this fact also contributed to his good command of the Arabic, in addition to the Persian language (Ghlonti 1983: 21 - 26). His familiarity with these languages greatly aided Gorgijanidze in compiling his multilingual *Georgian-Arabic-Persian Dictionary*. Undoubtedly, his lexicographic undertaking was motivated by practical necessities, for intense political, economic and diplomatic relations with Iran resulted in numerous Persian and Arabic loanwords appearing in the Georgian vocabulary, which naturally needed explanation, as far as they were barely understandable for the majority of the Georgian population.

Parsadan Gorgijanidze's multilingual dictionary lacks many features which we usually associate with modern, user-friendly lexicographic resources. The words included in the dictionary are not arranged alphabetically, nor are they organized according to any other readily identifiable system. Parsadan, as it seems, simply listed all foreign (Persian and Arabic) words which he could remember and which he deemed to be important for various reasons (religious and diplomatic terms, words routinely used in everyday life, and so on). Despite these shortcomings, the dictionary was a reliable resource on Persian and Arabic languages.

King Vakhtang (1675 – 1737), often referred to as Vakhtang the Scholar, had much to do with philology, literature, book-printing and lexicography. Vakhtang, who, not coincidentally, was educated by the pioneering Georgian lexicographer Sulkhan-Saba Orbeliani, was actively involved in lexicographic activities in addition to his general literary and scholarly pursuits. His lexicographic heritage involves two types of works: Persian-Georgian glossaries appended to his translations of Persian astronomical treatises; and an explanatory glossary appended to the printed edition of *The Knight in the Panther's Skin*.

The background of Vakhtang's contribution to the bilingual lexicography is as follows: Vakhtang translated from Persian two astronomical treatises. The first is Zij-i Sultani (often referred to by Georgian historiographers simply as Zij) by Ulugh Beg, the renowned Muslim astronomer and mathematician from Samarkand (in present-day Uzbekistan). Ulugh Beg's Zij is an astronomical table and star catalogue which was published by him in 1438–1439. Another astronomy-related book translated by Vakhtang from Persian is called Hidayat al-Nujum. In his glossaries, appended to both of his translations, Vakhtang translates and explains the Persian and Arabic words which he extensively used (transliterated into Georgian characters) in his translations. Obviously, these foreign borrowings were treated by Vakhtang as special terms from the field of astronomy and astrology, which required further explanation and elucidation. In the way Vakhtang explains the entries included in his word-list, we can feel the invisible presence of his famous mentor Sulkhan-Saba Orbeliani (Ghlonti 1983: 26 - 28).

2.4.2. Georgian Bilingual Dictionaries of the Seventeenth-Eighteenth Centuries with European Languages

Unlike bilingual dictionaries, composed with respect to Oriental languages, which were authored by Georgian scholars, European-Georgian dictionaries were mainly composed by foreign authors. The translation dictionaries from the seventeenth century are composed with respect to the Italian language and are authored by Italian missionaries who visited Georgia. The aggressive and expansionist policy of the neighbouring Muslim countries of that period urged Georgians to seek help from the Western nations. The Roman Catholic Church, for its part, was greatly interested in establishing its missionary centres in the East. Top-ranking Catholic clerics in Rome were convinced that by establishing such centres they would ensure the spread of the Catholic faith to the East. Georgia was among those countries which had attracted the attention of the Catholic Rome. In the seventeenth century, a number of missionaries were sent to Georgia from Rome. These missionaries showed a considerable interest in the Georgian language and culture and often even studied Georgian, for they believed that the language would greatly aid them in preaching and, of course, also in spreading Catholicism among the Georgian-speaking populace. This circumstance found its natural expression in the main trends which were prevalent in the seventeenth-eighteenth century bilingual Georgian lexicography.

Not surprisingly, taking the said trends into consideration, a *Georgian-Italian Dictionary* (*Dittionario giorgiano e italiano*) was printed in Rome in 1629 (DGI; Chikobava, Vateishvili, 1983). As the print on the cover of the book reads, the authors are Stefano Paolini, a prominent and experienced typographer of his time, and Nikoloz Cholokashvili, known in Italy as Niceforo Irbachi Giorgiano, a Georgian Orthodox priest and diplomat, who was then an ambassador of the Georgian monarch Teimuraz I to Europe. The dictionary was printed by the *Propaganda Fide* – a congregation of the Catholic Church in Rome, responsible for the missionary work and the spread of Catholicism. The dictionary contains 3084 words which extend over 181 pages of the printed book. Words in the dictionary are arranged in three columns. The first column includes Georgian words, second one – their transliteration in Latin characters, and the third column includes Italian translations of relevant Georgian words.

It is known that Stefano Paolini did not speak Georgian and had never visited Georgia. Presumably, the Georgian diplomat did not actively participate in the composition and publication of the dictionary either, for the latter contains numerous mistakes and errors both with respect to the Latin transliteration of Georgian words and with respect to the morphological and lexical equivalence of its Georgian and Italian parts.

In 1670, under the blessing of the Pope, **Bernardo Maria da Napoli**, a Capuchin monk from Italy, arrived in Georgia in order to conduct missionary activities. He stayed in Georgia for almost 10 years and composed two dictionaries: Italian-Georgian and Georgian-Italian ones. These dictionaries have never seen the light as printed books and their manuscripts are preserved in the National Library of Naples, Italy (Orlovskaya 1986: 94 - 110).

In the eighteenth century, the work on Italian-Georgian dictionaries still continued. In particular, an Italian missionary, whose name remains unknown and who is usually referred to as the **Anonym from Gori**, composed (presumably in 1724) an Italian-Georgian dictionary (Uturgaidze 1999). This dictionary is kept in the Georgian National Centre of Manuscripts (Tbilisi, Georgia). A previously unknown Georgian-Italian dictionary was discovered in 2012 in the Vatican Library. The information about the discovery was first disclosed to the participants of Batumi II International Symposium in Lexicography (Doborjginidze 2012: 77). Generally, the interest in Italy and the Italian language is clearly seen in Sulkhan-Saba Orbeliani's *Sitqvis Kona*. As we know, the Georgian headwords in Sulkhan-Saba's dictionary are, in addition to the definitions, supplied with their equivalents in three languages, including Italian.

At the beginning of the eighteenth century, there appeared the first bilingual dictionary / glossary with the Dutch language. The dictionary was composed by a Dutch statesman and orientalist **Nicolaas Witsen** (1641-1717) in collaboration with a Georgian Nobleman Al. Bagrationi. In 1705 Witsen published his book titled *North and East Tartary* (*Noord en Oost Tartarye*). In fact, Witsen treated in his work a wider spectrum of regions and countries than implied by its title, thus including in his survey the Caucasus, as well as Georgia. Witsen appended the chapter dedicated to Georgia with "The List of Georgian or Iberian[2] Language" or, in other words, a Dutch-Georgian glossary (Witsen 2013: 166 - 92). It is known that Alexander Bagrationi was on friendly terms with Peter I, King (Tsar) of Russia and accompanied him in his journeys to various countries. Together with the Russian Tsar, Al. Bagrationi visited Holland as well, spending a considerable period of time in this country. Exactly in this period he befriended Nicolaas Witsen and helped him compose his glossary. In the Dutch-Georgian Glossary, the words are not arranged either alphabetically or thematically. The words are displayed in three columns. The first column includes Dutch words, the second – the transliteration of Georgian words in Latin letters and finally, the third one – their Georgian translations. The dictionary includes 904 words, out of which 856 are the lexical units from the general word stock, while others are represented by numerals and names of months.

The eighteenth century also saw the interest of English authors in the Georgian language. In 1788, there was published in London a book by **George Ellis** titled *Memoir of Map of the Countries Comprehended Between the Black Sea, and the Caspian, with an Account of the Caucasian Nations and Vocabularies of their Languages* (Ellis 1788; Odzeli 1998: 32; Kikvidze, Pachulia 2021). The book describes the history, culture and religion of the Caucasian peoples and provides the information about the languages spoken in the Caucasus region. Along with other Caucasian countries, the book reviews in some detail Georgia as well. The author appends this chapter with a small comparative dictionary of Kartvelian languages.

It is noteworthy that the author shows interest not only in the Georgian language proper, but also in other Kartvelian languages. His book includes the material from Georgian, as well as from Mingrelian and Svan languages, the sister languages of Georgian. We can state that this book is the first known

---

[2] Iberia - An exonym for Georgian kingdom of Kartli (not to be confused with the eponymous Iberia - a peninsula / region in south-west Europe). Iberians is another name for Georgians.

example of studying the Georgian language in relation to English (Margalitadze, Tchighladze 2022). [3]

George Ellis was a broadly educated individual, who had graduated from the University of Cambridge. He was a historian, diplomat and Member of Parliament. Ellis himself had never visited the Caucasus or Georgia, but his interest in the region was caused by the fact that in 1782-1783 he had been on a diplomatic mission to Saint Petersburg, Russia. Ellis based his book mainly on Johann Anton Güldenstädt's itineraries on his travels to Russia and the Caucasus region, as well as on the description of Georgia by Jacob Reineggs, works of Peter Simon Pallas and Fr. Müller. In his book, Ellis also relied on the sources from classic antiquity.

As we learn from the foreword, Ellis's book was based on a minor comparative dictionary of world languages (*Linguarum totius orbis vocabularia comparativa*, or in Russian *Сравнительные словари всех языков и наречий*),[4] published on assignment from queen Elizabeth of Russia, which also comprises the material from Caucasian languages, including Georgian. The dictionary was written and published by the Russian Academy of Sciences in 1787 - 1789. In the foreword to his book, Ellis expresses regret that the dictionary lacks information concerning certain languages or dialects, as far as such information was not included in the original Russian dictionary. Ellis also regrets that English letters cannot adequately express the phonetic content of the Caucasian languages. The sounding of Caucasian phonemes was inadequately represented already in the Russian dictionary, because Russian lacks letters corresponding to some Caucasian sounds. The phonetic picture was further distorted when Ellis tried to transliterate Caucasian and Kartvelian phonemes by means of English letters. The dictionary often mixes up the terms *"language"* and *"dialect."* Svan language is regarded as a dialect, while Mingrelian words are said to represent the Imeretian dialect. These mistakes were transferred from the Russian dictionary, which caused many other inaccuracies as well (Ellis 1788).

2.5. Georgian Lexicography in the Nineteenth and Twentieth Centuries

2.5.1. The Nineteenth Century

The nineteenth century witnessed a dramatic change of the political situation in Georgia. The country was incorporated in the Russian Empire and since then, throughout the nineteenth century, Georgian bilingual lexicography

---

[3] Electronic version of the book by Margalitadze and Tchighladze is published on the following URL: https://margaliti.com/25/post19.htm

[4] Pallas, Peter Simon. *Linguarum totius orbis vocabularia comparativa* https://archive.org/details/bub_gb_mPBLAAAAcAAJ.

mostly produced Georgian-Russian dictionaries. Georgian was influenced by the Russian language as a result of Russia's domination in the country and Russian words started to enter the Georgian vocabulary without any control. Georgian writers, scholars and public figures were concerned with this fact and tried to produce dictionaries that would defend the Georgian language from corruption and uncontrollable borrowing processes.

Another foreign language, which appeared in the bilingual lexicography of the time, was the French language, the language popular among Georgian aristocracy. The Latin language was also used in some nineteenth-century dictionaries, predominantly in terminological ones.

In the nineteenth century, the interest of English authors towards the Kartvelian languages continued. In 1883 **Demetrius (Dmitri) Rudolph Peacock**, a Russian-born Englishman published his lexicographic endeavour, the full title of which is *Original Vocabularies of Five West Caucasian Languages compiled on the spot by Mr. Peacock*. D. R. Peacock was in service of the Russian Empire and, among other appointments, spent some time on administrative duties as a vice-consul to Batumi. He had also resided in Poti for some period of time. During his expeditions to various places of the Caucasus and Black Sea regions, Peacock, being commissioned by the Bengal Asiatic Society, collected the vocabularies of five, as he called them, West Caucasian languages, namely Georgian, Mingrelian, Svan, Laz and Abkhaz languages (Odzeli 1998: 33-34; Kikvidze, Pachulia 2019). In his book, the author shows a particular interest in the Svan language, erroneously referring to it, however, as to a Georgian dialect (probably after his predecessor G. Ellis).

Among the nineteenth-century English-Georgian word lists is **Marjory S. Wardrop's** unfinished *English-Georgian Dictionary*, which contains over 1000 words and is incorporated in *Etymological Dictionary of the English Language* by Chambers (CEDEL). M. Wardrop, an outstanding British Kartvelologist, the first translator of Shota Rustaveli's *The Knight in the Panther's Skin* in English, worked on the dictionary at the initial stage of the translation of the poem (Wardrop 2019). The manuscript of M. Wardrop's *English-Georgian Dictionary* was digitalized and published by the Lexicographic Centre of Tbilisi State University with bilingual English-Georgian introduction and commentaries in 2019 to commemorate the 150th anniversary of her birth.[5]

The nineteenth century is marked in the history of the Georgian lexicography by the lexicographic activities of Niko Chubinashvili and David Chubinashvili, prominent representatives of the Georgian lexicography of the time. They brought

---

[5] Electronic version of M. Wardrop's *English-Georgian Dictionary* is published online on the following URL: https://margaliti.com/EGD-web.pdf

the Georgian lexicography to a whole new level. Being well acquainted with Georgian lexicographic traditions and, especially, Sulkhan-Saba Orbeliani's lexicographic heritage, as well as with Russian and European lexicographic principles, they successfully introduced them into the Georgian lexicographic practice.

Niko Chubinashvili (1788-1845), a well-known Georgian lexicographer, archaeologist and translator compiled two dictionaries: *Georgian Dictionary with Russian Translations* (GDRT) and *Russian-Georgian Dictionary* (RGD) within the period of 1812 to 1825. Both dictionaries were published only in the 1960s under the editorship of A. Ghlonti.

Niko Chubinashvili's dictionary is based on the *Georgian Dictionary* by Sulkhan-Saba Orbeliani. In fact, the GDRT can be considered a substantially revised, corrected, edited and enlarged version of *Sitqvis Kona*. Entries in N. Chubinashvili's dictionary are provided with Russian equivalents of headwords. Some entries also contain equivalents of headwords in Turkish, Arabic, Armenian and other languages, transliterated in characters of the Georgian alphabet. Polysemous meanings of headwords are separated with two oblique lines (//), Russian equivalents are added not only to headwords, but also to each of polysemous meanings. Dictionary entries include references to sources, where the given word or any of its meanings are attested.

David Chubinashvili (1814-1891), a Georgian linguist, lexicographer and literary historian, was another outstanding representative of the nineteenth-century Georgian lexicography.

David Chubinashvili also composed two dictionaries: trilingual *Georgian-Russian-French Dictionary*, which he called *Treasury of the Georgian Language* (1840) and *Russian-Georgian dictionary*, which saw light in 1846 (Ghlonti, 1983, pp. 166 - 182).

D. Chubinashvili's *Treasury of the Georgian Language* contains 33 400 words and reflects the new lexical material which appeared in the vocabulary of the Georgian language as a result of the new generation of writers who had entered Georgian literary scene, numerous periodicals, belles-lettres books published, including the pieces of Old Georgian literature. It is noteworthy that in David Chubinashvili's dictionary entries are enriched with illustrational phrases and collocations, which is an important novelty for the Georgian lexicography of the nineteenth century. Niko and David Chubinashvili introduced a new principle for the lemmatization of the Georgian verb which has no infinitive in the Georgian language. In their dictionaries verb is regularly represented with a relevant verbal noun, so-called masdar, with its finite form (usually 3rd person singular, present or future tense) added in brackets.

2.5.2. The Twentieth Century

The twentieth century marked a significant upsurge in the Georgian lexicography which happened thanks to the foundation and activities of the Institute of Linguistics of Georgia (1941). There were produced various Georgian dictionaries, such as a comprehensive explanatory dictionary of the Georgian language, orthographic dictionaries, a dictionary of foreign words, phraseological, dialectal, comparative and etymological dictionaries, bilingual dictionaries, concordances, as well as dictionaries of scientific terms (*see* Dictionary section of Bibliography). The dictionaries were compiled according to the best lexicographic practice of the time.

The publication of ***The Explanatory Dictionary of the Georgian Language*** under the editorship of acad. Arnold Chikobava became a landmark event in the cultural life of Georgia (EDGL). The dictionary was composed in the 1950s and all prominent representatives of the Georgian linguistics of that period took part in its creation. The dictionary is based on the corpus of illustrational phrases and sentences selected from the Georgian literature, press, scientific literature and other sources and defines up to 113 000 words. As it is stated in the preface to the dictionary, this is far from representing the whole lexical wealth of the Georgian language.

The EDGL entries provide a detailed description of Georgian words, their polysemy, collocations and phraseological units, provide references to relevant sources. The dictionary comprises an ample amount of scientific terms. It should be noted that Georgian scientists from all fields were in active collaboration with the Editorial Board of the EDGL in order to ensure the adequate representation of scientific terminology in the nascent dictionary.

Explanatory Dictionary of the Georgian Language developed a new approach to the principles of lemmatization of the Georgian verb. Georgian language represents a language with complex morphology and especially complex is the categorial system of the Georgian verb (Shanidze 1973; Boeder 1968; Holisky 1981; Holisky 1979; Melikishvili et al., 2010). On the one hand, Georgian verb has inflectional categories such as person, number, mood, tense, iteration, sequence of action; on the other hand, it has derivational categories – aspect, voice, version, causative, location, direction-orientation (Shanidze, 1973). In order to adequately reflect these riches of the Georgian verb in the EDGL, Arn. Chikobava, the editor-in-chief, introduced in the dictionary as lemmas not only verbal nouns (e.g. *tesva* 'sowing'), but also finite forms of verbs reflecting grammatical categories of aspect, voice, version, causativeness, etc (e.g. *tesavs* 'sows he/she, it,' *itesavs* 'sows he/she, it for oneself,' *utesavs* 'sows he/she, it for smb.,' *atesvinebs* 'has smb. sow smth.,' *eteseba* 'will be sown,' *etc*). This principle was implemented throughout the eight volumes of the dictionary.

Later some dialectological dictionaries were compiled according to the same principle.

The terminological work in the twentieth-century Georgia deserves a special mention. The establishment of scientific institutes under the aegis of the Georgian Academy of Sciences (the 1940s – 1950s) significantly facilitated the conduct of terminological activities in the country. The Terminological Department of the Georgian Institute of Linguistics also took an active part in this. In the 1950s – 1990s, a number of terminological dictionaries were composed for practically all branches of science. These dictionaries were bilingual, explanatory or combined: bilingual-explanatory (see Dictionary section of References). It must be noted that Georgia in that period of time was an integral part of the Soviet Union and translation/bilingual lexicography inevitably continued to be practised in relation to the Russian language. Consequently, the majority of bilingual terminological dictionaries of that period of the Georgian history are Russian-Georgian.

In 1990, there was published an *Etymological Dictionary of the Kartvelian Languages* by Heinz Fähnrich and Surab Sardschweladse, which included the results of many years of comparative research and study in the field of the Kartvelian languages.

2.5.3. Bilingual Dictionaries of the Georgian Language in the Twentieth Century

During the twentieth century, various bilingual dictionaries were intensely compiled with respect to European, as well as to Oriental and Classical languages. In the 1930s, English-Georgian and Georgian-English dictionaries were composed almost simultaneously. The first English-Georgian dictionary (including 20,000 words) was published in Georgia in 1939. It was compiled by **Isidorè Gvarjaladze**, a Professor of the Pedagogical Institute of Foreign Languages in Tbilisi, Georgia. In the same year, **Eka Cherkesi** (Ekaterinè Cherkezishvili) completed in England the work on her Georgian-English dictionary. The publication of the book was, however, hindered by World War II and it was printed only in 1950 by the Oxford University Press (Margalitadze 2013). The same period of history saw the publication of dictionaries with various languages. It must be noted that the majority of translation dictionaries of that period were created on the initiative of individual specialists who, based on their own needs, strived to fill, as it were, the gaps and to meet the growing demand for the study of foreign languages in Georgia. Translation dictionaries, which were then composed by the lexicographers from Arnold Chikobava Institute of Linguistics, were mainly Russian-Georgian. In addition, the Institute had no department of European languages, which was another manifestation of the main trend in the Soviet ideology. The composition of comprehensive, academic bilingual dictionaries with respect to foreign languages, except for Russian, was not encouraged. Nevertheless, in the twentieth century there were composed several voluminous bilingual dictionaries, two of which were created abroad. These were *Georgian-German dictionary* by Kita Chkhenkeli, the *Comprehensive English-Georgian Dictionary* published by the Lexicographic Centre at Ivanè Javakhishvili Tbilisi State University (under editorship of Tinatin Margalitadze) and the *Comprehensive Georgian-English Dictionary* created under editorship of Donald Rayfield.

Kita Chkhenkeli (Tschenkéli) worked in Switzerland, namely at the University of Zurich. It was exactly in this university that his **Georgian-German Dictionary**, based on original lexicographic principles laid down by the author, was created. The publication of the dictionary began in 1961 and was carried out in fascicles. The last, 26th fascicle was published in 1974 by Yolanda Marchev, a disciple of Kita Chkhenkeli who, after the untimely death of her mentor, continued and successfully completed the project. After the publication of the dictionary in fascicles was over, the new printed edition in three volumes was published (GDW). The dictionary gained widespread approval among linguistic circles and was an enormous help to foreign Kartvelologists, who routinely used it to study the Georgian language. As already noted above, Georgian is characterized by complex morphology, while the lexicographic principles developed by Kita Chkhenkeli demonstrate the maximum structural models of Georgian words, systems of declension and conjugation, specificities of stem formation. The GDW entries list Georgian verbs by root, all forms of each particular verb are gathered in one cluster, where they are supplied with their relevant German translations. Roots, simple or complex stems, are highlighted in a way as to clearly demonstrate individual elements of a word, interrelations between the word's structural elements, system of stem modelling, root syncopation, truncation, etc. *The German-Georgian Dictionary* is a real novelty in the history of the Georgian lexicography. As an example, below is given an entry of the verb *tesva* 'sowing' from the GGD.

Inf. თესვა ‖ თესა

T' ვთესავ ‖ ვთეს s. *fut*

fut ~ s. და~; გან~ aussäen; *fig* zerstreuen, versprengen, auseinander-treiben, -jagen; გამ~ (zur Ausnützung freier Stellen) dazwischen an-säen od. -pflanzen (z. B. Bohnen in e-m Maisfeld); გადა~ von neuem besäen; და~ 1. (an-, aus-, ein-)säen (z. B. Korn) 2. be-, an-säen (z. B. Feld) 3. züchten (z. B. Bakterien) 4. *fig* den Keim zu et. (Gutem od. Schlechtem) legen, säen (z. B. Hass), einpflanzen (z. B. Liebe zu et.) 5. *fig* (umg.) vertun, verschleudern (z. B. Geld); მი~ 1. et. Unsorgfältig (irgendwo) säen 2. *fig* (umg.) vertun, verschleudern (z.B. Geld); მო~ 1. aus-, be-säen 2. *fig* ausstreuen, verbreiten (z. B. Gerücht); შე~ Bed. s.

გამო~; ჩა~ 1. Einsäen 2. *fig* den Keim zu et. (Gutem od. Schlechtem) legen, säen (z. B. Hass), einpflanzen (z. B. Liebe zu et.)

[*aor* -ვთესე *pf* -მითესავს ‖ -მითესია] ZP[1] (ს)თესია *fut* ეთესება (ეთესა, -) et. ist bei j-m (aus)gesät/(an)-gepflanzt (z. B. Korn in j-s Feld).

Meanwhile, the task of the creation of a ***Comprehensive English-Georgian dictionary*** was shouldered by the Chair of English Philology at Iv. Javakhishvili Tbilisi State University. This happened exactly because the Institute of Linguistics, as mentioned above, lacked a department of European languages. The creation of an English-Georgian Dictionary was planned as soon as the Chair of English Philology was established at the university in the 1960s. It was no easy task to work on the dictionary in an educational institution, which lacked any experience in the implementation of lexicographic projects. This resulted in numerous errors and mistakes both in the planning of the project and with respect to the selection of sources, etc. Working on the dictionary were the university teachers of English, who had no previous experience in lexicography.

In the 1980s, a small team of editors embarked upon the mission of fundamentally revising, expanding and updating the dictionary in order to prepare it for publication. The editors of the *Comprehensive English-Georgian Dictionary* (CEGD 1995-2014) decided to rely upon major English explanatory dictionaries as the source for their renewed dictionary. Namely, they chose *Oxford English Dictionary on Historical Principles* (OED), *Webster's Unabridged Dictionary* (WTNID), as well as other reliable English lexicographic sources which became their primary tool in researching the semantics of English words. With the spread of the Internet in Georgia, the editors started to use electronic corpora in their editorial work, as well as other modern methods of retrieving and processing data from corpora. This stage of the work on the dictionary continued for 35 years.

In 1995 there began the printed publication of the *English-Georgian Dictionary.* Not unlike the dictionary by Kita Chkhenkeli, the dictionary was published in fascicles, on a letter-by-letter basis. 14 fascicles of the dictionary have been published so far. In 2010 the online version of the dictionary (100,000 entries) was uploaded to the Internet. The primary purpose of the creation of the dictionary was to facilitate the translation of English literature (both belles-lettres/fictional and specialist) into Georgian. This is why the dictionary includes contemporaneous English vocabulary, as well as obsolete, archaic words and specialist terms (Margalitadze 2012).

There is a considerable semantic asymmetry between Georgian and English and editors of the CEGD confronted this problem at the early stage of their editorial work.

The Board of Editors of the CEGD developed different techniques for dealing with the problem of equivalence back in the 1980s independent of the lexicographic theories and practices of European lexicographers. In order to reflect the meaning of English words as precisely and accurately as possible, they established two levels of equivalence in the entries of the dictionary, namely the equivalents of meaning and translation/contextual equivalents. The combination of equivalents of meaning and translational/contextual equivalents, the application of certain principles of explanatory dictionaries and careful selection of illustrative material enabled the editors to describe all aspects, all nuances of meaning of English words. This is the novelty introduced by the team of the CEGD in the English-Georgian lexicography (Margalitadze, Meladze 2016).

It must be noted that the editorial team of the *Comprehensive English-Georgian Dictionary* founded at Tbilisi State University the Lexicographic Centre, which during its 25-year-long existence, implemented numerous bilingual lexicographic and corpus-related projects, introduced teaching of lexicography on all three university levels and promoted the process of transformation of lexicography into an academic discipline.[6]

The Comprehensive Georgian-English Dictionary under editorship of Donald Rayfield was published in London in 2006 by Garnett Press (CGED). Donald Rayfield is a well-known British Slavist and Kartvelologist. He is the author of a number of monographs on the Russian and Georgian Literature. He is also a skilful translator, including the translations of the pieces of Georgian literature into English.

When Prof. Rayfield presented his *Georgian-English Dictionary* to the academic society assembled at Batumi I International Symposium in Lexicography (2010), he said in jest that he had composed the dictionary solely for himself, for he could very well remember how difficult it was for him to study Georgian without having an adequate and reliable Georgian-English dictionary at hand. Thus he identified the target group, for which the *Comprehensive Georgian-English Dictionary* was primarily composed. This group includes foreign Kartvelologists, who study Georgian for various reasons. Georgian is interesting for foreign linguists because of the peculiarities of its morphological structure. Besides, they are interested not only in the Georgian language as such, but also in related Kartvelian languages. Historians are interested in the Georgian language in order to gain immediate access to and study Georgian historical sources, for the mediaeval history cannot be contemplated without taking the factor of

---

[6] This is the same working team which established in 2020 The Centre for Lexicography and Language Technologies at Ilia State University.

Georgia into account. The specialists in literature are interested in the language as they want to familiarize themselves with the rich Georgian literature, whose first specimens date from as early as fifth century CE. As Donald Rayfield himself writes in the preface to his history of the Georgian literature, the importance of the Georgian literature is out of all proportions to the number of speakers of the language (Rayfield 2000). This target group defined the selection of the vocabulary, which was included in the dictionary: the contemporary, as well as Old Georgian vocabulary, the word-stock of the Georgian dialects and related Kartvelian languages, the terms from specific branches of knowledge, and so on. The Dictionary includes virtually all the entries from the *Explanatory Dictionary of the Georgian Language*. The second major source was a database of the Georgian daily and weekly press (from 1999-2002). Thirdly, a searchable electronic version of forty substantial texts by contemporary writers, predominantly novelists was created and used. The fourth major source were Ilia Abuladze's and Zurab Sarjveladze's dictionaries of Old Georgian. There have been (selectively) used about thirty dictionaries of the various dialects of modern Georgian and dictionaries from various branches of science and technology. The Georgian-English Dictionary has also incorporated a substantial body of modern colloquial, including vulgar, expressions.

The CGED adopted Arn. Chikobava's approach to the Georgian verb and listed verbal noun / masdar and all the finite forms of the same verb in the dictionary, as it is in the EDGL. The CGED provides detailed grammatical labels to all the finite forms given in the dictionary. Donald Rayfield's dictionary includes 140,000 Georgian words and is published in two volumes.

2.6. Development of Digital Lexicography in Georgia

The development of digital technologies (including digital lexicography) in Georgia faced multiple obstacles during the country's troubled history throughout the twentieth century, overshadowed by the Soviet occupation with the inevitable domination of communist ideology.

The development of computing and digital technologies in the former Soviet countries (including Georgia) was greatly impeded by the fact that the Soviet ideology regarded cybernetics (as well as Mendelian genetics) as "pseudoscience." As a result, the development of computing and digital technologies in Georgia was considerably hampered.

The situation improved only during the period of the relatively liberal rule of Nikita Khrushchev, who led the general campaign for the de-Stalinization of the Soviet Union. The taboo previously imposed on cybernetics and genetics was lifted and since then both branches developed more or less normally.

Another hindrance to the smooth development of computing and digital technologies occurred after the collapse of the Soviet Union, when due to the ensuing political turmoil and civil war, Georgia was thrown into chaos and, for more than a decade, power outages and total blackouts (to say nothing of other major and minor inconveniences associated with that period of Georgia's history) became usual. This happened in the same period, when the world witnessed the advent of the Internet and the humanity was beginning to revel in the new-found opportunities offered by the World Wide Web.

As a consequence, the full-scale history of digital lexicography in Georgia begins only in the twenty-first century. It must be noted however that the digitalization of Georgian texts in order to compile the Georgian National Corpus (http://gnc.gov.ge/) began as early as the 1980s in collaboration of Georgian and German scholars under the scientific supervision of Prof. Jost Gippert from the Goethe University in Frankfurt am Main (Gippert, Tandashvili 2015). The development of corpus linguistics and digital humanities in Georgia gave impetus to the digitalization of the Georgian lexicography as well.

The development of digital lexicography in Georgia, like in the entire world, followed two main trends: (1) the digitalization of existing printed dictionaries and placing them on the Internet; and (2) the generation of digital dictionaries based on extensive databases, which are equipped with the functionality (i.e., control panel) allowing the constant reworking, revision, updating and complementation of the dictionary material.

A typical example of the first trend is the *Explanatory Dictionary of the Georgian Language* in 8 volumes, which is merely an electronic version of the original printed publication.[7]

The same trend is represented by the project, which has been implemented for many years by the National Parliamentary Library of Georgia. Practically all more or less important dictionaries existing in Georgia at the moment are digitalized within the framework of this project and are freely available to the general public.[8]

As for the second trend, dealing with the conceptual issues of the development of modern digital lexicography in Georgia is associated with the Lexicographic Centre at Tbilisi State University (TSU) and the editorial team of the *Comprehensive English-Georgian Dictionary*. In 2009, the editors of the CEGD decided to create its online version and to place it on the Internet. They studied the electronic

---

[7] *Explanatory Dictionary of the Georgian Language* (under the general editorship of Arnold Chikobava), available online on the following URL: http://www.ice.ge/liv/liv/ganmartebiti.php.

[8] Dictionaries are freely available to the general public on the following URL: https://www.nplg.gov.ge/geo/E-Dictionaries.

dictionaries existing at that time and decided to choose the CD version of the Oxford English Dictionary (OED) as a kind of template for their intended project. CEGD was uploaded to the Internet in 2010.[9]

The online version of CEGD has a wide range or search options. Search is possible by keywords, as well as by word combinations or phrases; it is possible to make search by headwords and make a full-text search; Georgian words and phrases can also be searched for. A control panel was specifically designed for the CEGD, which includes the following: the functionality to edit the wordlist of the dictionary; the one to insert new headwords / entries into the wordlist; functionality to store the logs of searches made by users; useful tools for editors, such as text generators and convertors. The control panel enables continual updating, correction and complementation of the dictionary.

In 2011–2014, the same technological framework was used for the new terminological dictionaries created by the Lexicographic Centre, namely for *English-Georgian Military Online Dictionary* (EGMOD) and *English-Georgian Biology Online Dictionary* (EGBOD).

In parallel with these projects, the next stage in the development of Georgian digital lexicography became clearly discernible: the composition of electronic and online dictionaries by the instrumentality of special Dictionary Writing Systems (DWSs), rather than on the basis of .doc files (Margalitadze, Keretchashvili 2013). Within such a system, the dictionary material is distributed to separate fields of the database, which enables the generation of online and electronic dictionaries of much higher quality.

This new trend was exemplified by another project of the Lexicographic Centre: *English-Russian-Georgian Online Dictionary of Technical Terms* (ERGTOD), which was uploaded to the Internet in 2016. It is a so-called "digitally born" dictionary, which was composed within the Multilingual Dictionary Management System (MultiDMS) as a database. The following fields were designed within the base: headwords (English, Russian, Georgian), definitions, field-specific labels, synonyms, related words, collocations, illustrative phrases, etc. The distribution of lexicographic data by appropriate fields resulted in the composition of a modern-type online dictionary equipped with multiform, versatile search systems for English, as well as Russian and Georgian languages. Besides, it became possible to automatically generate the following terminological pairs: English-Georgian, Georgian-English, English-Russian, Russian-English, Russian-Georgian, Georgian-Russian and, as a result, original 18,000 dictionary entries produced almost 87,000 additional six-language terminological pairs (Margalitadze 2018).

---

[9] *Comprehensive English-Georgian Online Dictionary* (editor-in-chief Margalitadze, Tinatin) is freely available on the URL: www.dict.ge.

An in-house dictionary writing system was also used in the composition of *The Georgian Dictionary* – an explanatory Georgian learner's dictionary (authors: G. Tsotsanidze, N. Loladze and K. Datukishvili), which was published in 2014 by Bakur Sulakauri Publishing. This made possible the creation of a rather adaptable and user-friendly online dictionary.[10]

Another important dictionary, representing this direction of Georgian digital lexicography is *the Online Dictionary of Idioms* (2014 - 2017), designed at Ilia State University (compilers - S. Berikashvili, I. Lobzhanidze, editorial board: Sh. Aphridonidze, S. Shamanidi). The dictionary, intended for specialists of Georgian and Modern Greek, takes an innovative approach to the representation of idiomatic information in electronic / web-based dictionaries. The dictionary can be described both as monolingual (Georgian) and bi-directionally bilingual (Modern Georgian-Modern Greek and vice versa). The Georgian part of the dictionary is supplied with authentic illustrative phrases and sentences from the "Corpus of the Georgian Language" created also at Ilia State University. It is equipped with user-friendly search tools enabling one to find necessary idioms, to realize their meanings and to see the specific contexts of their use. The dictionary is created in a professional Dictionary Writing System – Tlex. It is marked with the application of finite state technology for the morphological analysis of the modern Georgian language and the application of a morphological transducer intended to facilitate solving the problems of lemmatization and alphabetization often faced by the compilers of present-day Georgian dictionaries (Lobzhanidze 2019).

Modern Georgian lexicography is marked by development of new genres of lexicography. Professor Tamar Makharoblidze's several years of research at Ilia State University resulted in the publication of the *Georgian Sign Language Dictionary*, published by Ilia University Press in 2016.

Entirely corpus-based Georgian dictionaries opened a new page in the modern Georgian digital lexicography, marking a new development in this field. Here we would like to mention several recent Georgian dictionaries which are entirely corpus-based. They were composed specifically for the Frankfurt Book Fair 2018 within the framework of the project "Saba." These dictionaries are as follows:

>   (a) Three dictionaries of Georgian dialects, namely Tush, Imeretian and Fereydanian, were composed with their wordlists defined by means of a special corpus editor, which processed corpus data from the Georgian Dialect Corpus. The Georgian Dialect Corpus is being

---

[10] *The Georgian Dictionary* (authors: G. Tsotsanidze, N. Loladze and K. Datukishvili) is available online on the following URL: https://www.ganmarteba.ge.

composed and gradually complemented within the framework of the project "Linguistic Portrait of Georgia" since 2006 at the Department of Computer Processing of Linguistic Data of the TSU Arnold Chikobava Institute of Linguistics (Department supervisor - Marina Beridze). The corpus includes the data from various dialects of the Georgian language proper, as well as data from Zan (i.e. Mingrelian and Laz) and Svan, which are traditionally regarded as separate Kartvelian languages in their own right (Beridze, Lortkipanidze, Nadaraia 2015).

(b) Two learner's dictionaries, based on the frequency analysis were also composed within the framework of the same project "Saba:" Georgian-Abkhazian-English and Georgian-Ossetian-English. The frequency list was generated on the basis of the Georgian Web corpus (KaWaC, created by Dr. Sophie Daraselia from the University of Leeds, UK). These dictionaries are essentially multilingual, for each Georgian headword they include is supplied with its Abkhazian or Ossetian equivalents, which are followed by their English translations. The Georgian headwords and Abkhazian / Ossetian translations of these dictionaries are transliterated into Latin script (IPA adapted to Caucasian languages). Each headword is also supplied with grammatical information, such as its inflectional and derivational forms, etc. These, as well as other functionalities of the dictionaries in question, make them into a nice example of how the wide range of capabilities offered by the Internet and computer technologies in general can be creatively used in our modern-day digital humanities and digital lexicography.

One more important direction of modern Georgian digital lexicography is the application of lexicographic data in machine translation projects.

"It is no coincidence that we are witnessing an increasing need for high-quality lexicographical data. Language technology and artificial intelligence are moving into a phase where the word lists and morphological lexicons developed inside the NLP environment itself are insufficient to meet the demands for developing smarter and more sophisticated products. Automatic content summaries, domain classification and virtual assistants are but a few examples of applications that require 'knowledge' or some way of handling the semantics of human language. By far the best existing semantic descriptions of language are dictionaries, and for that reason, it is obvious that existing dictionaries are interesting for developers of such applications" (Trap-Jensen 2018).

A good example of cooperation between lexicographers and NLP specialists is "an English-Georgian Machine Translation Project," which is underway and which is a joint project of the "Centre for Lexicography and Language Technologies" at Ilia State University and "Text Technology Lab" at Goethe-University Frankfurt, Germany (Margalitadze, Pourtskhvanidze 2019).

With the modern processes of globalization underway, the Georgian language has to pass some difficult and demanding tests. Nowadays, the task of placing the Georgian language within the paradigm of modern technologies, which implies its full digitization and the development of adequate Georgian translation software, presents enormous and, at the same time, exciting new challenges to modern Georgian lexicographers and computer specialists.

Thus, the integration of the Georgian language into international digital translation products or programs, into various online or desktop applications, blogs and social network sites is the only way to ensure that the Georgian will retain its applied value and function in all spheres and domains.

This new tendency demands new approaches to dictionary data processing and data structuring issues that will increase the effectiveness of the application of lexicographic data not only for stand-alone dictionaries, but also for the NLP purposes. This is exactly the aim of transforming lexicography into a modern interdisciplinary branch of knowledge. This goal can be achieved by theoretical studies, as well as by educating a new generation of Georgian lexicographers at all three university levels, where lexicography will be taught in close relation with information technologies, computer linguistics, general linguistics and lexicographic practice (Sinclair 1984).

References

a. Standard References

Beridze, Marina, Liana Lortkipanidze, and David Nadaraia. 2015. "The Georgian dialect corpus: Problems and perspectives." In: Jost Gippert/Ralf Gehrke (eds.): *Historical Corpora. Challenges and Perspectives. Corpus Linguistics and Interdisciplinary Perspectives on Language,* Vol. 5. Tübingen: Narr.

Boeder, Winfried. 1968. "Über die versionen des Georgischen verbs." *Folia Linguistica,* Vol. 2 (1-2). Berlin: de Gruyter Mouton.

Chikobava, Arnold, and Juansher Vateishvili. 1983. *First printed books in Georgian* (in Georgian, Russian and English languages). Tbilisi: Khelovneba [In Georgian].

Doborjginidze, Nino. 2012. "Origins of Lexicological Method of Sulkhan-Saba Orbeliani." In: *Proceedings of the II International Symposium in Lexicography.* Batumi: Meridiani [In Georgian].

Ellis, George. 1788. *Memoir of Map of the Countries Comprehended Between the Black Sea, and the Caspian, with an Account of the Caucasian Nations and Vocabularies of their Languages.* London.

Ghlonti, Alexander. 1983. *Questions of Georgian lexicography.* Tbilisi: Sabtchota Sakartvelo [In Georgian].

Gippert Jost, Tandashvili Manana. 2015. "Structuring a diachronic corpus. The Georgian national corpus project." Gippert, Jost, Gehrke, R (eds). *Historical Corpora. Challenges and Perspectives. Corpus Linguistics and Interdisciplinary Perspectives on Language,* v. 5. Tübingen: Narr.

Hewitt, George. 1991. "Lexicography of the Caucasian languages I: Georgian and Kartvelian." *Handbücher zur Sprach- und Kommunikationswissenschaft: Woerterbücher*. Berlin: de Gruyter, pp 2415-2417.

Holisky, Dee Ann. 1981. "Aspect and Georgian medial verbs." *Anatolian and Caucasian studies*. Delmar, NY: Caravan Books.

—. 1979. "On Lexical aspect and verb classes in Georgian." In *Papers from the Conference on Non-Slavic Languages of the USSR* (eds: Paul R. Clyne, William F. Hanks, Carol L. Hofbauer). Chicago: University of Chicago, pp. 390 – 401.

Kikvidze, Zaal, and Levan Pachulia. 2019. "Demetrius Rudolph Peacock and the Languages of Georgia." *General and Specialist Translation / Interpretation: Theory, Methods, Practice: International Conference Papers*. Kyiv: Agrar Media Group.

—. 2021. "George Ellis' 130 English Words and Their Equivalents in Caucasian Languages (Evidence from his 18th c. book)." *General and Specialist Translation / Interpretation: Theory, Methods, Practice: International Conference Papers*. Kyiv: Agrar Media Group.

Lobzhanidze, Irina. 2019. "Computational Model of the Modern Georgian Language and Search Patterns for an Online Dictionary of Idioms." *In: Silva A., Staton S., Sutton P., Umbach C. (eds) Language, Logic, and Computation. TbiLLC 2018. Lecture Notes in Computer Science* 11456:187-208.

Makharoblidze, Tamar. 2015. "About the Georgian Sign Language Lexical Level." *Iberian Caucasian Linguistics,* vol.43. Arn. Chikobava Institute of Linguistics: Tbilisi. pp. 116-144 [In Georgian].

Makharoblidze, Tamar, and George Mirianashvili. 2016. "GESL lexical level and innovation technologies." *Proceedings of the XVII EURALEX International Congress: Lexicography and Linguistic Diversity.* Tbilisi: Ivane Javakhishvili Tbilisi State University. http://euralex.org/category/publications/euralex-2016/.

Margalitadze, Tinatin. 2012. "The Comprehensive English-Georgian online dictionary: methods, principles, modern technologies." Proceedings of *XV EURALEX International Congress*. Oslo: University of Oslo http://www.euralex.org/proceedings-toc/euralex_2012/.

—. 2013. "English-Georgian Lexicography." *The Kartvelologist.* Journal of Georgian Studies. Tbilisi: Tbilisi University Press.

—. 2018. "New Platform for Georgian Online Terminological Dictionaries and Multilingual Dictionary Management System." *Proceedings of the XVIII EURALEX International Congress: Lexicography in Global Contexts.* Ljubljana: Ljubljana University Press, Faculty of Arts.

—. 2022. *Introduction to Lexicography.* Tbilisi: Ilia State University Press [In Georgian].

Margalitadze, Tinatin, and George Keretchashvili. 2013. "From DOC Files to a modern online dictionary." Kosem, I., Kallas, J. et al (eds.). *Electronic lexicography in the 21st century: thinking outside the paper. Proceedings of the eLex 2013 conference.* Ljubljana/Tallinn: Trojina, Institute for Applied Slovene Studies/ Eesti Keele Instituut. http://eki.ee/elex2013.

Margalitadze, Tinatin, and George Meladze. 2016. "Importance of the Issue of Partial Equivalence for Bilingual Lexicography and Language Teaching." *Proceedings of the XVII EURALEX International Congress: Lexicography and*

Linguistic Diversity. Tbilisi: Ivane Javakhishvili Tbilisi State University. http://euralex.org/category/publications/euralex-2016/.

Margalitadze, Tinatin, Pourtskhvanidze Zakharia. 2019. "The Georgian Language in AI-based Translation Models: Cooperation of Lexicographers and NLP specialists." International conference *Lexicography at a Crossroads,* organized by TSU Lexicographic Centre and Consortium of European Master in Lexicography (EMLEX). https://margaliti.com/emlexweb.pdf.

Margalitadze, Tinatin, and Salomè Tchighladze. 2022. *Unknown Pages of English-Georgian Lexicography.* Tbilisi: Ilia State University Press [In Georgian].

Melikishvili, Damana, Daniel J. Humphries, and Maia Kupunia. 2010. *The Georgian verb: A Morphosyntactic analysis.* Hyattsville: Dunwoody Press.

Odzeli, Marika. 1998. *On the History of Georgian-English Literary Contacts.* Tbilisi: Tbilisi University Press [In Georgian].

Orlovskaya, Natalia. 1986. *Questions of the literary contacts of Georgia with the West.* Tbilisi: Tbilisi University Press [In Russian].

Rayfield, Donald. 2000. *The Literature of Georgia. A History.* London: Routledge.

Shanidze, Akaki. 1973. *Foundations of Georgian grammar.* Tbilisi: Tbilisi University Press [In Georgian].

—. 1999. "Explanatory dictionary of the Georgian language (critical notes)." *Questions of Linguistics.* v. 2. Tbilisi: Tbilisi University Press [In Georgian].

Shanidze, Mzekala. 1968. "Introduction to Eprem Mtsire's translation of Psalms (text and commentaries)." *Works of the Department of the Old Georgian Language.* v. 11, Tbilisi: Tbilisi University Press [In Georgian].

Sinclair, John. 1984. "Lexicography as an Academic Subject." R. R. K. Hartmann (ed.), *LEXeter '83. Proceedings.* Tübingen: Max Niemeyer, 13-30.

Trap-Jensen, Lars. 2018. "Lexicography between NLP and Linguistics: Aspects of Theory and Practice." Jaka Čibej, Vojko Gorjanc, Iztok Kosem, and Simon Krek (eds.). *Proceedings of the XVIII EURALEX International Congress: Lexicography in Global Contexts.* Ljubljana: Ljubljana. University Press, Faculty of Arts. https://euralex.org/publications/lexicography-between-nlp-and-linguistics-aspects-of-theory-and-practice/.

Tvaltvadze, Darejan. 2009. *Colophones of Eprem Mtsire.* Tbilisi: Nekeri [In Georgian].

Uturgaidze, Tedo. 1999. *History of the study of the Georgian language,* part I. Tbilisi: Georgian Language [In Georgian].

Wardrop, Marjory. 2019. *English-Georgian Dictionary.* Tbilisi: Tbilisi University Press.

Witsen, Nicolaas. 2013. *Noord en Oost Tartarye. Georgia of Iberia en Mengrelia.* (Trandslated into Georgian by A. Javakhadze and N. Javakhadze). Tbilisi: Universali.

b. Dictionaries:

[CEDEL] *Chambers's Etymological Dictionary of the English language:* A New and Thoroughly Revised Edition. 1882. Edited by A. Findlatter, M.A., LL.D. London and Edinburg.

[CEGD] *Comprehensive English-Georgian Dictionary,* fascicles I – XIV. Editor-in-chief Margalitadze, Tinatin. 1995 - 2014. Tbilisi: Lexicographic Centre.

[CEGOD] *Comprehensive English-Georgian Online Dictionary*. Editor-in-chief Margalitadze, Tinatin. 2010. Tbilisi: Lexicographic Centre. www.dict.ge.

[CGED] *A Comprehensive Georgian-English Dictionary* in 2 volumes. Editor-in-chief Rayfield, Donald. 2006. London: Garnett Press.

[DGI] *Dittionario Georgiano e Italiano* composto da Stefano Paolini con l'aiuto del M.R.P.D. Nicefore Irbachi, Giorgiano. Roma, 1629.

[EDGL] *Explanatory Dictionary of the Georgian Language* (under the general editorship of Arnold Chikobava). 1950 – 1964. I – VIII vols. Tbilisi: Mecniereba.

[EGBOD] *English-Georgian Biology Online Dictionary*. 2014. Tbilisi: Lexicographic Centre. http://bio.dict.ge.

[EGMOD] *English-Georgian Military Online Dictionary*. 2011. Tbilisi: Lexicographic Centre. http://mil.dict.ge.

[ERGTOD] *English-Russian-Georgian Online Dictionary of Technical Terms*. 2016. Tbilisi: Lexicographic Centre. http://techdict.ge.

[GDRT] Chubinashvili, Niko. 1961. *Georgian Dictionary with Russian Translations* (edited by A. Ghlonti). Tbilisi: Mecniereba.

[GDW] Tschenkéli, Kita, and Yolanda Marchev. 1965 - 1974. *Georgisch-Deutsches Wörterbuch*. Zürich.

[GRD] Chubinashvili, David. 1984. *Georgian -Russian Dictionary* (ed. A. Shanidze). Tbilisi: Sabtchota Sakartvelo.

Makharoblidze, Tamar. 2016. *Georgian Sign Language Dictionary*. Tbilisi: Ilia University Press [In Georgian].

[OED] *Oxford English Dictionary on Historical Principles*. 1989. Second edition on CD-ROM. Version 2.0. Oxford: Oxford University Press.

[RGD] Chubinashvili, Niko. 1971. *Russian-Georgian Dictionary*. In 2 volumes. Tbilisi: Sabtchota Sakartvelo.

[SSO] Orbeliani, Sulkhan-Saba. 1991. *Georgian Dictionary*. In 2 volumes. Tbilisi: Merani.

[WTNID] *Webster's Third New International Dictionary* (Unabridged). 1981. Merriam Webster Inc.

Abashidze, Simon, and Lado Abashidze. 1973. *Russian-Georgian Medical Explanatory Dictionary*. Tbilisi: Sabchota Sakartvelo.

Chabashvili, Mikheil. 1989. *Dictionary of Foreign Words*. Tbilisi: Ganatleba.

Chikobava Arnold. 1938. *Laz-Mingrelian-Georgian Comparative Dictionary*. Tbilisi: Mecniereba.

Dictionary of Philosophical Terms. 1987. Tbilisi: Sabtchota Sakartvelo.

Fähnrich Heinz, and Surab Sardschweladse. 1990. *Etymologisches Wörterbuch der Kartwel-Sprachen*. Leiden.

Imnaishvili, Ivanè. 1986. *Concordance of the Gospels*. Tbilisi: Tbilisi University Press.

Jorbenadze, Sandro. 1998. *Explanatory Dictionary of Terms of Intellectual Property*. Tbilisi: Samartali.

Kaukhchishvili, Simon. 1961. *Latin-Georgian Dictionary*. Tbilisi: Sabchota Sakartvelo.

Kereselidze, Nodar. 1988. *Multilingual Dictionary of Sociology*. Tbilisi: Metsniereba. *Legal terminology*. 1963. Tbilisi: Georgian Academy of Sciences Press.

Makashvili, Alexander. 1991. *Botanical Dictionary*. Tbilisi: Metsniereba.

Menabde, Tsiala. 1983. *English-Russian-Georgian Biological Dictionary.* Tbilisi: Metsniereba.

Neiman, Alexander. 1978. *Dictionary of Georgian Synonyms.* Tbilisi: Ganatleba.

Russian-Georgian Archaeological Dictionary (under the editorship of Andria Apakidze). 1980. Tbilisi: Tbilisi University Press.

Russian-Georgian Dictionary. In 3 volumes. 1959. Tbilisi: Georgian Academy of Sciences Press. *Technical terminology.* 1977. Tbilisi: Metsniereba.

Terminology of Geophysics. 1988. Tbilisi: Metsniereba.

Topuria, Varlam, and Ivanè Gigineishvili. 1998. *Orthographic Dictionary of the Georgian Language.* Tbilisi: Ganatleba.

Tsereteli, Giorgi. 1951. *Arabic-Georgian Dictionary.* Tbilisi: Mecniereba.

Uznadze, Nino. 1997. *English-Georgian Explanatory Dictionary of Psychoanalytical Terms and Concepts.* Tbilisi: Ganatleba.

Chapter 3

Modality and Negative *Ver* Particle
in the Georgian Language

Nino Sharashenidze

Ivane Javakhishvili Tbilisi State University, Georgia

Abstract

Modality and negation are universal categories. They have been the subject of many studies. In the Georgian language, these issues have yet to be studied, which will reveal many interesting scientific problems in Georgian and other languages from the group of Kartvelian languages. The issue is interesting from the typological point of view as well.

Negation in the Georgian language is a three-member system that involves neutral negation (particle *ar* – not), the negation of possibility (*ver* particle – can not) and the negation expressed by prohibition or request (particle *nu* – do not).

This chapter deals with the negation of possibility in the Georgian language. The analysis covers the aspects of negation and modality and points out the key feature related to the expression of negation and modality with the same form. Fields of application of the *ver* particle is wide. It is used with the forms of both indicative and subjunctive mood. The article provides the analysis of negation of possibility expressed by the *ver* particle, its collocations and semantics.

Keywords: Modality, modal form, modal meaning, negation, negative particle

***

3.1. Introduction

3.1.1. Category of Negation

From the cognitive point of view, negation involves a comparison between two situations: real, which lacks some element, and imaginary, which does not lack this element. Category of negation is expressed by different means: lexical, morphological, and syntactic. Negative expressions generally are marked. Usually, they are expressive because their purpose is to deny the fact, object, etc. into the human cognition. In natural languages, negation, as well as modality and quantifiers, play a role of the operator. The operator has its scope. It means that its meaning influences the components of the sentence. The influence may be expressed in the same clause or in the previous clause.

Negation is treated as a grammatical category. There are two main types of negation: rejections of suggestions and denial of assertion. Negation may be explicit and implicit (Tottie, 1991). Negation may cover the whole sentence (clausal negation) or some elements of the sentence (constituent negation). In Georgian language, it is expressed by the verbal and nominal negation (Advadze, 2018)

There are several purposes for expressing negation in languages: negation of existence, actions, facts, speech acts, etc. (Payne, 1985). Negation may be expressed by different grammatical parts of speech: particle, verb, noun, adjective, pronoun, adverb, preposition, quantifier, conjunction, complementizer (Wouden, 1997). Some lexical items are often used in collocation with negation. In fact, they contribute to its intensification, its strengthening. Their combination mostly expresses emphasis. Negation at the level of syntax also goes beyond the negative semantics. Besides the lexical units with negative semantics, this category includes some lexical units that are in collocation with or in the scope of negation.

In the Georgian Language the category of negation is expressed by both grammatical and lexical means.

> *u-* prefix can be attached to a noun (*uçigno* - *without book)*, an adjective (*ulamazo* - not nice), and a noun derived from the verb *(dauçereli - not written).*

The Georgian language uses a three-member system of particles for expressing negation.

> *ar* (not) expresses neutral or strong negation. This particle is used for verbs of all three types of mood: indicative – *ar aketebs* (*he doesn't make)*, subjunctive – *ar unda gaaketo* (*you shouldn't do)*, imperative - *ar gaaketo* (Don't do!). With some forms of verbs, the particle expresses a neutral negative result of the action: *ar gamiketebia* (*I have not done)*.

> *ver* (*can not)* particle in Georgian is considered to be the means of expressing possibility. The particle occurs only with the verbs of the indicative and subjunctive mood. The particle is never found with the verb in the imperative mood.

> *nu (do not!)* particle is used for expression of semantics of prohibition and request. It occurs with verbs of imperative semantics, with present and future tenses and it is never found with verbs in the past tense (Chumburidze 1970; Jorbenadze 1984; Sharashenidze 2015, Advadze 2018).

Table 3.1. Three-member system of negation and mood

Indicative mood	**ver** *(can not)*	
Subjunctive mood		**ar** *(not)*
Imperative	**nu** *(do not!)*	

3.1.2. Category of Modality

Modality as a grammatical category has been studied in linguistics for a long time. This category was introduced into linguistics by the same concept as in logic. Modality is based on the idea of subjective perception of the universe. Naturally, in all languages, there are linguistic means that convey the subjective perception of the universe or phenomena and, thus, modality is recognized as a universal category, although different languages have different linguistic means and systems of its expression. If we consider modality in a broader sense, there is not any sentence or discourse without modal content. The study of modality as a grammatical category involves the study of those linguistic means that constantly express the semantics of modality in languages. Modality as the attitude of a speaker towards the expression is manifested at all levels of the language system. Modality can be expressed by intonation, word order, sentence structures with complex hypotaxis, by adding modal verbs or some particles, or by the mood of the verb.

Modality is a cognitive, emotional aspect or will/desire of the speaker expressed by linguistic means in relation to the spoken discourse. The definition of modality implies semantics of the sentence. But it is important to consider that modality is not an analysis of a sentence taken out of the context. Sometimes, it is necessary to take into account the full text/discourse for determination of the essence of modality.

While studying modality, it is important to define concepts within the category itself. First of all, epistemic, deontic and dynamic modalities are distinguished (Von Wright 1951). The epistemic modality expresses the knowledge and belief of a speaker, while the deontic modality implies the content in which the subject performs an action. This action is conditioned by the speaker's desire or other motives (For example, law, morality, internal or external directives, etc.) (Lyons 1977; Palmer 1990, 2001; Frawley 1992; De Haan 1997; Van der Auwera and Plungian 1998; Portner 2009). Dynamic modality refers to ability, disposition. After extensive research have been created new terms for deontic modality: root modality, agent-oriented, speaker-oriented, and subordinating. The latter is used in subordinated sentence. The term agent-oriented denotes to all modalities where conditions are based on the agent, such as obligation, will, ability, permission, possibility. Speaker-oriented modality implies speech acts aimed at performance of something (imperative, directive, optative, permissive, prohibition). Epistemic modality refers to the whole statement (discourse) and expresses the position of a speaker in relation to the truth of the statement (Bybee 1985; Bybee and Fleischman 1995; Bybee, Perkins, Pagliuca, 1994). The notions may be presented in other terms, for example, agent-oriented modality is used for participant-oriented modality. It means that in some contexts, the subject is not an active agent of the action and only perceives the action. This kind of approach defines two more notions - participant-internal and participant-external modality (Van der Auwera and Plungian 1998). Participant-internal modality resembles dynamic modality - semantics of ability and need, as for participant-external modality, it is divided into participant-external deontic and non-deontic modality. In this sense, deontic modality is a subtype of participant-external modality and it covers permission and obligation of the speaker or other side. Non-deontic modality comprises possibility and necessity determined by the environment (De Haan 2005). Dynamic modality is divided into possibility due to the external (neutral) factors and internal possibility or acquired ability (subject-oriented) (Palmer 1990, 83; Portner 2009, 135).

The basic means of expression of modality are considered to be specific modal verbs, so-called modal auxiliary verbs. Among them are items expressing strong modality (must, deontic modality) and weak modality (may). The latter expresses permission (deontic modality) or possibility (epistemic modality). Thus, the same modal verb refers to both epistemic and deontic modality. This is a cross-linguistic phenomenon and it has diachronic bases, as epistemic meaning derives from deontic meaning (Traugott 2005). Such ambiguity, i.e., the use of one form for both strong and weak modality, is typical for German, Slavic, Roman and African languages (De Haan 2005). The same is observed in Georgian. The modal form, ***unda***, expresses both deontic and epistemic modality. The same refers to the modal particle, ***ver.*** It expresses dynamic modality, but there are some phrases where its meaning refers to epistemic modality.

There are different systems for the expression of modality in the old and modern Georgian language. In the old Georgian language, modal semantics were expressed by special verbs: ***ʒal-uʒs > ʒal-uc, ǯer-ars, qel-ečipebis, šesaʒlo ars, šemʒlebel ars***. Since the ninth century, we see modal forms of another type, like ***uʒlavs*** (Gambashidze, 2018). Since the fifteenth century, in middle Georgian, a new system was formed on the basis of grammaticalization.

The expression of modality has been imposed on modal particles, modal items that complement subjunctive and indicative forms and introduce modal semantics into the sentence (Sharashenidze, 2008, Makharoblidze 2018). But in view of the fact that the category of modality is not fully grammaticalized in the Georgian language, modal semantics, along with modal verbs and specific particles, are used for adverbs and other lexical units.

Table 3.2. Partial list of Georgian modals

Modal verbs	*ndoma, šeʒleba*
Impersonal modal verbs	*šeiʒleba, šesaʒloa, šesaʒlebelia*
Modal particles	*unda, ikneb, egeb, lamis*
Modal interrogative particles	*gana, nutu, aḳi*
Modal negative particles	*ver, nu*

Modal units precede verbal forms. Only a negative particle may be used between a verb and a modal particle. Usually, modal lexical units introduce modal semantics in the phrase though other grammar categories (tense, aspect) are expressed by a verbal form.

3.2. Modality in Georgian

The system of modality in the Georgian language underwent great changes: as a result of grammaticalization, the system of special modal verbs turned into the system of particles. Tense and mood form basis of the Georgian verb system. Therefore, when analyzing the category of modality, it is important to focus on the semantics of the modal form and the screeve form of the verb.

Grammaticalization led to the development of a new system in Georgian: systemic expression of the category of modality is closely related to the process of grammaticalization. In Old Georgian, modal semantics was expressed solely by means of special verbs (**ǯer ars** (should), **uqms** (must), **egebis** (may), **ʒalucs** (can)...). Beginning from the fourteenth-fifteenth centuries, great systemic changes of certain forms took place in the language. Out of these forms, the verb **ndoma** (want) underwent the most significant changes. Its formal and functional changes and numerous phenomena related to the grammaticalization of this form led to the development of the category of modality. The category of modality cannot be studied without analyzing the phenomenon of grammaticalization because this systemic change led to the development of numerous forms and new semantics.

Research of the process of grammaticalization embraces not only the analysis of the change of form but also the explanation of the semantic changes occurring in the language. In this regard, the semantic change of the form **unda** is of special interest. Grammaticalization implies loss of semantic features. However, the analysis of the **ndoma** form enables us to discuss the process of acquisition of new semantics. The initial semantics of the verb, **ndoma** (want/wish), formed the basis for an extremely diverse modal content. The first semantic shift is related to the second person form **gina / ginda**. The first step of grammaticalization of the verb **ndoma** (want) is the semantics of **free choice and absence of difference**. The decategorized **unda** form also reveals this semantics.

However, it later acquired additional semantics of debitive, obligation, deontic modality and epistemic necessity, which in itself embraced numerous other sub-semantics.

As a result of grammaticalization, several other modal particles were developed in Middle Georgian, namely **ikneb (possibly), egeb (maybe), lamis (almost)**. They were developed in the same way. The semantics of modal particles obtained as a result of grammaticalization was based on their lexical meaning. After they became invariant elements, they acquired more concrete modal semantics.

The contemporary Georgian system of expression of the category of modality has been developed since the fifteenth century as a result of grammaticalization. This system consists of elements of modal semantics (modal particles) and the main verb in this or that person form. Modal semantics changes as a result of the replacement of modal elements, but other categories and meanings are expressed by the main verb.

The category of modality in Georgian consists of the following types:

- **Epistemic possibility** – the main semantics of epistemic modality is **epistemic possibility**, which is based on the opinion and belief of the speaker. In contemporary Georgian, it is expressed by the modal form **šeiʒleba (may)**. **Modality of assumption-** epistemic possibility in Georgian also embraces the semantics of **assumption**. The assumption is based on the speaker's perception of the action, the possibility that something has happened or may happen, or the speaker's understanding of the fact. This central semantics is expressed by means of **egeb (maybe), iqneb (possibly)** deverbalized modal elements. In this regard, mention should also be made of the modal form, **albaT (probably)**. These modal forms express the semantics of **doubt, hope and request**, although assumption is a central semantics for the modality of this group. It can be paraphrased as: "it is probable," "it can be assumed that..."

- **Epistemic necessity** – the meaning is based on the content "it is necessary...," "as far as I know," "it is necessary," "I believe it is necessary." Epistemic necessity implies the attitude of the speaker based on their background knowledge, belief, and vision of the truth. The proposition of the utterance implies the speaker's opinion, experience and attitude based on knowledge, whereas the utterance expresses logical necessity of action. It is subjective modality which is based on the speaker's attitude. In Georgian, this semantics is expressed by the modal form, **unda** (must).

- **Deontic modality** – deontic modality is traditionally viewed as semantics of moral obligation and permission, with the meaning of possibility and necessity. Whatever is viewed as moral obligation and belongs to the field of necessity, is related to moral rules, and whatever is allowed and lawful, is considered possible. Deontic modality can be paraphrased as "it is necessary…," "it is possible…," "it is obligatory…." Apart from modal forms, the semantics of the utterance is enhanced by means of adjectives and adverbs with deontic content. There are several key semantics in the deontic modality, out of which the semantics of **permission** and **obligation** are central. In Georgian, deontic modality embraces the semantics of **permission, obligation and prohibition-request**. Permission implies those circumstances and situations which allow the action and make it possible. In Georgian, the semantics of deontic possibility is related to the modal form **šeʒleba** (can). One of the central semantics of deontic modality is **obligation**, which is expressed by means of modal form **unda** (must). This meaning implies the requirements related to rules and regulations, as well as moral obligations imposed by the society and ethical norms.

- **Dynamic modality** – dynamic modality denotes ability or necessity caused by internal or external state. It implies both mental and physical abilities. Dynamic modality embraces the semantics of dynamic necessity and dynamic ability (Palmer, 2001). Dynamic modality does not belong to subjective modality. It can be paraphrased as follows: "it is possible…" "it is necessary…" "I/he/she can…," "is able to…." In Georgian, dynamic modality chiefly embraces the semantics of ability and possibility and is expressed by **objective conjugation forms** of the modal verb **šeʒleba** (can): **šemiʒlia** *(I can),* **šegiʒlia** *(you can (second person singular)),* **šeuʒlia** *(he/she/it can),* **šegviʒlia** *(we can),* **šegiʒliat** *(you can (second person plural)),* **šeuʒliat** *(they can).* The modal form **unda** (must) also has the semantics of dynamic necessity if it expresses **necessity caused by objective reality**. In Georgian, a specific negative particle, **ver**, denotes the absence of dynamic ability.

- **The modality of desire** – the modality of desire (i.e., volitive) in contemporary Georgian embraces desire, expressed by the modal form **ikneb** (maybe), and a strong wish or dream, expressed by the modal form **neṭav** (if only).

Identification and classification of **modal indicators** and analysis of their relations with the types of modality enable us to draw a complete picture of expression of the category of modality in the Georgian language.

3.3. The *Ver* Particle in the Georgian Language

The *ver* particle is represented in two Kartvelian languages. The corresponding form of the *ver* particle is not found in the Svan language but it is restored at the stage of unification of Georgian and Zan languages. The relevant particle for *ver* in Mingrelian-Laz language is *var/va* (Fahnrich, Sarjveladze 1990). However, in the Mingrelian language, this particle does not convey the semantics of negation of possibility; it expresses only neutral negation. This data suggests that the development of the semantics of negation of the possibility is observed only in the Georgian language system.

We observe the *ver* particle from the ancient texts. By itself, it has not changed any form or function. We can say that this form is the oldest fixed expression of the modal semantics and negation in the Georgian language.

In the Georgian language, *ver* forms are not only for negation but quantifiers as well.

Table 3.3. Quantifiers with *ver* particle

		-c particle expressing focus and additive meaning	-ġa negative particle with the meaning of limitation	-ġa , -c
Animate (person) pronoun	*veravin*	*veravinac*	*veġaravin*	*veġaravinac*
Personal inanimate pronoun,	*veraperi*	*veraperic*	*veġaraperi*	*veġaraperic*
Indefinite pronoun	*veravitari*	-------------	*veġaravitari*	-------------
Negative temporal adverb	*verasdros, verasodes*	*verasdrosac,* -------------	*veġarasdros, veġarasodes*	*veġarasdrosac* -------------
Negative adverb of place	*versad*	*versadac*	*veġarsad*	*veġarsadac*
Conjunction		*verc ... verc*	*veġarc ... veġarc*	-------------

All forms with the particle, *ver*, can express semantics of negation of possibility. This semantics is well manifested in other opposite forms based on the three-member system of negation *(aravin - veravin - nuravin, araperi - veraperi - nuraperi, arsad - versad - nursad...),* The difference between them is determined by its initial semantics. **veravin, veraperi, versad** - may be translated as a neutral negative pronoun, but the difference between them in the Georgian language is essential. Excluding meaning and semantics in Georgian. There is a rule that in the case of double negation, each item of the three-member system activates the relevant derivation. There is no exception with regard to it.

In the case of double negation in Georgian, each negative particle (*ar, ver, nu*) always triggers the use of the relevant quantifier (*ar - arsad, ver - versad, nu - nursad*....).

> ### *arsad ar mivdivar (I don't go anywhere)*
> Adv Neg Loc   Neg **Go**V MedPass Pres Pv S:1Sg

> ### *versad ver mivdivar (I can not go anywhere)*
> Adv Neg Loc   Neg **Go**V MedPass Pres Pv S:1Sg

> ### *nursad nu midixar (Do not go anywhere)*
> Adv Neg Loc   Neg **Go**V MedPass Pres Pv S: 2Sg

3.3.1. *Ver* Negative Particle and Negation

The *ver* particle expresses dynamic modality and denotes the negation of possibility caused by physical and mental abilities or other circumstances. Semantics of collocations of "*ver* + verb" can be defined as neutral (caused by environmental conditions) as well as a "subject oriented" (internal or acquired ability) negation of possibility. In Georgian, *ver* expresses both neutral and subject-oriented negation: "*ver caval*" (I cannot go), "*ver gavaketeb*" (I cannot do) may mean negation of physical and mental ability, as well as negation caused by external factors. The semantics may be specified by a broad context and discourse but not by the collocation itself.

From the point of view of modality, there is one interesting example of the ancient Georgian language is that has not been developed; it has been established in the modern Georgian language in a different way. "*ver mižlavs*" (= *ar šemižlia, I cannot…*) expresses the negation of possibility of action where subject against his/her will be unable to perform the action.

> "*asoci clisa var da ver mižlavs me šemoslvad da gansvlad tkuen cinaše*" *(GNC)*

Here, a verb is presented with an objective marker and the particle, *ver*. This is an example of a dynamic modality that expresses the negation of possibility/ ability. The collocation is not currently used. In the modern Georgian language, a verb with an objective marker forms a combination with the particle, *ar*, and a verb with subjective marker – with the *ver* particle.

> ### ar *šemižlia – ver ševžleb*

The "*ver šemižlia*" combination has not developed. The reason may be the fact that the verb, *šemižlia*, with the meaning of dynamic modality and an objective marker, easily forms collocations with the particle, არ, which expresses neutral negation. The "*ver ševžleb*" combination means that negation of a subject's possibility/ability is based on knowledge; belief is a key feature of epistemic modality.

The semantics of the **ver** particle prevents the formation of some collocations. The **ver** particle never forms combinations with the meaning of deontic modality, as dynamic modality expresses ability and disposition while the **ver** particle negates it. It is common that the **ver** particle never forms a combination with the meaning of deontic modality. Accordingly, the fact that the particle is never used with imperative mood is determined by its semantics.

The ver particle, due to the semantics of dynamic modality, never forms combinations with some verbs. Primarily, these are verbs of physical and mental perception **(Verba Sentiendi)** and existential verbs. The limitation is caused by the verb semantics. Verbs of physical and mental perception express human feelings (hunger, thirst, pain, cold, love, hate, desire, will, hearing...). The use of the **ver** particle with these verbs contradicts the semantics of dynamic modality, as the feelings are natural phenomena for a human. Only the **ar** particle is used with these verbs. It expresses only neutral negation and negates a condition in a specific period of time (not the negation of ability, disposition and capability). This clearly indicates semantic blocking, the basis of which is the feature of dynamic modality.

The **ver** particle also does not occur with static verbs **(Stative Verbs)**.

Table 3.4. *ver* particle's incompatibility

Verbs of physical and mental perception **(Verbs of perception)**	*mšia* (I am hungry), *mcq̇uria* (I am thirsty), *mṭḳiva* (hurts), *mciva* (it is cold), *miq̇vars* (love), *mʒuls* (hate), *minda* (want), *mesmis* (hear)
Cognitive verbs	*vici* (I know)
Existential Verbs	*aris* (be), *arsebobas* (exist), *imq̇opeba* (is), *mdebareobs, akvs, hq̇avs* (have)
Stative Verbs	*ceria* (written), *abadia, gaačnia* (have), *avlia* (surrounded) *asxia, aq̇ria, aceria, axaṭia, axuravs, acqvia, atqvia, artqia, acvia, ačnia*

The **ver** particle is fully compatible with cognitive verbs (verbs with the meaning of knowledge, understanding, comprehension, application/analysis, synthesis, assessment/evaluation), as cognitive verbs express ability and disposition and **ver** relates to the degree of ability or possibility of its use. It should be noted that the verb, **codna (vici) (to know)**, is an exception; it never occurs with the particle, **ver**. It always forms a combination with the particle, **ar** (**ar vici**), which has the meaning of neutral negation. As knowledge is a factual phenomenon, the particle of negation of possibility is not used with this verb.[1] Cognitive verbs are used both with the particle, ***ver***, and the particle, ***ar***, of neutral negation, but they have different meanings: ***ver aǧcera*** *(= he could not describe)* – ***ar aǧcera*** *(= he did not describe)*, ***ver ҫarmoidgina*** *(he could not imagine)* - ***ar ҫarmoidgina*** *(he did not imagine)*. Cognitive verbs with the particle, ჴ6, are rarely used. They are mostly used with the conjunction, ***tu***, in conditional sentences. There was only one example found in **KAWAC** Corpus:

> ***mḳitxvels gauҫirdeba am suratis agkma, tu ar ҫarmoidgina dǧevandeli pilarmoniis adgilze morkaluli liandagi.*** *(KAWAC)*
> The reader will find it difficult to reproduce the view, if not to imagine the curved railway track on the site of today's Philharmonic.

According to the above-mentioned example, the ***ver*** particle is not used with existential verbs. Although, in the modern Georgian colloquial speech, there are two combinations with two meanings: *"ver aris"* - (1) Doesn't feel well, is not healthy. (2) Mental instability, mentally unhealthy. Therefore, we can say that the language removes the semantic blockade. This led to the change of the expression, a change in its semantics and the acquisition of an additional pragmatic aspect. The same semantic change is observed in the following phrases:

> ***ar mesmis*** *= I cannot hear, but:* ***ver mesmis*** *= I cannot comprehend, understand, realize it.* The examples represent additional pragmatic realization of the particle, ***ver***, and reveal the tendencies in the verbal discourse.

3.3.2. *Ver* Particle at the Syntactic Level

There are some cases of the use of the ***ver*** particle in the sentence:

1. ***ver*** negates an action or a state that doesn't happen due to the lack of opportunities associated with external or internal conditions. The ***ver*** particle always precedes a verb and negates the possibility of the action expressed by a verb. As it was noted, ***ver*** does not distinguish internal and external possibilities. The distinction is possible only at the lexical level or by the introduction of a subordinate clause.

> *(2)* ***gušin ana ver ҫavida teaṭrši.***
> *Adv Temp N Neg V Aor Pv S:3Sg N Dat Sg PP*
> *Yesterday Anna could not go to the theater.*

---

[1] ***vici*** verb is an exceptional case; only this verb forms ergative collocations in the present tense – ***icis man is.*** The verb moved form II series to I series with the same collocation in the old Georgian.

2. *vera* is used as an answer to a question and stands for the whole sentence.

(3) šeasrule davaleba? – vera.
V Act Aor Pv S:2Sg DO:3 N VN Pv Nom Sg - Neg L Pot
Have you done your assignment? – No, I couldn't.

3. Complicated forms (*verc, veġarc*) with the limited particle, "*ġa*," and the additive particle, "*c*," focus on the word with which they form a combination:

(4) verc me da verc šen ver gavaḳetebt amas.
Neg Pot Encl: Foc   Pron Pers 1 Nom Sg   Cj Coord   Neg Pot Encl: Foc
Pron Pers 2 Nom Sg   Neg   V Act Fut Pv S: 1Pl DO:3   Pron Pers 3 Dat Sg
Neither I nor you can do this.

(5) veġarc me gnaxet da veġarc tkven gvnaxet.
Neg Pot   Pron Pers 1 Sg   Cj Coord   Pron Pers 2 Nom Pl Encl:ʒ Foc
Pron Pers 2 Pl   V Act Aor S:2Pl DO:1Pl
Neither I could see you, nor you could see us

It must be noted that the *ver* particle forms the same syntactic collocations as other negative particles (Advadze, 2018); there are not any differences here. The main thing related to the three-member system of negation in Georgian is the semantics of negative particles.

3.3.3. *Ver* Particle and Double Negation

The Georgian language belongs to the group of languages in which double negation is used. There are several cases of using double negation in the Georgian language.

1. Double negation is required if a pronoun or an adverb are separated from a verb with another word(s).
2. Double negation is required if a negative pronoun or an adverb follows a verb.
3. Double negation is also required in case of a pronoun or an adverb with the particles "*ġa*" and "*c*".

Double negation cannot be used only when a negative pronoun or adverb immediately precedes a verb (Geguchadze 2007). However, it should be noted that the scientific literature indicates a case where the use of double negation is permissible, and this acquires a stylistic function - the use of a particle emphasizes the negation.

Generally, the use of multiple negations in a sentence does not comply with the rule of negation in logic. In logic, two negations cancel each other, and triple negation results in one negation. Linguistics distinguish several cases of multiple uses of negation. Double negation gives a single negation reading and intensifies it (Wouden, 1994). Interpretation of negation is related to the pragmatics. The use of double negation in natural languages has its prerequisites.

In this regard, it is interesting to analyze the data in languages that use double negation. Double negation is natural for Georgian and its use in a sentence is conditioned by activation of nominal and verbal negation.

In Georgian, double negation refers to two members of the sentence. On the one hand, we have a nominal negation, and on the other hand, verbal negation. Quantifiers with the *ver* particle are often used in sentences and, together with verbal negation, form nominal negation. In this case, negation of modality of possibility has a wider scope and refers to both a noun and a verb.

3.3.4. *Ver* Particle and Double Modality

As it was noted *ver* particle always precedes a verb and conveys the meaning of impossibility to perform the action presented by the verb. Accordingly, the collocation expresses modal semantics of the negation of possibility. The question is, how this collocation can take other modal forms? There are examples in the KAWAC Corpus where between *ver* particle and a verb stand modal forms - *unda* and *šeiʒleba*.

unda is a modal form that expresses epistemic necessity, while *šeiʒleba* expresses epistemic possibility. Collocations with *ver* particle conveys complicated modal semantics. Key point in this case is the location of a modal item and word order. For the analysis we provide a few cases from KAWAC and use the following symbols: N_{ver} - *ver* particle M_{unda} - modal form *unda*, modal form *šeiʒleba* - $M_{šeiʒleba}$, V = verb.

ver and *unda* modal forms - N_{ver} + M_{unda} + V: This order is the only one in the KAWAC (82 examples). There are not any cases with the inverse order. The analysis reveals two groups:

1. N_{ver} + M_{unda} + V − phrase expresses **negation of possibility or epistemic necessity**. In this case the scope of negation is wider and covers the semantics of epistemic necessity:

[**negation of possibility** + [epistemic **necessity**] + **verb**]
paṭara ver unda grʒnobdes, rom daʒabuli xart.
The little one shouldn't feel your tension.

Sometimes the co-occurrence is intensified with double negation:

> ***šesaçiravis moṭana <u>veravin ver unda mogaşcros</u> am ṭaʒartan.***
> *No one should forestall you in donation to this temple.*

> ***çesit, veranairad ver unda gaegot, sṗecrazmi rom apirebda oṗeraciis čaṭarebas.***
> *Really they were not obliged to know that the special-operations force was going to carry out this action.*

2. **Interrogative word + N$_{ver}$ + M$_{unda}$ + V** – the phrase expresses complex semantics: surprise + negation + epistemic necessity. i. e. the phrase in relation with the negation of epistemic necessity expresses the emotional attitude of surprise:
   [[**surprise** + [**negation** + [epistemic necessity] + verb]

> ***ocneba rogor ver unda aisrulo?!***
> *How can a man not realize his dream?!*

> ***raṭom ver unda daenaxa?***
> Why couldn't he have seen?

> ***raṭom ver unda xedavdnen isini?***
> Why can't they see it?

> ***cxrameṭi ̦clis bič̣ma rogor ver unda gadaçdviṭo ra unda kna mag dros?***
> *How can't a nineteen-year-old boy decide what to do in such a case?*

ver* and *šeiʒleba* modal forms**: In this group, we have a different situation: the negation of epistemic possibility (šeiʒleba.***) and dynamic possibility (***ver***) occurs in two sequences:

1. **M$_{šeiʒleba}$ + N$_{ver}$ + V** – in this sequence (81 examples in the Corpus) the scope of modal form is wider, as ***ver*** negates the possibility of the activity expressed by the verb. The semantics of the phase may be presented as the following: [**epistemic possibility** + [negation of possibility + verb]]:

> ***mat šeiʒleba ver gaigon čveni iumori.***
> *They may not be able to understand our humor.*

> ***adamianma šeiʒleba ver gauʒlos da uaresad daavaddes.***
> *A person may not be able to stand it and get sick even worse.*

> ***šeiʒleba ver iḋido iseti ram, rac namdvilad ş̌irdeboda sačukris mimǧebs.***
> *You might not be able to buy the one that the gift recipient really needed...*

*zogi/bevri **šeiʒleba ver mixvdes, razea saubari…***
Some/many *may not be able to* understand what this is about…

2. $N_{ver} + M_{šeiʒleba} + V$ – contexts with this order is limited. We have found only 6 cases in the KAWAC Corpus. The scope of the negative particle is wider and covers semantics of modality of epistemic possibility. [**negation of possibility** + [epistemic possibility + verb]]:

tu ara meḳobreoba, sxvanairad ver šeiʒleba šepasdes es gadaċqviṭileba.
If not piracy, then this decision cannot be assessed otherwise.

tu ara mekobreoba, sxvanairad ver šeiʒleba šepasdes gadaċqveṭileba rusetsa da apxazets šoris ṗirdaṗiri saaviacio mimosvlis šesaxeb.
*If not piracy, then otherwise it is **impossible to assess** the decision between Russia and Abkhazia on direct flights.*

es ar aris is cipri, romelic saxelmċipom ver šeiʒleba daparos.
*This is not a figure that a state **cannot repay.***

This group includes semantics of surprise as a result of use of an interrogative word, however, the proposal is presented in the affirmative form.

*gasagebia, **raṭom ver šeiʒleba daasaxelon mat rusi samxedroebis mier čadenili današaulis pakṭebi.***
*It is clear why they will **not be able** to call the crimes committed by Russian soldiers.*

The context of double negation is also confirmed:

ḳaṭegoriuli imperaṭivi aranairad da veranairad ver šeiʒleba idges ertmnišvnelovan mimartebaši češmariṭebastan.
*Categorical imperative in **no way and could not** stand unambiguously in relation to the truth.*

As a result, we can say that the use of double negation in Georgian is possible and the key point in this case is a sequence of modal forms: the scope of the first modal form is wider than the second one, as the latter refers to a verbal form only.

3.4. Conclusion

Negation and modality are universal categories that are common to all languages. Georgian a has three-member system of negation. The language uses the particle, არ (*ar*), for expressing neutral negation; the particle, ვერ (*ver*), expresses possibility; and the particle, ნუ (*nu*), expresses request/prohibition. არ (*ar*) is used with all forms of mood, ვერ (*ver)* is used with the indicative and conjunctive mood, and ნუ (*nu*) with the imperative mood. The particle, ვერ

(*ver*), represents a form with the semantics of both negation and modality. The expression of modality differs in the old and modern Georgian language: after grammaticalization, a new modal system has been formed through the particle, ვერ (*ver*), which is the oldest form of expression of negation and dynamic modality in the Georgian language. The particle has retained this function in the language. ვერ (*ver*) forms negative pronouns and adverbs that also have the modal semantics of negation of possibility. The scope of use of ვერ (*ver)* is determined/limited. It is not used with the verbs of perception, existential and static verbs. The ვერ (*ver*) particle always precedes a verb. The Georgian language is characterized by the expression of double plural. Plural expressed by ვერ (*ver*) is intensified with the complicated forms by use of particles ღა (-*ġa)* (expresses limited negation) and ც (-*c*) (expresses complementary function). Double negation in Georgian comprises both noun and verbal negation. As for the semantics of negation of possibility, it is extended with the complicated forms of negative pronouns and adverbs derived from the ვერ (*ver*) particle. Analysis of the contexts with ვერ (*ver*) has revealed phrases with double negation. In double negation, the scope of the first negative modal element is wider than the scope of the next modal element.

References

Advadze, Maia. 2018. *Nominal and verbal negation expressed by the particle "ver" in Georgian, Language and Culture.* Kutaisi. [In Georgian].

Bybee, Joan L., 1985. *Morphology: A study of the relation between meaning and form.* Amsterdam: Benjamins.

Bybee, Joan L., and Suzanne Fleischman, 1995. *Modality in Grammar and Discourse.* Amsterdam: Benjamins.

Bybee, Joan, Revere Perkins, and William Pagliuca. 1994. *The Evolution of Grammar, Tense, Aspect, and Modality in the Languages of the world.* Chicago: The University of Chicago Press.

Chumburidze, Zurab. 1970. *Negative particles in Georgian and stylistic features of their use, Georgian language and literature at school*, 1970, #2. Tbilisi. [In Georgian].

De Haan, Ferdinand. 1997. *The Interaction of Modality and Negation, A Typological Study.* New York: Garland.

—. 2005. *Typological Approaches to Modality, The Expression Cognitive Categories,* edited by William Frawley. Berlin: de Gruyter Mouton. https://pdfs.semantics cholar.org/f433/1055c9d78e29d7024f7d966fe22e5c749eac.pdf

Fahnrich, Haintz, and Zurab, Sarjveladze. 1990. *Etymological dictionary of Kartvelian languages.* Tbilisi. [In Georgian].

Frawley, William. 1992. *Linguistic Semantics.* Hillsdale, HJ: Lawrence Erlbaum.

Gambashidze, Maguli. 2018. "The verb *šeʒleba* (can) expressing dynamic modal semantics and related intransitive particles in written Georgian." *The International Symposium of the young scientists in humanities.* Tbilisi. [In Georgian].

Geguchadze, Leila. 2007. *About the wrong forms of single negation in modern Georgian. A collection of issues of the Georgian literary language: History and modernity.* Tbilisi [In Georgian].

Jorbenadze, Besaron. 1984. "For the variety of expressive forms of negation in Georgian." *Issues of Georgian speech culture*, VI, 1984. Tbilisi. [In Georgian].

Lyons, John. 1977. *Semantics*, v. I II, Cambridge: University of Cambridge Press.

Makharoblidze, Tamar. 2018. "Concerning Some Issues of Modality in Georgian." *Issues of The Structure of Kartvelian Languages* XIV. A. Chikobava Institute of Linguistics. Tbilisi. pp. 61-75.

Palmer, Frank Robert. 1990. *Modality and the English Modals*, second edition. New York: Routledge.

—. 2001. *Mood and Modality*. Cambridge: Cambridge University Press.

Portner, Paul. 2009. *Modality*. Oxford: Oxford University Press.

Sharashenidze, Nino. 2015. *The system of Negation in Georgian, General Analysis, Linguistic research*, XXXVIII, Tbilisi. [In Georgian].

Traugott, Elizabeth Closs. 2005. "Historical aspects of Modality." In *The Expression of Cognitive Categories*, edited by William Frawley. Berlin: de Gruyter Mouton.

Tottie, Gunnel. 1991. *Negation in English Speech and Writing: a Study in Variation.* New York: Academic Press, INC.

Van der Auwera, Johan, and Vladimir Plungian. 1998. "Modality's semantic map." *Linguistic Typology* 2, 79-124.

Von Wright, Georg H. 1951. *An Essay in Modal Logic.* Amsterdam: North-Holland Publishing Company.

Wouden, Ton van der. 1997. *Negative contexts: collocation, polarity and multiple negation.* London: Routledge.

GNC - The Georgian National Corpus, http://gnc.gov.ge/gnc/concordance

KaWaC – Georgian Corpus from the Web, http://corpus.leeds.ac.uk/internet.html

Chapter 4

The Linguistic Construal of Space
in Megrelian and Laz

Rusudan Gersamia

Ilia State University, Georgia

Abstract

Language encodes essential processes going on in the universe and provides
cognitive models being variously reflected crosslinguistically with respect to
various (for instance, socio-cultural and geographic and landscape-related)
factors.

A linguistic picture of space makes up a rather complex system in Megrelian
and Laz; hence, lexical and grammatical means for its representation is broad
and diverse. The linguistic representation of the cognitive model of space in the
languages in point involves substantives, verbs, and adverbs. Spatial features
are encoded in items at the lexical and grammatical levels: locative cases,
spatial preverbs and adverbs, deictic pronouns, adverbials of place. All
elements are satellites either inside or outside a verbal stem, making up a
complete linguistic picture of the world perception. Spatial relations can be
established by means of consideration and analysis of this system as a unity, as
far as elements of a language system are used not in an isolated way but rather
in interrelationship with other linguistic items. The chapter is an attempt to
represent a complete picture of spatial relations in Megrelian and Laz.

In the present chapter, stems with neutral roots referring to motion (movement)
and immobility (position) have been focused for the sake of establishing spatial
relations; they are the most essential and significant forms of human activities.
They are unique with respect to the fact that they pertain to the most ancient
layers of the Kartvelian lexicon, bearing their structural and semantic features.

Keywords: Spatial semantics, Motion and position verbs, Megrelian and Laz,
Preverb, Adverb

***

4.1. Introduction

Megrelian and Laz are non-written languages of the Kartvelian branch. Their historical differentiation occurred at the latest stage of the disintegration of Proto-Kartvelian (Deeters 1930; Gamkrelidze, Machavariani 1965; Klimov 1964; Fähnrich, Sarjveladze 2000). The theoretically postulated language, as a result of the divergence of which historical 'Megrelian' and 'Chan' (resp. Laz) emerged, has been referred to as Zan (Gamkrelidze, Machavariani 1965, 16), which seems to be rather a historical entity than the one functioning in present-day circumstances.

Megrelian and Laz linguistic systems, grammatical and semantic structures are much closer to each other than each of them to any language of the Kartvelian family, this having been conditioned by the fact that the differentiation of these languages pertains to a later period of the divergence of the Kartvelian languages (see G. Deeter's diagram; Deeters 1930).

Among the Kartvelian languages, Laz is the only one which is predominantly spoken outside Georgia, specifically, in Turkey; the only compact Laz settlement in Georgia is the border-line village of Sarpi; Laz is spoken beyond the border, along the Black Sea coast, from Hopa to Kemer, and its dialect differentiation is also evidenced along the coastline. The most effective means for the description of the language situation of Laz is a spatial-derivational model of language diversification based on the Wave Theory of linguistic changes and innovations (H. Schuchardt, J. Schmidt): a language feature spreads gradually, in a wave-like way from one location towards another so that it becomes difficult to draw sharp linguistic boundaries between them. Speakers residing in adjoining districts understand each other better and those residing in extreme peripheries hardly find each other's speech intelligible (Marr 1910; Chikobava 1936; Holisky 1991; Kutscher 2001, 2008; Kartozia 2005; Lacroix, R., 2009; Öztürk, Pöchtrager 2011; Kiria et al. 2015; Gersamia 2019).

The Megrelian language is spoken in Western Georgia. The two dialect varieties of Megrelian are rather close to each other, and Megrelians speaking distinct dialects from extremely remote areas freely understood each other a century ago (Kipshidze 1914, XVII), and they still do in our days.

Presently Megrelian- and Laz-speaking areas have no adjoining territories; they are split by the Gurian and Acharan dialects of Georgian. The Laz and Megrelian languages have had thirteen-century-long histories of independent development in different linguistic environments. These are the factors having played an essential role in turning Megrelian and Laz, dialects of the historical Zan language, into two individual languages.

Laz and Megrelians are bilingual; the Laz, living in Turkey, speak Laz and Turkish, and those living in Georgia speak Laz and Georgian, similarly to Megrelians who speak Megrelian and Georgian.

4.2. Some Basic Facts on Megrelian and Laz

According to L. Talmy's typological classification (Talmy 1985), Megrelian and Laz (resp. Kartvelian languages) pertain to the Satellite-framed languages with respect to the type of lexicalization, in which directions of motion in space and places of bodies' localization are represented beyond the verb root, by means of auxiliaries – satellites, being denoted in Verb-framed languages by the verb root itself (Talmy 1985, 85; Boeder 2004, 88-94). As for morphological structure, they are agglutinating languages. According to J. Greenberg's agglutination/fusion quantitative indices (Greenberg 1960), Megrelian and Laz have the highest scores of agglutination among the Kartvelian languages: Megrelian – 0.58 and Laz – 0.54 (Melikishvili 2010, 91).

The morphological structure of the Megrelian and Laz verb is a complex chain of morpho-syntactic elements providing a sequential presentation, to the left and to the right of the root, of morphemes, obligatory or character vowels, grammaticalized particles, modal elements (Gamkrelidze, Gudava 1981; Holisky 1991; Kutscher 2011; Lacroix 2009; Öztürk, Pöchtrager 2011; Asatiani 2011, 2018; Lomia, Gersamia 2012; Gersamia 2020). A verb root is a minimum morpheme with a conceptual structure1 encoding individual semantic components, concepts, the unity of which constitutes its meaning. A verb stem, not coinciding with a verb root, is morphologically construed entity with more morpho-syntactic information. A radical morpheme is neutral in terms of characterizing motion/immobility with any kind of locative features. A meaning which may be referred to by a root of motion is general and implies only a physical property of motion/immobility without which motion as such cannot happen, neither can immobility be described. A lexical meaning of a stem is determined by representants, functional satellites arranged around the root and, within an individual verbal construction, provide for the representation of specific lexical and grammatical meanings.

4.3. Construed Tri-Dimensional Space and Integral Processes of Dynamicity vs. Stativity

Space is a part of the universe which is associated with the physical existence of humans and living organisms at large, with the creation of the environment

---

1 For the term, see Jackendoff 1983; 1990.

necessary for organisms' vital activities; this is motion – a dynamic form of the existence of a matter.

In the recent decades, linguistic studies focused on linguistic representation of spatial relationships both in individual languages and cross-linguistically (Talmy 1985; Levinson 1996; Levinson 2003; Brown, Levinson 2003; Pederson et al. 1998; Langacker 1987; Lakoff 1987; Plungyan 2002; etc.).

In the languages in point, verbal stems pertain to different lexico-semantic classes; taking on linguistic devices (for instance, preverbs) encoding spatial relations has been constrained by meanings of verbal stems; (dynamic) verbs of motion and (stative) verbs of immobility/position demonstrate the most diverse picture in terms of the linguistic encoding of spatial relations. Therefore, it is with respect to these stems that it is plausible to completely establish the systemic relationships between spatial semantic elements associated with phenomena of motion/immobility and a linguistic form. Generally, investigations on spatial relations have predominantly been based on the interrelationships of motion and immobility, that is, dynamicity and stativity, as constituents of an integral process. With respect to this, every language is significant with its specific and universal features in terms of studies of both individual languages and cross-linguistic problems.

Dynamicity is a linguistic representation of an action, as of an ongoing process, and stativity is a linguistic representation of immobility, as of a process of being in one state (Shanidze 1980, 313). Notably, dynamicity / stativity has been regarded as the principal classification feature in Megrelian and Laz (Chikobava 1950, 105).

All basic kinds of motion (on land – to walk, to run, to crawl, etc., in water – to swim, to dive, etc., in air – to fly) are dynamic, while all basic verbs referring to spatial positions *(to sit, to lie, to be laid, to stand, etc.)* are stative, as well as items formed by means of spatial preverbs in Megrelian and Laz (Kobalava 2020, 6; Gersamia ibid., 47).

Another notable circumstance is that, based on mono-personal verbal roots referring to a position, relative-dynamic verbal stems are formed representing an action in motion, that is, in dynamics. Such a meaning is possible as a result of the mutual compatibility of conceptual (radical) and surface (form) elements, including the stem.

4.4. The Verbal Root Referring to Motion / Immobility and Representants Involved in the Construal of Space

In Megrelian and Laz, verbals roots are essentially neutral in terms of characteristics of motion/immobility by means of locative features, this being their peculiarity as of the Satellite-framed languages. This kind of information is conveyed beyond the root: within and/or beyond the stem; spatial features are encoded in lexical and grammatical entities:

- *locative cases,*
- *preverbs,*
- *adverbs and words used as adverbial modifiers of place,*
- *personal and demonstrative pronouns.*

The aforementioned means represent spatial relations from various angles and present a linguistic characteristics of a system of relations. Among them, spatial preverbs and adverbs acquire particular shades owing to the diversity of means of semantic representation.

4.4.1. Conceptualization of the Verbal Root

In the languages in question, verbal roots for motion and immobility contain such significant general features as: manner of motion or type of position (*to stand, to lie, to sit*), dynamicity or stativity, im/mobile figure (in/animate), volition (transfer semantics), tempo of motion, aspect (im/perfective), and Tense (Present, Past, Future) (Kobalava 2015, 495; Kobalava ibid., 43; Gersamia ibid., 45).

4.4.1.1. Motion (Dynamic) Verbal Roots

a)   Manner of motion (Talmy 1985). Differences among the kinds of motion have been essentially conditioned, on the one hand, by a subject's habitat – land, water, air, and by biological traits of an organism with respect to a habitat, on the other. This is primarily about motion *per se.* This is a motion being defined as a basic kind of motion of humans and animals moving on land. Owing to this feature, motion on land differs from verbal roots referring to motion in water and air:

Table 4.1. Verbal roots referring to neutral motion

	land – to go	water – to swim	air – to fly
Megrelian	*ul-a / rt-* R-MSD / R.AOR	*[n]čur-u-a* R-THM-MSD	*purin-u-a* R-THM-MSD
Laz	*o-l-v-a / o-xt-im-u* MSD1-R-THM-MSD1	*o-nčvi[r]-u* MSD1-R-MSD1	*o-putx-in-u* MSD1-R-THM-MSD1

b)   Figure. Following L. Talmy's 1985 definition, a figure is an object considered in relation to another object as either a mobile or immobile or localized entity. I. Kobalava views such a figure as a subject of motion which be either an animate or inanimate (active vs. inactive) organism, a physical phenomenon. Such an opposition plays a significant role in the semantic organization of nominal and verbal lexicon of the Kartvelian languages as those of carrying some features of active typology (Kobalava 2015, 496). An animate or active subject is referred to by substantives whose referents are characterized by vital activity, and objects devoid of activity are considered among lexico-semantic classes referring to non-living nature (Klimov 1974, 11-23; Kortava 2008, 65).

Hence, a class of living creatures in Megrelian and Laz incorporates humans, animals, and plants. Among them, predominantly one and the same verbs of motion/immobility are used to refer to humans and animals, as to animates, that is, for those capable of moving on their own:

Megr.   *k'oči / ǯoɣori   meurs* 'A man/dog goes.'
Laz   *k'oči / ǯoɣo[r]i   nulun* 'A man/dog goes.'

It is true that plants are not capable of moving on their own, but they are characterized by other vital activities being manifest, on the one hand, biologically, in salient vital processes (sprouting, nutrition, growth, fertilization of cells of the opposite sex) and, on the other, lexically; specifically, vocabularies related both to living organisms, at large, and, specifically, to the life cycle of plants are used to refer to the sprouting and further growth and development of plants:

(1a) Megr.   *ǯa / baɣana / ǯoɣori   irdu*

(1b) *Laz   ǯa / bere / ǯoɣoi   irdun*
        '[A] tree / child / dog grows.'

ǯaši tree. GEN ⎰
{
Megr. / Laz   *p'ir-ua* 'to bloom'

Megr. / Laz   *čan-ap-a* Megr. 'is planted,'
        Laz 'to be laden (with fruit)'

Megr. *bžɣirapa,*   Laz   *o-mži[r]-u* 'to wither'

Megr. *xumapa,*   Laz   *o-xomin-u* 'to dry up'
}

c)   Volition (casual or transfer semantics). A root renders information how a motion goes – by a subject's will or is caused by others; in the latter we mean not a morphologically marked causative forms but rather lexically conveyed causal meanings. Therefore, both roots referring to motion and a figure/subject of motion differ.

Motion/movement on one's own will, performed by a subject itself, is encoded by intransitive verb forms :

(2a)	Megr.	*k'oč-i*	*šara-s*	*me-ur-s.*
		man-NOM	road-DAT	PRV-R-THM-PRS.S3SG

(2b)	Laz	*k'oči*	*gza-s*	*n-ul-u-n.*
		man(NOM)	road-DAT	PRV-R-THM-PRS.S3SG

'A man walks on the road.'

A motion of *transfer sth/sb*, being caused or forced by someone else, is referred to by transitive verbs the use of which in a sentence, alignment of which with either a subject or an object is limited owing to semantic factors and depends on whether aligned actants are living (3a), (3b) or non-living (4a), (4b) ones:

(3a)	Megr.	*k'oč-k*	*baɣana*	*mid-e-ʔon-u* (< **mida-i-ʔon-u*).
		man-ERG	child(NOM)	PRV-APPL-R-AOR.S3SG

(3b)	Laz	*k'oči-k*	*bere*	*mend-i-q'on-u.*
		man-ERG	child(NOM)	PRV-APPL-R-AOR.S3SG

The man took the child.'

(4a)	Megr.	*k'oč-k*	*ʒa*	*mid-e-ɣ-u.*
		man-ERG	tree(NOM)	PRV-APPL-R-AOR.S3SG

(4b)	Laz	*k'oči-k*	*ʒa*	*mend-i-ɣ-u.*
		man-ERG	tree(NOM)	PRV-APPL-R-AOR.S3SG

'The man took the tree.'

d) Tempo of motion. In the Megrelian and Laz neutral verbal root referring to motion/movement a tempo of motion is not encoded; however, in Megrelian, the empty cells are filled in by phonosemantic (synaesthetic) verb stems containing a semantic component of tempo at the lexicalized stage of a root (Gersamia et al. 2016, 354-356); 'goes fast:' *meč'uminuns, mič'virtu*, etc.; 'goes slow:' *misakalu, miɣanɣalu*, etc. In Laz, the same meaning is conveyed by satellites outside a verb stem, adverbs:

(5a) *mani-mani* (ADV) *nunk'ap'ut'u* 'S/he was running fast-fast.'

(5b) *tamo-tamo* (ADV) *moxtu* (V) 'The s/he came slowly-slowly.'

e) Aspect and tense of motion. Generally, a process of motion may
    be viewed as a continuous, that is, ongoing, and discontinuous,
    that is, completed process. In their linguistic representations, the
    former is encoded by imperfective and the latter is encoded by
    perfective forms. The aspectual difference considerably modifies
    a diagram of motion and makes certain changes in meanings of
    related preverbs (Kobalava ibid., 43).

The association of the tense differences (Present, Past, Future) with the
aspectual ones in the Kartvelian languages, and in Megrelian and Laz, among
them, seems to be a relic of the time "when verb conjugation did not entail
alternations in the tense system, and conjugation was about encoding aspect,
that is, kinds of a process" (Chikobava 1948, 77); however, as far as tense is
realized differently in language with and without Aorist (Lyons 1978, 332-333),
in the Kartvelian languages, aspectual differences between forms of the Present
and Aorist groups has been encoded by means of dis/continuity of im/
perfective motion.

In Megrelian and Laz, there are several verbal roots referring to the basic kind
of motion on land ('to go') among which there is a grammatical distinction. In
forms of the Present-Future group of Series I, tense is encoded by means of the
imperfective root *ul-* (6a), (7b), while in perfective forms, there is the suppletive
root *rt-* (7a), (7b).

(6a) Megr.	*me-ur-s*	(6b) Laz.	*n-ul-u-n*
	PRV-go-PRS.S3SG		PRV-go-PRS.S3SG
	'S/he goes.'		'S/he goes'

(7a) Megr.	*mida-rt- u*	(7b) Laz.	*menda-xt-u*
	PRV-go-AOR.S3SG		PRV-go-AOR.S3SG
	'S/he went away.'		'S/he went away.'

A meaning of course, as a continuous process, will never be encoded by a
perfective form; however, a sector of motion, implying movement from one
point to another, will not stay 'empty' (Kobalava 2010, 242-243): the gap is filled
by various linguistic means in accordance with narrative requirements; for the
sake of this, the commonest is the Aorist form *id-* of the perfective root **vid* 'to
go' the meaning of which is slightly modified in Megrelian and Laz and encodes
imperfective aspect (Chikobava 1938, 274). This is enhanced by instances of the
repetition of the root *id-* (8a), (8b), occurring in the process of narration and
considerably enhancing the impression of continuity (Kobalava ibid., 45; for
the aforementioned tendency, see also Shanidze 1980, 506-508; Machavariani
1974, 120-121; Arabuli 1999, 50).

(8a)	Megr.	k'oč-k	i-d-u,	i-d-u,	i-d-u …
		man-ERG	MA:CV-to go-AOR.S3SG		

(8b)	Laz	k'oči(k)	i-d-u,	i-d-u,	i-d-u …
		man(ERG)	MA:CV-to go-AOR.S3SG		
		'The man walked, walked, walked …'			

4.4.1.2. Position (Stative) Verbal Roots

In Megrelian and Laz, position (stative) verbs and verbal roots have been analyzed in terms of their semantics and structure in Lomia and Gersamia (2010) and in Kutscher and Genç (2007). A figure's location in an area is encoded by position verbs whole roots already imply stativity. An immobile figure's position is based, on the one hand, on the aforementioned external factors, on topology of an area, and, on the other, seems to be conditioned by a physical constitution of a figure itself. A figure's position is horizontal (*to lie, to be put/to be chucked down*), vertical sheer (*to stand, to be planted*), vertical folded (*to sit*); in Laz and Megrelian, all the types are realized by means of mono-personal stative verbal roots.

Table 4.2. Stative verbal roots in Megrelian and Laz

	To stand	To sit	To lie	To be put	To be planted
Megr.	*dg-:*	*x-:*	*žan-:*	*ʒ-:*	*čan-:*
	dg-u(n)	*xe(n)*	*ž-an-u*	*ʒu*	*č-an-s*
	'S/he stands.'	'S/he sits.'	'S/he lies.'	'It is put.'	'It is planted.'
Laz	*dg-:*	*x-:*	*žan-:*	*ʒ-:*	*čan-:*
	dg-u-n	*xe-n*	*ž-an-s*	*ʒin*	*č-an-s*
	'S/he stands.'	'S/he sits.'	'S.he lies.'	'It is put.'	'It thrives.'

Essential conceptual components, which may be contained by structures of position verbal roots, makes up the semantic oppositions: a) animate -- inanimate, b) living – non-living, c) human – non-human.

a) only animate: Megr.-Laz. *xe / xen* 'S/he sits,' *žan* 'S/he lies;' animate / inanimate: *dgu / dgin* - 'S/he stands;' only inanimate: *ʒu / ʒin* 'It is put;' for the encoding of animates' position, Megrelian uses preverbal forms of the existential verb *re(n)* 'is:' *ge-re* 'X stands onto Y,' *gila-re(n)* 'X stands beside Y,' *c'imo-re(n)* 'X stands ahead of Y,' *muk'o-re* 'X stands behind Y,' etc. It is up to a preverb to specify a figure's location and reference with an object.

b) the groups of animates included plants together with the rest of animates. The stative root referring to plants' vertical position is *čan-: čans* 'It thrives' the meaning of which is shifted in Laz referring to 'bearing of fruit.' The class of inanimates includes all inanimate figures excluding plants.

c)   position verbs, used for the class of humans, are: *xe(n)* 'S/he sits,' *žan* 'It lies, Megr. *ge-re(n)* 'S/he stands.' (*k'oči gere* 'A man stands.'), Laz. *dgin-* 'S/he stands.' (*k'oči dgin* 'A man stands.'); all other instances are about the rest except humans.

4.5. Direction, Spatial Reference and Topology of Place

In Megrelian and Laz, a motion conveyed by a verb is performed in a sheer way along horizontal and vertical axes, or in an inclined trajectory; the latter is particularly peculiar to Megrelian being conveyed by means of a certain group of preverbs and adverbs.

In the languages in point, directions in space can be conveyed in a more complex way, with respect to a relatum as well, and, hence, a picture of geometric configurations of mobile or immobile bodies in space can be defined. Therefore, a motion referred to by dynamic verbs (a location, in case of stative verbs) is referential in relation to an axis of motion of other bodies or a figure (horizontal, vertical, inclined).

A frame of reference is a coordination system used for detecting an object's location. *relative* and *absolute* frames of reference have been distinguished (Levinson 1996; Pederson et al. 1998). Each of them is defined with respect to a type of a relatum. Both man-made artifacts, natural objects, and even a human body may be used in the function of a relatum.

In Megrelian and Laz, all the types of reference are used and encoded in satellites inside and outside of the stem, in preverbs and adverbs. A greater part of combined preverbs encode the relative reference and, generally, presents a diagram of the configuration of things in space. With a vertical direction, the reference is absolute and is determined with respect to a fixed landmark, viz., to the earth's surface (see 11a-15b).

A preverb is a prefix having an adverbial meaning and occurring as a dominant means for the encoding of spatial relations in the languages in question. It is taken on by verbal roots referring to motion and location and represents a locative picture of the spatial distribution of dynamic and stative processes: bodies' motion or location in an area, a specific direction of motion, provides information about an area in which a motion takes place; besides, it encodes a place of bodies' localization, provides its typological characteristics and also involves information about a place in point or specific arrangement, geometry between bodies (where, by what, in what, on what, how, etc.) (Kobalava ibid., 49; Gersamia ibid., 67).

Spatial adverbs are notional lexical items, satellites outside a verbal stem, which define in what circumstances and with what features an act conveyed by a verb takes place (Kobalava ibid., 72). Within a sentence they occur as adverbial modifiers of place and refer to a direction of movement and a place of bodies' localization in relation to mobile or immobile landmarks / relata localized in an area. Adverbs seldom provide topological characteristics of a place.

4.5.1. A System of Spatial Preverbs in Megrelian and Laz: Structure and Classification

In the system of the agglutinating verbal stem, a position of preverbs is stable occupying the third slot from the left in Laz and the fifth slot in Megrelian.

Table 4.3. Structure of verbal prefixal morphemes

Lang.	-7	-6	-5	-4	-3	-2	-1	0
Megr.	NEG	AFF /PRF	PRV	IMPF	EVD	S/O	FV	R-
Laz				NEG/ AFF/ PRF	PRV	S/O	FV	R-

Preverbs, included in a verbal stem, seldom appear in their complete phonological form in Megrelian; constituting vowels undergo phonetic transformations (they either alter or are deleted) as a result of the influence of vowels of a following morpheme (Kipshidze 1914; Chikobava 1936; Kartozia et al. 2010; Kiria et al. 2015; Lomashvili 2015). The structure of Laz preverbs is much more stable and their alterations mostly occur at an absolute final position of a cluster (for details, see Öztürk, Pöchtrager 2011, 100-101).

Structures of preverbs are simple, derived, and compound (Kobalava ibid., 12; Gersamia ibid., 68); simple or primary preverbs are mono-syllabic and their structure is either V or CV; they are few: {*o-, e-, ge-, go-, do-, me-, mo-*} + {*a-, da-, še-, ga-*}. Derived preverbs are formed not as a result of the combination of the simple ones, as it happens in Georgian compound preverbs (preverb + preverb: *a+mo-, še+mo-, ga+mo-, c'a+mo*, etc., encoding only an oriented direction), but rather of combinations of simple preverbs and adverbial (locative) particles which come into effect only after they are taken on by simple preverbs, making up a preverb as an entirety (for tables of derived preverbial combinations, see Asatiani 2015; Kiria et al. 2015; Rostovtsev-Popiel 2016; Lacroix 2009; Öztürk, Pöchtrager 2011; Kobalava, Gersamia 2020); accurate estimation of independent meanings of the aforementioned particles within preverbs seems to be rather conditional. Difficulties arise from the semantics of the particles in question; specifically, one and the same particle occurs with distinct, sometimes with opposite meanings with different preverbs (cf. Gudava, Gamkrelidze 1981; Ivanishvili, Soselia 2014, 183-192).

Table 4.4. Adverbial particles in Megrelian and Laz

Megr.	-la	-ša	-k'o	-c'o	-da	-ma	-mo	-no	-to		
Laz	-la,	-ša	-k'a	-c'a	-da	-ma	-mo	-na		-ia /-ža	-xo

The numbers of such preverbs reach forty in each language (Kipshidze 1914; Asatiani 2015; Kajaia 2000; Kartozia et al. 2010; Kiria et al. 2015; Ezugbaia 2011; Ivanishvili, Soselia 2014; Kobalava ibid.; Gersamia ibid.).

Some preverbs follow the Georgian rule of combination; therefore, they may be considered to be compound: Megr. *mi+da-, gi+mo- / gi+ma-, c'i+mo-, k'i+no-, k'i+la-;* Laz. *me+nda-, k'o+na-, go+na-* (Gersamia ibid., 69).

Generally, it is a multi-functional entity in the Kartvelian languages (Veshapidze 1967; Shanidze 1973; Chikobava 1936; Makharoblidze 2016; Makharoblidze 2018; Kobalava ibid.; Gersamia ibid.); they have derivational and grammatical functions.

In their grammatical function, preverbs derive perfective Aorist and Future forms based on imperfective ones (Chikobava 1936; Kartozia 2005; Kartozia et al. 2010; Asatiani 2015; Kiria et al. 2015). They derive numerous semantically various stems. All the functions of preverbs can not be simultaneously compatible either in Megrelian or in Laz.

4.5.2. Spatial Features of Preverbs

Spatial features are established based on meanings attested with preverbs in the linguistic representation of spatial relations. I mean that verbal roots referring to motion (dynamicity) and immobility (stativity) take on various preverbs, thus enabling to establish meanings of preverbs with a maximum accuracy.

Two types are distinguished among spatial preverbs: directional, that is, orienting, and locative.

Directional preverbs (being structurally simple) are taken on by verbal stems referring to motion and encode direction, define a vector of motion. Addition of such preverbs to positional verbs is limited, generating specific meanings.

Alongside direction, locative preverbs (being structurally simple) provide additional information about a place of motion/immobility, topology, geometric arrangement of figures, spatial reference (Kobalava ibid., 11, 13; Gersamia ibid., 72).

4.5.2.1. Types of Direction of Motion and Spatial Location Encoded in Preverbs

Megrelian and Laz preverbs are apt to detalize well the horizontal and vertical zones (Kobalava and Gersamia 2020). A vector of motion, encoded by a preverb, is directed in space either vertically or horizontally. With a vertical direction, an inclined trajectory is rendered well, being encoded by spatial preverbs, adverbs and adverbials of place. Laz preverbs, unlike their Megrelian counterparts, are unable to encode an inclined trajectory.

Below I will discuss examples for the three directions:

Among the directions encoded *in a horizontal area*, the simplest one is *hither-thither*, towards the first person or an area where the first person is (9a), (9b) – from the first person or from the area where the first person is (10a), (10b);[2] it is about a course of motion determined by a deictic orientation without obstacles.

(9a) Megr. *boši-k*   *muš*   *ʔude-ša*   *mola-rt-u.* [Kipsh. 31.3]
            boy-ERG   his   house-ALL   PRV-go-AOR.S3SG
            'The boy went to his house. '

(9b) Laz   *xoʒa*   *ku-mo-xt-u.* [Chik. II. 130.19]
            mullah(NOM)   AFF-PRV-go-AOR.S3SG
            'The mullah came.'

(10a) Megr. *mažira*   *dγas*   *me-ul-a(n)* *išo*   *k'ic'ia-ša.*
            second   Day   PRV-go-   thither(ADV:DR)   Kitsia-ALL
                      (ADV:T) S3PL
            'On another day, they go   [Lol. 122.25]
            to Kitsia.'

(10b) Laz   *bee*   *ko-me-xt-u.*
            Boy (NOM) AFF-PRV-go-AOR.S3SG
            'The boy came there.'   [Kal. 41.30]

Among the directions of motion, encoded *in a vertical area*, the simplest one is a direction downwards or upwards. A direction of motion is defined in relation to the earth surface and occurs as an absolute landmark. A motion may start from the earth surface upwards (11a), (11b), or from the earth depth till its surface (12a), (12b); in the opposite direction, from above downwards: till the

---

[2] In (9a), (9b), (10a), (10b), a moving figure is grammatically encoded by means of the 3rd person, towards which a motion is directed, 1st person, that is, a speaker invovled in a communicative situation – "I/we;" alternatively, the 1st person, that is, a speaker is in an area towards which a motion is directed. (9a) is a representation of the situation in question: *the boy's*, that is, the 3rd person's motion is directed towards *his home*, and the describer, that is, the 1st person person, i.e. a speaker is in that area; the same can be stated for (9a). As for (10a) and (10b), the moving figure, denoted by the 3rd person, is distanced either from the 1st person, that is, a speaker or from the area where the 1st person is located. Hence, in motion a deictic persion is basic, while other persons' motion is determined from the position occupied by the 1st person: either by motion towards a speaker or from a speaker.

earth surface (13a), (13a) or from the surface towards its depth (14a), (14b), which is represented by distinct preverbs in Megrelian, while, in Laz, the situation is not drastically different:

{vertical motion *from below upwards* + landmark: till the earth surface}:

(11a) Megr. *[dixa-še]*   *eše-el-u*   *ndem-k.*   [Kipsh.
                                                                        60.23]

        [earth-ABL]   PRV-go-AOR.S3SG   ogre-ERG
        'The earth split and an ogre came up.'

(11b) Laz   *ask'ili*   *k-e-xt-u.*   [Kal. 250.14]
               dog-rose   AFF-PRV-go-AOR.S3SG
               'The dog-rose hipped.'

{vertical motion *from below upwards* + landmark: from earth surface}:

(12a) Megr. *iše-el-u*   *č'adari-ša.*   [Kart.19]
               PRV-go-AOR.S3SG   plane-tree-ALL
               'S/he climbed the plane-tree.'

(12b) Laz   *t'ooǯi*   *yova-šen*   *yše-putx-u.*
               pidgeon(NOM)   nest-ABL   PRV-fly-
                                                         AOR.S3SG
               'The pidgeon flew up from the nest.'

{vertical motion *from above downwards* + landmark: till earth surface}:

(14a) Megr. rošap'i-k   kua-š   c'van-s
               Roshapi-ERG   stone-GEN   sharp point-DAT
               ki-gi-a-ntx-u.   Khub. 62,29]
               AFF-PRV-SPRS-fall-AOR.S3SG
               'Roshapi fell on the sharp point of the stone.'
                                                                [Kal. 223.10-11]

(14b) Laz   *ka-ge-xt-u*   *cxeni-šen.*
               AFF-PRV-go.AOR.S3SG   horse-ABL
               'S/he came down from the horse and opened the door.'

{vertical motion from above *downwards* + landmark: from earth surface}:

(15a) Megr. čil-i   do   komonž-k
                   wife-NOM   and   husband-ERG
                   dini-l-es   *dinaxale.*   [Khub. 36, 27]
                   PRV- go-AOR.S3PL   inside(ADV)
                   'The wife and husband went down into [sth].'

(15b) *Laz*   *k'ui-s*   *ge-i-l-u.*   [Zhg. 107.31]
                   pit-DAT   PRV-PASS-go-AOR.S3SG
                   'S/he went down into the pit.'

The vertical direction is either sheer or inclined. The above examples (11a-15b) are for sheer motion. An inclined trajectory implies motion on inclined surfaces – downhill, mountain slope, inclined shore, etc., (not on the stairs). In this case, a motion from below upwards is grammatically encoded in two stages: for instance, from the water up to the shore (to climb the earth's surface) (15c) and to go uphill from the earth's surface (15d); in both instances, the earth's durface is a natural landmark (Kobalava, ibid, 27-28).

(15c) Megr. *t'ariel-k*   *gek'o-nčur-u*   *ʒga-ša* .   (Kipsh. 103.27)
                   Tariel-ERG   PRV-swim-AOR.S3SG   shore-ALL
                   'Tariel swam up onto the shore.'

(15d)   *gvala- ša*   *gek'o-rt-u.*
                   mountain-ALL   PRV-climb-AOR.S3SG
                   'S/he climbed the mountain.'

On the other hand, motion along both a horizontal and vertical axes and *in an inclined trajectory* as well is encoded in a more complex way; it takes place either in a closed or open area, either from outside inwards or from inside outwards, and rendering not only a direction but also a relation to another object, either mobile or immobile (I. Kobalava: *relative orientation*; R. Gersamia: *object reference*). The relations in question are encoded in locative particles and their function is to convey locativity: *ahead – behind, on top – beneath, inside – outside, around* (Kobalava ibid., 73; Gersamia ibid., 31).

Any spatial adverb is a combination of spatial features, a semantic unity, which can only be divided into simple semes. The componential analyses of Megrelian and Laz preverbs have established the following basic combining rules:

For dynamic (motion) verbs:

    I.   {direction + orientation + object deixis / absolute landmark}

II.   {direction + orientation + person deixis / variable landmark}
III.   {targetless motion with no landmark}

For stative verbs

IV.   {location + object deixis / referent}

Locative and landmark features of an area also appear in the semantic structure of preverbs. A seme of visibility is also encoded in a handful of preverbs.

Thus, Megrelian and Laz spatial preverbs are described with respect to all the semantic components likely encoded in a specific preverb, this making up a rather complex and diverse synthesis of meanings (see Table 4.5).

Table 4.5. Meanings of preverbs when combined with verbal roots of motion

Laz	
ama-	From below upwards + inwards.
eša-/ešk̢a	From below upwards to the earth surface and from the earth surface.
moža-	From above upwards, sharp ascending motion.
ge-/ʒe-	1. Motion from above downwards, oriented to the earth surface, to a specific point of an area 2. From above downwards from the earth surface into the depth or just into a circumscribed area.
dolo-	From above downwards, inside a closed or semi-closed area.
geša- / geška-	From above downwards, circumscribed area.
meša- / meška-	Motion from outside inwards between two points of an area.
goša- / goška-	From inside outwards, motion from a center.
moc'a-	From inside outwards + forward (straight ahead).
geža/o	From above downwards on a surface of an object, onto.
ek̢a-/ek̢o-	Motion behind an immobile referent.
mok̢a	Deictic [I <] motion behind a referent.
mek̢a-	Motion beside a referent (to pass by).

Megrelian	
eša-	Motion from below upwards till or from the earth's surface.
miša-	Motion from outside inwards towards a closed area or a tight area.
giša-	Motion from inside outwards from a closed area towards an open one or b. from the center of a tight area.
ela-	Inclined trajectory from the edge of a referent/from its outlying point; motion beside a referent.
gino-	Motion from a deictic center by way of overcoming a certain obstacle.
ek̢o-	Motion behind a referent; motion along an inclined surface from above downwards.
dik̢o-	Motion from above downwards along an inclined surface.
dino-/ ino-	Motion from a visual center downwards towards a closed area.
ec'o-	Motion in front of a referent.
mik̢o-	Motion from a deictic center beside another immobile or moving referent.
muk̢o-	Motion towards a deictic center beside another immobile or moving referent.

4.5.3. Locative Preverbs and Representation of Stativity in Dynamics

A considerable part of Megrelian and Laz locative preverbs are of shared use for dynamic/motion and stative/position verbs. Such preverbs are also capable, by means of adding to verbal roots of position (*to sit, to stand, to lie*), of presenting stativity in dynamics, that is, of transforming stative forms into dynamic ones (ST>DIN). In such circumstances, a preverb is unchanged and semantic components of a locative particle, included in a locative preverb, are essentially retained, irrespective of the fact that the suffix structure of a verb is changed. Simple preverbs, as structural constituents of a locative preverb, do not demonstrate such features with respect to their function – to determine the direction of motion.

In order to illustrate the aforementioned, I will pick one example with the Laz locative preverb *dolo-*, with respect to the Megrelian preverb *dino-* having the same meaning.

Laz *dila-* / Megr. *dino-* – taken on by both dynamic/motion (16) and stative/ position (17) bases. In (18), the verb implies that stativity, being referred to by the verbal root *xed-* 'to sit,' is an outcome of a certain action which is conveyed by the entire structure of the verb, and the preverb Laz *dolo-* / Megr. *dino-* encodes a direction of motion and a topology of place, specifically, the direction from above downwards of a figure's vertical motion is encoded in the simple preverbs: Laz *do-*, Megr. *di- (<*do-)*, which make up a combined preverb; the particlea *-lo, -no* provide information about a type of area (deep circumscribed, almost a closed area; for instance, a pit, a box, deepness of sea, river, etc.).

(16) Laz   *mzoγa-s*   *dolo-xt-u*   [Chik. 34.26]
             sea-DAT   PRV-go-AOR.S3SG

      Megr. *zγva-ša*   *dino-rt-u*
             sea-ALL   PRV-go-AOR.S3SG
             'S/he went into the sea.'

(17) Laz   *mu*   *dolo-x-e-n*   *iašik'i-s?* [Zhg.
                                                                                78.9]
             what(NOM) PRV-sit–CV:STAT-PRS.S3SG box-DAT

      Megr. *mu*   *dino-x-e(-n)*   *iašik'i-s?*
             what(NOM) PRV-sit–CV:STAT(-   box-DAT
                         PRS.S3SG)
             'What is sitting here inside the box?'

(18) Laz   *yašik'i-s …*   *Ɖadišai*   *ko-dol-i-nžir-u*   [Zg. 77.34]
            box-DAT   padishah(NOM)   AFF-PRV-FV-lie-AOR.S3SG

      Megr. *iašik'i-s*   *Ɖadišahi-k*   *dini-nžir-u*
            box-DAT   padishah-ERG   PRV-lie-(AOR.S3SG)
            'The padishah lay down into the box.'

In (16), the structure of the preverbs Laz *dolo-*, Megr. *dino-* taken on by a dynamic verb, is described by Set (a), and, in (17), a stative verbal root takes on Set (b) of the structure of the same preverbs; in the case of STAT>DIN, Set (a) is retained.

(a) DIN: {VERT: motion +TR: vert + TR: sheer + DIR: from above downwards + inside a closed area, towards depth / end point + visual factor)
(b) STAT: {VERT:position + IN (vert)+ closed area + inside + visual factor }

Table 4.6. Common preverbs for stativity and dynamicity

AT, IN FRONT OF		IN, INTER		ON, ALONG THE SURFACE		AROUND	UNDER		BACK
Megr.	Laz	Megr.	Laz	Megr.	Laz	Megr. Laz	Megr.	Laz	Megr. Laz
ala-muk'o-mik'o-	*ela-mok'a-mek'a-*	*[d]ino-aša-miša-muša-*	*dolo-eša-meša-moša-ama-*	*ge-gela-gima-*	*g/že-g/žela-me(y)a-*	*go-*	*mito-eto-*	*ec'a-gec'a-*	*ek'a-/ek'o-*

The question arises: why do stative (position) and dynamic (motion) verbal stems take on one and the same preverb? Why do we say that stativity and dynamics are parts of one and the same process? As far as in Megrelian and Laz, stativity is encoded where there is either a starting and an end point of a dynamic verb, a connecting sector of the point, which is a process of motion, will not have stativity (Kobalava 2015).

4.5.4. System of Spatial Adverbs in Megrelian and Laz: Structural and Semantic Classifications

Megrelian and Laz spatial adverbs are satellites outside a stem. Spatial distribution by means of them occurs as a very complex picture. Adverbs denote:

a. location of a figure in its immobility (stativity) (question: where?)
b. starting point (point of departure (question: where from?) and orientation towards an endpoint of motion, or convey terminativity (question: where to?) in motion (dynamics).

Three different models of adverbs have been distinguished in Megrelian and Laz:

1. Simple or primary, basic adverbs which are not divisible into constituting elements: Megr. *ži*, Laz. *ži[n]* 'above;' Megr. *tudo*, Laz. *tude* 'below, beneath.' Adverbs with the initial deictically opposed vowels *a-* and *e-* : Megr. *[a]t-a-k* 'here' – *[e]t-e-k* 'there;' *a-šo* 'hither' – *i-šo* 'thither;' Laz. [h]a-k-o – [h]e-k-o 'here' – 'there;' *[h]a-š-o* 'hither' – *[h]i-š-o* 'thither.' Adverbial stems, borrowed from Turkish, are also considered to be simple (Gabunia 1993; Gersamia ibid.).

2. Derived adverbs are etymologically segmentable entities and incorporate such inflectional and derivational elements with spatial features as functionally differing particles, case markers, postpositions, certain preverbs: their combination are predominantly sequential and stable (Kobalava, Gersamia, ibid., 110). Sometimes homo-functional element are repeated in a sequence which must be due to the desemantization of a preceding element (Gersamia ibid., 205).

3. Compound – duplicated structure providing information about widening-narrowing of an area; duplicated forms of opposition adverbs referring to place encode widening of a deictic area in both directions: Megr. *eše-gime* 'upwards-downwards,' Laz *ži-tude* 'above-below,' and reduplicated forms encode widening of a deictic area in a single direction: Megr. *eše-eše* 'upwards-upwards,' *gime-gime* 'downwards-downwards, Laz *ži-ži* 'above-above,' *tude-tude* 'below-below.'

4. Spatial adverbs encode horizontal, vertical, and inclined trajectories either in relation to a landmark or without a landmark, and this is due to the physical peculiarities of motion (dynamic) and immobility (stativity) in these languages and to specific traits occurring in their linguistic representation.

With respect to their relation to a landmark, adverbs make up semantic groups of oriented and independent (occurring with no landmark) among which opposition pairs are distinguished in the former: deictic – non-deictic, proximal – distal; independent adverbs have no opposition. In terms of the representation of spatial relations, there are three groups: locative (with and without deixis), directional (with an orienting component), and geometric-topological. The first one encodes location / stativity either in relation to a certain landmark (deictic) or without it (without deixis); the second one encodes direction / dynamics, including an orienting component as well; the third one is totally devoid of an orienting component providing only a topological characteristics of a place (Kobalava ibid.; Gersamia ibid.).

4.6. Morpho-Syntactic Models of the Construal of Space

Elements of a language system and preverbs among them, are used not in an isolated way but rather in interrelationship with other linguistic items. In Megrelian and Laz, they are associated with certain categories of the noun and the verb, with other parts of speech: adverbs and pronouns. Without considering these associations it is impossible to represent a complete picture of spatial relations because a direction (and an orientation), as well as a place of motion, encoded by a preverb, is just a hint to spatial relations. Their individual (lexico-grammatical) meanings are specified at the morpho-syntactic level whereby respective grammatical categories are involved. This is equally true of the encoding of both horizontal and vertical directions (Kobalava ibid, 20).

4.6.1. Encoding of a Starting and End Point of a Figure's Motion and of Its Course in an Area

For the sake of the complete representation of motion / movement of both horizontal and vertical directions, it is essential to provide a tri-dimensional picture of an area. In the diagram of a horizontal direction, three phases (phase: I. Kobalava) should be logically expected: Beginning, as a starting point of motion, End, as a completion of motion and, hence, its final point, and Course, describing the period between the two points and a process of dynamics itself. Three phases are not identifiable in a vertical area owing to the gravitational character of motion. In Megrelian and Laz, the three phases have been linguistically encoded. In terms of form and meaning, they are mutually independent, that is, they are capable of existing independently of each other and there is no necessity for their amalgamation. However, in the process of natural communication, within a sentence, they are amalgamated around one and the same moving subject; this is quite logical with respect to narrative principles (Kobalava ibid., 14-15; Gersamia ibid., 57).

In Megrelian and Laz, the three phases are linguistically encoded: "They are independent of each other in terms of the fact that none of them necessarily implies an occurrence of the rest; however, in the process of communication, there is a possibility for their unification within a single cycle: based on a logic of motion and long-standing practical experience, they merge within a sentence, around one and the same mobile subject (Kobalava ibid., 15).

In Megrelian and Laz, a grammatical element (be it an affix or a root) is not able to encode an entire path of motion, movement from point A to point B. actually, each of them encodes three independent, time-spanning periods or phases: Beginning of motion (19a), (20a), Course of motion (19b), (20c), and End of motion (19c), (20c). This is a logical unity of motion being encoded morpho-syntactically in these languages.

Laz

ph- I _	(19a)	k'oči(k)	avli-še	ko-gama-xt-u
Beginning		man(ERG)	yard-ABL	AFF-PRV-go-AOR.S3SG
ph- II_	(19b)	i-d-u, i-d-u		do
Course		MA:CV-go-AOR.S3SG		and.CONJ
ph- III_	(19c)	ko-me-xt-u		daγi-ša
End		AFF-PRV-go-AOR.S3SG		forest-ALL

(19a) 'A man left the yard, (19b) walked, walked and (19c) came up to a forest.'

Megrelian

ph- I _	(20a)	k'oč-k	oze-še	gini-l-u
Beginning		man-ERG	yard-ABL	PRV-go-AOR.S3SG
ph- II _	(20b)	i-d-u,	i-d-u	do
Course		MA:CV-go-AOR.S3SG		and.CONJ
ph- III_	(20c)	ki-me-rt-u		tya- ša.
End		AFF-PRV-go-AOR.S3SG		forest-ALL

(20a) 'A man crossed the yard, (120b) walked, walked and (20c) came up to a forest.'

Laz (19a-c) and Megrelian (20a-c) examples are a complete clause morpho-syntactically representing an entire path of motion in an area. Meanwhile, the three phases are independent and linguistically encoded by means of different devices with various and specific functions.

In (19a) and (20a), the semantics of the phase of Beginning is grammatically encoded by the ablative markers -iše and -še and by the locative preverb gama-. The ablative markers are taken on by an adverbial modifier of place, while the preverb – by the verbal (dynamic) roots of motion -xt and -rt.

In (19c) and (20c), the phase of End is encoded by the allative marker –sa, which also conveys an adverbial modifier of place, and by the deictic preverb me- rendering a motion starting from the first person and is taken by the roots of motion -xt and -rt.

In (19d) and (20d), the phase of course is represented by the repetition of preverbless verbal form (*idu* 'went'), conveying an imperfective, continuous action, thus referring to a course of motion as a process.

(21a-b) and (22a-b) are actually existing contexts in which a phase picture of motion is incomplete: either the phases of Beginning and Course ((21a) and (21b)) or of Course and End ((22a)and (22b)) are present.

(21a) Megr. *koč-k*   *ʔude-še*   *gini-il-u*
               man-ERG   house-ABL   PRV-go-AOR.S3SG
               do   *mida-rt-u*
               and   PRV-go-AOR.S3SG

(21b) Laz.   *koči*   *oxori-še*   *gama-xt-u*
               man (NOM)   house-ABL   PRV-go-AOR.S3SG
               do   *menda-xt-u*   /   *i-gzal-u.*
               and   PRV-go-AOR.S3SG   /   PASS-travel-
                                                      AOR.S3SG

               'The man left the house and went away.'

(22a) Megr. *šara-s* *mi-i-š-es*   *Mešareep-i*
               road-   PRV-CV-go.IPV-S3PL   passenger-PL-NOM
               DAT
               do   *ke-me-rt-es*   *arti*   *oxori-ša.*
               and   AFF-PRV-go-AOR.S3SG   one(DEF)   house-ALL

(22b) Laz   *gzamšine-pe-k*   *gza-s*   *ulu-t'-es*
               passengers-PL-ERG   road-DAT   go-IPV-PL.S3SG
               do   *ar*   *oxori-ša*   *ko-me-xt-es.*
               and   one(INDF)   house-ABL   AFF-PRV-go-S3PL

               'Passengers walked along the road and came to a house.'

Analyses of similar contexts help identify morpho-syntactic features for individual phases during motion both in a horizontal and a vertical direction. Grammatical devices by means of which the semantics of the beginning, course, and end of motion in an area are represented in Megrelian and Laz are diverse and systemic. Basic translocative and transfer verbal roots are applied in both phases.

Phase of Beginning is encoded by

1. locative case form of adverbials, viz. is encoded by the ablative[3] and answers the questions: *from where, from whom / from what*; it is encoded by various suffixes being used for different word classes:

    a) the suffix *-de* occurs in the singular and plural with 1st and 2nd person pronouns (Megr.-Laz. *čkim-de* 'from me,' *skan-de* 'from you[SG],' *čkin-de* 'from us,' *tkvan-de* 'from you[PL]'); the questions: *from what, from whom*. The derivator *-de / -do*, taken on by Laz adverbs, seems to have the same function in certain contexts: *galende* 'from outside,' *žilen-do* 'from above,' *hakolendo* 'from here,' *hekolendo* 'from there;' however, it performs a function of the allative as well according to another part of contexts (for details, see Gersamia ibid., 93, 95; 160). Megrelian adverbs do not take on such a derivator. They answer the question: *from where*.

    b) *- iše / -še* – with all substantives used as an adverbial modifier of place, as well as with spatial adverbs (Megr.-Laz. *xolo-še* 'from nearby,' Megr. *šor-še* 'from far away,' *gale-še* 'from outside,' *dinaxle-še*, Laz. *doloxe-še* 'from inside') and with the 3rd person pronoun (Megr. *ti-še* 'from him/her,' *tinep-iše* 'from them,' Laz. *hemu-še* 'from him/her,' etc.); their questions are: *from where, from whom, from what*.

    c) a starting point is also encoded by means of a certain group of simple, derived, and compound preverbs. They are the Megrelian *gito-, giša, gino-, gimo-, k'ila-, c'imo, mida-*, etc., the Laz *goša-, meda-, menda-, gama-*, etc. in horizontal motion.

    d) with imperfective verbal roots / stems of motion / movement: Megr. *ul-: gini-l-u*, (20a), (21a), Laz. *xt-: gama-xt-u* (19a), (21b).

Phase of End:

It is encoded by a locative case form of adverbials of place, viz. in the function of allative and illative; the questions: *where, where to*. It is represented by various suffixes used for a different class of words:

    a) The suffix *-da* occurs in the singular and plural with 1st and 2nd person pronouns (Megr.-Laz *čkim-da* 'towards me,' *skan-da* 'towards you[SG],' *čkin-da* 'towards us,' *tkvan-da* 'towards you[PL]'); questions: *towards what, towards, whom, with whom*.

---

[3] The encoding of opposite meanings of the locative cases – ablative and allative by means of a single form has been repeatedly evidenced in linguistics works (Chikobava 1936, 51; Kutscher 2010, 256-257; Kiria et al. 2015, 56).

b)   *-iša* / *-ša* – with all substantives used as an adverbial modifier of place, as well as with spatial adverbs (Megr.-Laz *xolo-ša* 'till nearby,' Megr. *šor-ša* 'far away,' Laz *mendra-ša* 'far away,' *gale-ša* 'till nearby) and with the 3ʳᵈ person pronoun (Megr. *ti-ša* 'towards him/her," Laz *hemu-ša* 'with/towards him/her,' etc.); The question of adverbs is *till where* and that of pronouns is *with whom / what, towards whom what.*

c)   with spatial adverbs: the derivator *-le* (Megr. *židole*, Laz *žindo-le(n)* 'upwards,' Megr. *tudo-le*, Laz *tudendo-le(n)* 'downwards') and in interrogative pronouns (*so-le(n)* 'where to') (Kutscher 2010, 256-257); the derivator *-x* which is of a postpositional origin and is assumed as an Abkhazian loan (Lomtatidze 1943, 974; Gudava 1947,188-189; Gabunia 1993, 67): Megr. *mino-x* 'on this side,' *gino-x* 'on that side,' etc.; the derivator *-do* (Laz. *melendo* 'on that side,' *molendo* 'on this side').

d)   by means of certain groups of simple, derived, and compound preverbs (Megr. *me-, mito-, miša-, mila-, mino*, etc., Laz *me-, melo-, meša-* / *mešk'a-*, etc.), the affirmative *ko-*, the prefix *ge-*, forming the perfect (Kobalava 2010, 237).

e)   perfective verbal roots/stems of motion/movement:

Phase of Course:

Course is a continuous dynamic process with a directed vector, demonstrating orientation/reference and ending without an implication of a beginning and an end. Coutse, that is, motion *per se* cannot be encoded by perfective verbal forms; therefore, it is realized by means of imperfective verbal stems. For the sake of this, the following have been most widely used in Megrelian and Laz:

a)   Perfective, Present Group forms of motion verbs (both *per se* and transfer).

b)   Aorist forms of perfective roots which are more diverse in Laz: Megr.-Laz. *idu* (19b), (20b), Laz. *igzalu, goxtu* (23). The semantics of the verbs in question has been shifted encoding imperfective aspect, while Aorist in form (A. Chikobava). The perception has been intensified by instances of the repetition of stems in a syntactic construction creating an impression of continuity.

(23)   laz   *go-xt-u, go-xt-u*   *ia*   *ǯoɣoi-k.*   [Kal. 31.3]

PRV-go- AOR.S3SG   s/he.ERG   dog- ERG

'The dog walked, walked…'

Phases are characteristic of a vertical motion as well; however, in a horizontal motion, individual phases are independent while, in a vertical one, the phases of Beginning and End merge with that of Course: a) {Beginning+Course}, b) {Course+End}; the aforementioned is due to a different diagram of motion in an vertical area and corresponds to the conditions of gravity (I. Kobalava).

The same grammatical means are used for describing the phase structure of a vertical motion as for a horizontal one:

1. Preverbs indicating a vertical direction, either an inclined or a sheer trajectory; the vector of motion is directed from below upwards (11a), (11b), (12b), (26): Megr. *e-, eša-, ela-, ek'o-*, Laz. *e-, eša-, ela-, ec'a[1]-, ešk'a-/ eška-* or from above downwards (14b), (15a), (15bs); Megr. *ge-, do-, ino-, ala-, gela-…* Laz. *ge-, do-, mec'a-, gec'a-, ec'a[2]-, goc'a-, geša-, gela-, dolo-, ek'a.[2]*

2. The phases of Beginning and End are encoded by respective preverbs (Beginning: Megr.-Laz. *e-, eša-, ela-…* End: *ge-, do-, ino-…*) or by an ablative (11a), (12b), (14b) and allative (12a) forms of nouns (as well as pronouns and adverbs) used as an adverbial modifier of place (Megr. *ži-še*, Laz. *žin- še* 'from above,' *tudo- še* 'from below'…, *žin- ša* 'upwards'…), or locative nouns (14a) in dative used as adverbial modifiers of place and locative adverbs (12b).

3. The principles of temporal and aspectual opposition are the same; only the use of roots referring to motion is limited owing to their spatial shades. In both languages, the roots *purin-* (Megr.), *putx-* (Laz.) 'to fly' and *ur- / rt-* (Megr.), *ul- / xt-* (Laz.) are widely used to refer to vertical motion.

4.6.2. Encoding Points of a Figure's Location in an Area

In Megrelian and Laz, a place of a figure's location is encoded in locative preverbs and locative adverbs (*here – there, up – down*, etc.); it is morpho-syntactically represented in dative forms of nouns and locative adverbs used as adverbial modifiers of place (Megr.-Laz *ʒga-s / mʒga-s* 'on the shore,' *škas-s* 'in the middle,' *xolo-s* 'near,' Laz *orta-s* 'in the middle,' *yani-s* 'near'). Locative preverbs are taken on by both positional (stativity) and movement (dynamics) verbal roots.

Megrelian locative preverbs have been analyzed in detail by I. Kobalava (ibid.), and those of Laz in Kutscher and Genç (2007) and Kutscher (2011).

a) a place of location is encoded by locative adverbs: Megr. *tak - tek*, Laz. *[h]ak – [h]ek* 'here – there,' Megr.-Laz *mele – mole* 'on that side – on this side,' Megr. *c'oxle - uk'axle* 'ahead – behind,' Laz *c'oxle* 'ahead' – *ukvačxe* 'behind,' *ži – tudo* 'up – down,' etc. The picture of the spatial distribution is diverse as well: up – down, ahead – behind, beside, outlying, around, to the left – to the right, etc. (Kobalava ibid.; Gersamia ibid.).

b)   a place of location is encoded by dative forms of locative adverbs; e.g. Megr. *xasilas*, Laz *mʒgas* provide information about a place of location; this is an area in the vicinity of **x**, that is, beside it. The preverb *ela-* has the same meaning; however, there is a difference: in the form *e+la*, being received as a result of the combination of a simple preverb and a locative particle, the *e-* is an orienting component encoding the direction from below upwards (24a), (24b), and the locative particle denotes a location

(24a)   Megr.   *boši*   *xasilas*   *k-ile-rin-u*   [GOL. II.522]
                      boy(NOM)   beside   AFF-PRV-be-AOR.S3SG
                                               (ADV:DAT)
                      'S/he put the boy beside him/her.'

(24b)   Laz   *t'et'eli*   *xuvarda*   *mʒgas*
                      Naked (NOM)   lover(NOM)   beside(ADV:DAT)
                      ela-dgi-t'-u.   [Kipsh. 43]
                      PRV-stand-IMP-S3SG
                      'The naked lover was standing in the corner.'

c)   a location is also encoded by a dative case forms of a noun: *c'vans* 'on a sharp point,' (25a), *k'uis* 'into the pit;' it is true that a verb root is dynamic and a direction of a preverb is from above downwards, a location, whereby a figures motion is discontinued, is encoded by a dative form.

(25a)   Megr.   *rošap'i-k*   *kua-š*   *c'van-s*
                      Roshapi-ERG   stone-GEN   sharp point-DAT
                      ki-gi-a-ntx-u.   [Khub. 62.29]
                      AFF-PRV-SPRS-fall-AOR.S3SG
                      'Roshapi fell on the sharp point of the stone.'

(25d)   Laz   *k'ui-s*   *ge-i-l-u.*   [Zhg. 107.31]
                      pit-DAT   PRV-PASS-go-AOR.S3SG
                      'S/he went down into the pit.'

4.7. Conclusion

The present paper is a discussion of how space is construed linguistically in Megrelian and Laz, as the most closely related languages within the Kartvelian family. Based on the verbal stems referring to motion and immobility, it is demonstrated how deep semantic structures of space are represented by means of surface structures in the languages in point.

According to L. Talmy's classification, Megrelian and Laz are Satellite-framed languages, that is, spatial relation are encoded not in a root, as it happens in Verb-framed languages, but rather in satellites outside a verbal root, predominantly in spatial preverbs, as well as in external satellites of a verbal stem, that is, a lexicalized entity, in deictic pronouns, and adverbs. For the sake of the description of a complete picture of a tri-dimensional area, the languages in point make use of lexical and grammatical categories which are dealt with in the paper.

The semantic analysis of motion (dynamics) and immobility (stativity) verbs has established the conceptual structure of a verbal root and semantic components of spatial preverbs.

The Megrelian and Laz verbal root is a minimum morpheme with a conceptual structure (R. Jackendoff), encoding divided semantic components, concepts the unity of which is represented by a root meaning. Verbal roots are essentially neutral in terms of characteristics of motion/immobility by means of locative features, acquiring this status together with other morphemes, thus turning into a stem. Information associated with spatial relations is conveyed beyond the root: within and/or beyond the stem, in locative cases, preverbs, adverbials of place, deictic pronouns. The aforementioned means represent spatial relations from various angles and present a linguistic characteristics of a system of relations.

In the languages in question, verbal roots for motion and immobility contain such significant general features as: manner of motion (*to go, to swim, to fly*) or type of position (*to stand, to lie, to sit, to be put, to be planted*), dynamicity or stativity, im/mobile figure (in/animate, non-/living), volition (transfer semantics), tempo of motion, aspect (im/perfective), and tense (Present, Past, Future). Few exceptions, being encoded in a root by means of spatial features, do not change the general picture in these languages.

A preverb is a satellite morpheme of a root, a prefix with a poly-functional adverbial meaning, encoding a local picture of the spatial distribution of dynamic and stative processes: a preverb may define a direction of a moving figure (vertical, horizontal, sheer), spatial reference, that is, relation to either a moving or immobile relatum (to person, among them), topology of place (15d), (15c), that is, geo-morphology of an area, and type (open, closed, semi-open) (16), (17), (18), in some instances a figure's location with respect to visualization (see Table 6). A simple preverb, which is independent or is included in a derived structure (PRVsmlp + ADV loc), defines a direction, and all the other functions, associated with rendering spatial semantics, are performed by a locative particle. Spatial preverbs are described as sets of semantic components the synthesis of which establishes a meaning of a preverb in question.

A motion conveyed by a verb is performed along horizontal and vertical axes, either in a sheer or in an inclined trajectory. The latter is particularly specific for Megrelian and is encoded by specific preverbs (*ela-*, *dila-*).

Preverbs are selectively combined with a verbal root of motion according to which phase of motion is to be encoded: Beginning, End, or Course; on the other hand, an entire picture of a motion, that is, a figure's movement in an area, cannot be described only by means of preverbs; it can be made possible by means of systemic analyses of deictic pronouns, adverbials of place, and adverbs correlating with a preverbed verb within a syntactic construction.

Most of the locative preverbs are common for motion (dynamic) and position (stative) verbs presenting a process of stativity-dynamics as a unified one in the languages in point. In the three-phase system of motion, stativity is encoded where a dynamic process either begins or ends, that is, in locative points. It is also important that, being taken on by position (*to stand, to lie, to sit, to be put, to be planted*) verb roots, preverbs are capable of presenting stativity in dynamics, that is, of transforming stative forms into dynamic ones (STAT>DIN), whereby all essential spatial features of a locative preverb has been retained, while a simple preverb, as its constituent, encodes a vector of motion, and a suffix structure of a verbal root has been modified.

Preverbs are used not in an isolated way but rather in interrelationship with other linguistic items. In Megrelian and Laz, they are associated with certain categories of the noun and the verb, with other parts of speech: adverbs and pronouns. Only with respect to these correlations it is possible to represent a complete picture of spatial relations because spatial features, encoded by preverbs, are only a general hint to spatial relations. Their individual linguistic (lexico-grammatical) meanings are specified at the morpho-syntactic level whereby respective grammatical categories are involved. They are adverbs, satellites beyond a stem, encoding a figure's location in its immobility (stativity) and specifying starting, final, and target points in spatial motion. The former is encoded by locative adverbs with a simple structure, a dative form of a noun or adverb, and the latter – by a derivator, taken on by an adverbial stem of a derived structure, or by ablative (*-iše* / *-še*) or allative (*-iša* / *-ša*) markers, which, when combined with 1st and 2nd person pronouns, occur with the morphemes *-de* (ABL) and *-da* (ALL).

It should also be noted that the rules of the construal of adverbs and preverbs in Megrelian and Laz are essentially different from those of the other Kartvelian languages. Whereas a derived preverb is a combination of a simple preverb and a locative particle, derived adverbs is a linguistic entity produced as a result of combinations of various elements (derivators, preverbs, root of a simple adverb).

In Megrelian and Laz, a construction of a phrase conveying to spatial semantics is a certain sequence of lexical and grammatical entities, involving the distribution of individual functions, as well as their merging, this being for, on the one hand, the detalization of spatial linguistic data, and for a complete representation of the linguistic state of the art.

Table 4.7. Map of space Linguistic representations in Megrelian and laz

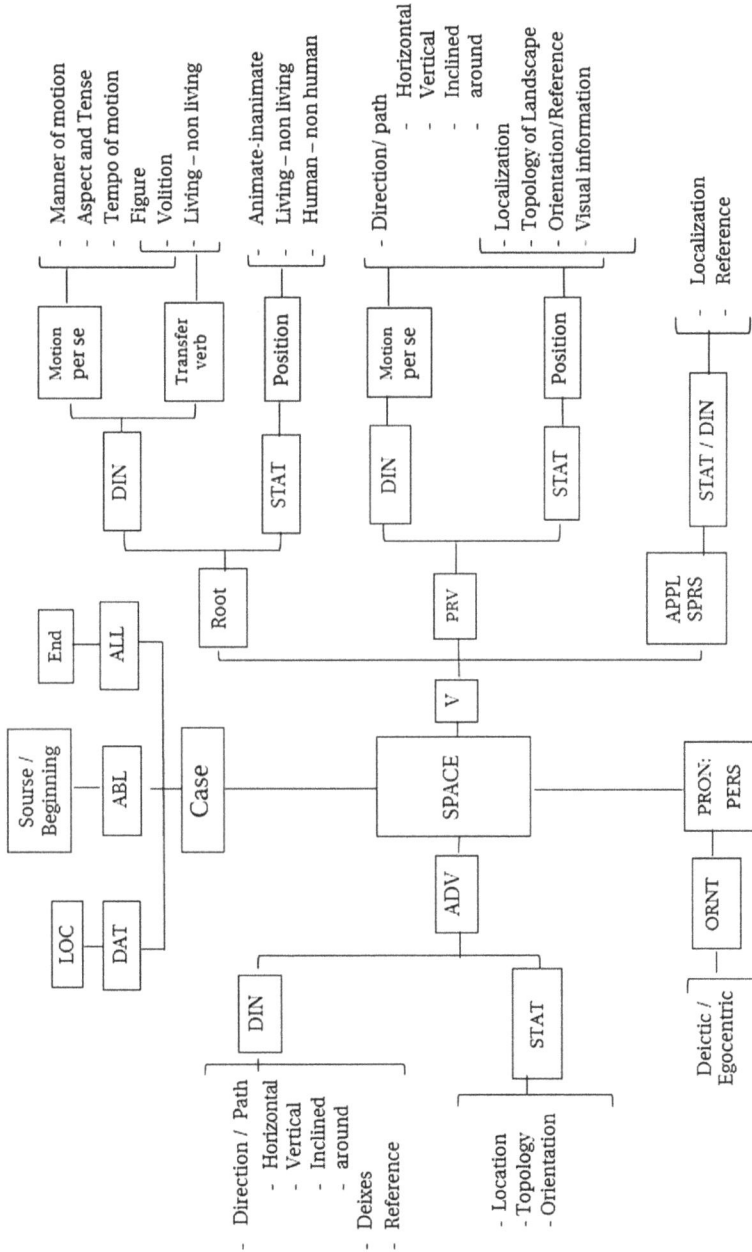

ABL	Ablative case	MA	Medio-Active voice
ADV	Adverb	MSD	Masdar
AFF	Affirmative / Affirmative particle	NEG	Negative particle
ALL	Allative	NOM	Nominative case
AOR	Aorist	0	Object
APPL	Applicative	PASS	Passive voice
CONJ	Conjunction	PL	Plural
CV	Character vowel	POT1	Potential
DAT	Dative case	PP	Postposition
DEF	Definite	PRS	Present / Present Tense
DIN	Dynamics	PRV	Preverb
DIR	Direction (path)	R	Root
ERG	Ergative	S	Subject
EVID 1	Evidential	SPRS	Superessive
FV	Vowel prefixes / Functional vowels	STAT	Stativity
GEN	Genitive case	THM/ TS	Thematic marker
IMPF	Imperfect	TR	Trajectory
IPV	Imperfectiv	VRT	Vertical
INDF	Indefinite	[1] [2] [3]	Sets of obligatory person markers
LOC	Locative / Locative adverb		

References

Arabuli, Avtandil. 1999. "On the problem of a number of conjugable items of a verb in Georgian." *Issues of Linguistics* 1. Tbilisi. [In Georgian].

Asatiani, Irina. 2012. *A Dictionary of Laz.* Tbilisi: Artanuji.

—. 2015. *Prepositions in the Zan (Megrelian-Chan) Language.* Tbilisi: Tbilisi State University Press. [In Georgian].

Asatiani, Rusudan. 2011. *A Synopsis of Laz Grammar.* Tbilisi: Universal. [In Georgian].

—. 2018. "Morphological structure of the Laz verb." *Issues of Linguistics*: 5-20. Tbilisi. [In Georgian].

Boeder, Winfried. 2004. "Lexicalization patterns." *Proceedings of the Chair of the Old Georgian Language* 31. [In Georgian].

Brown, Penelope, and Stephen Levinson. 2003. *Space in Language and Cognition. Explorations in Cognitive Diversity.* Cambridge: Cambridge University Press.

Chikobava, Arnold. 1936. *A Grammatical Analysis of Chan.* Tbilisi. [In Georgian].

—. 1938. *A Chan-Megrelian-Georgian Comparative Dictionary.* Tbilisi.

—. 1948. *Problems of an Ergative Construction in the Ibero-Caucasian Languages.* Tbilisi. [In Georgian].

—. 1950. "A general linguistic characteristic of the Georgian language." *Explanatory Dictionary of the Georgian Language* 1. Tbilisi. [In Georgian].

Deeters, Gerhard. 1930. *Das Khartwelische Verbun.* Verglichende Darstellung des Verbalbaus der Sudkaukasichen Sprachen. Band 1, Leipzig: Markert and Petters.

Ezugbaia, Lali. 2011. "Topology of space based on Megrelian-Laz preverbs." *Linguacultural Studies* 1, (ed. by I. Chantladze, E. Soselia, N. Mgeladze), 2011, pp. 143-146. [In Georgian].

Fähnrich, Heinz, and Zurab Sarjveladze. 2000. *Etymological Dictionary of the Kartvelia n Languages.* 2nd edition. Tbilisi: Tbilisi State Pedagogical University. [In Georgian].

Gabunia, Kakha. 1993. *Formation and Functions of the Adverb in the Kartvelian Languages.* Tbilisi: Metsniereba. [In Georgian].

Gamkrelidze, Tamaz, and Givi Machavariani. 1965. *The System of Sonants and Ablaut in Kartvelian Languages.* Tbilisi: Mecniereba. [In Georgian].

Gersamia, Rusudan. 2019. "Problems of Division of Laz into Dialects and Peculiarities of Khopa-Chkhala." *Issues of Linguistics.* Tbilisi: Tbilisi State University. [In Georgian].

—. 2020. *Space and Motion in Language Representation (Analyses of Laz Linguistic Data).* Tbilisi: Ilia State University.

Gersamia, Rusudan, Zaal Kikvidze, Maia Lomia, and Medea Saghliani. 2016. *Phonosemantic Vocabulary in Kartvelian Languages.* Tbilisi: Ilia State University. [In Georgian].

Greenberg, Joseph. 1960. "Quantitative Approach to the Morphologycal Typology of Language," *International Journal of American Linguistics* Vol. XXVI, 3.

Gudava, Togo. 1947. "An Abkhazian postposition in Zan." *Bulletin of the Georgian Academy of Sciences,* vol. 8. Tbilisi. [In Georgian].

Gudava, Togo, and Tamaz Gamkrelidze. 1981. "Consonant clusters in Megrelian." In *Tbilisi University to Akaki Shanidze.* Tbilisi. [In Georgian].

Holisky, Dee Ann. 1991. "Laz." In Harris, A. C. (ed.), *The indigenous languages of the Caucasus.* Volume 1: The Kartvelian languages, 395-472. Delmar, New York: Caravan Books.

Ivanishvili, Marine, and Eter Soselia. 2014. "Preverbs in Megrelian." *Issues of Linguistics:* 182-193. Tbilisi. [In Georgian].

Jackendoff, Ray. 1983. *Semantics and Cognition.* Cambridge, MA: MIT Press.

—. 1990. *Semantic Structures.* Cambridge, MA: MIT Press.

Kartozia, Guram. 2005. *Laz Language and Its Place among the System of the Kartvelian Languages.* Tbilisi: Nekeri. [In Georgian].

Kartozia, Guram, Rusudan Gersamia, Maia Lomia, and Taia Tskhadaia. 2010. *Linguistic Aanalysis of Megrelian.* Tbilisi: Meridian. [In Georgian].

Kipshidze, Ioseb. 1914. *A Grammar of the Megrelian (Iverian) Language with a Reader and a Vocabulary.* Saint-Petersburgh. [In Russian].

Kiria, Chabuka, Lali Ezugbaia, Omar Memishishi, and Merab Chukhua. 2015. *Laz-Megrelian Grammar, 1. Morphology.* Tbilisi: Meridian. [In Georgian].

Kajaia, Otar. 2000. *A Megrelian-Georgian Dictionary,* vols. 1-3. Tbilisi: Nekeri.

Klimov, Georgij. 1964. *Etymological Dictionary of the Kartvelian Languages.* Moscow: Academy of Sciences of USSR. [In Russian].

—. 1974. "On the Character of Active Languages." *Linguistics* 131: 11-13. [In Russian].

Kobalava, Izabela. 2010. "On one peculiarity of the present stem in Megrelian (grammatical and semantic aspects)." *Issues of Linguistics* I-II. Pp. 234-250. Tbilisi. [In Georgian].

—. 2015. "The semantics of the verb *ula* 'to go' in Megrelian." *Typological Studies* VII. Tbilisi. [In Georgian].

—. 2020. *Space and Motion in Language Representation (Analysis of Megrelian Linguistic Data)*. Tbilisi: Ilia State University. [In Georgian].

Kobalava, Izabela, and Rusudan Gersamia. 2020. "Semantic Components of Adverbs in Megrelian and Laz." *Bulletin of the Georgian National Academy of Sciences.* vol. 14, no. 2; pp. 109-113. [In Georgian].

Kortava, Iuri. 2008. "Active order." In *Encyclopeadia "Georgian language,"* comp. by I. Kobalava, ed. by G. Kvaratskhelia. Tbilisi: Erovnuli mtserloba. [In Georgian].

Kutscher, Silvia. 2001. "Nomen und nominales Syntagma im Lasischen. Eine deskriptive Analyse des Dialekts von Ardesen." (Lincom Studies in Caucasian Linguistics 17.) München: Lincom Europa.

—. 2008. "The language of the Laz in Turkey: Contact-induced change or gradual language loss?" *Turkic Languages* 12, 82-102.

—. 2010. "When 'towards' means 'away from:' the case of directional-ablative syncretism in the Ardesen variety of Laz (South-Caucasian)." *Language Typology and Universals*, Vol 63. Issue 3. Bremen: Academie Verlag.

—. 2011. "On the Expression on Spatial Relations in Ardeşen-Laz." *Linguistic Discovery* 9, 2: 49-77.

Kutscher, Silvia, and Sevim Genç. 2007. "Laz positional verbs: semantics and use with inanimate figures." *Linguistics* 45, 1029-1064.

Lacroix, Rene. 2009. *Description du Dialecte Laze d'Arhavi* (caucasique du sud, Turquie). Grammaire et textes. PhD Dissertation. Manuscript.

Lakoff, George. 1987. *Women, Fire, and Dangerous Things. What Categories Reveal about the Mind.* Chicago and London: The University of Chicago Press.

Langacker, Ronald. 1987. *Foundation of Cognitive Grammar,* vol. 1: Theoretical prerequisites. Stanford: Stanford University Press.

Levinson, Stephen. 1996. *Space in Language and Cognition: Explorations in Linguistic Diversity.* Cambridge: Cambridge University Press.

—. 2003. *Space in Language and Cognition: Explorations in Cognitive Diversity.* Cambridge: Cambridge University Press.

Lomashvili, Leila. 2015. "Morphonology of Mingrelian Prevernal Markers and Structure of PF." *Advances in Language and Literary Studies* Vol. 6 No. 1; pp. 172-179.

Lomia, Maia, Gersamia Rusudan. 2012. *Interlinear Morphemic Glossing (Morpological Analysis of Megrelian Texts).* Tbilisi: Ilia State University. [In Georgian].

Lomtatidze, Ketevan. 1943. *Principal Kinds and Shape of Local Preverbs in Abkhazian and Abaza.* Tbilisi. [In Georgian].

Lyons, John. 1978. *An Introduction to Theoretical Linguistics.* Moscow. [Translated from English into Russian] / Lyons J. 1977. *Semantics.* Cambridge: Cambridge University Press.

Machavariani, Givi. 1974. "The Category of aspect in the Kartvelian languages." *Issues in the Structure of Kartvelian Languages* IV. Tbilisi. [In Georgian].

Makharoblidze, Tamar. 2016. "On Kartvelia preverbs." *Ibero-Caucasian Linguistics* LXIV. Tbilisi. [In Georgian].

Makharoblidze, Tamar. 2018. "On Georgian Preverbs." *Open Linguistics*, Vol. 4: Issue 1.

Marr, Nikolai. 1910. *A Grammar of the Chan (Laz) Language (with a reader and vocabulary)*. Saint-Petersburg. [In Georgian].

Melikishvili, Irine. 2010. "On inflectionality (fusionality) in the Kartvelian languages." *Issues of Linguistics* I-II. Tbilisi. [In Georgian].

Öztürk, Balkiz, and Marcus Pöchtrager. 2011. *Pazar Laz*, Munich: LINCOM Europa.

Pederson, Eric, Eve Danziger, Stephen Levinson, Sotaro Kita, Gunter Senft, and David Wilkins. 1998. "Semantic typology and spatial conceptualization." *Language* 74(3): 557–589.

Plungyan, Vladimir. 2002. "On the specific character of expressing of nominal spatial peculiarities in the verb: the category of verb orientation." *Grammaticalization of Spatial Meanings*, ed. by V. A. Plungyan. Moscow. [In Russian].

Rostovtsev-Popiel, Alexsander. 2016. "Kartvelian Preverbs in a Cross-Linguistic Perspective." *VII International Symposium on Kartvelian Studies Georgia in the Context of European Civilization*: 94-97. Tbilisi.

Shanidze, Akaki. 1980. *Foundations of Georgian Grammar*. Works in twelve volumes. III. Tbilisi: Tbilisi State University [In Georgian].

Talmy, Leonard. 1985. *Toward a Cognitive Semantics*, Vol. 1 and 2. Cambridge. MIT Press.

—. 1991. "Path to Realization: A typology of event conflation." *Berkeley Working Papers in Linguistics*: 480-519.

Veshapidze, Irakli. 1967. *Preverb in Old Georgian*. Tbilisi: TSU Press. [In Georgian].

Abbreviations of texts

Kipsh.	Kipshidze, I. *A Grammar of the Megrelian (Iverian) Language with a Reader and a Vocabulary*. Saint-Petersburgh, 1914.
Chik. II.	Chikobava, Arn. *A Grammatical Analysis of Chan*. Tbilisi: Georgian Academy of Sciences Press, 1936. / Chikobava, Arn. *Works*, III. Tbilisi: Institute of Linguistics, 2008.
Lol	Lola nana (Megrelian texts with Georgian translations), compiled by M. Todua and L. Basilaia. Tbilisi, 2007.
GOL.I	*Georgian Oral Lore, Megrelian Texts* II; texts prepared for publication by C. Danelia and A. Tsanava. Tbilisi, 1991.
Kal.	Kalandia, T. *Laz Texts (with interlinear translations)*. Tbilisi: Artanuji, 2008.
Kart.	Kartozia, G. *Megrelian and Laz Texts*. Tbilisi: Nekeri, 2008.
Khub.	Khubua, M. *Megrelian Texts*. Tbilisi, 1937.
Zhg.	Zhgenti, S. *Chan Texts; Arkabe Sub-dialect*. Tbilisi: Georgian Academy of Sciences Press, 1938.
Duméz.	Dumézil, G. *Laz Folk Tales and Legends*. The Georgian version of Laz folk tales prepared and the vocabulary compiled by M. Bukia. Tbilisi: Institute of Linguistics, 2009.

Chapter 5

On the Representation of Morphosyntactic Predictions: ERP Evidence from Georgian

Ellen Lau

University of Maryland College Park

Maria Polinsky

University of Maryland College Park

Nancy Clarke

Amazon AWS AI

Michaela Socolof

McGill University

Abstract

Much recent work in psycholinguistics argues that comprehenders rapidly generate expectations about the upcoming input. But so far, we know little about the representational format of these expectations. Do predictive inferences have the same status as more direct inferences from bottom-up input? We investigate this question using the case of morphosyntactic prediction in an ERP (event-related brain potential) study in Georgian. Our experimental design makes critical use of the grammatical properties of Georgian, a split-ergative language in which an ergative-marked nominal is most commonly found in the aorist (typically translated as past tense). Combining the ergative with temporal adverbials like 'tomorrow,' which strongly predict a clause with non-past interpretation, allows us to create a situation in which the cues conflict not in themselves, but in the constraints that they place on the upcoming verb tense. If these cues drove predictive, incremental updates to the syntactic representation in the same way as bottom-up input, we might expect to see an immediate response to the conflict. However, the results of our ERP experiment provide no positive evidence of processing difficulty when contextual cues motivate conflicting predictive inferences about the tense of the upcoming verb. The late positivity ERP response associated with processing difficulty is only observed when direct evidence of unacceptability is encountered at the verb itself.

Keywords: context, ergativity, event-related brain potentials (ERP), Georgian, morphosyntactic cues, prediction, split ergativity

***

In investigations of the human cognitive architecture that supports language comprehension, the majority of experimental studies have focused on just a few languages. However, more and more the field of psycholinguistics has come to recognize that less-commonly studied languages can afford unique opportunities to answer fundamental questions about these processing mechanisms. In this paper we describe such a case. We show how the grammatical properties of Georgian allowed us to investigate the representation of syntactic predictions in a way that would be possible in few other languages, in what to our knowledge is the first electroencephalographic (EEG) study of language processing in Georgian. To anticipate our conclusions, while our findings may be in need of further replication, it nonetheless seems simultaneously both astonishing and satisfying that brain responses could be consistent across typologically diverse languages.

5.1. Background

Psycholinguistic research in the last two decades has come to the conclusion that *prediction* is an important component of language comprehension. But, what is prediction? Several possibilities are on offer.

One weaker use of the concept of prediction simply equates it with context-sensitive comprehension. For example, imagine a toy comprehension system whose goal is to estimate the meaning intended by the speaker. Imagine that it is equipped with knowledge of the world, and knows, for instance, that events of the chasing of rabbits by dogs are more commonly viewed and discussed than events of the chasing of flies by dogs. Now imagine that the system is presented with the language input 'I saw a dog chasing a rabbit' or 'I saw a dog chasing a fly.' If, after receiving the last word of the sentence, the system uses world knowledge about what events are more likely to 'boost' the intended message representation in the rabbit-sentence, and if this results in the system 'selecting' this representation more quickly and effortlessly than in the fly-sentence, it would be an example of 'predictive language comprehension' under this relatively permissive view. Even simple lexical frequency effects might count as 'prediction' under this view, if the occurrence of a word or concept contributes to boosting a message because a word or concept that occurs frequently in the broadest context (all prior experience) is more likely to be intended than one that occurs less frequently.

A stronger use of the concept 'prediction'—stronger in the sense of characterizing a smaller set of processing models—uses it to refer to cases in which the context impacts the estimation of an external cause before that external cause has actually generated any sensory input. For example, imagine that in the above example the sentence is presented incrementally, and at the point of receiving the input 'chasing,' the system not only infers the lexical item (syntactic root) for 'chase' on the basis of this acoustic input, but also infers the lexical item for 'rabbit.' Even if these inferences both turn out to be correct, they can be distinguished by the fact that in one case the inferred lexical item 'chase' has already impacted the acoustic input, and in the other, the inferred lexical item 'rabbit' has not yet had any impact on the acoustic input. And we can thus use the word 'prediction' to pick out this second class of inferences.

In this study, we adopt the stronger concept of prediction and investigate the hypothesis that comprehenders generate morphosyntactic predictions. We will explore questions that follow from this hypothesis about the representation of the predictive inferences. It could be that, at the level of the syntactic representation being constructed during parsing, predictive (context) and non-predictive (direct evidence) inferences have qualitatively similar impacts—that is, predicting a morphosyntactic feature from context could have exactly the same kind of impact as hearing some direct acoustic or visual evidence for that feature. Alternatively, it could be that the impact of predictive inferences is qualitatively different because context is a less reliable cue.

One simple thing we know about direct evidence for morphosyntactic features is that when direct acoustic/visual evidence conflicts with the syntactic representation inferred from the prior context, there is strong and immediate processing disruption in behavioral and neural responses. For example, in ergative languages like Hindi and Georgian, an ergative-marked subject cannot appear with a verb in the imperfective (Hindi) or present tense (Georgian). If an ergative-marked subject is followed by an imperfective verb in the same clause, we immediately see reaction time slowdowns and increased amplitude of an event-related brain potential (ERP) late posterior positivity response associated with processing difficulty incurred by grammatical computation (see Dillon et al., 2012, for Hindi, and see Swaab et al., 2012 for a general overview of ERP techniques in language).

Here, we asked whether analogous effects of processing difficulty are observed when the conflict is between two strong predictive inferences. If predictive inferences about morphosyntactic features have the same cognitive status as non-predictive inferences from direct evidence, then a cue that *generates a predictive inference* that conflicts with the prior context should cause immediate processing difficulty, just as direct acoustic/visual evidence for a morphosyntactic feature that conflicts with the prior context causes processing difficulty.

The experimental design we use to explore this question in Georgian is inspired by the observation by Dillon et al. (2012) that in ergative languages, both temporal adverbials and case-marking of the subject can serve to generate predictive inferences about the same morphosyntactic features of the upcoming verb. Dillon et al.'s ERP experiment was conducted in Hindi, where an ergative-marked subject can only co-occur with perfective verb forms. They showed rapid and robust ERP sensitivity to the ungrammaticality that arises when an ergative-marked subject was followed by a non-perfective future verb form (an early negativity and a late positivity). They also showed rapid ERP sensitivity when the contextual conflict was instead induced by a mismatching temporal adverbial (e.g. 'yesterday' followed by the same non-perfective future verb form), although with slight differences in the spatial profile of the response. Although Dillon et al. (2012) were interested in the nature of those subtle differences between the adverbial and case-marking cues, here we abstract across them to focus on a different question: what happens when their predictions conflict?

Georgian has the same form of contingency between the ergative subject marker (∂(ა)/-*m(a)*) and (aorist) tense morphology, as in (1-2) (although debate exists in the theoretical literature over whether the marker –*m(a)* in fact encodes ergative case vs. an Agent whose form is conditioned on the verb's tense).[1] Two other grammatical forms compatible with the ergative are the relatively infrequent optative and future, which we discuss more below.

Before we proceed with the data, a note on terminology is in order. The ergative (form in ∂(ა)/-*m(a)*) is sometimes referred to as the narrative, and the nominative (the form often but not always ending in -o/-*i*) is also referred to as the absolute. In what follows, we will be using the terms *ergative* and *nominative*, although nothing hinges on this terminology.

Case Match:

(1) თბილის-ში კაც-მა   ბარ-ში დალი-ა   ღვინო და...
     tbilis-ši k'ac-ma   bar-ši dali-a   γvino da...
     tbilisi-in man-ERG bar-in drink-AOR wine and
     'In Tbilisi, the man in the bar drank wine and...'

Case Mismatch:

(2) *თბილის-ში კაც-მა   ბარ-ში დალი-ევს   ღვინო და...
     tbilis-ši k'ac-ma   bar-ši dal-evs   γvino da...
     tbilisi-in man-ERG bar-in drink-FUT wine and
     'In Tbilisi, the man in the bar will drink wine and...'

In our study, instead of examining the violation responses at the verb, we focus on what would happen *prior* to the verb if the predictions generated by the

---

[1] See Klimov and Alekseev (1980), and see Harris (1981); Legate (2008); Nash (2017); Polinsky (2020) for discussion in English and further references.

temporal adverbial and subject marker conflicted with each other—in other words, if a future temporal adverbial like 'tomorrow' predicting a non-aorist verb was followed by the ergative-marked noun whose primary prediction is that of aorist morphology. The other grammatical forms compatible with the ergative and future-oriented adverbs, such as 'tomorrow' are the relatively infrequent optative and future. In the corpus data that we were able to check, the ratio of ergative-assigning verbs in the aorist and in the optative is about 6 to 1; the ratio of ergative-assigning verbs in the aorist and in the future is also about 6 to 1. If we combine all the instances of ergative-assigning verbs that are compatible with the future, the aorist forms are three times more likely to occur with the ergative subject than these future-oriented forms.[2] These counts allow us to assume that the expectation of the optative or future is lower than that of the past-oriented aorist. This set up is less categorical than what is observed in Hindi (Dillon et al., 2012), where the perfective is the only form compatible with ergative marking, but nevertheless, the association between the ergative and the aorist is higher than its association with the optative and the future.

Therefore, if comprehenders immediately computed the constraints of both the adverbial and the case and if predictive inferences about morphosyntactic features have the same cognitive status as non-predictive ones, we would expect to observe activity at the case-marked noun, associated with shifting the prediction for the rarer optative or future morphology.

Cue-conflict Control:

(3) ხვალ   კაც-ი   ბარ-ში დალი-ევს   ღვინო და...
    xval   k'ac-i   bar-ši dal-evs   ɣvino da...
    tomorrow man-NOM   bar-in drink-FUT   wine and
    'Tomorrow, the man in the bar will drink wine and...'

Cue-conflict Mismatch:

(4) *ხვალ   კაც-მა   ბარ-ში დალი-ევს   ღვინო და...
    xval   k'ac-ma   bar-ši dal-evs   ɣvino da...
    tomorrow man-ERG   bar-in drink-FUT   wine and
    'Tomorrow, the man in the bar will drink wine and...'

Having outlined the linguistic background of the experimental work presented here, we will now describe the methods and results of the study.

---

[2] We are grateful to an anonymous reviewer for detailed corpus data on the distribution of aorist, optative, and future.

5.2. Participants

EEG data were collected from a total of 46 participants, for which they received monetary compensation. All the participants were right-handed native speakers of Georgian. Written informed consent was obtained from all participants. Datasets from 15 participants had to be excluded from further ERP analysis due to excessive artefact during the epoch (artefact identification procedures detailed below). This number is slightly larger than typical for EEG studies, primarily because imperfect climate control during the hot Georgian summer resulted in large sweat artefacts in a significant number of participants. Data from the remaining 31 participants (9 male, mean age 23.6y) were carried forward for subsequent analysis.

5.3. Materials

Our experiment was originally designed to include six conditions: (1-4) above, as well as two further conditions to confirm Dillon et al.'s (2012) observation that standard processing difficulty effects arise with tense-mismatching adverbials, here a past-tense adverbial (and nominative subject) with a present-tense verb. Therefore, we created 180 cue-type sets of six items each. All items began with a clausal adverbial, followed by the first noun which was rotated across a list of approximately 30 professions, followed by a locative, followed by the critical transitive verb, and a direct object; the first clause was always followed by a second clause connected to the first with a connective such as and/but/because. Unfortunately, due to experimenter error, the two extra adverbial conditions were accidentally created in such a way that items from both conditions appeared in an unacceptable form (specifically, in the 'acceptable' condition, 'yesterday' + nominative subject was combined with a past-tense perfective instead of an imperfective). Since this error made the contrast between those two extra conditions uninformative, we do not discuss them further in this paper.

In addition to the experimental items, there were 120 fillers and 60 items from another experiment (Lau et al., submitted). The 60 items from the other experiment, as well as half of the fillers, began with either a locative adverbial or a temporal adverbial, followed by a noun (similar to the relative clause stimuli used in another ERP experiment we conducted—see Lau et al., submitted). The remaining 60 fillers were sentences that began in other ways, usually with a sentence initial noun or a subordination marker.

The 180 item sets were distributed across six lists in a Latin Square design, such that each item could appear in each condition, but only one of these versions would occur on any given list. The 180 items from each list were combined and randomized with the 180 additional items, such that each participant saw a total of 360 items in the experimental session, where half of the items were designed to be judged acceptable and half were designed to be judged unacceptable.

5.4. Procedure

The experiment was conducted at the Institute for Theoretical and Applied Linguistics at the Ivane Javakishvili Tbilisi State University. During the experiment, participants were seated in a chair in a quiet room. Stimuli were visually presented on a computer monitor in white 18-point text on a black background. Each trial began with a 1000ms fixation cross. After a 200ms blank screen, the words of the sentence were presented with a constant 600ms stimulus onset asynchrony (SOA), where each word appeared for 500ms separated by a 100ms blank screen.

The final word stayed on the screen for a duration 600ms, followed by a blank screen of 200ms. Then the probe screen appeared, asking whether the sentence was acceptable or not. Participants responded using the 'F' and 'J' keys on the keyboard, where 'F' indicated acceptable and 'J' indicated unacceptable. The experiment was preceded by a brief practice session with filler sentences to ensure that participants understood the task and were comfortable with the presentation format. Five breaks were evenly spaced across the experiment to allow participants to rest.

5.5. Electrophysiological Recording

Sixteen Ag/AgCl electrodes were held in place on the scalp by an elastic cap (BrainVision): AFz, F7, F3, Fz, F4, F8, FC5, FC6, Cz, CP5, CP6, P7, P3, Pz, P4, P8. Bipolar electrodes were placed above and below the left eye and at the outer canthus of the right and left eyes to monitor vertical and horizontal eye movements. Responses were referenced to the left mastoid. The ground electrode was positioned on the scalp between Fz and Cz. Impedances were maintained at less than 10 kΩ for all scalp and ocular electrode sites and less than 2 kΩ for the mastoid site. The EEG signal was amplified by a portable BrainVision V-Amp system and continuously sampled at 512 Hz by an analogue-to-digital converter.

5.6. Analysis

As our recordings were conducted in an environment without electrical shielding, two notch filters were applied offline to the continuous data (50Hz and 100Hz) to minimize line noise. We also applied offline a more standard bandpass filter (Butterworth, order 2) of .1-20Hz. We then extracted epochs time-locked to the onset of the critical word from -100:1000ms. Averaged ERPs were formed from these epochs, after rejecting trials with ocular and muscular artefact, using preprocessing routines from the EEGLAB (Delorme and Makeig, 2004) and ERPLAB (Lopez-Calderon and Luck, 2014) toolboxes. Muscle potential, sweat, and alpha wave artefacts were identified using the peak-to-peak artefact rejection routine provided by ERPLAB (specifically, the *pop_artmwppth()* function), and eye-blink and eye-movement artefacts were identified using the step function artefact rejection routine provided by ERPLAB (specifically, the *pop_artstep()* function), followed by visual confirmation of the identified artefacts by the experimenters and exclusion. Participants for whom more than 50% of trials contained artefacts were excluded from further analysis. In three datasets, one electrode (different for each dataset) contained a disproportionate number of epochs containing peak-to-peak fluctuations of 100 μV or more and was therefore replaced with an interpolated value from surrounding electrodes, using the *eeg_interp()* function provided by EEGLAB with the default method of spherical interpolation. A 100-ms pre-stimulus baseline was subtracted from all waveforms, and a 40-Hz low-pass filter was applied to the ERPs offline.

We conducted Type III SS repeated-measures ANOVAs on mean ERP amplitudes between 800-1000ms for the late positivity. For the latter, we focused on the later end of the traditional time-window in which late positivities are observed (~600-1000ms) because the complexity of Georgian morphology would be likely to increase the processing time associated with basic morphological decomposition, and because a syntactic violation manipulation in the other sub-experiment elicited a late positivity in this later time-window (Lau et al., submitted); however, we note that the use of a less standard time-window means that the conclusions that can be drawn from the late positivity results are more tentative. In order to quantify the topography of the effects, we included the factor of anteriority in all analyses (anterior electrodes: AFz, F7, F3, Fz, F4, F8, FC5, FC6; posterior electrodes: Cz, CP5, CP6, P7, P3, Pz, P4, P8).

5.7. Results

As expected, we observed significant late positivity effects of unacceptability at the verb in both condition sets when the ergative case marker was followed by a future-tensed verb (Figure 5.1), both in the simple ergative control pair (significant interaction between condition and anteriority: $F(1,30) = 12.8$, $p < .05$) and in the future adverbial + ergative comparison of interest of interest (significant interaction between condition and anteriority: $F(1,30) = 8.6$, $p =.05$).

Our question of primary interest was whether neural effects of processing difficulty would be observed earlier in the sentence when an aorist-predicting ergative subject followed a non-aorist a conflicting adverbial, one that predicted a future tense. We saw no evidence of such processing difficulty; there were no reliable differences during the late positivity time-window (no main effect of condition, nor an interaction between anteriority and condition; $ps > .1$), and little numerical difference in the waveforms anywhere in the response to the subject noun.

Figure 5.1. Scalp topoplots and ERP waveforms at electrode Pz time-locked to the verb position in the four conditions

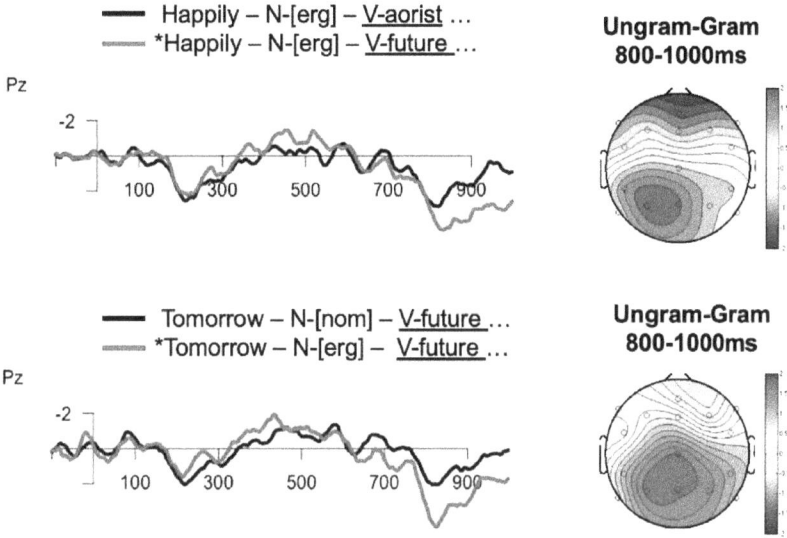

Happily – N-[erg] – V-aorist ...
*Happily – N-[erg] – V-future ...

Pz

Ungram-Gram
800-1000ms

Tomorrow – N-[nom] – V-future ...
*Tomorrow – N-[erg] – V-future ...

Pz

Ungram-Gram
800-1000ms

Figure 5.2. Scalp topoplots and ERP waveforms at electrode Pz time-locked to the noun position in the cue-conflict condition and its control

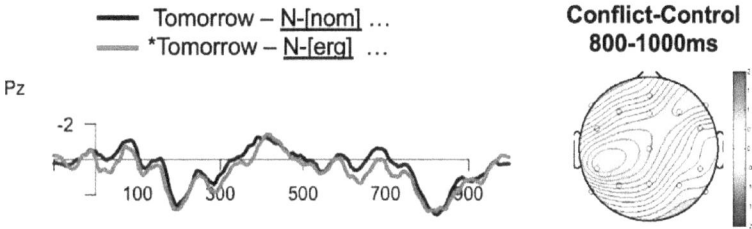

Tomorrow – N-[nom] ...
*Tomorrow – N-[erg] ...

Pz

Conflict-Control
800-1000ms

We also examined the responses to the end-of-sentence acceptability judgment. Responses to the simple ergative cue control pair showed a robust contrast in acceptability judgments: 69% of the ergative + aorist judgments were acceptable, while only 17% of the ergative + future judgments were acceptable. However, in the cue-conflict pair, while the unacceptable ergative + future sentences yielded low ratings (10%), so did the acceptable nominative + future sentences (11%). In revisiting the stimuli, we realized that due to experimenter error, a tense mismatch systematically occurred in this condition well after the critical region, in the second clause of the sentence. Thus, even though the critical first clause was acceptable, the sentence was globally unacceptable. Below we discuss whether this post-critical region error could have had an indirect impact on responses to earlier parts of the sentence.

5.8. Discussion

The results of our ERP study failed to show evidence that a morphosyntactic prediction that conflicts with the context generates the same processing difficulty as direct evidence for a conflicting morphosyntactic feature. We observed standard late positivity ERP effects of conflict when an ergative-marked subject was followed by direct evidence of unacceptability, in the form of a future-tensed verb. However, we saw no difference in the ERP response when a future-tense predicting temporal adverbial (e.g., 'tomorrow') was followed by an aorist-predicting ergative subject.

The most interesting explanation for these results is that predictive morphosyntactic inferences from context and direct morphosyntactic inferences from bottom-up phonological input do not have the same cognitive status. In other words, morphosyntactic prediction is not just an 'early version' of the same operations that would be triggered by direct evidence. How might the consequences of predictive cues be different? One example would be a parser that has something akin to 'parallel activation' and 'selection' stages, where predictive cues could act to weight the support of some parses higher or lower during a stage in which multiple parses remain under consideration, while direct evidence not only updates their weights but also triggers the selection of a particular parse (compare Toscano et al., 2010, for a similar approach to the parsing of sound signals). Then, the late positivity might be taken to be diagnostic of hitting a selection problem when the direct evidence from the non-aorist verb has ruled out other grammatically acceptable analyses. In contrast, the predictive cue from the ergative subject acts to markedly shift weight away from the future-tensed analysis, but does not trigger selection. This kind of explanation plays out the common intuition that predictive cues provide less solid evidence than direct bottom-up input, and thus that their role in parsing is accordingly weaker: they serve to bias rather than to choose.

Another possibility is that the particular kind of predictive inference we tested, morphosyntactic prediction, simply isn't routinely computed at all. This explanation would be interesting because according to some popular 'Bayesian' or 'predictive coding' approaches, prediction is an inherent architectural property of cognition, and should be observed whenever reliable cues are available. Clear evidence for morphosyntactic prediction is difficult to obtain because processing difficulty when a prediction is violated can usually be equally well explained by a bottom-up view where the direct evidence forces selection of an infrequent/low-probability analysis. In older work, one of us has argued that morphosyntactic prediction for verbal agreement explains certain error patterns in agreement comprehension known as agreement attraction (e.g. 'The key to the cabinets are on the table;' see Wagers, Lau and Phillips, 2009), yet later work has suggested that these error patterns are variable (Hammerly, Staub and Dillon, 2019). A case that has received a lot of attention recently in the ERP literature is the dependence of the form *a/an* in English on the predicted phonological form of the subsequent word (e.g., 'On a windy day the boy flew a/*an kite'). Delong et al. (2005) and Urbach et al. (2020) have observed ERP sensitivity at the determiner as a function of the predicted form of the noun. However, note that this case (and parallel ones manipulating grammatical gender on a prenominal marker) involves prediction of lexical information (the form or gender of a predicted noun) rather than the prediction of grammatical properties like the tense or aspect of the clause.

A third possibility is that predictive morphosyntactic inferences are generated, but that our materials were presented too rapidly to detect them, or that the conflicts they generated were resolved too easily. For example, because the temporal adverbial was immediately followed by the ergative subject, it could be that there was not enough time to generate the prediction for a future-tense verb at the adverbial. In this case, the parser would be effectively receiving the adverbial cue and the ergative marker cue simultaneously and trying to use them jointly to predict the continuation. Or, it could be that the one low-probability form consistent with both the future adverbial and the ergative marker, namely, the optative, was still accessible enough that it was not especially costly to shift from a future-tense prediction to an optative prediction when the ergative-marked subject was encountered. To address this possibility in future work, it would be helpful to start with simple sentence-continuation experiments which could show how often Georgian speakers combine the ergative and the optative. A reviewer points out that interestingly, there is suggestive evidence that the ergative marker does rapidly trigger predictive *semantic* inferences (for assigning agentive argument role), as disruption is immediately observed at the ergative argument in simple Hindi or Georgian SOV clauses when the argument is inanimate (Choudhary et al., 2007; Bornkessel-Schlesewsky and Schlesewsky, 2008; Foley and Wagers, 2020; Foley, 2020).

A fourth possibility is that predictive morphosyntactic inferences are generated, but only in response to certain cues and not others. In the current experiment, the temporal adverbial cue exerts contextual constraint on the grammatical tense of the clause in a somewhat indirect way: the temporal adverbial indicates that the current clause is likely to express a meaning about an event in the future, which in turn indicates that the verb phrase is likely to be specified with future tense or another non-aorist form like the optative. And perhaps more indirect contingencies of this type do not generate predictive morphosyntactic inferences. On the other hand, contextual constraint from a grammatical cue like ergative case might be thought to be more 'direct,' for example, by virtue of it needing to be grammatically licensed by a subset of tenses, and perhaps this more 'direct' relation does result in a predictive inference. In fact, Dillon et al.'s (2012) original study in Hindi was partly motivated by the related question of whether semantic vs. syntactic cues to tense lead to different kinds of processing error signals. In a similar vein, a reviewer wonders whether cue-conflict effects might emerge when the cue order is reversed (ergative case cue generates a predictive inference an aorist-tensed clause, and then a future-oriented adverb is encountered which is inconsistent with the sentence meaning that accompanies that grammatical inference). We think this is an interesting idea. If only certain kinds of information can trigger the generation of grammatical predictions, that would raise a host of new questions for parsing models about which ones and why.

Finally, it is important to acknowledge several shortcomings and errors in our experimental design that could suggest less interesting explanations for our failure to observe a cost for prediction conflict. First, our original design included an additional pair of conditions designed to confirm standard processing difficulty effects when combining a future adverbial alone with an aorist verb, but errors in stimuli creation compromised this pair. Second, due to an unfortunate error, the grammatical control conditions with the nominative-marked subject and a future-tensed verb often continued with a conjoined second clause in the past tense, resulting in global unacceptability later in the sentence. This error occurred well after the analysis regions, and the late positivity observed at the critical verb shows that these post-critical errors did not lead to participants adopting a strategy of 'giving up' on analyzing the sentences in general. However, it remains possible that these errors or other general properties of our stimuli set altered the predictive inferences that participants generated such that the results don't generalize to the case of natural language comprehension.

Converging evidence with analogous configurations is certainly needed, and evidence from behavioural designs may be especially helpful as there it is possible to present many fewer items per condition than in ERP. In a pilot online self-paced reading experiment (n=33) using similar items, we have similarly observed no clear evidence of reading time slowdown associated with the cue conflict created by the future adverbial and the ergative-marked subject, even though those trials were now much rarer (5 out of 186 total sentences).[3]

5.9. Conclusions

We hope that this paper illustrates the untapped potential of languages with rich morphological systems like Georgian for investigating central questions about the language comprehension architecture. Here the properties of Georgian allowed us

---

[3] It is worth noting that in the self-paced reading experiment, all items were designed to be acceptable, and therefore the five future-adverbial + ergative sentences continued with the acceptable optative verb. However, the rarity of these trials together with the presence of 20 fillers where the future adverbial was followed by the more frequent future tense, makes us dubious that participants learned an 'optative/future strategy' within the experiment.

to ask an important and relatively unexplored question in psycholinguistics: do morphosyntactic predictive inferences from the context have the same cognitive status as direct inferences from the input? Although our conclusions are tentative, we hope our investigation, the first-ever neurolinguistic study of Georgian, paves the way to further work on an important question for researchers that are committed to a predictive processing architecture.

Acknowledgments

This work was supported in part by NSF grant BCS-1619857 to Maria Polinsky, NSF grant BCS-17949407 to Ellen Lau, and by the College of Arts and Humanities at University of Maryland. We would like to thank Anna Namyst and Bill Idsardi for technical assistance and Steven Foley, Cass Lowry, and two anonymous reviewers for detailed comments on an earlier draft of this paper. We are grateful to Rusudan Asatiani, Zurab Baratashvili, Irina Lobzhanidze, Tamar Makharoblidze, and Irakli Salia for help with the Georgian data. We are indebted to the faculty of the Institute for Theoretical and Applied Linguistics at the Ivane Javakishvili Tbilisi State University for help with participant recruitment and the administration of the experiment. All errors are our responsibility.

References

Bornkessel-Schlesewsky, Ina, and Matthias Schlesewsky. 2008. "The role of prominence information in the real-time comprehension of transitive constructions: A cross-linguistic approach." *Language and Linguistic Compass* 3(1): 19–58.

Choudhary, Kamal Kumar, Matthias Schlesewsky, Dietmar Roehm, and Ina Bornkessel-Schlesewsky. 2007. "The role of animacy in the processing of ergative constructions: Evidence from Hindi." Paper presented at the 13th Annual Conference on Architectures and Mechanisms for Language Processing, Turku, Finnland.

DeLong, Katherine A., Thomas Urbach, and Marta Kutas. 2005. "Probabilistic word pre-activation during language comprehension inferred from electrical brain activity." *Nature neuroscience*, 8(8): 1117-1121.

Delorme, Arnaud, and Scott Makeig. 2004. "EEGLAB: an open source toolbox for analysis of single-trial EEG dynamics including independent component analysis." *Journal of Neuroscience Methods* 134(1): 9-21.

Dillon, Brian, Andrew Nevins, Andrew Austin, and Colin Phillips. 2012. "Syntactic and semantic predictors of tense in Hindi: An ERP investigation." *Language and cognitive processes* 27(3): 313-344.

Foley, Steven. 2020. *Case, agreement, and sentence processing in Georgian*. Ph.D. thesis, University of California Santa Cruz.

Foley, Steven, and Matt Wagers. 2020. "Prominence scales guide incremental sentence comprehension in Georgian." Poster presented at the 33rd Annual

CUNY Conference on Human Sentence Processing (CUNY 33). University of Massachusetts Amherst, Amherst, MA. March 19–21.

Hammerly, Chris, Adrian Staub, and Brian Dillon. 2019. "The grammaticality asymmetry in agreement attraction reflects response bias: Experimental and modeling evidence." *Cognitive psychology* 110: 70-104.

Harris, Alice C. 1981. *Georgian syntax: A study in relational grammar.* Cambridge: Cambridge University Press.

Klimov, Georgij A., and Mikhail E. Alekseev. 1980. *Tipologija kavkazskix jazykov.* Moscow: Nauka.

Lau, Ellen, Michaela Socolof, Nancy Clarke, Rusudan Asatiani, and Maria Polinsky. Submitted. *A subject relative clause preference in a split-ergative language: ERP evidence from Georgian.*

Legate, Julie A. 2008. "Morphological and Abstract Case." *Linguistic Inquiry* 39 (1): 55–101.

Lopez-Calderon, Javier, and Steven J. Luck. 2014. "ERPLAB: an open-source toolbox for the analysis of event-related potentials." *Frontiers in human neuroscience*, 8, 213.

Nash, Lea. 2017. "The structural source of split ergativity and ergative case in Georgian." In Jessica Coon, Diane Massam, and Lisa Travis (eds.) *The Oxford Handbook of Ergativity,* 175-203. Oxford: Oxford University Press.

Polinsky, Maria. 2020. "Introduction." In Maria Polinsky (ed.) *The Oxford Handbook of Languages of the Caucasus,* 1-25. Oxford: Oxford University Press.

Swaab, Tamara Y., Kerry Ledoux, C. Christine Camblin, and Megan A. Boudewyn. 2012. "Language-related ERP components." In Emily Kappenman and Steven J. Luck (eds.), *Oxford library of psychology. The Oxford handbook of event-related potential components,* 397–439. Oxford: Oxford University Press.

Toscano, Joseph C., Bob McMurray, Joel Dennhardt, and Steven J. Luck. 2010. "Continuous perception and graded categorization: electrophysiological evidence for a linear relationship between the acoustic signal and perceptual encoding of speech." *Psychological Science* 21(10): 1532-1540.

Urbach, Thomas, Katherine DeLong, Wen-Hsuan Chan, and Marta Kutas. 2020. "An exploratory data analysis of word form prediction during word-by-word reading." *Proceedings of the National Academy of Sciences* 117(34): 20483-20494.

Wagers, Matt W., Ellen Lau, and Colin Phillips. 2009. "Agreement attraction in comprehension: Representations and processes. "*Journal of Memory and Language* 61(2): 206-237.

Chapter 6

Merged Functionality of Absolutive and Nominative in Georgian

Svetlana Berikashvili

Georg-August University of Göttingen; Ilia State University

Irina Lobzhanidze

Ilia State University

Abstract

This article examines the relationship between Georgian absolutive and nominative cases focusing on the differences and/or similarities between their morphosyntactic representation and functionality in Old and Modern Georgian. The description of theoretical knowledge is applied to the computational rule-based morphosyntactic annotation of Georgian and, from this perspective, the most important is to identify the definition of lemma sign for a concrete token not only in Modern, but in Old Georgian and to assess how the functions of nominative and absolutive coincide between each other diachronically. The lemmatization of Georgian nominals does not reveal any problems in case of Modern Georgian, but the existence of absolutive declared by some scholars in Old Georgian affects the common processing of data. So nominative and absolutive cases are examined diachronically focusing on their 1) lexical pecularities, 2) morphological case markers including so-called 'zero morph,' and 3) syntactic functionality of nominal phrases paying special attention to subjects and objects. The results are considered from the viewpoint of dependency analysis.

Keywords: Georgian Language, case markers, Absolutive, Nominative, morphosyntactic analysis

***

6.1. Introduction

Georgian language belongs to the morphologically rich agglutinating languages. This means that its morphological structure reveals a large number of inflectional categories, a large number of elements that verb or noun paradigms can contain, an interdependence in the occurrence of various elements, and a large number of regular, semi-regular and irregular patterns. There are many Natural Language Processing (NLP) systems used for treating languages with concatenative-type morphology like Georgian. One of the best-known approaches to the morphological analysis of such languages is the finite state technique as described by Beesley and Karttunen (2003). The finite-state technique was efficiently adopted for the compilation of the tokenizer and morphological analyser of Georgian and applied to tokenization, sentence splitting, morphological analysis and named entity recognition (Lobzhanidze 2019). The morphological analyser of Modern Georgian has been developed as a bi-directional transducer by means of the Xerox calculus tools *xfst* and *lexc*. The analyser combines the following four main factors:

- Quantity of morphemes/slots per paradigm;
- Internal changes between or within morphemes/slots;
- Linguistic theory used for reference; and,
- Type of dictionary(ies) used.

The transducer provides lemmatization, assignment of PoS tags and determination of other morphological features. The morphological analyser was tested on the Georgian language corpus (Doborjginidze et al. 2012; 2014) compiled to promote corpus-based approaches to the Georgian language. The corpus is freely available online at http://corpora.iliauni.edu.ge/ and covers approximately 13 million words.

The tokenization and morphological analysis can be considered as an initial stage in the description of the main characteristics of the Georgian language:

- A well-developed system of word inflection and derivation;
- Agglutinating and inflecting structures supposing use of a huge variety of grammatical affixes and from time to time internal inflection of a stem; and,
- The ergative construction of sentences.

At the same time, the description of Modern Georgian is not enough to provide - the whole scale processing of Georgian texts. An additional transducer for the annotation of Old Georgian is important to cover distinctions between Old, Middle and Modern Georgian with regards to the following:

- Alphabets (*Asomtavruli, Nuskhuri* and *Mkhedruli*) reflected by Unicode Ranges 10A0–10FF and 2D00–2D2F (Everson 1991-2019);
- Vocabulary;
- Some phonological items, for instance non-syllabic /û/ (so-called *ubrjgu*) (*t'ûali* 'eye,' *mkûdari* 'dead,' *t'agû* 'mouse' etc.) substituted

initially by the bilabial spirant /w/ and then by the consonant /v/, falling (descending) and rising (ascending) diphthongs represented by means of the phonemes /y/ and /uˆ/ etc.;

- Some morphological elements, for instance, *Suffixaufnahme* generated on the basis of the genitive case and connected to the position of forms in the genitive case in relation to their nominal heads (*želisaman* 'made of wood,' *mkisaysa* 'of the harvest,' *abrahamisit'gan* 'from Abraham' etc.) etc.

Still, a description of Old Georgian is possible using finite-state morphology similar to the Modern. The morphological rules of Old Georgian are encoded in a way to generate Old Georgian forms from the digitized version of Abuladze's dictionary (1973), enriched by other words collected from various online and offline sources for the corpus of Georgian language. The transducer used for the morphological analysis of Old Georgian is constructed in a way to provide morphological analysis for each token of the input text. The output of the analyser represents a lemma sign assigned by convention to a concrete PoS or a lemma with multicharacter symbols, including the plus sign used by Xerox convention to convey morphological or syntactic features (1, 2).

(1) სული:სულ-ი+Noun+Com+Inanim+Sg+Nom 'soul'
(2) რაჲ:რა+Pron+Int+Sg+Nom 'what'

Identification of a lemma sign is, firstly, a starting point for the generation of a paradigm, and, secondly, is a base for the further distinguishing of types and tokens by means of corpus-based approaches. Accordingly, the analysis providing lemmatization, assignment of PoS tags and determination of other morphological features could be used for future annotation from within the Text Encoding Initiative (3, 4).

(3) <w lemma="სულ-ი" ana="Ncnsd">სულს</w> 'soul'
(4) <w lemma="რა" ana="Ncnsn">რაჲ</w> 'what'

In accordance with the Morpho-syntactic Annotation Framework (MAF), a lemma is a lemmatized form class of inflected forms differing only by inflectional morphology. In European languages, the lemma is usually the /singular/ if there is a variation in /number/, the /masculine/ form if there is a variation in /gender/, and the /infinitive/ for all verbs. In some languages, certain nouns are defective in the singular form, in which case the /plural/ is chosen. In Arabic, for a verb, the lemma is usually considered to be the third person singular with an accomplished aspect (MAF Standards 2012).

Following the above-mentioned definition, the nominal paradigm of Georgian language presupposes the use of nominative singular for lemmatization purposes. Modern Georgian strictly follows this rule, as seen in the clear morphosyntactic functions and concrete markers of the nominative case. But in Old Georgian, some scholars (Imnaishvili 1956; Shanidze 1976, and others) distinguish the so-called absolutive (*crp'elobit'i*) case. Sometimes referred to as *absolute* (Rayfield 2006, and others), *nominal root* (Vogt 1968), *nominative without marker* (Sarjveladze 1997), etc. This is not to be confused with the syntactic absolutive, i.e., the case of nouns in ergative-absolutive languages used as the subject of intransitive and object of transitive verbs.

This paper describes a lemmatization problem with regards to the distinction between Old and Modern Georgian morphosyntactic apparatus paying special attention to nominative and absolutive cases from the viewpoint of their functions, markers and terminal operations needed for computational processing.

The paper is divided into the following parts: 1. Introduction; 2. Functional differences: absolutive vs nominative; 3. Morphological analyser and lemmatization; 4. Conclusions.

6.2. Functional Differences: Absolutive vs Nominative

Belonging to an open class of items, nominals refer to things, persons, etc., and can be classified in various ways. There are four PoS-es in Georgian determined as nominals: nouns, adjectives, pronouns and numerals, and additional verbal forms like participles and verbal nouns (masdars). All these forms follow the principles of nominal inflection, require the morphological category of case, and share a similar sequence in slots combination. Generally, the computational generation of nominal inflection depends on the part of speech in accordance with the following schemes:

Noun
Type -> number markers -> case markers and/or clitics [postpositions] -> emphatic vowel -> clitics [auxiliary verb, markers of indirect speech]

Adjective
Type -> degree -> number markers -> case markers and/or clitics [postpositions] -> emphatic vowel -> clitics [auxiliary verb, markers of indirect speech]

Pronoun
Type -> number markers -> case markers and/or clitics [postpositions] -> emphatic vowel -> clitics [auxiliary verb, markers of indirect speech]

Numeral
Type -> number markers -> case markers and/or clitics [postpositions] -> emphatic vowel -> clitics [auxiliary verb, markers of indirect speech]

The quantity of slots differs depending on the part of speech, cf. nouns – 8 slots (12 in Old Georgian), adjectives – 11 (12 in Old Georgian), numerals – 12, pronouns – 9 (Boeder 1979; 2005; Hewitt 1995; Shanidze 1973; Vogt 1968; 1971, and others). For all nominals, case and number are morphologically specified characteristics of the nominal inflection used to show the relationship between nominals and other parts of speech within a given phrase, clause or sentence. These occupy slots directly after the nominal root. The first slot after the nominal root is occupied by a number marker represented by an empty morph in singular, and by the -*eb*-, -*n*-, -*t*- markers in plural, while the second one is occupied by case markers. The sequence of slots after the nominal root differs between Old and Modern Georgian. For instance, in Modern Georgian, the structure reveals the following units:

Table 6.1. Distribution of slots after the nominal root[1] in Modern Georgian

0	1	2	3	4	5	6	7	8
Root (R)	Number marker (Nbr)	Case marker (Case)	Emphatic vowel (Emph)	Post-position (Posp)	Emphatic vowel (Emph)	Particle (Ptl)	Auxiliary verb (Aux)	Indirect Speech marker (IS)
	eb	*i*	*a*	*vit'*	*a*	*c'*	*a*	*met'k'i*
	n	*ma, m*		*ze*		*c'a*		*t'k'o*
	t'[2]	*s*		*t'an*		*ġa*		*o*
		is		*ši*		*ġac'*		
		it'		*gan*		*ve*		
		d, ad		*t'vis*		*me*		
		v, o		*ken*		*mc'*		
				ebr				
				t'anave				
				urt'				
				dan				
				mde				

While in Old Georgian, it consists of the following units:

Table 6.2. Distribution of slots after nominal root in Old Georgian

0	1	2	3	4	5	6	7	8	9	10	11	12
R	Case	Emph	Nbr	Nbr	Case	Emph	Case	Emph	Posp	Emph	Ptl	Aux

The main difference between Old and Modern Georgian with regards to the nominal paradigm lies in the first five slots. In Old Georgian, the first five slots are occupied by a combination of case and number markers, indicating the

---

[1] This scheme does not include slots before the nominal root as happens in the case of adjectives, where slots before and after the nominal root are occupied by degree markers.

[2] -*t* marker in Georgia reflects not only number, but also oblique case value, namely: ergative, dative and genitive.

doubling of plural numbers (5) and doubling or sometimes tripling of case
markers generated on the basis of the genitive case (6). The case marker
occupying the first slot precedes the number markers.

(5)   *saxl-eb-n-i* 'houses,' *saxl-eb-t'-a* 'houses' etc.[3]
      house-pl-pl-nom, house-pl-pl.nnom-emph

(6)   *k'al-is-a-t'-a* 'of women, *k'al-∅-is-ad* 'for a woman' etc.
      woman-gen-emph-pl.nnom-emph, woman-sg-gen-adv

There are differences with regards to the markers of the ergative (-*man*),
genitive (-*is*, -*ys*) and instrumental (-*it'*, -*yt'*) cases, but it is out of the scope of
this paper, as the main interest lies in the morphotactics of the case and
number markers from a diachronic point of view, and their relation to the
nominal root and functions of the cases. Modern Georgian, following case-
marking strategies, distinguishes nominative and dative cases as subjective or
oblique cases, and ergative as subjective. But in Old Georgian some scholars
distinguish an additional absolutive case (Shanidze 1976; Imnaishvili 1956;
Tschenkeli 1956, and others). So, the main questions to be answered are:

1.   What are nominative and absolutive cases from a morphosyntactic
     point view?

2.   How do they coincide with the lemma definition from the viewpoint
     of computational analysis?

3.   Is a lemma sign equal to a nominal root?

6.2.1. Case Markers and the Nominal Root

In Modern Georgian, the nominative case is represented by means of an -*i*-
marker added to consonant-final nominals, and a 'zero-marker' added to
vowel-final nominals (7), while in Old Georgian – by means of -*i*- added to
consonant-final nominals, and a 'zero-marker' or -*y*- added to vowel-final
nominals. However, those that end in -*e* followed by the case marker -*y*- merge
in *ē*, while those that end in a non-syllabic *û* followed by a case marker -*i*- are
merged in '*w* or have a parallel form just with *û* (8).

(7)   In Modern Georgian:
      nišan-∅-i 'sign,' *cit'el-∅-i* 'red' etc.
      sign-sg-nom, red-sg-nom
      abra-∅ 'signboard,' *mo-cit'al-o-∅* 'reddish' etc.
      signboard-sg.nom, cmpr>red< cmpr-sg.nom

---

[3] In the following and unless otherwise stated, examples are of the authors; glosses are
given according to the Leipzig Glossing Rules (Comrie, B. et al. 2008) and Eurotyp
Guidelines (Bakker et al. 1993); transliteration follows the ALA-LC transliteration system
for Georgian scripts (Johnson 2011).

(8) In Old Georgian:

msaxur-Ø-i 'servant,' *maġal-Ø-i* 'high' etc.

servant-sg-nom, high-sg-nom

mt'a-Ø-y 'mountain,' *że-Ø-y‖żē-Ø* 'son,' *borcû-Ø‖ borcû-Ø-i* -> *borc'w-Ø* 'hill' etc.

mountain-sg-nom, son-sg-nom // son- sg.nom, hill-sg.nom

In both cases, the case markers are attached to the nominal root, which, depending on the final character, triggers the subdivision of the nominals (noun, adjective, pronoun and numeral) into different declension types, i.e., those which undergo syncope and those which undergo truncation, as in the following:

Table 6.3. Nominal root

Nominal root	Processes
Consonant-final	Non-syncopating (e.g. *asul* (in Old Georgian) ‖ *asuli* (in Old and Modern Georgian) 'mainden' etc.)
-l, -r, -m, -n- consonant-final preceded by *-a, -e* and *-o*	Generally syncopating in genitive, instrumental and adverbial cases in singular, and in all cases in plural with the *-eb-* marker (e.g. *zamt'ar* (in Old Georgian) ‖ *zamt'ari* (in Old and Modern Georgian) 'winter' -> *zamt'ris* 'of winter,' *irem* (in Old Georgian) ‖ *iremi* (in Old and Modern Georgian) 'deer' -> *irmis* 'of deer,' *p'ot'ol* (in Old Georgian) ‖ *p'ot'oli* (in Old and Modern Georgian) 'leaf' -> *p'ot'lis* 'of leaf' etc.)
Consonant-final roots with alternations	*o->v* in Modern Georgian (e.g. *mindori* 'meadow' -> *mindvris* 'of meadow' etc.) and *o->û* in Old Georgian depending on the century (e.g. *monazon ‖ monazoni* 'nun' -> *monazûnis ‖ monazvnis* 'of nun' etc.) alternations in genitive, instrumental and adverbial cases in singular and in all cases in plural with the *-eb-* marker
-a-final	Non-truncating in singular (e.g. *lurja* 'dark grey horse' -> *lurjas* 'of dark grey horse' etc.)
-o and *-u-* vowel-final	Non-truncating (e.g. *abano* (in Old and Modern Georgian) ‖ *abanoy* (in Old Georgian) -> *abanos* (in Modern Georgian), *abanoys* (in Old Georgian), *ku* (in Old and Modern Georgian) ‖ *kuy* (in Old Georgian) -> *kus* (in Modern Georgian), *kuys* (in Old Georgian) etc.)
-a-final	Truncating in genitive and instrumental cases in singular and in all cases in plural with the *-eb-* marker (e.g. *żma* (in Old and Modern Georgian) ‖ *żmay* (in Old Georgian) 'brother' -> *żmis* 'of brother' etc.)
-e-final common nouns	Truncating in genitive and instrumental cases in singular (e.g. *dġe* (in Old and Modern Georgian) ‖ *dġē* (in Old Georgian) 'day' -> *dġis* (in Old and Modern Georgian) 'of day' etc.)
Consonant- and vowel-final proper nouns, especially, personal names	Non-syncopating and non-truncating (e.g. *iakob* ‖ *iakobi* 'Jacob' -> *iakobis* 'of Jacob,' *mart'a* 'Marta' -> *mart'as* (in Modern Georgian) ‖ *mart'ays* (in Old Georgian) 'of Marta' etc.) etc.)
Exceptions	There are some exceptions in Old Georgian, like the syncopating *šurduli* 'catapult,' truncating *ġwno* 'wine,' etc.

In Modern Georgian, the nominal root cannot be considered as a form associated only with the nominative case, as, depending on the part of speech, it also appears in other cases (ergative, dative, genitive, instrumental, adverbial and vocative). In particular, the nominal root is used separately as a determiner or modifier if a nominal occurs together with a noun, or a noun phrase. In Modern Georgian, a nominal root can be represented by an adjective (9), a pronoun (10), a numeral (11) and/or a proper noun (12).

(9)

    cit'el-∅   kaba-∅-s
    red:sg.dat   dress-sg-dat
    'red dress' etc.

(10)

    am-∅   cign -∅-s
    this:sg.dat   book -sg-dat
    'this book' etc.

(11)

    ot'x-∅   pir-∅-s
    four:sg.dat   person-sg-dat
    'four people' etc.

(12)

    luarsab -∅   t'at'k'ariże-∅-s
    Luarsab:sg.dat   Tatkaridze-sg-dat
    'Luarsab Tatkaridze' etc.

In Old Georgian, the use of the nominal root is slightly different. Proper nouns, 'especially, personal names' forms use a nominal root for cases different from the nominative, and, generally, the case of the personal name is determined by the head of the nominal phrase (13, 14). Numerals show parallel forms with and without case markers (15), while the other PoS-es require markers of concrete cases (16, 17).

(13)

    pavle-∅   moc'ik'ul-∅-s
    Paul:sg.dat   Apostle-sg-dat
    'to Paul the Apostle' etc.

(14)

> *cmida-Ø-man*   *šušanik-Ø*
> holy-sg-erg   Shushanik:sg.erg
> 'the Holy Shushanik' etc.

(15)

a.   *sam-Ø-s-a*   *kac'-Ø-s-a*
      three-sg-dat-emph   man-sg-dat-emph
b.   *sam-Ø*   *kac'-Ø-s-a*
      three:sg.dat   man-sg-dat-emph
c.   *kac'-Ø-s-a*   *sam-Ø-s-a*
      man-sg-dat-emph   three-sg-dat-emph
      'to three men' etc.

(16)

> *cmida-Ø-s-a*   *mocame-Ø-s-a*
> saint-sg-dat-emph   martyr-sg-dat-emph
> 'to the Saint Martyr' etc.

(17)

a.   *ama-Ø-s*   *kac'-Ø-s-a*
      this-sg-dat   man-sg-dat-emph
      'to this man' etc.
b.   *cign-Ø-s-a*   *em-s-a*
      book-sg-dat-emph   my-dat-emph
      'to my book' etc.

From the diachronic point of view, special attention should be paid to the nominal root and the declension paradigm of personal names. In Old Georgian, there are three main rules: firstly, proper nouns require the nominal root to be used in the nominative, ergative and vocative cases; secondly, they do not require an emphatic vowel; and, thirdly, they do not form plural (Sarjveladze 1997; Shanidze 1976, and others). Nominative case markers have been observed since the seventh century, ergative – since the ninth century, and vocative – since the tenth century. This means that the language reveals allomorphs: 'zero morph' and/or case markers. In Modern Georgian, the declension of personal names also requires allomorphs: 'zero morph' and/or nominative and vocative case markers. And despite the fact that the 'zero morph' could be used rarely with the ergative case, and with vowel-final nominals acting as determiners and modifiers, scholars do not consider it as an allomorph (Gogolashvili et al. 2011).

6.2.2. Functions of Nominative and Absolutive Cases

In accordance with the widely-known definitions, the absolutive case does not have a special marker and is equal to the nominal root, while the nominative case has special markers different for consonant- and vowel-final nominal roots (Shanidze 1976, Imnaishvili 1956 and others). From the syntactic point of view, absolutive is defined as a case that groups together intransitive subjects (S) and transitive objects (O) in ergative-absolutive languages (see Comrie 1978; Dixon 1979; 1994; Marantz 1984; Aldridge 2008; Deal 2015; Polinsky 2016 among many others on the properties of ergative languages). At the same time, the absolutive and nominative reveal similar syntactic features in Old and Modern Georgian (see table 2.4)

Morphologically, the absolutive case is not represented in Modern Georgian, while the nominative case has its own functions in Old Georgian and preserves them in Modern. Forms in nominative singular are considered as headwords in Old (Rukhadze and Koplatadze 2008; Abuladze 1973) and Modern Georgian dictionaries (Chikobava 1950-1964; Tsotsanidze et al. 2014). This theoretical background affects the compilation of the morphological analyser, presupposing the use of nominative singular for annotation purposes and considering it as a lemma of the inflectional paradigm.

Modern Georgian strictly follows the Morpho syntactic Annotation Framework (MAF) rule (see section 1), because of the clear morphosyntactic functions and concrete markers of the nominative case. But in the case of Old Georgian, some scholars (Imnaishvili 1956; Shanidze 1976, and others) distinguish the so-called absolutive case. The form of the absolutive case is equal to the nominal root and closer to the definition of the MAF indicating number (singular), without additional case markers. So, the main questions to answer are the following:

1. Are there any functions which distinguish absolutive and nominative cases?

2. Is there any sense considering a zero-morph of the vowel- or consonant-final nominal root as a separate case in Old Georgian?

3. What are the conditions for using the nominal root as a lemma in the case of Old Georgian?

There are different opinions with regards to the differentiation of absolutive and nominative cases. Following Danelia (1998), the absolutive was used from the fifth until the ninth centuries, and was then replaced by the nominative. Yet, according to some scholars, the functions of absolutive are similar to nominative (Sarjveladze 1997; Uturgaidze 1986; Topuria 1956; Chikobava 1940, and others), and absolutive is considered to be just a nominal root or an unmarked nominative. Other scholars (Danelia 1998; Shanidze 1976; Imnaishvili 1956, and others) describe some functions of the absolutive as distinct from, shared with, and replaced by nominative case markers (-*i*- with consonant-final and -*y*- with vowel-final nominals) in Old Georgian texts.

Morphosyntactically, Georgian belongs to the ergative-absolutive languages. It has been revealed in the literature (Ura 2001; 2006; Legate 2008; Bobaljik and Wurmbrand 2009; Polinsky and Preminger 2014; Rezac et al. 2014, among many others) that ergativity is not a unified phenomenon worldwide, and that there is a considerable variation among the languages with ergative case marking. Thus, ergative languages can be divided into: (a) syntactically and morphologically ergative; (b) pure ergative and split-ergative; (c) split ergative based on a tense+aspect distinction or a full DP/pronouns distinction; (d) those which have nominative as an object case or absolutive (default); (e) those which assign ergative with unergative predicates: obligatory (Georgian), optionally (Hindi, see Bobaljik 2008), or showing the dialectical variation (Basque, see Rezac et al. 2014) and those that do not (Samoan, see Tollan 2018).

For our purposes, the differentiation between ergative languages based on the notion of the absolutive case (Legate 2008) is interesting. According to Legate's (2008) analysis, ergative languages can be subdivided into two groups: ABS=DEF and ABS=NOM languages. In ABS=DEF languages, T assigns the nominative Case to S and v^4 assigns the accusative Case to O, these Cases are realized as default (=ABS) at the morphological level. This happens because the languages lack nominative and accusative case morphology. In ABS=NOM languages, absolutive corresponds to the abstract nominative Case, assigned by T to both S and O. Georgian is provided as an example of such a language. Although our main purpose at this point is not a theoretical evaluation of Legate's (2008) assumptions about Georgian, the analysis of the functions of absolutive and nominative cases in Old Georgian and comparison with Modern Georgian provided in this section show that the Georgian absolutive has mixed properties of nominative and morphological default, thus highlighting that not all Legate's arguments (2008) are borne out for Georgian. We will mention just some of them. First, if absolutive is just abstract nominative, it must be limited only to subject and object (this was predicted by Legate's analysis 2008: 67–69), but this is not the case for Georgian. Nominative/absolutive is

---

[4] Different theories have been proposed in generative grammar about how the accusative case is actually assigned. It can be analyzed as assigned under government with V (Chomsky 1981), by Voice (Kratzer 1996), which is generally referred to as v, under agree with Voice, which is different from v (Legate 2014) or even by the dependent case rule (Marantz 2000 [1991], Baker 2015, Baker and Bobaljik 2017 etc.). See also Preminger to appear for further discussion. Legate's analysis (2008) is based on the commonly accepted idea in the minimalist framework that accusative is assigned by v.

used as an object of postposition (18-19), or as time adjunct (20-21), both in Modern and Old Georgian (see Kvachadze 1996: 229; Gogolashvili et al. 2011: 130-131 for functions of nominative/absolutive in Georgian).

(18)

> Modern Georgian
>
> *nik'a-m   mariam-i-vit'   lamaz-i   kal-i*
> Nika-ERG Mariam-**NOM/ABS**-as beautiful-NOM/ABS WOMAN-**NOM/ABS**
> *nax-a.*
> see- 3.SG.SBJ:AOR
> 'Nika saw a woman as beautiful as Mariam.'

(19)

> Old Georgian, (Galat. 2,14, Abuladze 1973)
>
> *carmart'-Ø-ebr da   ara   Huria-Ø-ebr   c'xovn-d-eb-i*
> pagan-   and   not   Jew-**ABS/NOM**-like live-PASS-THM-
> ABS/NOM-like   PRS.IND:2SG
> 'You live not like Jews, but like pagans.'

(20)

> Modern Georgian
>
> *sam-i   ts'el-Ø-i   ar   m-i-nax-av-s   megobar-Ø-i.*
> three-   year-SG-   NEG   1SGOBJ-VERS.RFL-   friend-SG-NOM
> NOM/ABS **NOM/ABS**   see-TS-
>   3SGSBJ:PF.IND
> 'I have not seen my friend for three years.'

(21)

> Old Georgian, (Lives of Holy Fathers, Dvali 1974)
>
> *[...]mravalžam-Ø   a-i-žul-eb-d-es   mas*
> *[...]*many_times-   PV-PRV-FORCE-TS-EM-   this:3SG.DAT
> NOM/ABS   3PLSBJ:IMPF
> *t'xrob-Ø-ad, [...]*
> story-telling- SG-NOM *[...]*
> '…many times, they forced him to go on with story.…'

Second, the diagnostics of case alternation in non-finite environments used in the literature to prove that Georgian lacks absolutive and as a result of this property it is assumed to have an inherent ergative case (Legate 2008), or to prove that Georgian ergative is structural, because it is not attested in the non-finite environment (Nash 2017), cannot be applied to Georgian. This happens because Georgian has no infinitive as such, and it uses nominalization in the non-finite contexts mentioned by Legate (2008: 66). However, this nominalization happens at V-level and not at vP-level, thus creating simple possesive construction – a DP, which consists of a noun in genitive + nominalized verb or better to say derived nominal. This derived nominal has nominal and not verbal properties in that it is unable to introduce external argument and assign structural accusative, because it lacks v. In order to address the issue as to whether absolutive or nominative should be used as a lemma for the Old Georgian morphological analyser, the functions of absolutive in Old Georgian should be presented in detail.

Functions shared with nominative and replaced afterwards are as follows:

a) The grammatical function (GF) of the **subject** represented by a nominal root with verbs denoting being (*ars* 'to be') (22), and if a nominal root is used with indefinite pronouns or numerals (23). A nominal part of the complex predicate acting as a subject is precisely described in scientific literature (Danelia 1998; Imnaishvili 1956).

(22)

(C. 18, 18; Abuladze 1973)

[…] ramet'u	*qinel*	*iqo [...]*
[…] because	cold-abs	be:3sgsbj.aor.ind [...]

'Because it was cold'

(23)

(Sin. 36, 250v; Abuladze 1973)

da	*ag̃-vid-a*	*xut'-∅*	*kac'-∅*	*simag̃le-∅-d.*
and	prev-go-3sgsbj	five-abs	man-abs	height-sg-adv

'And five men went up.'

b) The GF of the **subject** represented by a nominal root with verbs denoting possession (*esua* 'to have' etc.), doing (*ik'ms* 'to do' etc.) and naming (*ecoda* 'to name' etc.) (Danelia 1998: 528), as indicated in the examples (24).

(24)

(C, 27; Abuladze 1973)

a.
e-rk'u-a	*agarak-∅-s-a*	*mas*	*agarak-∅*	*sisxl-∅-is.*
vers-name-3sgsbj:aor.ind	field-sg-dat-emph	this:3sg.dat	field-abs/nom	blood-sg-gen

'It was named as Field of Blood.'

b.
e-cod-a	*agarak-∅-s-a*	*mas*	*agarak-∅-i*
vers-name-3sgsbj:aor.ind	field-sg-dat-emph	this:3sg.dat	field-sg-nom

sisxl-∅-is-a-y.
blood-sg-gen-emph-nom

'It was named as Field of Blood.'

c)   The GF of the **direct object** represented by a nominal root, with verbs
     denoting possession, naming (*hrk'ua* 'to name' etc.) (25-26) (Danelia
     1998: 528), etc. And in spite of Imnaishvili's assumption (1956) that
     these cases are not regular, the data express regularities in the use of
     the nominal root to indicate the GF of a direct object.

(25)

(I, 9,13; Imnaishvili 1956)

...adgil-Ø-s-a	*mas,*	*rt̄-s-a*	*h-rk'w-an*
place-sg-dat-emph	3sg:dat	that-dat-emph	3sg-name-3pl:aor.sbjv

k'vap'enil-Ø
pavement-abs/nom
'...to that place, which was named pavement'

(26)

(Ier, 29, 6JO; Danelia 1998)

...u-sxen-i-t'	*že-t'-a*	*t'k'uen-t'-a*	*c'ol-Ø*
prv-bring-ts- 2sgSbj:aor	son- pl.dat- emph	you-2pl.gen- emph	wife- abs/nom

'...bring wives to your sons'

A function described as distinct from the nominative is also that of the **object**,
but incorporated into the verb:

d)   A nominal root (absolutive of an object) is incorporated into a verb, as
     shown in (28, 29). Several kinds of verbs participate in this process (*-qop'a*
     'to do,' *-c'ema* 'to bit,' *-ġeba* 'to take,' *-dgma* 'to place,' *-č'ena* 'to show,'
     -cip'eba 'to be able') as stated by Danelia (1998). The result of this
     incorporation can be observed in Modern Georgian, cf.: *uar-qop's ->*
     uarqop's 'denies smth.,' *uar-qop'a -> uarqop'a* 'denial' etc. At the
     same time, the examples of incorporated nouns cannot be considered
     as independent syntactic units neither in Old nor in Modern Georgian,
     and, as a result, they can be considered as a nominal root, but not as
     an inflectional form of a noun.

(27)

(II Tim., 2, 12; Abuladze, I., 1973)

ukuet'u	*uar-v-q-o-t',*	*man-c'-a*
whether	denial:abs-1sgsbj-do- sbjv-pl:plup	3sg.erg-ptl- emph

uar-m-qv-n-es	*uen*
denial:abs-1sgdobj-be- pl-aor	1pl.nom

'If we deny him, he will also deny us.'

(28)

(M. sc., 169, 1; Abuladze, I., 1973)

mis	*cil-∅*	*h-brżvan-an*	*da*
3sg.gen	instead-abs/nom	3sg.obj-speak-pl:prs.ind	and

pativ-u-qop'-en	*sixarul-∅-it'.*
respect:abs-vers.3iobj-do-pl:prs.ind	joy-sg-ins

'They speak for him, and show their respect with joy.'

Additionally, some scholars (Imnaishvili 1956, Danelia 1998) describe the functions of the absolutive case used:

e) As **adjuncts**: time adjuncts (29), adverbials denoting condition (30), objects used with postpositions (32).

(29) (A-144; Abuladze 1973)

ramet'u	*žam-∅*	*ert'-∅*	*p'art'oeba-∅-s-a*	*iqv-n-es*
while	time-abs/nom	one-abs/nom	plain-sg-dat-emp	be-pl-3plsbj:aor.ind

'Once they were on the plains.'

(30) (G; M Isu N. 10, 6; Abuladze 1973)

a.

aġmo-ved	*č'uen-da*	*mscrap'l-∅*
prev.pfv-come:aor.ind	1pl-ptl	quickly-abs/nom

'Come up to us quickly'

b.

aġmo-ved	*č'uen-da*	*mst'u-ad*
prev.pfv-come:aor.ind	1pl-ptl	quickly-adv

'They came quickly to us'

Further, the verbs (*codeba* 'to call,' *c'ema* 'to punch, to give,' *-ġeba* 'to take,' *-dgma* 'to place' etc.) required a nominal root to show the functions of the adverbial case (Sukhishvili 2019) (31).

(31) (L, 6,1; L 6,13 so-called *Khanmeti* type of text; Sukhishvili 2019)

a.

gamo-i-rč'in-a	*at'ormet-n-i*	*mat'-gan-n-i,*
prev-vers.refl-choose-3sgsbj:aor.ind	twelve-pl-nom	3pl.gen-from-pl-nom

romel-t'-a-c'a	*moc'ik'ul-∅*	*u-cod-a*
that-pl.dat-emph-ptl	Apostle-abs/nom	vers.3iobj-call-3sgsbj:aor.ind

'Twelve of them were chosen and called the Apostles.'

b. *[...]*   *romel-t'-a-c'a moc'ik'ul-ad x-u-cod-a*

    [...]   that-pl.dat-   Apostle-adv   3sgdobj- vers.3iobj-call-
          emph-ptl   3sgsbj:aor.ind

'... called the Apostles.'

The example provided below (32) shows objects used in absolutive with the postposition *-ebr* 'as, like.'

(32)

    (C, 19, 20; Abuladze 1973)

    ceril-Ø iqo   *ebrael-Ø-   p'romin- da   berżl-Ø.*
                           ebr,   Ø-ebr

    letter-   be:3sgsbj.aor.ind   Jewish-   Latin-   and   Greek-
    abs/nom   abs/nom- abs/nom-   abs/nom
                               like   like

    'The letter was like Jewish, Latin and Greek.'

f)   As denoting the main functions of nominative (33, 34), ergative (35) and/or vocative (36) cases with proper nouns, paying special attention to the fact that in Old Georgian, proper nouns used in the nominative, ergative and vocative cases are represented by a nominal root and do not require case markers.

(33)

    Syntactic abs/morphologically nominal root (Kim. 52,15; Imnaishvili 1956)
    rĩ-s-a   *e-cod-eb-od-a*   *likinioz-Ø*
    that-dat-emph   vers.3iobj-call-ts-impf-   Likinioz-abs/nom
                    3sgsbj

    'Who was called Likinioz...'

(34)

    Syntactic nom/morphologically nominal root (Kim. 54,20; 59,22; Imnaishvili 1956)
    likinioz-Ø   *še-u-vrd-a*   *p'erx-t'-a...*
    Likinioz-nom   prev.pfv-vers.3iobj-fall-   foot-pl.dat-emph
                     3sgsbj:aor.ind

    'Likinioz fell at his/her feet...'

(35)

    Syntactic ERG/morphologically nominal root (Kim. 52,25-26,29; Imnaishvili 1956)
    mi-u-g-o   *likinioz-Ø...*
    prev.pfv-vers.3iobj-say-3sgsbj:aor.ind   Likinioz-erg

    'Likinioz answered...'

(36)

> Syntactic voc/morphologically nominal root (Kim. 52,24; Imnaishvili 1956)
>
> *saquarel-∅-o*   *likinioz-∅*
> dear-sg-voc   Likinioz-voc
> 'Dear Likinioz...'

The use of a nominal root in different cases in Old Georgian resulted in constructions where a subject and object (if expressed by personal names) did not show any difference from the morphological point of view. The distinction between the subject and object was made only in accordance with their syntactic position in the clause, i.e., the subject occupied the first position, while the object the second (37).

(37)

> Mt, 2v.
>
> *abraham-∅*   *šva*   *isak-∅*
> Abraham-erg   give_birth:3sg.sbj.aor.ind Isak-abs
> 'Abraham gave birth to Isaak.'

Although syntactically both cases are different, morphologically they are unmarked. Thus, on the surface level, we get the same root forms for both core arguments. This is impossible in the languages where absolutive corresponds just to abstract nominative case, but possible in the ABS=DEF languages, where any DP bearing an abstract Case feature that is blocked at the morphological level, can be realized as the morphological default.

From the above-mentioned functions of Old Georgian absolutive, it can be observed that absolutive is mostly used to denote core arguments: subjects and objects, the function that is characteristic to nominative and that puts Georgian in the groups of languages, where absolutive is equal to nominative. However, the additional functions of adjuncts (time adjuncts, adverbials, instruments) and objects with postpositions, as well as two morphologically default DPs per clause puts Georgian into the group of languages where absolutive is equal to a morphological default, thus showing mixed properties.

All these peculiarities in the description of so-called absolutive and its functions in Old Georgian affect the rule-based approach to the modeling of Georgian morphosyntax, and require a more thorough analysis of Old and Modern Georgian data with regards to the comparison of functions and their equivalence.

Table 6.4. Comparison of functions in Modern and Old Georgian

Functions	Modern Georgian Nominative	Old Georgian Nominative	Old Georgian Absolutive
Real subject	1. With transitive verbs in the first series and with intransitive verbs in all series; 2. A nominal part of complex predicate	1. With transitive verbs in the first series and intransitive verbs in all series; 2. A nominal part of complex predicate	1. With transitive verbs in the first series and intransitive verbs in all series; 2. A nominal part of complex predicate
Direct object	With transitive verbs in the second and third series and with *experiencer* and *non-volitional* verbs in all series (excluding some verbal forms)	With transitive verbs in the second and third series	1. With transitive verbs in the second and third series; 2. Incorporated noun into verb.
Adverbial modifier	1. Denoting time; 2. Denoting situation; this form requires the postposition -*vit* - 'like'	1. Denoting time; 2. Denoting situation; this form requires the postposition -*vit* - 'like'	1. Denoting time; 2. Denoting situation; this form requires postposition -*ebr, -ebriv* 'like, as'

6.2.3. Interim Summary

As can be seen in the table above, the nominative and so-called absolutive cases reveal similarity in syntactic functions, the only distinction depends on the morphological markers used in the case of nominative and replaced by 'zero morph' in so-called absolutive. Thus, while there are no prerequisites to declare the existence of an additional case in Old Georgian if its syntactic functions are equal to those of the nominative, there is a prerequisite to consider the lemma forms for Old and Middle Georgian in the following way:

1.   Consonant-final common nouns, adjectives, numerals and pronouns require a lemma in the nominative singular ending in -*i*-;

2.   Vowel-final common nouns, adjectives, numerals and pronouns require a lemma in the nominative singular ending in 'zero' or -*y*-;

3.   Consonant- and vowel-final propers nouns require a lemma in the nominative singular ending in 'zero morph.'

To summarize, the representation of a lemma form in accordance with the rules mentioned above allows us to preserve a common syntactic frame for Old, Middle and Modern Georgian, and to offer more concrete procedures with regards to dependency analysis determining the subject, object and modifier.

6.3. Morphological Analyzer and Lemmatization

As it was mentioned previously, the morphological analyser of the Georgian language is constructed in a way to provide morphological analysis and to identify the lemma sign for each token of the input text (Lobzhanidze 2022). The analysis provides lemmatization, assignment of PoS tags, and determination of other morphological features. The extended lexicons, morphological guessers and additional rules improved the coverage of the analyser.

6.3.1. Lemmatization

With Georgian, the identification of the lemma sign is associated with the so-called "lemmatizaton problem" (Lobzhanidze 2019). Generally, lemmatization refers to dictionaries and morphological analyses of words presented in dictionaries. By convention, the lemma for the nominal paradigm as represented in Georgian dictionaries is nominative singular, but Georgian verbs do not have an infinitive, and there is no clear rule with regards to the headwords of verbal paradigms. Thus, lemmatizaton is associated with two types of discrepancy with regards to the MAF standard (MAF Standards 2012):

1. The headwords of nominal entries are represented in the nominative singular. The main problem originates with regards to Old Georgian dictionaries. As mentioned above, in Old Georgian, the nominative singular depending on the type of stem, is associated with two morphs -*i*- (for consonant-final stems) and -*y*- (for vowel-final stems) and there is a so-called nominal root declared by some scholars as the absolutive case. The dictionaries never represent nouns in the absolutive form (they do not include proper nouns), and never represent forms with -*y*- for vowel-final stems; the vowel-final stems are represented following the headword compilation principles of Modern Georgian, i.e., without a nominative case marker. These inconsistencies are avoided by using the 'zero morph,' considering it as a nominative case at the lexical level and removing all types of nominative case markers at the surface level for the generation of nominal inflection;

2. The headwords of verbal entries are represented in Modern Georgian dictionaries in different ways: a) the verbal noun, the so-called masdar (Tsotsanidze et al. 2014, Chubinashvili 1940); b) the root-based form, the so-called abstract root (Tschenkeli 1965), and c) the third person singular in the present or future indicative (Rayfield 2006, Chikobava 1950-1964, and others). The Old Georgian dictionaries prefer the first option, i.e., that headwords are represented as verbal nouns (Rukhadze et al. 2008, Abuladze 1973). These differences affect the lexicon of the morphological analyser, provoke the generation of different output, and require different strategies with regard to the generative models of concrete classes, especially in the case of participles and verbal nouns (masdars), which inflect according to nominal paradigms. These problems are avoided by reducing the headwords of verbal entries in dictionaries to the forms in second person singular closely associated with the stems.

6.3.2. Morphological Analyser and Generator of Georgian

The analyser is written by means of two tools *lexc* and *xfst*. *lexc* is a high-level declarative programming language used as a lexicon compiler for defining finite-state automata and transducers, while *xfst* is a compiler for regular expressions and is used to manipulate networks (automata and transducers) previously described by *lexc*. In other words, *lexc* is associated with the morphotactics of a language, while *xfst* with the phonological and orthographical alternation rules. A finished bi-directional transducer of Georgian language covers morphosyntactic peculiarities and its output consists of lemmata with morphosyntactic features of the Georgian language and of different finite-state transducers associated with concrete PoS-es and replace-rule transducers.

The *lexc* modules (verb.txt, noun.txt etc.) consist of lexicons and continuation classes represented in accordance with the following syntax:

    Form   continuation class ;

The form is subdivided into two parts: lexical, corresponding to the upper level, and surface, corresponding to the lower level. The lexical part consists of a lemma sign assigned by convention to a concrete PoS, and appropriate tags used to provide morphological analysis of a concrete form. A lemma sign represented at the surface level is a base for the further generation of the whole inflection according to the appropriate continuation classes already defined. The *xfst* modules (verb.script, noun.script etc.) trigger replacement processes like truncation, syncopation and others. Triggers are special tags attached to the intermediate level and associated with concrete replacement processes.

Table 6.5. Structure of bi-directional transducer

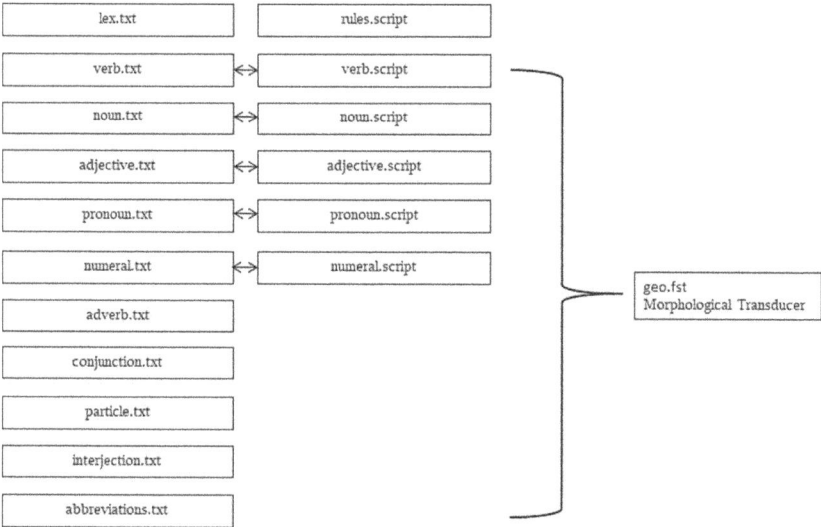

Table 6.6. Lexical, intermediate and surface levels

	Modern Georgian	Old Georgian	
Lexical	ma+Noun+Sg+Gen	ma+Noun+Sg+Gen	ma-y+Noun+Sg+Gen
Intermediate	ma^Sis	ma^Sis	may^Sis
Surface	mis	mis	mis

An upper level '*a*' is mapped to a lower level '0' followed by the trigger '^S' and the genitive case marker *-is*. As a result, the '^S' symbol triggers the truncation process, and, afterwards, removes '*a*' or '*ay*' from the surface level. All these levels are covered by the transducer and the morphological analysis, where each analysis contains a word form followed by its lemma, its PoS category and morphosyntactic features are as follows (38):

(38) In Modern Georgian: ძმის:ძმა+Noun+Sg+Gen

In Old Georgian: ძმის:ძმა+Noun+Sg+Gen or ძმის:ძმა-ჲ+Noun+Sg+Gen

Disambiguation of the material is necessary if the morphological analysis of a concrete word gives more than one option (39). It means that disambiguation requires consideration not only of the token taken separately, but its place in the context, paying special attention to the dependencies between words.

(39) და:და+Conj+Coord

და:და+N+Com+Anim+Sg+Nom or და:და-ჲ+N+Com+Anim+Sg+Nom

It means that the output of the analyser is to be disambiguated for each token in the input string. Such type of disambiguation is closely connected to the identification of the dependency relations and syntactic functions using Constraint Grammar (Karlsson et al. 1995) within the VISL CG-3 compiler/parser (Didriksen et al. 1996-2021). To provide a dependency analysis of Georgian, it is crucial to annotate the verb and its arguments with special grammatical markers for subject, objects, etc., and to have an appropriate theoretical understanding of the grammatical function of subjects and objects not only in the case of Modern, but also in the case of Old Georgian. In both cases, the most important thing is to constrain the grammatical functions of the cases: nominative, ergative, genitive (in case of doubling and tripling of cases in Old Georgian), and dative, using all available information about them: 1) lexical, including use of personal pronouns, 2) morphological, such as case markers available, e.g. in the case of the nominative, attention should be paid to 'zero morph' and case markers used in Old and Modern Georgian, and, 3) syntactic, for instance, word order within DP.

6.3.3 Interim summary

The computational rule-based approach to the morphosyntactic analysis of Old and Modern Georgian depends on different factors, including the type of dictionary entries, morphological markers and syntactic relations. These factors are of special importance for syntactic disambiguation to be held in future, and special attention needs to be paid to the three main cases associated with subjects and objects: nominative, ergative and dative.

6.4. Conclusions

The main question addressed in the paper was whether absolutive or nominative should be used as a lemma for the Old Georgian morphological analyser. Based on the similarity of nominative and so-called absolutive in syntactic functions, we have shown that the only distinction is based on the existence of morphological markers in the nominative and 'zero morph' in the so-called absolutive. In Modern Georgian, nominative is one of the main cases used for identification of subject and object. Additionally, its functions are distributed to adjuncts. The functions of nominative are the result of long-term language development throughout time. In Old Georgian, the functions of nominative were somehow similar to the Modern, but the distinct representation of nominals at the morphological level led to the different opinions with regards to the nominative case, and provided a background for the description of the so-called absolutive case. Although the existing grammars of the Old Georgian data provide arguments to support both views, we have demonstrated that there are no prerequisites to declare the existence of an additional case in Old Georgian if its syntactic functions are equal to those of the nominative. Moreover, the computational rule-based approach to morphosyntactic analysis – tokenization, morphological analysis, and, especially, disambiguation of the output data, requires preservation of the common processing of both Old and Modern Georgian data.

Glosses

ABS absolutive

ADV adverbial

AOR aorist

CMPR circumphix

DAT dative

DOBJ direct object

EM extension marker

EMPH emphatic vowel

ERG ergative

GEN genitive

IND indicative

IOBJ indirect object
IMPF imperfect indicative
INS instrumental
NEG negation
NNOM non-nominative
NOM nominative
PF perfect
PL plural
PLUP pluperfect
PRS presence
PRV preradical vowel
PST past
PTL particle
PV preverb
RFL reflexive
SBJ subject
SBJV subjunctive
SG singular
TM thematic suffix
VERS version

Morphological Feature Tags

+N noun
+Conj conjunction
+Coord coordinating
+Com common
+Anim animate
+Inanim inanimate
+Sg singular
+Nom nominative
+Pron pronoun
+Int interrogative
+Gen genitive

Abbreviations

II P. Acts of Peter
II Tim Epistle to Timothee
A-144 Readings from the Writings of St. John Chrysostom
C The Adysh Gospels (Adishi Four Gospels)
Galat. Bible, New Testament
G The Gelati Bible
Kim. Kimen
L Gospels of Luke
Mt. Gospel of Matthew
M Isu N. the Book of Jesus Nave
M. S. Teachings of the Holy Fathers
Sin. Manuscripts from Georgian collection of St. Catherine's Monastery

Funding and Acknowledgments

The authors would like to express special gratitude to an anonymous reviewer for very helpful comments and suggestions. For Svetlana Berikashvili this article is part of a joint project of the Georg August University of Göttingen and Ilia State University (2018-2021), funded by the Volkswagen Foundation and supported by the Shota Rustaveli National Science Foundation of Georgia (SRNSFG) [grant number N04/46, project number N93569].

References

Abuladze, Ilia. 1973. *Dictionary of Old Georgian Language.* Tbilisi: Science. [In Georgian].

Aldridge, Edith. 2008. "Generative approaches to ergativity." *Language and Linguistic Compass 2(5)* 966–995.

Apridonidze, Shukia, and Chkhaidze, Levan. 2004. *From Georgian and into Georgian. Transliteration of Georgian Alphabet.* 4 June. Accessed January 15, 2020. http://laag.iatp.org.ge/article/008.htm.

Baker, Mark. 2015. *Case: Its principles and its parameters.* Cambridge: Cambridge University Press. DOI: https://doi.org/10.1017/CBO9781107295186.

Baker, Mark, and Jonathan Bobaljik. 2017. "On inherent and dependent theories of ergative case." In *The Oxford Handbook of Ergativity,* by Jessica Coon, Diane Massam and Lisa Demena Travis, 111–134. Oxford: Oxford University Press. DOI: https://doi.org/10.1093/oxfordhb/9780198739371.013.5.

Bakker, Dik, Östen Dahl, Martin Haspelmath, Maria Koptjevskaja-Tamm, Christian Lehmann, and Anna Siewierska. 1993. *Eurotyp Guidelines.* European Science Foundation in Language Typology.

Beesley, Kenneth, and Lauri Karttunen. 2003. *Finite-State Morphology: Xerox Tools and Techniques.* Stanford: CSLI Publications.

Bobaljik, Jonathan David. 2008. "Where's phi? Agreement as a postsyntactic operation." In *Phi theory: Phi-features across modules and interfaces*, by Daniel Harbour, David Adger and Susana Béjar, 295–328. Oxford: Oxford University Press.

Bobaljik, Jonathan David, and Susi Wurmbrand. 2009. "Case in GB/Minimalism." In *The Oxford Handbook of Case*, by Andrej Malchukov and Andrew Spencer, 44–59. Oxford: Oxford University Press.

Boeder, Winfried. 1979. "Ergative syntax and morphology in language change: the South Caucasian languages." In *Ergativity: towards a theory of grammatical relations*, by Frans Plank, 435–480. Orlando: Academic Press.

—. 2005. "The South Caucasian languages." *Lingua 115* 5–89.

Chikobava, Arnold. 1950-1964. *Georgian Explanatory Dictionary.* Tbilisi: Academy of Sciences. [In Georgian].

—. 1940. "The oldest mark of the third subject in Kartvelian languages." *Bulletin of the Institute of language, history and material culture, V-VI* 36–38. [In Georgian].

Chomsky, Noam. 1981. *Lectures on government and binding.* Dordrecht: Foris.

Chubinashvili, David. 1940. *Georgian-Russian-French Dictionary.* Saint-Petersburg: Imperial Academy of Sciences.

Comrie, Bernard. 1978. "Ergativity." In *Syntactic typology: studies in the phenomenology of language*, by Winifred (ed.) Lehman, 329–394. Austin: University of Texas Press.

Comrie, Bernard, Haspelmath, Martin, and Bickel, Balthasar. 2008. *The Leipzig Glossing Rules: Conventions for Interlinear Morpheme-by-morpheme Glosses.* Leipzig: Max Planck Institute for Evolutionary Anthropology.

Danelia, Korneli. 1998. "To the place of Absolutive case in the system of Georgian cases." In *Essays from the history of Georgian literary language*, by Korneli Danelia, 525–533. Tbilisi: Tbilisi State University. [In Georgian].

Deal, Amy Rose. 2015. "Ergativity." In *Syntax – Theory and analysis: An International Handbook, vol.1.*, by Tibor Kiss and Artemis Alexiadou, 654–707. Berlin: de Gruyter Mouton.

Didriksen, Tino, and Eckhard Bick. 1996-2021. *VISL CG-3.* Accessed February 12, 2021. https://visl.sdu.dk/cg3.html.

Dixon, Robert M. W. 1994. *Ergativity (Cambridge Studies in Linguistics 69).* Cambridge: Cambridge University Press.

—. 1979. "Ergativity." *Language 55(1), DOI: https://doi.org/10.2307/412519* 59–138.

Doborjginidze, Nino, Irina Lobzhanidze, and Irakli Gunia. 2012. *Georgian Language Corpus.* 19 12. Accessed 10 30, 2019. http://corpora.iliauni.edu.ge/.

Doborjginidze, Nino, Irina Lobzhanidze, and George Mirianashvili. 2014. *Corpus of Georgian Chronicles.* 24 02. http://corpora.iliauni.edu.ge/.

Dvali, Manana. 1974. *Old Georgian translations of the Medieval Novels, Alphabet-Anonymous Lives of the Holy Fathers.* Tbilisi: Science. [In Georgian].

Everson, Michael. 1991-2019. *Georgian Supplement, Range: 2D00-2D2F.* Accessed July 16, 2019. https://unicode.org/charts/PDF/U2D00.pdf.

—. 1991-2019. *Georgian, Range: 10A0-10FF.* Accessed July 16, 2019. https://unicode.org/charts/PDF/U10A0.pdf.

Gogolashvili, George, Avtandil Arabuli, Murman Sukhishvili, Mariam Manjgaladze, Nino Chumburidze, and Nino Jorbenadze. 2011. *Morphology of Modern Georgian language*. Tbilisi: Meridiani. [In Georgian].

Hewitt, George. 1995. *Georgian: A Structural Reference Grammar.* Amsterdam: John Benjamins.

Imnaishvili, Ivane. 1956. "To the issue of Absolutive case in proper nouns." *To the history of declension in Kartvelian languages* 59–75. [In Georgian].

Karlsson, Fred, Atro Voutilainen, Juha Heikkilä, and Arto Anttila. 1995. *Constraint Grammar: A Language-Independent System for Parsing Unrestricted Text.* Berlin and New York: de Gruyter Mouton.

Kratzer, Angelika. 1996. "Severing the external argument from its verb." In *Phrase structure and the lexicon*, by Johan Rooryck and Laurie Zaring, 109–137. Dordrecht: Kluwer Academic Publishers.

Kvachadze, Leo. 1996. *Syntax of Modern Georgian Language.* Tbilisi: Rubikoni. [In Georgian].

Legate, Julie Anne. 2008. "Morphological and abstract Case." *Linguistic Inquiry 39 (1).* 55–101.

—. 2014. "Split ergativity based on nominal type." *Lingua 148, DOI: https://doi. org/10.1016/j.lingua.2014.06.002* 183–212.

Lobzhanidze, Irina. 2019. "Computational Model of the Modern Georgian Language and Search Patterns for an Online Dictionary of Idioms." *Language, Logic, and Computation. TbiLLC 2018. Lecture Notes in Computer Science, vol 11456* 187–208.

—. 2022. *Finite-State Computational Morphology: An Analyzer and Generator for Georgian.* Cham: Springer.

Marantz, Alec. 1984. *On the nature of grammatical relations.* Cambridge, MA: MIT Press.

—. 2000 [1991]. "Case and licensing." In *Arguments and Case, explaining Burzio's generalization*, by Reuland Eric, 11–31. Amsterdam/Philadelphia: John Benjamins Publishing Company.

Nash, Léa. 2017. "The structural source of split ergativity and ergative case in Georgian." In *The Oxford handbook of ergativity*, by Jessica Coon, Diane Massam and Lisa Demen Travis, 175–205. Oxford: Oxford University Press, DOI: https://doi.org/10.1093/oxfordhb/9780198739371.013.8.

Polinsky, Maria. 2016. *Deconstructing ergativity, Two types of ergative languages and their features.* Oxford: Oxford University Press.

Polinsky, Maria, and Preminger, Omer. 2014. "Case and Grammatical Relations." In *The Routledge Handbook of Syntax*, by Andrew Carnie, Yosuke Sato and Daniel Siddiqi, 150–167. London and New York: Routledge.

Preminger, Omer. To appear. "Taxonomies of case and ontologies of case ." In *On the place of Case in Grammar*, by Elena Anagnostopoulou, Christina Sevdali and Dionysios Mertyris, Oxford: Oxford University Press, lingbuzz/005463.

Rayfield, Donald. 2006. *A Comprehensive Georgian-English Dictionary.* London: Garnett.

Rezac, Milan, Albizu, Pablo, and Etxepare, Ricardo. 2014. "The structural ergative of Basque and the theory of Case." *Natural Language and Linguistic Theory 32* 1273–1330.

Rukhadze, Geore, and Koplatadze, Gvantsa. 2008. *Unified Dictionary of Old Georgian Language.* Tbilisi: Georgian Patriarchate. [In Georgian].

Sarjveladze, Zurab. 1997. *Old Georgian Language.* Tbilisi: Tbilisi State Pedagogical University Press. [In Georgian].

Shanidze, Akaki. 1973. *Foundations of Georgian Grammar, Morphology, I.* Tbilisi: Tbilisi State University. [In Georgian].

—. 1976. *Old Georgian Language.* Tbilisi: Tbilisi State University. [In Georgian].

Shanidze, Mzekala. 1956. "To the function and place of which pronoun in Old Georgian." *To the history of declension in Kartvelian languages,* 140–143. [In Georgian].

Standards, ISO. 2012. *Language Resource Management – Morpho-syntactic Annotation Framework (MAF), No 24611.* https://www.iso.org/standard/51934.html.

Sukhishvili, Murman. 2019. "Marked and unmarked forms of direct object replaced by instrumental and adverbial cases in Old Georgian." *Iberian-Caucasian Linguistics, XLVII* 147–156. [In Georgian].

Tollan, Rebecca. 2018. "Unergatives are different: Two types of transitivity in Samoan." *Glossa: a journal of general linguistics 3(1), 35* 1–41.

Topuria, Varlam. 1956. "To Vocative case." *To the history of declension in Kartvelian languages,* 36–48. [In Georgian].

Tschenkeli, Kita. 1965. *Georgisch-Deutsches Wörterbuch.* Zürich: Amirani-Verlag.

Tschenkeli, Stefane. 1956. "To the inflection of proper nouns in the book of Kings accroding to the Oshkhi Manuscript." *To the history of declension in Kartvelian languages,* 76–128. [In Georgian].

Tsotsanidze, George, Loladze, Nana, and Datukishvili, Ketevan. 2014. *Georgian Dictionary.* Tbilisi: Bakur Sulakauri. [In Georgian].

Ura, Hiroyuki. 2006. "A parametric syntax of aspectually conditioned split-ergativity." In *Ergativity: Emerging issues (Studies in Natural Language and Linguistic Theory 65),* by Alana Johns, Diane Massam and Juvenal Ndayiragije, 111–141. Dordrecht: Springer.

—. 2001. "Case." In *The Handbook of Contemporary Syntactic Theory,* by Mark Baltin and Chris Collins, 334–373. Oxford: Blackwell.

Uturgaidze, Tedo. 1986. *Morphophonological analysis of Georgian noun.* Tbilisi: Science. [In Georgian].

Vogt, Hans. 1968. "Case system in Old Georgian." *Reviewer* 251–284. [In Georgian].

—. 1971. *Grammaire de la langue géorgienne.* Oslo: Universitetsforlaget.

Chapter 7

Diasystemic Modelling of the Verbal Inflection System in the Western Georgian Dialects (Kartvelian)

Yidian She

Université Paul Valéry Montpellier

Abstract

Kartvelian inflectional system exhibits the interaction of morphosyntactic features, morphosemantic features and inflection-class traits (Makharoblidze and Léonard, 2020). Considering the structural complexity of Kartvelian inflection system, it could hardly be described by an incremental and morpheme-based model in a parsimonious way. In recent years, linguists have adopted in the domain of Kartvelian linguistics the *Paradigm Function Morphology* (PFM) model which relies on a realisational and paradigm-based approach to inflectional morphology and provides a more holistic point of view. Makharoblidze and Léonard (2020) have adapted the PFM model to Standard Georgian and have proven that PFM is efficient to "disentangle the structural complexity of the inflectional system of Georgian verbs." By adopting Makharoblidze and Léonard's analysis model, which is initially conceived for Standard Georgian, the present paper tackles the verbal inflection in the diasystem of five western Georgian dialects, *i.e.*, *Upper Imeretian*, *Lower Imeretian*, *Gurian*, *Adjarian* and *Taoan*. At first, the fourfold division of inflection classes is seized as a constant feature in the diasystem of western Georgian dialects, and the stem-distribution patterns turn out to be efficient to highlight the clear-cut distinctions among inflection classes. Then, the exponence paradigms, which are considered as a source of divergence in diasystem, are used to distinguish subgroups of the four inflection classes. Finally, the dynamic relations of the verbal inflection system in the western Georgian dialects are depicted in an implicational graph.

Keywords: western Georgian dialects, verbal inflection, PFM, Principal Parts, diasystemic modelling

***

7.1. Introduction

Kartvelian languages exhibit complex inflectional systems in which, as indicated by Makharoblidze and Léonard (2020), the "morphosyntactic features, morphosemantic features and inflection-class traits" interact. This multilevel interaction could hardly be represented by an incremental and morpheme-based model in a parsimonious way (*cf.* Stump, 2016). In recent years, linguists begin to consider Kartvelian verbal inflection with a more holistic point of view (*cf.* Makharoblidze and Léonard, 2020; Tran Ngoc, 2020). Within a realisational-inferential approach which allows to consider the *complexity* of inflectional system, Makharoblidze and Léonard (2020) have adapted *Paradigm Function Morphology* (henceforth PFM) model to Standard Georgian and obtained plausible results. The present paper will adopt Makharoblidze and Léonard's model. By applying this model to analyse the verbal inflectional system (or conjugation) of western Georgian dialects, I will propose a diasystemic modelling of the conjugation of western Georgian dialects.

The family of Kartvelian languages comprises four groups: Georgian, Megrelian, Svan and Laz which are mainly spoken in the Republic of Georgia and in the north of the Republic of Turkey. Among these languages, the modern Georgian has the most speakers whose number reaches five million (Tran Ngoc, 2020). According to Tuite (1998: 138-139), there are about 15 Georgian dialects which generally exhibit mutual intelligibility. The present paper will be interested in five of the Georgian dialects spoken in western Georgia and the neighbouring regions in northern Turkey, *i.e.*, *Upper Imeretian* (ზემოიმერული კილოკავი), *Lower Imeretian* (ქვემოიმერული კილოკავი), *Gurian* (გურული კილო), *Adjarian* (აჭარული კილო), and *Taoan* (ტაოური კილო). Upper Imeretian and Lower Imeretian are classified by Tuite (1998) into the northwest subgroup of Georgian dialects, and Gurian and Adjarian into the southwest subgroup, while Taoan is not mentioned in Tuite's nomenclature. By contrast with the four other dialects which are spoken in modern Georgian territory, Taoan is used in the historical province of Tao that is nowadays a part of Republic of Turkey. (Chokharadze et al., 2018). Chokharadze et al. (2018) indicate that Taoan exhibits a significant distinction with literacy Georgian and other Georgian dialects. However, such distinction does not prevent Taoan speakers from communicating with speakers of other Georgian dialects.

By focusing on the inflection system of the western Georgian dialects, the present paper attempts to answer the following questions. What are the constant features in the inflection system of the western Georgian dialects? What are the parameters by means of which dynamic relations among dialects could be observed? How the diasystemic dynamics of the western Georgian dialects could be modelled in a reader-friendly way? To reply to these questions, I will first demonstrate in section 2 the theory and method adopted by the present paper and the corpus on which my analysis is based. After having explained the methodologic and theorical background, I will indicate in section 3 a constant feature in the realm of stem throughout the western Georgian dialects and Standard Georgian, that is, the *fourfold division* of stem-distribution patterns which corresponds to four verbal inflection classes. Then, the realm of exponence will be considered as a source of divergence and the subclasses of four inflection classes will be carried out by means of exponence patterns. In addition, I will introduce the concept of *Principal Parts* (Finkel and Stump, 2007, 2009) that allows the forms of each inflectional subclass to be deduced and represented in a parsimonious way. Finally, but not least, an implicational graph which demonstrates the sources of convergence and divergence in western Georgian diasystem will be presented in section 4. With this graph, I will try to highlight the dynamic relations among the verbal inflection systems of the western Georgian dialects. Then, further prospects will be given in the concluding section.

7.2. Method and Corpus

7.2.1. PFM Theory and Makharoblidze and Léonard's Analysis Model

Stump (2016) distinguishes two pairs of opposed approaches to inflection, *i.e.*, incremental approach vs. realisational approach and morpheme-based approach vs. paradigm-based approach. Regarding the incremental approach and the realisational approach, the former tends to consider that "exponents introduce morphosyntactic properties," but for the latter, it is the morphosyntactic properties that determine "the introduction of exponents" (Stump, 2016: 14, footnote 6). For example, in an incremental approach, the Georgian verbal form *shegik'era* ("he/she sewed it for you") could be segmented as below:

she-	g-	i-	k'er	-a
Preverb	P2.Object	Version.marker	Root.Past	P3.SG.Subject

"He/she sewed it for you."
(Harris, 1981: 87, gloss modified)

The prefix *she-* is a *preverb* that conveys perfect aspect, and the prefix *g-* is an object marker of second person. As to the vocalic prefix (or *version marker*) *i-*, it operates in verbal valency/voice and makes the monovalent verb stem bivalent. Finally, the suffix *-a* is a subject marker of third person singular. Thus, according to the incremental approach, it is these affixes (or exponents) that introduce the morphosyntactic properties of the verbal form *shegik'era*. However, my explication above is reductionist. In fact, the preverb *she-* is polyfunctional and can expose not only aspectual meaning, but also directional meaning (from outside to inside) and valency expansion (Makharoblidze, 2018). Furthermore, it can convey aspectual meaning only when it prefixes an aorist verb stem. Version markers also have multiple functions: apart from valency expansion, they can reflect the *Speech-act Participant* traits of arguments and convey possessive-destinative relations between arguments in other contexts. Thus, it seems that an incremental approach, which implies that the whole is merely the sum of its components, could hardly seize interactions among exponents and interactions between stem and exponents.

On the contrary, the realisational approach has a reverse view and would think that it is the morphosyntactic properties of the given verb that introduce exponents. More precisely, once the verb stem (X) has been determined, the morphosyntactic properties of the verb such as {Tense: Aorist}, {Aspect: Perfect}, {Mood: Indicative} and {Agreement: {Subject: 3; Number: Singular}; {Object: 2; Number: Singular}} trigger the exponents *shegi*-X(aorist)-*a*. In this case, exponents are treated in a holistic way, and the effect of interactions among different exponents is taken into account.

As to the second opposition – the morpheme-based approach and the paradigm-based approach, in the former, morphology is reducible to a series of syntagmatic relations, so that "paradigms are epiphenomenal" in inflectional morphology. However, in the latter, the paradigmatic dimension is considered as an irreducible domain in morphology as well as the syntagmatic dimension. For example, regarding the impersonal verb in French, such as *pleuvoir / il pleut*, the defectivity is intrinsic to this kind of verb. But one might ignore this interaction between the morphosyntactic level and morphosemantic level by adopting an exclusively syntagmatic approach. The same can be said of Georgian verbs, there are numerous verbal properties, such as defectivity, stem-distribution patterns and their interactions with morphosemantic and inflectional-class traits, that could only be observed from a paradigmatic point of view. Makharoblidze and Léonard (2020) demonstrate the (systemic) *complexity* in the inflectional system of the Standard Georgian verbs. [1] A *complex system* is "a system composed of a great number of constituents which interact among each other in a non-linear way" (Picard, 2019: 13, own translation). A complex system is not only defined by the sum of all its components, but also by the permanent interactions of components in their contexts (ibid.: 14). Thus, according to Makharoblidze and Léonard (*op. cit.*), the inflection of Georgian verbs is also based on a complex system, and an incremental and morpheme-

---

[1] Henceforth, the terms *complexity* or *complex* that I use in this paper always denote the *systemic complexity* instead of the descriptive/constitutional complexity of a language (*cf.* Dahl, 2004, as cited in Picard, 2019: 12)

based model could hardly be sufficient to describe the Georgian inflectional system which is characterised by the non-linear interactions among the morphosyntactic level, morphosemantic level and inflectional-class traits. Therefore, Makharoblidze and Léonard (2020) suggest that PFM is able to describe the Kartvelian verbal infection in a sufficient and parsimonious way. PFM is above all a realisational and paradigm-based model and allows us to take into account non-linear interactions in analyses. The PFM model adapted to Georgian verbal inflection comprises three sets of rules. Firstly, for a given lexeme, that is, an "unrealised" theorical abstraction, *Rules of Stem Choice* (henceforth RSC) selects a stem in the corresponding stem paradigm of this lexeme, according to the morphosyntactic (or/and morphosemantic) properties associated with this lexeme. Secondly, *Rules of Exponence* (henceforth RE) affix the selected stem by the exponents determined by the morphosyntactic (or/and morphosemantic) properties associated with this lexeme in question and finally obtain the realised form. It is noteworthy that the exponents are considered as a whole in RE. Eventually, a third set of rules called *Morpho-(pho)nological Rules* (henceforth MPR) could resolve the "controversial issues in the segmentation of stems and chains of affixes or clitics" (Makharoblidze and Léonard, 2020).

To illustrate these three sets of rules, consider the example of the realisation of Taoan verbal form *shuuch'amia* (apparently, he/she has eaten it). The lexeme CH'AM (to eat) has a stem paradigm of four stems, that is, $X_1 = \sqrt{}$ech'am, $X_2 = \sqrt{}$ich'am, $X_3 = \sqrt{}$uch'am and $X_4 = \sqrt{}$sch'am. [2] Each stem corresponds to an RSC:

RSC1 Stem (L, σ: {{Aspect: {Pluperfect} ∧ Mood: {Evidential}} ∨ {Aspect: {Perfect} ∧ Mood: {Subjunctive}}}) = ⟨ech'am, σ⟩ = X_1

RSC2 Stem (L, σ: {Aspect: {Perfect} ∧ Mood: {Evidential} ∧ Person: {1 ∨ 2}}) = (⟨ich'am, σ⟩) = X_2

RSC3 Stem ((L, σ: {Aspect: {Perfect} ∧ Mood: {Evidential} ∧ Person: {3}}) = (⟨uch'am, σ⟩) = X_3

RSC4 Stem (L, : {Tense: {Present Future Aorist} Aspect: {Imperfect} ∨ Mood: {Conditional ∨ Optative}}) = (⟨sch'am, σ⟩) = X_4[3]

---

[2] Traditionally, the stems *ech'am, ich'am*, and *uch'am* could be segmented as *e-ch'am, i-ch'am*, and *u-ch'am* of which *e-, i-*, and *u-* are called *version vowels*. However, in Makharoblidze and Léonard's model, version vowels are considered as part of stem, because they are more lexical/derivational than inflectional. More details will be mentioned in Section 3.1.

[3] Abbreviation, symbols, and operators:

The formula RSC1 means that when the morphosyntactic and morphosemantic properties associated with the lexeme CH'AM consist of evidential pluperfect or perfect subjunctive, the stem X_1 will be selected. Then, according to RSC2, when lexeme is associated with first person evidential perfect or second person evidential perfect, the stem X_2 will be selected. When lexeme is associated with third person evidential perfect, the stem X_3 will be selected, as exhibited in RSC3. Moreover, according to RSC4, when lexeme is associated with present or future or aorist tense, or else, when it is associated with imperfect aspect or conditional or optative mood, the stem X_4 will be selected. The order of rules is not arbitrary but follows Pāṇini's rules: when two or several rules are in competition, it is the narrowest rule that will be applied (Bonami and Stump, 2016). Given that in the case of the verbal form *shuuch'amia*, the lexeme CH'AM is associated with third person evidential perfect, RSC3 is finally applied and the stem X_3 is chosen.

Once the relevant stem has been selected, RE affix this stem according to the morphosyntactic and morphosemantic properties of lexeme. There are two RE that are eligible to affix the stem X_3, as shown below:

RE1 X_3, σ: {Aspect: {Perfect} ∧ Mood: {Evidential} ∧ Person: {3} ∧ Number: {Singular}} = *she* + X_3 + *ia* = *sheuch'amia*

RE2 X_3, σ: {Aspect: {Perfect} ∧ Mood: {Evidential} ∧ Person: {3} ∧ Number: {Plural}} = *she* + X_3 + *ian* = *sheuch'amian*

As shown in RE1 and RE2, when lexeme is associated with third person singular and evidential perfect, the exponents *she*-X-*ia* are affixed to stem. However, when lexeme is associated with third person plural and evidential perfect, it is *she*-X-*ia* that is affixed to stem. Given that the lexeme CH'AM is associated with third person plural, RE1 is applied.

It is noteworthy that the form **sheuch'amia* is not yet the final realisation. In this case, it requires the application of MPR:

MPR1 $\langle V_{Pv} \rangle \rightarrow \langle V_V \rangle / \_\langle V_V \rangle$

According to MPR1, the final vowel of preverb (Pv) is assimilated by the version vowel (V) of stem. Thus, in the unrealised form **sheuch'amia*, the final

---

L   lexeme
σ   property set
p ∧ *q* *p* and *q*
p ∨ *q* *p* or *q*
p = *q* *p* equals *q*
(*cf.* Stump, 2016)

vowel of the preverb *she-* is assimilated by the version vowel *u-* of the stem *uch'am*, which finally gives the realised form *shuuch'amia*.

7.2.2. Corpus and Analysis

All the written corpora used in the present paper are from the book entitled ახალი ქართული ენა წიგნი IV – დიალექტების მორფოლოგია: პარადიგმები [*New Georgian Language Vol. 4 – Morphology of Dialects: Paradigms*]. Corpora and their authors are listed below:

Lower Imeretian: N. Sharashenidze

Upper Imeretian: N. Sharashenidze and G. Ch'auch'idze

Gurian: G. Dgebuadze

Adjarian: N. Surmava

Taoan: M. Paghava and N. Ts'ets'khladze

In addition, my analysis was also based on the recording carried out by Prof. Jean Léo Léonard in Georgia in 2018. In this recording, Prof. Nino Sharashenidze, as a native Lower-Imeretian speaker, pronounces inflectional forms of the Lower-Imeretian written corpus.

Furthermore, a large part of the analyses of the present paper, especially the analyses about exponence patterns and principal parts, were carried out with the help of *Principal-part Analyzer Tool*, a programme written in Perl by Prof. Raphael Finkel.

7.3. Verbal Inflection Classes of the Western Georgian Dialects

7.3.1. Delimitation of the Realm of RSC and the Realm of RE

This section focuses on the classification of verbal inflection in the western Georgian dialects and tries to find out convergence and divergence throughout the inflection systems of these dialects. Before getting into the substance of this matter, I would like first to clarify the delimitation of the realm of RSC and the realm of RE in these dialects.

The Georgian verb template is constituted by 14 slots: three prefixal slots, one slot dedicated to verb root and eight suffixal slots. (see Table 7.1) This template initially conceived for Standard Georgian, which is based on the Kartlian-K'akhetian dialect (Tuite, 1998: 138), is also applicable to western Georgian dialects such as Lower Imeretian, Upper Imeretian, Gurian, Adjarian and Taoan. My corpus does not comprise passive nor causative forms so that I cannot assert if slot +1 and slot +3 are adequate for above-mentioned western

Georgian dialects. But apart from these two slots, the Georgian verb template can perfectly describe verbs of the five western Georgian dialects. Otherwise, Makharoblidze and Léonard (2020) divide these slots into two categories, that is, inflectional and derivational (or lexical) categories. Verb root (slot 0), passive marker and causative marker are considered as derivational. As to the slots of preverb (slot -3) and version marker (slot -1), they have both inflectional and derivational values. And the remaining slots are inflectional.

Table 7.1. Georgian verb template

SLOT	LEXICAL	INFLECTIONAL
-3	Preverb	
-2		Prefixal nominal marker
-1	Version marker	
0	Root	
+1	*Passive marker*	
+2		Thematic suffix
+3	*Causative marker*	
+4		Imperfective marker
+5		Mood / row marker
+6		Auxiliary verb
+7		Suffixal nominal marker
+8		Plural marker

(Makharoblidze and Léonard, 2020, modified)

One might say that the verb template is based on an incremental approach to inflection, and it seems that such a model tends to flatten the Kartvelian inflectional system in which interact the morphosyntactic proprieties, morphosemantic proprieties and inflection-class traits. However, this model turns out to be perfectly compatible with the realisational and paradigm-based approach, since appellations like "preverb (-3)," "version marker (-1)" and "thematic suffix (+2) do not explicitly convey any morphosyntactic meanings or contents. Furthermore, the verb template is useful to delimit the realm of stem and that of exponence for PFM analysis.

In PFM analysis, above-mentioned derivational slots generally belong to the realm of stem, while inflectional slots belong to the realm of exponents. However, as indicated in Table 7.1, preverb and version marker are both polyfunctional. According to Makharoblidze (2012; 2018) and Makharoblidze and Léonard (2020), preverbs can convey spatial contents and operate in tense, aspect, mood, and verbal valency. They can also produce new verbs. Thus, preverbation affects different levels such as the morphosyntactic level, morphosemantic level and derivational level. In Makharoblidze and Léonard's analysis model, preverbs are treated as proclitics instead of prefixes and the preverbs without derivational value are considered relevant to the realm of RE.

As regard version markers, they are also linked to morphosyntactic, morphosemantic and lexical levels. Version markers reflect the *Speech-act Participant* (henceforth SAP) traits of arguments, convey possessive-destinative relations between arguments, and operate in verbal valency. Makharoblidze and Léonard's model resolves the polyfunctionality of version by treating inflectional and derivational version markers as a part of stem which prefixes verb root. Otherwise, thematic suffixes, which are classified in inflectional category by Makharoblidze and Léonard, also turn out to be polyfunctional in southwestern dialects according to the analysis of the present paper. For example, in many transitive verbs of Taoan and several transitive verbs of Adjarian, thematic suffixes have an inflectional value. As indicated in Table 7.2 that shows a part of conjugation of the Taoan transitive verb TS'ER (to write), in present indicative, the thematic suffix *-av* is a component of the stem *sts'erav*, so that in this case the thematic suffix has a lexical value. However, in aorist, the thematic suffix *-ev* belongs to the realm of exponents and is combined with the preverb (-3) *da-*, the nominal suffix (+7) *-i*, and if necessary, the nominal prefix of 1st person *v-* or/and plural suffix *-t* in RE. The introduction of *-ev* is in fact licensed by SAP traits.

Table 7.2. Partial conjugation of Taoan transitive verb TS'ER (to write)

SCREEVE	PRESENT INDICATIVE						AORIST					
SLOT	-3	-2	0	+2	+7	+8	-3	-2	0	+2	+7	+8
1SG		*v*	*sts'er*	*av*			*da*	*v*	*sts'er*	*ev*	*i*	
2SG			*sts'er*	*av*			*da*		*sts'er*	*ev*	*i*	
3SG			*sts'er*	*av*	*s*		*da*		*sts'er*		*a*	
1PL		*v*	*sts'er*	*av*		*t*	*da*	*v*	*sts'er*	*ev*	*i*	*t*
2PL			*sts'er*	*av*		*t*	*da*		*sts'er*	*ev*	*i*	*t*
3PL			*sts'er*	*av*	*en*		*da*		*sts'er*		*es*	

Transliterated in Latin alphabet and segmented by the author of this article. The visualisation of this table follows the model of Tran Ngoc (2019).

Thus, by adopting the delimitation of the realm of RSC and the realm of RE suggested by Makharoblidze and Léonard (see Table 7.1), the present paper would also suggest distinguishing the lexical thematic suffix from the inflectional thematic suffix, because the former is a component of the verb stem, while the latter belongs to exponents. Consequently, the realm of RSC and that of RE in the five western Georgian dialects are shown below in Table 7.3.

Slots belonging to stem, *i.e.*, the realm of RSC, are shaded, while the remaining slots belong to exponents, *i.e.*, the realm of RE. As passive marker (+1) and causative marker (+3) are not attested in my corpus of western Georgian dialects, they will not be discussed in the present paper.

Table 7.3. The realm of stem and the realm of exponence

SLOT	LEXICAL	INFLECTIONAL
-3	Preverb	Preverb
-2	Prefixal nominal marker	
-1	Version marker	Version marker
0	Root	
+1	*Passive marker*	
+2	Thematic suffix	Thematic suffix
+3	*Causative marker*	
+4		Imperfective marker
+5		Mood / row marker
+6		Auxiliary verb
+7		Suffixal nominal marker
+8		Plural marker

(Makharoblidze and Léonard, 2020, modified)

7.3.2. Convergence: Stem Distributions

Linguists generally distinguish four verbal inflection classes in Standard Georgian (*cf.* Harris, 1981; Makharoblidze and Léonard, 2020). Georgian verbs could be classified by means of morphosemantic and morphosyntactic criteria. The first inflection class (henceforth IC1) comprises transitive and telic verbs, the second inflection class (IC2) comprises intransitive and passive verbs. For verbs of IC1 and IC2, the preverbation distinguishes forms of present subseries from forms of future subseries. As to verbs of the third inflection class (IC3), they are intransitive and atelic and are also called medio-active verbs. And the fourth inflection class (IC4) comprises medio-passive verbs which could convey affective, static, or epistemological meanings, etc. Moreover, verbs of IC2 and IC4 trigger enclitic copula in Series III, while verbs of IC1 and IC3 trigger oblique agreement in Series III (Makharoblidze and Léonard, 2020; Harris, 1981, 1991). Criteria by which different inflection classes are defined could be heterogenous. In fact, the distinction among different inflection classes involves morphosyntactic proprieties and morphosemantic proprieties at the same time. As also mentioned by Makharoblidze and Léonard (2020), inflection-class traits of Georgian verbs are the by-product of the interaction between morphosyntactic level and morphosemantic level. Therefore, the complexity of Georgian inflection system also has an impact on the classification of verbal inflection.

Furthermore, according to my analysis of corpus, the same fourfold division of verbal inflection in Standard Georgian is found anew in all the five western Georgian dialects. Consequently, the objectives of this subsection are twofold: on the one hand, I will demonstrate the stability of the fourfold division of verbal inflection throughout the western Georgian dialects and show that this *quadripartition* of verbal inflection could be a "constant" in the diasystem of western Georgian dialects. On the other hand, I will prove that the PFM model can tackle the complexity of inflection classes from a holistic point of view. By visualising the stem-distribution patterns, I will show the clear-cut distinction among the four inflection classes in a more reader-friendly way.

Lexemes are theorical abstractions instead of linguistic forms (Stump, 2016). They are realised by means of the application of RSC and RE. Precisely, RSC selects a stem in the corresponding stem paradigm of the lexeme, according to morphosyntactic (or/and morphosemantic) properties associated with this lexeme. For example, the Upper-Imeretian verb MO_K'REP ("to pluch," IC1) has a stem paradigm of five stems, as shown below in Table 7.4.

Table 7.4. Upper Imeretian: MO_K'REP

STEM	SLOTS IN VERB TEMPLATE		
	-1	0	+2
X_1	*e*	*k'rip*	
X_2	*i*	*k'rep*	
X_3	*u*	*k'rep*	
X_4		*k'rip*	
X_5		*k'rip*	*am*

The Upper-Imeretian verb MO_K'REP has a stem paradigm of five stems.

According to Makharoblidze and Léonard's model, the distribution of these stems could be determined by RSC1-5:

RSC1   Stem (L, σ: {{Aspect: {Pluperfect} ∧ Mood: {Evidential}} ∨ {Aspect: {Perfect} ∧ Mood: {Subjunctive}}}) = ⟨ek'rip, σ⟩ = X_1

RSC2   Stem (L, σ: {Aspect: {Perfect} ∧ Mood: {Evidential} ∧ Person: {+SAP}}) = (⟨ik'rep, σ⟩) = X_2

RSC3   Stem ((L, σ: {Aspect: {Perfect} ∧ Mood: {Evidential} ∧ Person: {-SAP}}) = (⟨uk'rep, σ⟩) = X_3

RSC4   Stem (L, σ: {Tense: {Aorist} ∨ Mood: {Optative}}) = (⟨kr'ip, σ⟩) = X_4

RSC5   Stem (L, σ: {Tense: {Present ∨ Future} ∨ Aspect: {Imperfect} ∨ Mood: {Conditional}}}) = (⟨k'ripam, σ⟩) = X_5

As mentioned above, the application of RSC follows Pāṇini's rules. RSC1 means that when the lexeme MO_K'REP is associated with morphosyntactic proprieties such as evidential perfect or perfect subjunctive, then the stem *ek'rip* (X_1) will be chosen to produce the realised form of MO_K'REP. And the remaining RSC could be interpreted in the same manner.

I also illustrate the stem distribution of the verb MO_K'REP in the third colon of Table 7.5.

Table 7.5. Stem distribution of several Upper-Imeretian verbs

LEXEME		MO_K'REP	BOCH'	TES	CH'ER	Q'OL
PRESENT SUBSERIES	PRESENT	*k'ripam*	*boch'am*	*tesam*	*ch'ri*	*q'am*
	IMPERFECT					
	PRESENT SUBJUNCTIVE					
FUTURE SUBSERIES	FUTURE					*eq'oleb*
	CONDITIONAL					
	FUTURE SUBJUNCTIVE					
AORIST SERIES	AORIST	*k'rip*	*boch'*	*tes*	*ch'(e)r*	*eq'ol*
	OPTATIVE					
PERFECT SERIES	PERFECT	*ik'rep* *uk'rep*	*iboch'(n)* *uboch'(n)*	*ites(n)* *utes(n)*	*ich'r* *uch'r*	*q'ol*
	PLUPERFECT	*ek'rip*	*eboch'*	*etes(n)*	*ech'r*	
	PERFECT SUBJUNCTIVE					

MO_K'REP, BOCH,' TES, and CH'ER belong to IC1, while Q'OL belongs to IC4.

As indicated in Table 7.5, apart from MO_K'REP, there are other transitive verbs, that is, verbs of IC1, share the same stem-distribution pattern, such as BOCH' ("to pick up"), TES ("to plant"), and CH'ER ("to cut"). As to Q'OL ("to have," inanimate), a IC4 verb, its stem distribution is however different from that of IC1 verbs. Moreover, by analysing the corpus of the western Georgian dialects, I found out four patterns of stem distributions which correspond to the four inflection classes, respectively.

Figures 7.1 – 7.5 illustrate the stem-distribution patterns of all the verbs of the western Georgian dialect corpus. Two screeves that share a same stem are linked by a line. The number labelled on the line indicates the number of verbs that have the same stem in the two screeves in question in the corpus.

Figure 7.1. Stem distribution of IC1 verbs

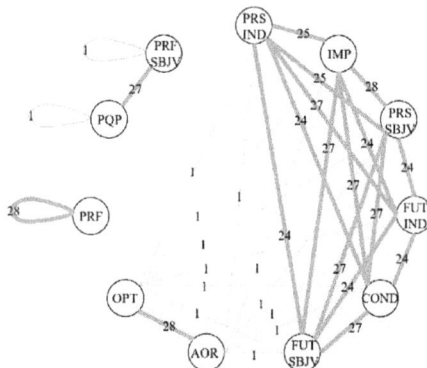

The visualisation of stem distributions illustrated in Figures 7.1 – 7.5 follows the visualisation model elaborated by Guérin et al. (2019). Figure 7.1 illustrates the stem distribution of 28 IC1 verbs.

Figure 7.2. Stem distribution of IC2 verbs

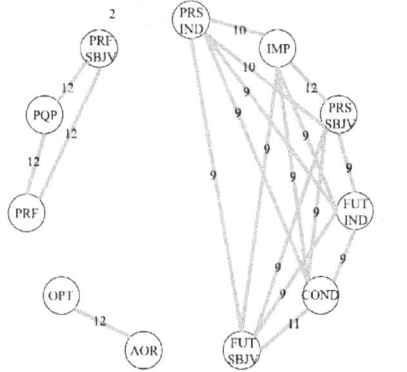

The visualization of the stem distribution of 12 IC2 verbs.

Figure 7.3. Stem distribution of IC3 verbs

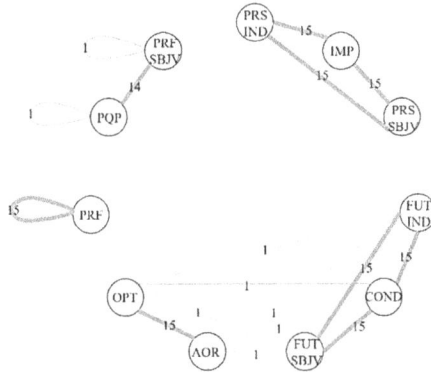

The visualization of the stem distribution of 15 IC3 verbs.

Figure 7.4. Stem distribution of IC4A verbs

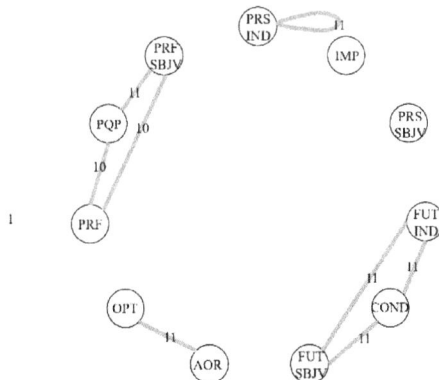

The visualization of the stem distribution of 11 IC4A verbs.

Figure 7.5. Stem distribution of IC4B verbs

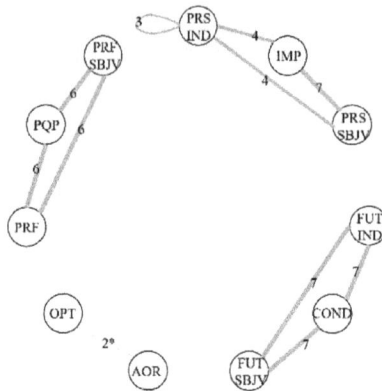

The visualization of the stem distribution of 7 IC4B verbs. The Upper-Imeretian IC4B verb Q'OL ("to have") and the Taoan IC4B verb ND ("to want") are not defective in Series II, i.e., aorist and optative.

As shown in Figures 7.1 – 7.5, there are four stem-distribution patterns, which correspond to the four inflection classes in western Georgian dialects. Figure 7.1 illustrates the stem-distribution pattern of IC1 verbs. IC1 verbs generally have five stems: a stem shared by six screeves of Series I, *i.e.*, present indicative, imperfect, present subjunctive, future indicative, conditional and future subjunctive; a stem shared by two screeves of Series II, *i.e.*, aorist and optative; a +SAP stem and a -SAP stem used in perfect of Series III; and a stem shared by pluperfect and perfect subjunctive of Series III.

Regarding Figure 7.2 which illustrates the stem distributions of IC2 verbs, there are only three stems: each series has a single stem.

Figure 7.3 illustrates the stem-distribution pattern of IC3 verbs which involves six stems: a stem for Present subseries; a stem for Future subseries; a stem for Series II; a +SAP stem and a -SAP stem used in perfect of Series III; and a stem shared by pluperfect and perfect subjunctive of Series III.

Figure 7.4 and Figure 7.5 illustrate the stem-distribution pattern of IC4 verbs. Since IC4 verbs are subdivided into two groups: IC4A verbs are defective in imperfect and present subjunctive, and IC4B verbs are defective in aorist and optative (*cf.* Makharoblidze and Léonard, 2020), the stem-distribution pattern of IC4 verbs is also divided into two subtypes. The stem-distribution pattern in Figure 7.4 corresponds to IC4A verbs: a stem is merely used in present indicative, since these verbs are defective in other screeves of Present Subseries; a stem for Future Subseries; a stem for Series II; and a stem for Series III. Figure 7.5 illustrates the stem-distribution pattern of IC4B verbs: Present Subseries, Future Subseries and Series III have respectively three distinct stems.

To conclude on this point, I would like to affirm that the fourfold division of inflection classes exhibits a certain degree of stability throughout the five analysed dialects and could be considered as a constant in the diasystem of western Georgian dialects.

Furthermore, results shown in this subsection also prove that the PFM model is efficient in analysing the inflection classes of western Georgian dialects. As already shown in Makharoblidze and Léonard's model, unlike the criteria of verbal classification based on syntagmatic dimension, which could be heterogeneous, stem-distribution patterns, as a criterion based on paradigmatic dimension, turn out to be able to highlight the clear-cut distinction among the four inflection classes of western Georgian dialects in a concise manner.

In addition, it is noteworthy that Lower Imeretian have a fourth series which comprises screeves conveying present tense and evidential mood. But for a given verb of any inflection classes, its inflectional forms of the fourth series share a single and peculiar stem. Thus, as the stem-distribution pattern in the fourth series is the same for verbs of any inflection classes, the presence of the fourth series in Lower Imeretian does not impact nor modify the fourfold division of inflection classes.

7.3.3. Divergence: Exponence Paradigm

In above subsection, it is demonstrated that all verbs of the five western Georgian dialects could generally be classified into four inflection classes according to a sole criterion, that is, stem-distribution pattern. Now I will show in this subsection that the four inflection classes could be subdivided into subclasses, according to the paradigms of the exponents affixed to selected stems. In other words, for a given stem-distribution pattern (or inflection class), there are one or more corresponding exponence patterns (or exponence paradigms). The number of these corresponding exponence paradigms determines the number of subclasses within the inflection class in question. The corpus used by the present paper, which is, admittedly, quantitively limited, shows that within an inflection class, exponence paradigms vary quantitatively and qualitatively. Thus, exponence paradigms turn out to be one of the points of divergence in western Georgian dialects. Before getting into the substance of this matter, I would like to explain how exponents are treated with the help of the PFM model. Given that PFM suggests a holistic approach to the inflectional morphology, exponents are always considered as a whole[4] as shown in the example of the Gurian transitive verb CH'AM ("to eat"):

---

[4] For the time being, the present article only conceives a sole block of RE for the five western Georgian dialects.

(1) CH'AM: first-person plural form in imperfect

    a.   v-a-ch'm-ev-d-i-t

        P1-version.marker-root-thematic.suffix-imperfect.marker-row.marker-plural

    b.   RE: X σ {Agreement: {PERS: 1, NUM: SG}; Aspect: {Imperfect}}

        => v + X + evdit = (⟨vach'mevdit, σ⟩)[5]

(1a) represents an incremental approach to the segmentation of exponents. According to the analysis in (1a), it is the exponents that introduce morphosyntactic and morphosemantic proprieties. By contrast, (1b), which illustrates RE of Makharoblidze and Léonard's model, treats exponents as a whole, and the introduction of exponents is licensed by morphosyntactic and morphosemantic proprieties (Stump, 2016: 14).

With such a holistic approach, 13 exponence paradigms could be found in Upper-Imeretian. The results are shown in Table 7.6 as an illustrative example.

Table 7.6. Exponence paradigms and dynamic principal parts of Upper-Imeretian verbs

IC	Example	Present			Imperfective		Present Subjunctive	
		1sg	3sg	3pl	1sg	3sg	1sg	3sg
IC1-A	MO_TIB ("to mow")	v-	-s	-en	v-di	-da	v-de	-des
IC1-B	SV ("to drink")	v-	-s	-en	v-di	-da	v-de	-des
IC1-C	TES ("to plant)	v-	-s	-en	v-di	-da	v-de	-des
IC1-D	CH'ER ("to cut")	v-	-s	-an	v-di	-da	v-de	-des
IC2	XMAR ("to help")	v-i	-a	-ian/ien	v-odi	-oda	v-ode	-odes
IC2/3	Q'VIR ("to shout")	v-var	-s	-an	v-odi	-oda	v-ode	-odes
IC3-A	TKV ("to say")	v-	-s	-en	v-di	-da	v-de	-des
IC3-B	NAX ("to see")	v-	-s	-en	v-di	-des	v-de	-des
IC4-A	TS'V ("to lie")	v-var	-s	-an	/	/	/	/
IC4-B	Q'OP ("to be")	v-	-a	-ian	/	/	/	/
IC4-C	KON ("to have *inanimate*")	m-	-	-t	m-(d)a	-(d)a	m-des	-des
IC4-D	ND ("to want")	m-a	-a	-at	m-oda	-oda	m-odes	-odes
IC4-E	Q'OL ("to have *animate*")	m-s	-s	-t	m-da	-da	m-des	-des

---

[5] This RE function follows Makharoblidze and Léonard's analysis model.

IC	Example	Future			Conditional		Future Subjunctive	
		1sg	3sg	3pl	1sg	3sg	1sg	3sg
IC1-A	MO_TIB ("to mow")	PVv-	PV-s	PV-en	PVv-di	PV-da	PVv-de	PV-des
IC1-B	SV ("to drink")	PVv-	PV-s	PV-en	PVv-di	PV-da	PVv-de	PV-des
IC1-C	TES ("to plant)	PVv-	PV-s	PV-en	PVv-di	PV-da	PVv-de	PV-des
IC1-D	CH'ER ("to cut")	PVv-	PV-s	PV-an	PVv-di	PV-da	PVv-de	PV-des
IC2	XMAR ("to help")	PVv-i	PV-a	PV-ian/ien	PVv-odi	PV-oda	PVv-ode	PV-odes
IC2/3	Q'VIR ("to shout")	PVv-	PV-s	PV-en	PVv-di	PV-da	PVv-de	PV-des
IC3-A	TKV ("to say")	v-	-s	-an	v-di	-da	v-de	-des
IC3-B	NAX ("to see")	v-	-s	-en	v-di	-da	v-*di*	*-da*
IC4-A	TS'V ("to lie")	v-i	-a	-an	v-odi	-oda	v-ode	-odes
IC4-B	Q'OP ("to be")	v-i	-a	-ian	v-oi	-oda	v-ode	-odes
IC4-C	KON ("to have *inanimate*")	m-a	-a	-at	m-oda	-oda	m-odes	-odes
IC4-D	ND ("to want")	m-a	-a	-at	m-oda	-oda	m-odes	-odes
IC4-E	Q'OL ("to have *animate*")	m-a	-a	-at	m-oda	-oda	m-odes	-odes

IC	Example	Aorist			Optative		Perfect		Perfect Subjunctive
		1sg	3sg	3pl	1sg	3sg	1sg	3sg	1sg
IC1-A	MO_TIB ("to mow")	PVv-e	PV-a	PV-es	PVv-o	PV-os	PVm-ia	PV-ia	PVm-os
IC1-B	SV ("to drink")	PVv-i	PV-a	PV-es/en	PVv-a	PV-as	PVm-ia	PV-ia	PVm-as
IC1-C	TES ("to plant)	PVv-e	PV-a	PV-en	PVv-o	PV-os	PVm-ia	PV-ia	PVm-os
IC1-D	CH'ER ("to cut")	PVv-i	PV-a	PV-es/en	PVv-a	PV-as	PVm-ia	PV-ia	PVm-as
IC2	XMAR ("to help")	PVv-e	PV-a	PV-en	PVv-o	PV-os	PVv-ivar	PV-ia	PVv-ode
IC2/3	Q'VIR ("to shout")	PVv-e	PV-a	PV-es	PVv-o	PV-os	PVm-ia	PV-ia	PVm-os
IC3-A	TKV ("to say")	-i	-a	-an	-a	-as	m-ia	-ia	m-as
IC3-B	NAX ("to see")	PVv-e	PV-a	PV-es/en	PVv-o	PV-os	m-ia	-ia	m-os
IC4-A	TS'V ("to lie")	v-i	-a	-en	v-e	-es	v-var	-a	v-iq'o
IC4-B	Q'OP ("to be")	v-i	-o	-en	v-o	-os	v-var	-a	v-iq'o
IC4-C	KON ("to have *inanimate*")	/	/	/	/	/	m-ia	-ia	m-odes
IC4-D	ND ("to want")	/	/	/	/	/	m-ia	-ia	m-odes
IC4-E	Q'OL ("to have *animate*")	m-a	-a	-at	m-os	-os	m-ia	-ia	m-odes

The data of this table are carried out with the help of Principal-part Analyzer Tool, programme written in Perl by Prof. Raphael Finkel.

As indicated in Table 7.6, Upper-Imeretian exponence paradigms allow distinguishing four subclasses in IC1, two subclasses in IC3, and five subclasses in IC4. In addition, the lexeme Q'VIR ("to shout") exhibits heteroclisis. In other words, the exponence paradigms of Q'VIR is split: exponents of Present Subseries belong to IC2, while exponents of other Series belong to IC3.

In the diasystem of western Georgian dialects, the number and the type of exponence paradigms of each inflection class vary from one dialect to another and could be impacted by multiple features. Firstly, varieties within the slot of preverb (-3) trigger the variation of exponence paradigms. For example, preverb is absent in the conjugation of IC4 verb NDOMA ("to want") in Standard Georgian as it is in Upper Imeretian, while in the conjugation of the Taoan cognate of NDOMA, the preverb takes an inflectional value: it is absent in Present Subseries and present in all other Series. Secondly, the slots of nominal prefix (-2) and plural marker (+8) also trigger the variation of exponence paradigms throughout dialects. Adjarian and Taoan, contrary to three other dialects studied by the present paper, have two series of exponence paradigms in competition. For one of the competing pair, the exponents introduced by 1st person plural are characterised by the prefix *gv-* (slot -2) in a synthetic manner. By contrast, for the other competing series of exponence paradigms, the exponents introduced by 1st person plural are characterised by the nominal prefix *m-* (slot -2) and the plural suffix *-n* (slot +8). Moreover, inflectional thematic suffixes (+2) which reflect SAP traits also play an important role in the variation of exponence paradigms. In Series I of Gurian transitive verbs, the default exponence paradigms of IC1 reflect SAP traits by means of the opposed desinences (slots +5, +6, +7, and +8). As shown in the example of the transitive verb mal in Table 7.7[6], the +SAP forms have no desinence in the singular and are characterised by *-t* (+8) in the plural, while the -SAP forms are characterised by *-s* (+7) in the singular and by *-en* (+7/+8) in the plural. Apart from the default exponence paradigms, there is a series of exponent paradigms which reflect SAP traits in an *overmarked* manner. As shown in the example of the transitive verb RETSX ("to wash") in Table 7.7[7], the SAP traits is not only reflected by desinence in slots +5, +6, +7, and +8, but also reflected by the presence of the inflectional thematic suffix (+2). The thematic suffix *-av* reflects the +SAP value, while its absence reflects the -SAP value.

---

[6] The slots belonging to stem are shaded. In this instance, the stem of the lexeme MAL comprises deux components, *i.e.*, the root *mal* and the thematic suffix *-av*.

[7] In this instance, the stem of RETSX comprises only the verb root *retsx*. The thematic suffix *-av* does not belong to stem but to exponents.

Table 7.7. Lexical thematic suffix vs. inflectional thematic suffix in Gurian

LEXEME	MAL ("to hide")						RETSX ("to wash")					
SCREEVE	FUTURE INDICATIVE						FUTURE INDICATIVE					
SLOT	-3	-2	0	+2	+7	+8	-3	-2	0	+2	+7	+8
1SG	*da*	*v*	*mal*	*av*			*ga*	*v*	*retsx*	*av*		
2SG	*da*		*mal*	*av*			*ga*		*retsx*	*av*		
3SG	*da*		*mal*	*av*	*s*		*ga*		*retsx*		*s*	
1PL	*da*	*v*	*mal*	*av*		*t*	*ga*	*v*	*retsx*	*av*		*t*
2PL	*da*		*mal*	*av*		*t*	*ga*		*retsx*	*av*		*t*
3PL	*da*		*mal*	*av*	*en*		*ga*		*retsx*		*en*	

Stems are shaded.

The Series II of Taoan and Adjarian transitive verbs exhibits similar phenomenon with the respect of Series I of Gurian transitive verbs, as already indicated in Table 7.2. These above-mentioned features that trigger the variation of exponence paradigms will be treated in a systematic way in section 4 by means of the diasystemic modelling.

Furthermore, in order to represent the exponence paradigms in a parsimonious way, it is necessary to introduce the conception of *Principal parts* developed by Finkel and Stump (2007, 2009). Finkel and Stump (ibid.) indicate the fact that Latin students deduce all inflectional forms of a verb from only four principal parts and affirm that principal parts are not only interesting in the domain of language pedagogy, but also in the domain of typological variation in morphology. Finkel and Stump (2007) define principal parts of an inflection class as "the minimum of forms needed to deduce all remaining […] forms" in this inflection class. Moreover, Finkel and Stump (2009: 3-5) distinguish two types of principal parts: static principal parts and dynamic principal parts.

Firstly, in a static principal-part scheme, "the same sets of morphosyntactic proprieties [(henceforth MS sets)] identify the principal parts for every inflection class." Finkel and Stump (*op. cit.*) think that the principal parts used in traditional Latin pedagogy are typical static principal parts.

Table 7.8. Principal parts of five conjugations (inflection classes) in Latin

Conjugation	1SG present indicative active	Infinitive	1SG perfect indicative active	Perfect passive participle
1st	laudō	laudāre	laudāvī	laudātum
2nd	moneō	monēre	monuī	monitum
3rd	dūcō	dūcere	dūxī	dūctum
3rd (mixed)	capiō	capere	cēpī	captum
4th	audiō	audīre	audīvī	audītum

(Finkel and Stump, ibid.: 1)

One could find this kind of conjugation table in most Latin language textbooks (See Table 7.8). In fact, for a Latin verb, once these four forms (in 1SG present indicative active, infinitive, 1SG perfect indicative active, and perfect passive participle) have been given, the whole conjugation of this verb can be deduced. It is noteworthy that in this case the most important is not the whole conjugated forms, but the exponents of these four forms. In other words, by memorising the exponents of these four MS sets, one can predict the whole exponent paradigm of a given verb. As the MS sets used to identify principal parts are the same for all five inflectional classes, the principal parts in Latin are called static principal parts by Finkel and Stump (2007, 2009).

Since the conception of principal parts has a universal value, it is also applicable to the inflection classes of the western Georgian dialects. I choose to demonstrate the principal parts of Upper-Imeretian inflection classes as an illustrative example[8]. As indicated in the first rows of Table 7.6, 22 representative MS sets are taken into account in principal-part analysis. Unlike Latin which requires four static principal parts to predict the whole exponent paradigm, Upper Imeretian only needs three static principal parts. With the help of Finkel's *Principal-part Analyzer Tool*, I got 19 possible groups of MS sets which are eligible to identify the static principal parts of Upper Imeretian, as shown below:

Table 7.9. Possible analyses of static principal parts in Upper Imeretian

Possible analyses	1st principal part	2nd principal part	3rd principal part
1.	1SG PRESENT	3PL FUTURE	3PL AORIST
2.	3PL PRESENT	3PL IMPERFECT	3PL AORIST
3.	3PL PRESENT	1SG FUTURE	3PL AORIST
4.	3PL PRESENT	3SG FUTURE	3PL AORIST
5.	3PL PRESENT	3PL FUTURE	3PL AORIST
6.	3PL PRESENT	1SG CONDITIONAL	3PL AORIST
7.	3PL PRESENT	3SG CONDITIONAL	3PL AORIST
8.	3PL PRESENT	1SG FUTURE_SUBJ	3PL AORIST
9.	3PL PRESENT	3SG FUTURE_SUBJ	3PL AORIST
10.	3PL PRESENT	1SG AORIST	3PL AORIST
11.	3PL PRESENT	3PL AORIST	1SG OPTATIVE
12.	3PL PRESENT	3PL AORIST	3SG OPTATIVE

---

[8] Since exponents of 2nd person could generally be deduced by those of 1st person and exponents of 1st and 2nd person plural by corresponding singular forms, for the time being, only exponents of 1st and 3rd person singular, and 3rd person plural of several morphosyntactic propriety sets are taken into account in the principal-part analysis in the present paper.

13.	3PL PRESENT	3PL AORIST	1SG EVIDENTIAL PERFECT
14.	3PL PRESENT	3PL AORIST	3SG EVIDENTIAL PERFECT
15.	3PL PRESENT	3PL AORIST	1SG PERFECT SUBJUNCTIVE
16.	1SG IMPERFECT	3PL FUTURE	3PL AORIST
17.	3PL IMPERFECT	3PL FUTURE	3PL AORIST
18.	1SG PRESENT_SUBJ	3PL FUTURE	3PL AORIST
19.	3SG PRESENT SUBJUNCTIVE	3PL FUTURE	3PL AORIST

There are 19 possible groups of MS sets eligible to identify the static principal parts of Upper Imeretian.

I would like to choose the first group of MS sets (1sg present, 3pl future, and 3pl aorist) to make an illustrative example. For a given Upper-Imeretian verb, regardless of its inflectional class, the whole exponent paradigm of this verb can always be deduced from its exponents of 1sg present, 3pl future, and 3pl aorist (See Table 7.10).

Table 7.10. Static principal parts of the Upper-Imeretian inflectional classes

Inflectional Class	Present 1SG	Future 3PL	Aorist 3PL
IC1-A	v-	PV-en	PV-es
IC1-B	v-	PV-en	PV-es/en
IC1-C	v-	PV-en	PV-en
IC1-D	v-	PV-an	PV-es/en
IC2	v-i	PV-ian/ien	PV-en
IC2/3	v-var	PV-en	PV-es
IC3-A	v-	-an	-an
IC3-B	v-	-en	PV-es/en
IC4-A	v-var	-an	-en
IC4-B	v-	-ian	-en
IC4-C	m-	-at	/
IC4-D	m-a	-at	/
IC4-E	m-s	-at	-at

The whole exponent paradigm can be deduced from the exponents of 1SG PRESENT, 3PL FUTURE, and 3PL AORIST.

Secondly, under the dynamic principal-part scheme, the MS sets and the number of MS sets used to identify the principal parts vary from one inflection class to another. According to Finkel and Stump (2007: 4), the dynamic principal-part scheme turns out to be more parsimonious than the static scheme. In the instance of Upper Imeretian, the dynamic conception of principal parts only requires one or two MS sets to identify principal parts, unlike the static conception of principal parts that always requires three MS sets for every inflectional class. One of multiple dynamic principal-part analyses is shown in Table 7.11, in which the principal parts of each inflection class are shaded.

As indicated in Table 7.11, three inflectional classes (IC1-a, IC1-b, and IC1-c) need two dynamic principal parts to deduce all remaining forms, while the other inflectional classes need only a single dynamic principal part.

Table 7.11. Dynamic principal parts of the Upper-Imeretian inflectional classes

IC	Present		Imperfect	Future	Conditional		Future Subj.	Aorist		Num
	1SG	3PL	3SG	3PL	1SG	3SG	1SG	1SG	3PL	
IC1-A	v-	-en	-da	PV-en	PVv-di	PV-da	PVv-de	PVv-e	PV-es	2
IC1-B	v-	-en	-da	PV-en	PVv-di	PV-da	PVv-de	PVv-i	PV-es/en	2
IC1-C	v-	-en	-da	PV-en	PVv-di	PV-da	PVv-de	PVv-e	PV-en	1
IC1-D	v-	-an	-da	PV-an	PVv-di	PV-da	PVv-de	PVv-i	PV-es/en	1
IC2	v-i	-ian/ien	-oda	PV-ian/ien	PVv-odi	PV-oda	PVv-ode	PVv-e	PV-en	1
IC2/3	v-var	-an	-oda	PV-en	PVv-di	PV-da	PVv-de	PVv-e	PV-es	1
IC3-A	v-	-en	-da	-an	v-di	-da	v-de	-i	-an	1
IC3-B	v-	-en	-des	-en	v-di	-da	v-*di*	PVv-e	PV-es/en	1
IC4-A	v-var	-an	/	-an	v-odi	-oda	v-ode	v-i	-en	1
IC4-B	v-	-ian	/	-ian	v-oi	-oda	v-ode	v-i	-en	1
IC4-C	m-	-t	-(d)a	-at	m-oda	-oda	m-odes	/	/	1
IC4-D	m-a	-at	-oda	-at	m-oda	-oda	m-odes	/	/	1
IC4-E	m-s	-t	-da	-at	m-oda	-oda	m-odes	m-a	-at	1

Requiring no more than two MS sets to identify principal parts, the dynamic principal-part scheme turns out to be more parsimonious than the static scheme.

7.4. Diasystemic Modelling of the Western Georgian Dialects

I have demonstrated in section 3 the four stem-distribution patterns in the realm of RSC, which turn out to be a stable constant in the western Georgian dialects, and I have mentioned several features in the realm of RE such as the preverbation, the reanalysis of 1st person plural forms, and the inflectional thematic suffix, which trigger variations of exponence paradigms throughout the western Georgian dialects. In this section, convergence and divergence in the diasystem of the western Georgian dialects will be described in a more systematic manner. The main morphophonological processes operating in the dynamic relations of diasystem are depicted in the below figure (Figure 7.6).

Figure 7.6. Implicational graph: dynamic relations of the diasystem of western Georgian dialects

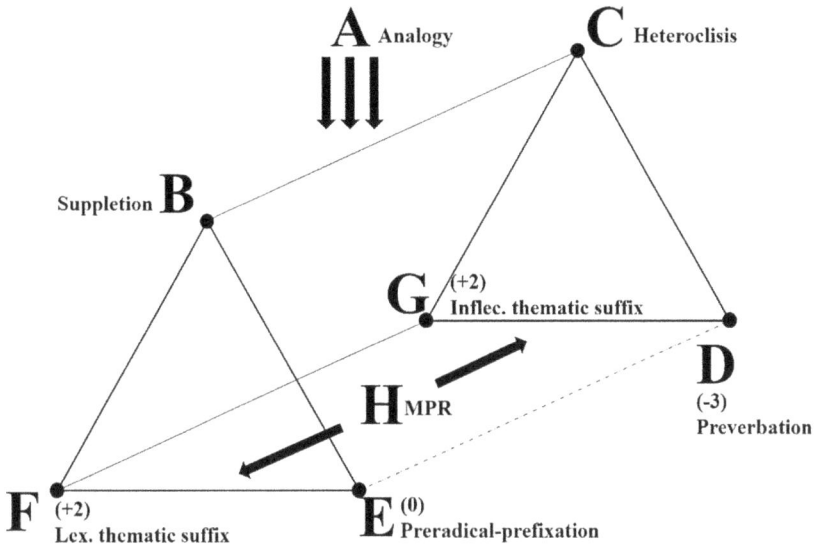

The letters A – H represent the morphophonological processes that operate in the diasystem of western Georgian dialects.

As depicted in Figure 7.6, there are two triangles: B – E – F and C – D – G. On the one hand, the triangle B – E – F represents the morphophonological processes which especially operate in the realm of stem. This does not mean that the robustness of stem distributions in the diasystem might be eroded by the application of these morphophonological processes. In fact, the processes of the triangle B – E – F only affect stems' forms on the morphophonological level, but never modifies stem distributions on the paradigmatic level. In other words, the stem-distribution patterns and the fourfold division of inflection classes are not affected by these processes and remain stable throughout the diasystem. Hence the convergence in the diasystem of the western Georgian dialects. On the other hand, the triangle C – D – G represents the morphophonological processes which generally operate in the realm of exponents. These processes, namely *heteroclisis, preverbation*, and *inflectional thematic suffix*, affect not only exponents' forms on the morphophonological level, but also exponent paradigms: some paradigms are syncretised (heteroclisis), some paradigms are partially changed (preverbation), and other paradigms become especially sensitive to an MS set (inflectional thematic suffix). All these processes trigger the subdivision or variation of exponent paradigms, namely, the divergence of exponent paradigms throughout the diasystem of the western Georgian dialects.

Table 7.12. Dynamic relations of the diasystem of western Georgian dialects

INDEX	Morphophonological Process	Slot(s) involved	Example
A	Analogy	Stem and exponents	**Adjarian** IC2 MAL ("to hide"): Aor1sg *de=vmalevi*, Aor2sg *de=ymalevi*, Aor3sg *de=ymala* vs. Prf1sg *da=vmalul=var*, Prf2sg *da=malul=xar*, Prf3sg *da=malul=a*
B	Suppletion	Stem	**Gurian** AR ("to walk"): *ar* in Present Subseries and Series II~III, Future Subseries *vl* vs. **Adjarian** AR ("to walk"): *ar* in Series I~III
C	Heteroclisis	Exponents	**Lower Imeretian** IC3 PIKR ("to think"): Prs1sg *pikrob=var* > IC2/4 vs. **Gurian** IC3 PIKR ("to think") Prs1sg *v-pikrav*
D	Preverbation	-3	**Lower Imeretian** IC4 ND ("to want"): -PV in Series I~III vs. **Taoan** IC4 ND ("to want"): +PV in Future Subseries, Series II, and Series III
E	Preradical-prefixation	0	**Taoan** IC1 CH'AM ("to eat"): *sch'am* in Series I and II, *ch'am* in Series III vs **Gurian** IC1 CH'AM ("to eat"): *ch'am* in Series I~III
F	Shift of lexical thematic suffixes	+2	**Lower Imeretian** IC4 DG ("to stand"): Fut3sg *idg-om-il-eb-a* vs. **Gurian** IC4 DG ("to stand"): Fut3sg *idg-eb-a*
G	Inflectional thematic suffixation	+2	**Taoan** IC1 CH'AM: Aor1sg *v-sch'am-ev-i*, Aor2sg *sch'am-ev-i*, Aor3sg *sch'am-a* vs. **Gurian** IC1 CH'AM: Aor1sg *v-ch'am-e*, Aor2sg *ch'am-e*, Aor3sg *ch'am-a*
H	Morphophonological Rules: Assimilation/dilation and Dissimilation	Stem and exponents	Assimilation/dilation: **Taoan** IC1 SU ("to drink"): Fut1sg *she=vsuam*, Fut2sg *she=suam*, Fut3sg *she=suams* vs. Prf1sg *shi=mismia*, Prf2sg *shi=gismia*, Prf3sg *shu=usmia* Dissimilation: **Lower Imeretian** IC4 D ("to sit"): Prf3pl *m dar=alien* vs. Prs3pl *dam=arien*
*	Isoglossic Rules	Stem and exponents	**Upper Imeretian** IC3 K'REP ("to pluck"): Prs2sg *k'ripam* vs. **Lower Imeretian** IC3 K'REP ("to pluck"): Prs2sg *k'ripav*;

This table specifies the slot(s) involved in each of the morphophonological processes presented in Figure 7.6 and gives illustrative examples.

In the rest of this section, I will explain the morphophonological processes respectively, with the help of illustrative examples in the Table 7.12.

In Table 7.12, the morphophonological processes that operate in diasystemic dynamics are outlined. **Analogy**, which affects the realm of stem as well as the realm of exponents, comprises all phenomena about "the 'type-changing' of a stem [or an exponent] or the fusion of two types" (Léonard, 2020: 115, translated by the author of the present paper). For example, in the realm of RE, the inflectional forms of the Adjarian verb MAL ("to hide") have the proclitic preverb *da=* in aorist. Regarding the 2nd person and 3rd person forms, since the preverb *da=* (slot -3) precedes the version vowel *i-* (slot -2), *da=i-* forms a single syllable and becomes *de=y-* due to the morphophonological rule of assimilation. As to 1st person forms, although the preverb *da=* precede a consonant, *i.e.*, the nominal prefix *v-* (slot -2), and does not satisfy the condition for the application of the morphophonological rule of assimilation, it is replaced by *de=* by analogy with the 2nd and 3rd person forms of aorist. Moreover, it seems that the above-mentioned reanalysis of 1st person plural exponents of oblique agreement in Taoan is also produced by analogy with the 2nd and 3rd person plural forms.

Within the triangle B – E – F, **suppletion**, indexed by "B," could involve all slots in the realm of stem. Then, the **preradical prefixation** (E) affects slot 0, that is, the verb root. In Taoan and Adjarian, the verb roots of some lexemes are prefixed by fricatives like *s-* or *h-* in Series II or/and Series III, by contrast with their cognate in other dialects. The **shift of lexical thematic suffixes** (F) affects slot +2. For example, the Series-I stem of the Taoan verb TS'ER ("to write") comprises the lexical thematic suffix *-av* (X = *sts'er-av*), while its cognate form in Standard Georgian has no lexical thematic suffix (X = *ts'er*). Moreover, the stem of the Gurian verb DG ("to stand") in Future Subseries comprises a single lexical thematic suffix *-eb* (X = *dg-eb*), while its cognate form in Lower Imeretian exhibits a recursiveness of thematic suffixation (X = *dg-om-il-eb*). However, it is noteworthy that all these processes generally affect all stems of a given Series, so that the stem distributions remain *de facto* unchanged.

As to the triangle C – D – G, *sensu stricto*, **heteroclisis** (C) refers to split exponence paradigms which exhibit properties of distinct inflection classes. The Gurian medio-active verb PIKR belongs to IC3, and its exponent of 1st person singular in present indicative is *v-*. By contrast, its cognate in Lower Imeretian triggers auxiliary verb in present indicative, which is a property of IC2 or IC4 verbs. In addition, it should be noted that heteroclisis can coexist with suppletion (*cf.* Stump, 2016: 184-188). Then, diasystemic differences could also be triggered by the process of **preverbation** (D) which affects the slots -3. As already indicated in Table 7.12, inflectional preverbs are absent in the inflection of the Lower-Imeretian verb ND ("to want"), while for its Taoan cognate, the preverb *ma-* has an inflectional value: *ma-* is absent in Present Subseries but present in all other Series. Moreover, the process of **inflectional thematic suffixation** (G), which is closely linked to SAP traits, plays an important role in the diasystem of the western Georgian dialects. As already mentioned in section 3, for a group of transitive verbs in Taoan (in Series II), Adjarian (in Series II) and Gurian (in Series I), the +SAP value triggers the introduction of inflection thematic suffixes. All these processes trigger the multiple variations of exponent paradigms throughout the diasystem.

Finally, the **Morphophonological Rules** operate between the realm of stem (triangle B – E – F) and the realm of exponents (triangle C – D – G). Firstly, **assimilation/dilation** turns out to be a source of divergence in the diasystem. Assimilation/dilation has a strong impact on Adjarian and Taoan. As shown in the example in Table 7.12, the vowels of preverbs are completely assimilated by the version vowel of stem. However, relatively, assimilation/dilation has little impact on dialects such as Gurian. In comparison with assimilation/dilation, **dissimilation** seems to be relatively trivial. As shown in the example in Table 7.12, in Lower Imeretian, the enclitic copula ⟨*arien*⟩ becomes ⟨*alien*⟩ because of the final consonant of the stem.

Besides, I also mentioned the **Isoglossic Rules** (IR) in Table 7.12, but it should be noted that IR plays a peripherical role in the dynamic relations of diasystem.

7.5. Conclusion and Further Prospects

To reply the questions related to the convergence and divergence of the western Georgian dialects asked in section 1, the present paper has first demonstrated in section 3 the clear-cut and robust fourfold division of verbal inflection by means of the visualisation of stem distributions. While the multilevel interaction of inflection system and the polyfunctionality of morphemes like preverbs, version markers, and thematic suffixes could hinder the analyses of the structural complexity in the syntagmatic dimension, the analyses based on the paradigmatic dimension provide an alternative point of view that allows the perception of the whole system. In section 3, the analyses of stem-distribution patterns and exponence patterns prove that the paradigm-based approach and the holistic point of view suggested by PFM are efficient to model and visualise the inflection classes in the western Georgian dialects. Meanwhile, the analyses in section 3 prove that, as also indicated by Makharoblidze and Léonard (2020), even though the traditional "Screeves-Series" model and the verb template elaborated by Georgian grammarians seem to be initially based on an incremental and morpheme-based approach, they are *de facto* plausibly compatible with realisational and paradigm-based models such as the PFM model. Therefore, in section 4, the implicational graph that depicts the dynamics of diasystemic variation is also based on the Georgian verb template. By revealing eight morphophonological processes that operate in the inflection system of diasystem, the present paper tried to highlight the underlying simplex features of the complex structure.

The corpus of the present paper is quantitively and qualitatively limited and does not comprise the bi-personal (sagittal) conjugation of IC1 and IC3 verbs.

Besides, this paper has not treated the principal-part properties of each dialect in terms of typological comparison (*cf.* Finkel and Stump, 2007, 2009). Further research should be based on more complete corpora and consider how the principal-part properties of Georgian dialects operate in the dynamic relations of diasystem.

Acknowledgement

I would like to express my sincere gratitude to Prof. Jean Léo Léonard for his precious and inspiring advice. And I am also grateful to Enos Lam who proofread this paper.

Further reading:

Makharoblidze, Tamar. 2012. *The Georgian Verb.* Lincom Studies in Caucasian Linguistics, 20. München: Lincom Europa.

Léonard, Jean Léo. 2020. "Esquisse de Modélisation Diasystémique de la Conjugaison Slovène," *Verbum XLII*, 2020 (1-2). p.85-129

References

Bonami, Olivier, and Gregory Stump. 2016. "Paradigm Function Morphology," In Andrew Hippisley and Gregory Stump (eds.), *Cambridge Handbook of Morphology.* Cambridge: Cambridge University Press. p. 449-481.

Chokharadze, M., Shota Rodinadze, and Natia Abashidze, N. 2018. "Taoan Dialect of Georgian Language and Linguistic Space of Collective Memory in the Chorokhi Basin," *Journal of Arts and Humanities, 7 (10).* p. 65-72.

Dahl, Östen. 2004. *The Growth and Maintenance of Linguistic Complexity.* John Benjamins Publishing. Cited in Picard (2019: 12).

Finkel, Raphael, and Gregory Stump. 2007. "Principal parts and morphological typology," *Morphology*, 17. p. 39-75.

—. 2009. "Principal parts and degrees of paradigmatic transparency," In James P. Blevins and Juliette Blevins (eds.), *Analogy in grammar: Form and acquisition.* Oxford: Oxford University Press. p. 13-53.

Guérin, Maximilien, Louise Esher, Jean-Léo Léonard, and Sylvain Loiseau. 2019. "Modélisation diasystémique de la conjugaison dans le domaine du Croissant (gallo-roman) : classes flexionnelles, espaces thématiques et exponence." Study Day "Modélisation diasystémique et typologie," Apr 2019, Paris, France.

Harris, Alice. 1981. *Georgian Syntax: A Study in Relational Grammar.* Cambridge: Cambridge University Press.

—. 1991. *The Indigenous languages of the Caucasus, 1: The Kartvelian languages.* Caravan Books.

Léonard, Jean Léo, and Tamar Makharoblidze. 2021. "Disentangling Structural Complexity in a (Challenging) Inflectional System: The Georgian Verb." Unpublished manuscript.

Makharoblidze, Tamar. 2012. "On the Category of Version," *Kadmosi, 4*. Tbilisi: Ilia State University. p. 154-213.

—. 2018. "On Georgian Preverbs," *Open Linguistics, 4 (1)*. p. 163-183. https://doi.org/10.1515/opli-2018-0009.

New Georgian Language Vol. 4 – Morphology of Dialects: Paradigms. Tbilisi: Ivane Javakhishvili Tbilisi State University Arnold Chikobava Institute of Linguistics. [In Georgian].

Picard, Flore. 2019. "Morphologie flexionnelle verbale des langues sames : modélisation de la complexité diasystémique d'un système flexionnel." Doctoral dissertation. Paris: Université Sorbonne Université – Ecole doctorale 5.

Stump, Gregory. 2016. *Inflectional Paradigms: Content and Form at the Syntax-Morphology Interface*, Cambridge: Cambridge University Press.

Tran Ngoc, Anaïs. 2019. "La flexion verbale du géorgien et du svane, une analyse des catégorisations grammaticales des langues kartvéliennes." Master's dissertation. Paris: Sorbonne Université.

—. 2020. "Application d'une modélisation diasystémique à la conjugaison svane (kartvélien): catégorisation et visualisation," *Verbum XLII*. Manuscript submitted for publication.

Tuite, Kevin. 1998. *Kartvelian Morphosyntax: Number agreement and morphosyntactic orientation in the South Caucasian languages*, Lincom Studies in Caucasian Linguistics, 12. München: Lincom Europa.

Chapter 8

Correlatives and Other Relatives in Georgian

Léa Nash

Université Paris 8/CNRS, France

Abstract

This work presents a unified analysis of two types of correlatives in Georgian, with and without an internal head in the left-peripheral clause RC. I argue that in both cases, RC is a nominal constituent, namely an internally-headed relative clause. The internal head is overt in one type and silent in the other. These internally-headed relatives are generated as left-peripheral topics and are resumed by a demonstrative phrase in the matrix clause. The analysis brings support to uniformity approaches to correlativisation whereby correlatives do not result from a distinct way of relative clause composition that is not already employed for forming other relative types in a language. Specifically, it confirms Cinque's (2009, 2020) thesis according to which correlatives are instances of relative clause left-dislocation. I further show that prenominal relative clauses in Georgian are also configurations where an internally headed relative adjoins to a demonstrative phrase. This reduces four relativisation strategies attested in Georgian to two: postnominal relatives with external head, and all other types of relatives—prenominal, head-internal, correlative—with internal head. The two syntactic operations that underlie all these constructions, externalisation of head in overt syntax vs. its externalisation at the logical form, have interpretative consequences: postnominal relatives are set restrictive, whereas all other relative clauses are maximalising.

Keywords: relative clauses, correlatives, internally headed relatives, demonstrative phrase, demonstrative requirement, prenominal relative clauses, postnominal relative clauses, reconstruction, island (constraints), left-dislocation, left-dislocated, headless relatives

***

8.1. General Introduction

This chapter presents an analysis of a relativisation strategy in Georgian where (i) the relative clause precedes its head, and (ii) these two elements are not adjacent. This type of relative clauses is known in typological studies as a *correlative construction*, widely attested in the Indo-Aryan language family and in a great variety of languages (cf. Lipták 2009 for an overview). The term describes configurations in (1) where: (i) the clause RC and the nominal expression it modifies, the correlate coNP, are not adjacent; (ii) RC precedes coNP and is positioned in the left periphery of the sentence; (iii) RC contains a relative pronoun, (iv) coNP is a demonstrative (pro)nominal. [1]

(1) [RC Relative Clause] [TP … [coNPcorrelate NP]…]

Georgian has two relative constructions, extensively used in the spoken register, where two parts of a relative clause are discontinuous. I will refer to underlined RCs in (2-3) as headless-RC and head-internal-RC respectively, as their only difference is the presence of head in (3). The coNP is in italics in each sentence: the demonstrative can be optionally combined with noun.[2]

(2) [ketos   rom   daek'arga   [ninom   *is*   *(c'igni)*   ezoši'   ip'ova
     Keto.D   that   lost   Nino.E   Dem   book.N   yard.in   found
     "Nino found the book that Keto lost"
     Lit. "that Keto lost, Nino found that book"

(3) [ketos   rom   c'igni   daek'arga] ninom   *is*   *(c'igni)*   ezoši   ip'ova
     Keto.D   that   book.N   lost   Nino.E   Dem   book.N   yard.in   found
     "Nino found the book that Keto lost"
     Lit. "the book that Keto lost, Nino found that book"

The constructions in (2-3) do not have all the properties commonly attributed to correlatives cross-linguistically. Importantly, RCs in (2) or (3) do not contain a relative pronoun or a determiner, and RC in (2) does not have a head. However, coNP must be a demonstrative NP in (2-3), and this demonstrative requirement constitutes the hallmark of correlative constructions. (cf. Srivastav 1991)

(4) * [ketos   rom   (c'igni)   daek'arga] ninom   *c'igni/erti c'igni*   ezoši   ip'ova
       Keto.D   that   book.N   lost   Nino.E   book.N/onebook.N   yard.in   found
       "Nino found the/one book that Keto lost"

---

[1] Abbreviations: 1,2,3=1st,2nd,3rdperson; adv=adverbial; ACC=accusative; cop=copula; CP=embedded clause; .D=dative; D=determiner; Dem=demonstrative; DP=nominal (phrase); E=ergative; GEN=genitive; N=nominative; Q=quantifier; pl=plural; rel=relative marker; sg=singular; TP=sentence.

[2] When the distal demonstrative is not combined with a noun, it functions as a 3rd person pronoun. (cf. Nash 2020).

Downing (1973) states that correlatives are found in 'loose' OV languages, or languages with free word order, and Georgian easily fits this description. Moreover, it has been often observed in typological surveys of relative clauses that correlative strategy is never the only way to construe a relative clause in a language, (Keenan 1985). Indeed, besides the constructions in (2-3), three types of relative clauses are possible in Georgian: postnominal relatives, prenominal relatives and internally headed relatives. Therefore, constructions in (2-3), albeit typologically unusual, can be taken to illustrate that correlative constructions also make part of Georgian grammar. In short, all four universally attested relative clauses are attested in Georgian: postnominal, prenominal, internally headed and correlative.

As correlatives generally co-exist with another relative type in a language, most studies aim to elucidate whether a derivational link can be established between the two. Uniformity approaches advocate for structural parallelism between correlatives and other relatives, whereas non-uniformity approaches support the idea that correlatives are construed by a special strategy that is not used in relative clause formation in the language. The following questions are addressed by proponents of each approach:

- What constituent is RC in (1)? Is it a relative clause CP of the same kind found in externally headed relative clauses, that is not adjacent to the head?

- What is the source of RC in (1)? Is it generated in its surface position in the left periphery, or is it moved from the matrix clause, and specifically from coNP?

- What is the structural and semantic relation between RC and coNP?

Transposing these questions to Georgian correlatives in (2-3), it is also important to establish whether RC is the same constituent in both constructions, whether it has the same structural origin in (2-3), and whether RC and coNP in both cases stand in the same relation. In short, we need to know not only how (2) and (3) are construed but also what properties set them apart.

I argue in this work for a unified analysis of correlatives in (2) and (3). In both constructions, RC is a nominal constituent, and so is the coNP. In both constructions, RC is a relative clause without external head, i.e. it is an internally headed relative clause. The internal head is overt in RC in (3) and silent in RC in (2). Therefore, their purely descriptive labels as *headless* and *head-internal* RCs are structurally misleading,— both are internally headed. RC is generated in its surface position as an adjunct in the left periphery of the matrix clause. The coNP in each configuration is a (pro)nominal bound by its antecedent RC. This relation between RC and coNP is different from standard intersection semantic link that exists between the head and the relative clause CP in postnominal relatives, confirming that (2-3) are instances of correlativisation, where RC behaves as a generalized quantifier. (Srivastav 1991, Grosu and Landman 1998). But RC in (2) with silent head and RC in (3) with overt head do not entertain the same structural relation with coNP. While coNP in (3) can be deeply embedded and separated by sentential boudaries (islands) from RC, locality restrictions hold for RC and coNP in (2). This difference is due to the fact that headless RC contains a silent internal head which is too deficient to externalise at LF, unlike its overt counterpart in head-internal RCs. Therefore RC in (2) can only be locally licensed by an external nominal, the coNP, that moves out of the matrix clause at LF.

The present analysis promotes the uniformity approach to correlativisation, and specifically lends support to Cinque's (2009, 2020) thesis according to which correlatives are instances of relative clause left-dislocation. Georgian correlatives result from topicalisation of internally headed relative clauses resumed by a demonstrative phrase. I further show that prenominal relative clauses in Georgian are also configurations where an internally headed relative adjoins to a demonstrative phrase. This reduces Georgian relativisation strategies to two: postnominal relatives with external head, and all other types of relatives—prenominal, internally-headed, correlative—with internal head. The two syntactic operations, externalisation of head in overt syntax or at the logical form, have interpretative consequences: postnominal relatives are set restrictive, all other relatives are maximalising.

Before the roadmap, some precisions about terminology on relative clauses are in order. I use the term relative(s) and relative clause(s) to refer to nominal constituents modified by an embedded clause. Relative clause CP refers to the embedded clause, and (relative) head refers to the noun or noun phrase that the relative clause CP is composed with.

(5) [$_{DP}$relative (clause) the [$_{NP}$head interesting book] [$_{CP}$relative clause CP that a friend translated]]

The paper is organised as follows. In Section 8.2, I present four types of relative clauses in Georgian, and argue that only postnominal relatives involve overt head-externalisation. While all four types contain the same relative clause CP, *rom*-clause does not flesh out the same constituent in each type: in postnominal relatives, *rom*-clause is a CP, whereas in all other relative types it is a DP with null external nominal structure that embeds CP, or in other words, it is an internally headed relative. Section 8.3 investigates the structural relation between RC and coNP in correlatives. It is shown that RCs do not move from the matrix clause. Moreover, RC and coNP are not subject to same locality restrictions in (2) and (3). This asymmetry is attributed to the deficient nature of the silent NP head in headless RC. Section 8.4 concludes the study.

8.2. Four Relativisation Strategies in Georgian

All four universally attested relativisation strategies exist in Georgian: postnominal, prenominal, internally headed (circomnominal) and correlative. Postnominal relatives are used in written Georgian, while other types of relatives are characteristic of spoken register. The general subordinating complementizer *rom* is employed in every type of relative clauses, but one type of postnominal relatives is based on relative pronouns. The main focus of this work are *rom* based relatives, as correlatives in (2-3) involve this subordinator.[3]

8.2.1. Postnominal Relative Clauses

There are two types of postnominal relative clauses in Georgian, roughly parallel to *that-* and *wh-*relatives in English.[4] The *wh-*strategy is also employed in free relatives in Georgian, not discussed in this work, while *that-*strategy underlies correlatives, prenominal and internally headed relatives too.

8.2.1.1. *Romel-*Relatives

This is a "standard" strategy, and the oldest. The relative clause CP follows the head noun and contains the relative determiner/pronoun, often *romel* "which," as its initial element.[5] Georgian relative pronouns are constituted of a *wh-*element (used in interrogatives) and the relative suffix –*c*, which also

---

[3] Correlatives with relative pronouns are also possible in Georgian, (i), where RC is formally identical to free relatives. They are not studied in this work.

(i) a. romeli c'igni-c   ginda,   is (c'igni)   iq'ide
     which book.N-rel 2.want, Dem book.N 2.buy
     "Which(ever) book you want, buy that book"

  b. ra-c   viq'ide,   ketis   is   gavat'ane
     what.N-rel 1.bought Keti.D Dem 1.make.take
     "What I bought, I made Keti take it"

[4] Boeder (2005, 71) regards *wh-*relatives to be the only option of relativization in literary Georgian. *That-*strategy is more characteristic of spoken register (cf. Hewitt 1995, 606). On the scale from mostly spoken strategies of relativisation to mostly written ones, correlatives would appear on the leftmost end, followed by externally headed *that-* relatives, and *wh-*relatives on the rightmost end.

[5] The relative determiner/pronoun *romel* is morphologically related to the general subordinator *rom*: the extra morpheme -*el-* is an adjectivizer and could roughly express the sense of kind, as in *p'ariz-el* 'Paris-ian'. The diachronic evidence points to the derivation of *rom* from *romel*, (Harris 1993). This resonates with Kayne's (2010) analysis of subordinator *that* in English as a reanalysed relative pronoun.

functions as a focalising additive marker 'also.'[6] -*c* is optional at the end of the relative phrase if the genitive relative pronoun is followed by independent noun phrase or postposition, (6b, 7b).

(6) a. romel-i-c
    which-N-rel
    'which'

  b. romlis   gamo-(c)
    which.GEN cause-rel
    'for which, because of which'

(7) a. *kalaki* [romeli-c   p'oet'ma daatvaliera] lamazia
    city.N which.N-rel poet.E   visited   beautiful.is
    "(A/The) city which the poet visited is beautiful"

  b. momc'ons *xe*   [romlis   kveš-(ac) bavšvebi sxedan]
    1.like   tree.N which.GEN under-rel children.N sit
    "I like (a/the) tree under which (the) children are sitting"

Romel-relative clause CPs can extrapose.

(8) me *kali*   gavicani [romeli-c   londonši   cxovrobs]
    I   woman.N met   which.N-rel London.in lives
    "I met a/the woman who lives in London"

8.2.1.2. *Rom*-Relatives

Compared to *romel*-relatives, *rom*-relatives are more "colloquial" where *rom* is often reduced to *ro-*. The complementizer *rom* 'that,' which also functions as a standard subordinator in finite clauses, cannot be the initial constituent in the CP that follows the head. It can be placed anywhere except the initial position, and must precede the verb.

(9) *kalaki* [(*rom) p'oet'ma (rom) gušin (rom) daatvaliera (*rom)] lamazia
    city.N (that) poet.E   yesterday visited   beautiful.is
    "A/The city that the poet visited this morning is beautiful"

The relative clause CP in *rom*-relatives, henceforth referred as *rom*-clause, can be extraposed. In general, regardless of the relativisation strategy, the extraposition of the relative clause CP is obligatory if the relative head-noun is

---

[6] It is tempting to unify the two semantic functions of -*c*, as relativizer and as additive marker. Intuitively, the marker can be considered to link the head inside the relative clause to the external head. Instead of signalling identification between the two, the particle conveys that the external head has an additional function inside the relative clause: a book which Nino likes=a book *which book-also* Nino likes. A more detailed investigation of the particle -*c* awaits further research.

focalised in the preverbal field, (Nash 1995, Skopeteas et al. 2009, Skopeteas and Fanselow 2009, 2010).[7]

(10) vanom   *kali*   dainaxa   [xis   kveš   rom   ijda]
     Vano.E   woman.N   saw   tree.GEN   under   that   sat
     "Vano saw *a/the woman* that was sitting under a tree'

Two main ways to derive postnominal relatives have emerged from the impressive body of research on relative clauses: head-raising and head-matching. According to the head-raising approach, the external NP head is raised from the relative clause CP, (cf. Vergnaud 1974, Kayne 1994). Matching analyses propose that the external head is base-generated outside CP and is matched with the internal deleted/null head, (cf. Chomsky 1965, Sauerland 1998). I adopt here the head-raising analysis for both types of postnominal relative clauses in Georgian, and contend that the relative clause CP contains a gap left by the moved head.

(11) postnominal relatives: [$_{DP}$ D NP [$_{CP}$ *romel-/…rom…..*NP ….]]

8.2.2. Prenominal Relative Clauses

The *rom* relative clause CP can also precede the external head, which must contain a demonstrative (cf. Nash 1995). With respect to the demonstrative requirement, prenominal relative clauses behave like correlatives in (2-3).

(12) a. ketis   [p'oet'ma rom gušin   daatvaliera] *(is)* lamazi   kalaki uq'vars
        Keti.D poet.E   that yesterday visited]   Dem beautiful city.N love
        "Keti loves the beautiful city that the poet visited yesterday"
     b. keti   [xis   kveš rom ijda] *(im) prang kals   icnobs
        Keti.N tree.GEN under that sat   Dem French woman.ACC knows
        "Keti knows the French woman that sat under a tree"

The prenominal relative clause CP and the demonstrative nominal behave as one constituent and can be coordinated, (cf. Bhatt 2003 for same facts in Hindi). Each conjunct is pronounced as one prosodic unit in spite of its phonological heaviness, without a break at the right edge of RC.

(13) [[xis   kveš rom ijda]*is   kali*]   da   [[mak'as rom elap'arak'eba]
     treeGEN under that sat Dem woman.N and   Maka.D that speaks
     is   k'aci]   col-kmari-a
     Dem man.N   wife-husband.N-cop
     "The woman that is sitting under the tree and the man that is speaking to Maka are husband and wife"

---

[7] More generally, postnominal relative clauses under focus can either split, as in (10), or occur after the verb, unsplit.

The prenominal relative clause CP can contain the internal head. Such structures are stylistically marked but well-formed.

(14) [[xis   kveš rom *kali*   ijda *is*   *kali*]   da [mak'as rom *k'aci*
     treeGEN under that woman.N sat Dem woman.N and Maka.D that man.N
     elap'arak'eba] *is*   *k'aci*]   col-kmari-a
     speaks   Dem man.N   wife-husband.N-cop
     "The woman that is sitting under the tree and the man that is speaking to
     Maka are husband and wife"

Concerning their internal structure, it is tempting to analyse prenominal relatives as a mirror image of postnominal relatives in (11), with the relative clause CP preceding the external head. However, *rom*-clause in postnominal relatives cannot contain an internal head.[8]

(15) *miq'vars *(ori)*   *kalaki* [vanom rom kalaki   daatvaliera]
     1.love   two   city.N Vano.E that city.N   visited
     "I love two cities that Vano visited"

In the next section, I present internally headed relatives and argue that prenominal relatives in Georgian are not stricto sensu *prenominal*. What looks like their external head is in fact a demonstrative DP, adjoined to the relative clause. And what looks like the relative clause CP is the relative clause itself. Therefore, prenominal relatives are analysed as nominal constituents where internally headed relative is *adjoined* to demonstrative phrase.

8.2.3. Internally Headed Relatives

*Rom-clause*s with internal head, but not combined with the external head, are also possible in Georgian. They occupy argument positions, which indicates that they are DPs. In (16b), the internally headed relative functions as the object of verb *burn* that can only take DP objects.

---

[8] If the external head in postnominal relatives is preceded by a demonstrative, the relative clause CP with internal head is more acceptable, and even gets better with extraposition. These facts suggest that what looks like extraposition in (ii) may very well be a right-field adjunction of the head-internal RC in (3) to the matrix clause.

(i) ??me miq'vars *is*   *kalaki* [vanom rom kalaki   daatvaliera]
    I   1.love   Dem city.N Vano.E that city.N   visited

(ii) ?me *is kalaki*   miq'vars [venom   rom   kalaki   daatvaliera]
     I   Dem city.N 1.love   Vano.E that   city.N   visited
     "I love that city that Vano visited"

(16) a. [ketom rom *gogo* gaicno] universit'et'ši mušaobs
Keto.E that girl.N met   university.in works
"The girl that Keto met works at the university"

b. vanom dac'va [ketom rom *c'igni* ip'ova]
Vano.E burnt Keto.E that book.N found
"Vano burnt a/the book that Keto found"

Internally headed relatives can coordinate between them, and with a simple nominal, which further confirms that these relative clauses are DPs.

(17) [ketim rom *gogo* gaicno], [ninos *k'aci* rom elap'arak'eba], da *tkveni*
Keti.E that girl.N met   Nino.D man.N that talks   and your
ekimi amxanagoben
doctor.N befriend
"A/The girl that Keti met, a/the man that is talking to Nino, and your doctor are friends"

Internally headed relatives can be left-dislocated in a sentence. In (18a-b), the initial relative functions as a topic, prosodically separated from the main clause. In general, internally headed relatives make good topics that (re)introduce a new referent into the current discourse, (18b)

(18) a. [ketim rom *gogo* gaicno], vanos egona   rom tkven gest'umrebodat
Keti.E that girl.N met   Vano.D believed that you 2.would.visit
"A/The girl that Keti met, Vano believed that she would pay you a visit"

b. moedanze *xe*   roa]   asi   c'lis uk'an q'opila darguli
square.on tree.N that.cop hundred year.G ago   has.been planted
"A tree that there is at the square, it was apparently planted 100 years ago"

Internally headed relatives clearly behave as nominal constituents in Georgian, in spite of the absence of an external head. Cole (1987) argues that this relative type contains a phonologically silent external nominal head that functions as a null anaphor. The internal head must abstractly move out of the clause at LF and adjoin to the null anaphor for proper binding. For Williamson (1987), internally headed relatives are DPs, where the internal noun must covertly raise to the edge of the relative clause CP below D for proper quantification.

Harris (1993, 1994) proposes an interesting account of Georgian internally headed relatives according to which they are diachronically derived from prenominal relatives. The external head has been reanalysed as the internal head due to inverse case-attraction. Namely, instead of the case assigned in the matrix clause, the external NP head is marked with the case of the embedded clause. I adopt Harris' conclusion and contend that internally headed relatives in modern Georgian have been realised from true prenominal relatives, and occur at the present within null nominal functional shell. I remain vague about the detailed architecture of this inaudible shell, and just state that it contains at least the D head, (cf. Borer 2005 for in-depth analysis of nominal functional structure). I assume that D is always initial in Georgian, even in internally headed relatives, which are generally but not exclusively found in head-final languages (de Vries 2002).

How can this conclusion be accommodated with facts presented in Section 8.2.2? Does Georgian have true prenominal relatives with overt external final head along with internally headed relatives with covert external head? The answer to the last question is negative. I contend that what looks like prenominal relatives in the previous section, are not relative clauses with externalised post-CP head, but rather 'big-DP' [$_{DP}$DP^DP] adjoined structures where the internally headed relative is left adjoined to the demonstrative phrase.

(19) a. internally headed relative: [$_{DP}$ D [$_{CP}$..*rom* ..N...]]
     b. prenominal relatives: [$_{DP}$ [$_{DP}$internally headed relative] [$_{DP}$Dem N]]

While the structure in (19b) can be easily adopted for prenominal relatives where *rom*-clause contains internal head as in (14), it is less straightforward for structures like (12). There is no internal head in the clause that precedes Dem N; *rom*-clause in (12) is formally identical to the relative clause CP in postnominal relatives as in (9). In the next section, I argue that this resemblence is misleading: postnominal and prenominal *rom*-clauses have different properties and accordingly must be analysed differently. While postnominal *rom*-clauses are analysed as CPs with a gap, prenominal *rom-clause*s are larger units. They are relative clauses, i.e. nominals, that contain the relative clause CP. If a prenominal *rom* clause does not contain an internal head, it is still analysed as (19a), except one difference: the internal head in such case is there, but it is silent. Therefore, *all* prenominal relatives in Georgian can be viewed as adjunction structures, where the internally headed relative is adjoined to demonstrative phrase. In other words, what superficially looks like their external head is not the head of a relative clause. A necessary step towards this analysis consists in proving the nominal status of *rom*-clauses without an overt internal head.

8.2.3.1. Dual Analysis of *Rom*-Clauses

We have seen that Georgian prenominal relatives can be of two types: the lefthand *rom*-clause is often headless but it can also contain internal head.

(20) a. keti   [[xis   kveš   rom ijda] *im*   *prang*   *kals*]   icnobs
         Keti.N tree.GEN under that sat   Dem French woman.ACC knows
         "Keti knows the French woman that sat under a tree"
     b. keti   [[xis   kveš   rom *kali* ijda]*im*   *prang* kals*]   icnobs
         Keti.N tree.GEN under that sat   Dem French woman.ACC knows
         "Keti knows the French woman that sat under a tree"

In (20b), the lefthand *rom*-clause is identical to an internally headed relative clause. The nominal status of internally headed relatives have been demonstrated in Section 8.2.3: internally headed relatives can coordinate with simple DPs and occupy argument positions. Therefore, the prenominal relative with internally headed relative clause in (20b) can be viewed as a combination of two DPs, as proposed in (19b). On the other hand, the prenominal relative clause in (20a) contains a headless *rom*-clause, which is formally identical to the postnominal relative clause CP in (11). The question is whether the relative in (20a) is closer to (20b) or to a postnominal relative.

One reason why postnominal and prenominal *rom*-clauses cannot be analysed in the same way has been provided by the ill-formedness of (15),— postnominal *rom*-clauses may not contain internal head while the prenominal *rom*-clause can. Moreover, lefthand *rom*-clauses must obey the demonstrative requirement, while postnominal *rom*-clauses do not have to.

(21) a. ketim c'aik'itxa [*ori c'igni*   [<u>vanom rom gadatargmna</u>]]
      Keti.E read   two book.N   Vano.E that   translated

   b. *ketim c'aik'itxa [[<u>vanom rom gadatargmna</u>] *ori   c'igni*]
       Keti.E read   Vano.E that translated   two   book

   c. ketim c'aik'itxa [[<u>vanom rom gadatargmna</u>] *is   ori   c'igni*]
      Keti.E read   Vano.E that translated   Dem two   book
      "Keti read two books that Vano translated"

Prenominal relatives and postnominal relatives hence have distinct properties. This asymmetry can be attributed to the link that exists between the external head and the CP in each case. I analysed postnominal relatives in (11): the head is extracted from *rom*-clause CP and subsequently can be merged with any type of determiner. The same is not true for prenominal relatives. Consider the derivations in (22). If the CP from which the head NP has been previously externalised raises above D, it is unclear why the sequence (22a) *CP-two-women* is ill-formed in (21b). An alterternative scenario in (22b) where CP raises above the externalised NP below D would again yield a never attested *(two)-CP-women* sequence. Therefore, I conjecture that the prenominal *rom*-clause is not a preposed CP.

(22) a. [$_{DP}$[$_{CP}$...*rom*..t$_{NP}$..] D NP [$_{CP}$...*rom*..t$_{NP}$...]]

   b. [$_{DP}$ D [$_{CP}$...*rom*...t$_{NP}$..] NP [$_{CP}$...*rom*..t$_{NP}$...]]

The issue is to determine whether *rom*-clauses without internal head can flesh out another constituent than CP. Bare *rom*-clauses in (23b), unlike internally headed relatives in (23a), cannot occupy argument positions.

(23) a. vanom dac'va [ketom rom   *c'igni*   ip'ova]
      Vano.E burnt Keto.E that book.N found
      "Vano burnt a/the book that Keto found"

b. *vanom dac'va [ketom rom ip'ova]
   Vano.E burnt Keto.E that found
   Intended reading: "Vano burnt (thing/whatever) that Keto found"

However, *rom*-clauses can function as short answers in contexts where a nominal is expected.

(24) Question: ninom *romeli cigni*   unda gadatargmnos?
                Nino.E which book.N must translate
                "Which book must Nino translate?"
   Answer 1: [me rom   davc'ere]   Answer 2: idiot'i
              I   that wrote   idiot.N
              "The one that I wrote" (lit: "that I wrote")   "The Idiot"

They can be members of lists, coordinated with other headless *rom*-clauses or with nominals. In list contexts, the nominal head of the list must be available in the immediate context; ommiting 'three cakes' results in ungrammaticality in (25). The example (25a) shows that *rom*-clauses are interpreted as indefinites, while (25b) indicates that their definite interpretation is also available.

(25) a. st'umrebs *(sami namcxvari) mivartvit: [me rom gamovacxve],
        guests.D three cake.N   1pl.served I   that baked
        [iam rom iq'ida], da pranguli mak'aronebi
        Ia.E that bought and French macarons.N
        "We served three cakes to the guests: 'one' that I baked, 'one' that Nino bought, and French macarons"

   b. st'umrebs *(im otx namcxvridan sami) mivartvit: [me rom gamovacxve],
       guests.D that four cake.from three 1pl.served I   that baked
       [iam rom iq'ida], da pranguli mak'aronebi
       Ia.E   that bought and French macarons.N
       "We served three out of those four cakes to the guests: the one that I baked, the one that Nino bought, and French macarons"

These facts suggest that *rom*-clauses can function as nominals, even if they are too deficient to surface in argument positions. I propose to analyse *rom*-clauses in (24-25) as internally headed relatives where the relative clause CP is embedded in a nominal structure. The CP contains a silent head with the denotation PERSON, THING. (cf. Kayne 2005 on silent heads). In this sense, *rom*-clauses in (24-25) minimally differ from standard internally headed relatives in (19).

The two structures of nominal *rom*-clauses are presented in (26). While the overt internal head in (26b) moves out of the clause at LF to license the null nominal shell, as standardly assumed in the literature on internally headed relatives, the silent head in (26a) is too deficient to licence the external null anaphor in the sense of Cole (1987) or to provide nominal range for D to quantify over, in the sense of Williamson (1987) or Basilico (1996). As Georgian is a language without articles, we can hypothesize that D, which is always null, needs a lexical nominal support, even at LF. For this reason, relatives that contain silent internal heads need to be licensed by other locally present DPs in order to be interpreted as referential nominal expressions. In the case of lists and short answers, this external licenser is in the immediate discourse, and in the case of prenominal relatives, the licenser is the adjoined demonstrative phrase. In this sense, the null head THING/PERSON is akin to Δ_{NP} in elliptical structures.[9]

(26) a. relatives internal-headed by silent noun
   [$_{DP}$ D [$_{CP}$..*rom* ..THING/PERSON...]]

   b. relatives internally headed by overt noun
   [$_{DP}$ D [$_{CP}$..*rom*..N...]]

To conclude, I have shown that bare *rom*-clauses can be analysed as two different constituents: in postnominal relatives, they are relative clause CPs with a gap of externalised head; in prenominal relatives, in lists and as short answers, they are internally headed relatives with relative clause CP embedded in DP. In the latter, *rom*-clauses contain an internal silent head, while in the former, they contain a trace of the externalised overt NP.

(27) a. *rom*-clauses in postnominal relatives
   [$_{CP}$...*rom*...NP...]

   b. *rom*-clauses in prenominal relatives
   [$_{DP}$D [$_{CP}$...*rom*...THING/PERSON..]]

8.2.4. Correlatives

We turn next to the last type of relative clauses, correlatives. (Nash 2002, Foley 2013). Universally, correlatives contain two elements: the clausal element in the left periphery and the demonstrative pro(noun) in the matrix clause. In Georgian correlatives, a specific boundary pause can be detected after the clausal element which is pronounced with a rising pitch. As regards to coNP, it is not isolated or made intonationally salient in the main clause. (Cf. Borise 2020 and sources therein on Georgian prosody).

---

[9] To strengthen the idea that the null head in (26a) is akin to the elided NP, consider (i) where the second relative clause can be "headless" given the salient NP antecedent in the first relative. I am grateful to an anonymous reviewer for providing this test case.

(i) cudat   gvakvs   sakme! [šeša   [vanom ro   dagvit'ova]] ver vnaxe, [*ketom mezobels*
   bad.adv 1pl.have business firewood.N Vano.E that us.left   can't 1.find Keto.E neigbour.D
   ro   gamoartva] k'i mak'os   uk've   dauc'via
   that took.from   yes Mak'o.D already burned
   "Bad news! The fire logs that Vano left us, I couldn't find, whereas [~~those~~ [*that Keto took from the neighbour*]], Mako has apparently already burned!"

In (2-3), we saw that the clausal element, RC, can be a head-internal *rom*-clause, which is an internally headed relative, or a headless *rom*-clause, which can either be analysed as CP in (27a) or as DP in (27b). Correlatives are subject to the demonstrative requirement, which prenominal relatives must obey too. Therefore, we expect headless *rom*-clause in (28) to behave as structures in (27b).

Constructions in (28) are identical to correlatives in (2), as they display key properties attributed to this type of relativisation: RC in the left periphery is discontinuous from the head, coNP, obligatorily spelled out as a demonstrative phrase.[10]

(28) a. [me rom davc'ere] nino   *im*   c'igns   k'itxulobs
        I   that wrote   Nino.N Dem book.ACC reads
        "Nino is reading the book that I wrote"

    b. [xis   kveš rom ijda] vano   *im*   kalze   pikrobda
        tree.GEN under that sat   Vano.N Dem woman.on thought
        "Vano was thinking about the woman that was sitting under the tree"

Left-peripheral RC discontinous from Dem+N can contain the internal head, as shown in (3). We already saw in (18) that an internally headed relative can be placed in the left periphery. In the same position, it can also be associated with

---

[10]*Rom*-clauses must contain an overt pronoun if the elided/silent head in the relative clause CP functions as a complement of P or is marked with oblique case. If the elided/silent head is a dative argument in the embedded clause, the dative pronoun is optional. (cf. Hewitt 1995:606-608). This strategy to insert an overt pronoun to salvage a derivation is common in languages which build relative clauses without relative pronouns. (cf. Shlonsky 1992 on Hebrew resumptive pronouns).

(i) a. [me rom *imas-tan* vmušaob] ninos   *is gogo*   uq'vars
        I   that 3sg.D.-with 1.work   Nino.D Dem girl.N loves
        "Nino loves the girl I work with", (lit:"That I work with-her, Nino loves that girl"

    b. [me rom *(?imas)* velap'arak'ebodi] ninos   *is gogo*   uq'vars
        I   that 3sg.D   spoke   Nino.D Dem girl.N loves
        "Nino likes the girl that I was speaking to" (lit:"That I was speaking to, Nino loves that girl")

This situation is not unique to correlatives. Postnominal and prenominal *rom*-clauses are subject to the same resumptive pronoun strategy.

(ii) a. gavicani *erti* *msaxiobi* [q'vela   rom *imaze* ocnebobs]
         1.me   one   actor.N   everyone.N that 3sg.on dreams

    b. gavicani [q'vela   rom *imaze* ocnebobs] *is*   *msaxiobi*
         1.met   everyone.N that 3sg.on dreams   Dem   actor.N
        "I met a/that actor that everyone is dreaming about (her)"

coNP, which yields a correlative configuration. The minimal pair in (29) summarizes this optionality; only (29a) is a correlative.[11]

(29) a. [me rom *c'igni*   davc'ere] ninom *is*   *c'igni*   unda gadatargmnos
        I   that book.N wrote   Nino Dem book.N must translate
        "A/The book that I wrote, Nino must translate that book"

    b. [me rom *c'igni*   davc'ere] ninom unda gadatargmnos
        I   that book.N wrote   Nino.E must translate
        "The book that I wrote, Nino must translate"

Internally headed relatives in (29) function as topics, resumed or not. In other words, a structure where an internally headed relative in the left-periphery is resumed by a nominal in the matrix conforms to the definition of a correlative construction. Notice that resuming by a demonstrative phrase is not limited to topicalized relative clauses but is also frequent with simple DP topics, as in (30b).[12]

(30) a. [me rom vak'cina   davic'une], rusetši   turme   q'velas   mart'o
        I   that vaccin.N snubbed   Russia.in apparently everyone.D only
        im   *vak'cinas*   uk'eteben
        Dem vaccine.ACC do
        "The vaccine I snubbed, apparently in Russia they only inject that vaccine to everyone"

    b. sp'ut'nik'i, rusetši   turme   qvelas   mart'o *im vak'cinas*
        Sputnik.N Russia.in apparently everyone.D only   Dem vaccine.ACC
        uk'eteben
        do
        "Sputnik, apparently in Russia they only inject that vaccine to everyone"

We conclude that correlatives with head-internal RCs are structures which involve a relative clause in the left periphery, resumed by a demonstrative phrase in the matrix.

---

[11] The sentences in (29) are not used in the same discourse context. (29a) is a felicitous answer to the question where coNP is under narrow focus: *Which book must Nino translate?* The internal head in (29b) cannot function as the focus of the main clause.

[12] An anonymous reviewer inquires whether the demonstrative used in coNPs must be distal, as all the examples in this article suggest. Georgian distinguishes three types of demonstratives: proximal *es/eg*, distal but close to the discourse situation or to the interlocuter *mag*, distal *is*. While *mag* can be encountered in the same contexts as in (30), the proximal *es/eg* may not. This asymmetry is due to the fact that the deictic slot of the distal demonstrative can be identified and bound by the discourse salient topic, while the deictic component of the proximal demonstrative is bound by the situation operator of type *here*. (cf. Elbourne 2013)

(31) correlatives with head-internal RC: [DP D [CP ... rom....N...]] [TP .....[DP Dem N]....]

The question is whether the same analysis can be extended to correlatives with headless RCs. For this to be possible, we must show that *rom*-clause RC is similar to *rom*-clause in prenominal relative clauses and not to *rom*-clause in postnominal relative clauses.

While it is easy to posit for Georgian that extraposition in relative clauses is the result of right-hand movement of *rom*-clause CP from postnominal relatives, the same type of movement is difficult to maintain for *rom*-clauses found in correlatives.

The external head in postnominal relatives has the same properties as the external head in extraposition configurations: it does not have to be preceded by determiners and *may* be preceded by a demonstrative or by a quantifier.

(32) a. vano   icnobs *gogos/   or gogos/   im gogos   [ias rom mosc'ons]
        Vano.N knows girl.ACC/ two girl.ACC/ Dem girl.ACC Ia.D that like

   b. vano   *gogos/   or gogos/   im gogos   icnobs [ias   rom
      Vano.N girl.ACC/ two girl.ACC/ Dem girl.ACC knows Ia.D   that
      mosc'ons]
      like
      "Vano knows a/the/those/two girl(s) that Ia knows"

In correlatives, on the other hand, *rom*-clause can only be associated with coNP that is modified by demonstrative (33a). The example in (33b) shows that the same holds for correlatives with internally headed RCs and (33c) reminds us that exactly the same situation is observed for *rom*-clauses in prenominal relative clauses.

(33) a. [ias   rom mosc'ons] vano   *gogos/   *or gogos/ ^{ok}*im gogos*
        Ia.D   that like   Vano.N girl.ACC/ two girl.ACC/Dem girl.ACC
        icnobs
        knows

   b. [ias   rom *gogo(eb)I* mosc'ons] vano   *gogos/   *or gogos/
      Ia.D   that girl(s).N   like   Vano.N girl.ACC/ two girl.ACC/
      ^{ok}*im gogos*   icnobs
      Dem girl.ACC knows

   c. Vano   [ias   rom mosc'ons] *gogos/   *or gogos/ ^{ok}*im gogos*
      Vano.N Ia.D   that like   girl.ACC/ two girl.ACC/ Dem girl.ACC
      icnobs
      knows
      "Vano knows a/the girl/two girls/that girl that Ia likes"

The demonstrative requirement holds for correlatives. In fact, the demonstrative requirement is unanimously recognized as the hallmark of correlativisation. (Keenan 1985, Srivastav 1991, Belyaev and Haug 2020). This requirement and the possibility of having an internal head unifies prenominal relatives and correlatives, and sets them apart from postnominal relatives. Therefore, headless RC in correlatives and *rom*-clause in prenominal relatives must be structurally identical. In both constructions, *rom*-clause is an internally headed relative clause, where the internal head is realised as a silent noun.

(34) correlatives with headless RC:

[$_{DP}$D[$_{CP}$..rom..THING/PERSON..]][$_{IP}$..[$_{DP}$Dem N]...]

To summarize, four types of relative clauses are attested in Georgian: postnominal, prenominal, internally-headed, and correlatives. Apart from postnominal *romel*-relatives, which are not the focus of this work, all other relatives involve the embedded clause with subordinator *rom*. The external head must be preceded by a demonstrative if the embedded clause is prenominal. If the embedded clause does not follow the external head, it may contain the internal head. The table in 8.1. summarizes these important properties of each relative type with *rom*-clause.

Table 8.1. *rom*-relative clauses

Type	embedded clause	internal head	determiner on external head	structure
Postnominal	*rom*-clause	No	Ø; Q; Dem	[$_{DP}$D NP [$_{CP}$...*rom*...NP..]]
Prenominal	*rom*-clause	Yes	Dem	[$_{DP}$[$_{DP}$D[$_{CP}$...*rom*...NP$^{o/s}$..]][$_{DP}$Dem (N)]]
Internally-headed	*rom*-clause	Yes	/////////////////	[$_{DP}$D [$_{CP}$...*rom*...NP$^{o/s}$..]]
Correlative	*rom*-clause	Yes	Dem	[$_{DP}$D[$_{CP}$...*rom*...NP$^{o/s}$..]][$_{IP}$...[$_{DP}$Dem(N)]...]

Only two types of relatives, prenominal and correlative, consistently show parallel behaviour: they can contain internal heads and they obey the demonstrative requirement. They share the first property with internally headed relatives. I argued that the prenominal and correlative strategies are extensions of the head-internal strategy, and result from left-adjunction of internally headed relative to DP or TP, respectively. This proposal presupposes the structural ambiguity of *rom*-clauses, which flesh out either bare CPs or CPs embedded in the phonologically null nominal structure. The *rom*-clause qua bare CP contains a gap and is found in head-external postnominal relatives. The *rom*-clause qua DP involves nominal structure which embeds CP with internal head; it constitutes an internally headed relative. An important property of internally headed relatives in Georgian is that the internal head can be overt or silent, specified by superscript in Table (35). When it is silent, DP *rom*-clauses are formally identical to CP *rom*-clauses. To conclude, two relativisation strategies, postnominal and internally-headed, exist in Georgian. The former is based on *overt* head-externalisation and the latter on *covert* head-externalisation (cf. Cole 1987, Culy 1990)

Having established the structural identity of RC and coNP in correlatives, we need to determine their topology. Are correlatives discontinuous/split prenominal relatives that result from the movement of DP *rom*-clause to the left periphery stranding Dem-N in the matrix? If this is what happens in Georgian, it can provide support to theories which view correlativisation as a split variant of another strategy of relative clause formation used in the language. The next sections show that this turns out *not* to be the case in Georgian. Rather, correlatives result from generating internally headed relatives in the left periphery of clauses and resuming them by coNP in the matrix. This suggests that correlativisation in Georgian can be reduced to topicalisation, a widely attested operation in the language and cross-linguistically.

8.3. Topology of Correlatives

The literature on correlatives centers on whether these constructions are derived from externally headed relatives or whether they involve base-generation of RC, which is not the relative clause but rather an embedded proposition in the left periphery. The former type of conclusion is known as uniformity approach, and the latter, as non-uniformity approach.

According to uniformity approach, RC is generated in the left periphery and is a relative clause with null/deleted external head (Cinque 2009, 2020). The coNP is an independent coreferent demonstrative phrase.

Non-uniformity approaches are based on meaning differences between headed relatives and correlatives: the denotation of correlatives involves quantification rather than noun modification typical of externally headed relatives. RC and coNP do not form a constituent, the former is a left-peripheral generalized quantifier CP that binds into a variable in coNP. (Dayal 1996, Izvorski 1996, Lipták 2012). The important difference between this type of non-uniformity approach and the uniformity approach based on the peripheral generation of RC lies in the constituency of RC: it is nominal (DP) in the uniformity approach and clausal (CP) in non-uniformity approaches. A noteworthy mix of two approaches has been put forth by Bhatt (2003): RC is a CP moved from the main clause where it is base-generated as an adjunct to coNP. But this scenario does not exclude that [RC-DemP] constituent out of which RC moves to the left periphery is a prenominal head-external relative clause, i.e. DP.

Which of these approaches is the most adequate for Georgian correlatives? We have established that RC is an internally headed relative, i.e. a nominal. Therefore non-uniformity analyses cannot be applied to Georgian correlatives. The analysis put forth in this work is compatible with the uniformity approach because RC is a head-internal relative clause. RC can be the first nominal moved out of the big DP [DP DP DemP] in the matrix clause. Alternatively, RC can be a base-generated DP in the left-periphery. In the next section, I show that RC is not moved from the matrix. Therefore, only the scenario à la Cinque (2009, 2020) is applicable to Georgian correlatives: RC is a *head-internal* relative clause base-generated in the left-periphery and coindexed with coNP in the matrix clause.

8.3.1. RC Does Not Move

In an important analysis of Hindi correlatives, Bhatt (2003) proposes that RC starts out as a CP, left-adjoined to the matrix DP, and subsequently moves to the left periphery. Three pieces of evidence in favor of the low origin of RC are provided: firstly, [RC-coNP] are DP constituents and can be coordinated in Hindi. Secondly, RC can be reconstructed into the matrix clause, and thirdly, coNP cannot be too deeply embedded and separated from RC by islands. In Georgian, [RC-coNP] sequences, aka prenominal relatives, can also be coordinated, as was shown in (14). However, RC in correlatives cannot reconstruct, suggesting that RCs do not originate in the matrix clause.

Bhatt (2003) shows that in Hindi a name in RC cannot be coreferent with a pronoun in matrix clause that c-commands coNP. This ban is due to the fact that the RC reconstructs back at LF into its original site within the prenominal relative and is c-commanded by a pronoun.

(35) Hindi: *[RC ...Name$_k$ ...] [TP ...Pronoun$_k$ ...[DP RC-coNP] ...]

With respect to reconstruction, Georgian correlatives do not show the same effects, and side with correlatives in Bulgarian (Izvorski 1996) and Hungarian (Lipták 2012). Both head-internal and headless RCs may contain names coreferent with a pronoun that c-commands coNP.

(36) a. [mak'as$_k$ rom misc'eret], iman$_k$ is   c'erili   gazetši
        Maka.D that 2pl.wrote 3sg.E Dem letterN newspaper.in
        gamoakveq'na
        published
        "Maka published the letter you wrote to her in the newspaper"
        lit: What you wrote to Maka, she published that letter in the newspaper"

   b. [mak'as$_k$ rom c'erili   misc'eret] iman$_k$ is   c'erili   gazetši
        Maka.D that letter.N 2pl.wrote 3sg.E Dem letter.N newspaper.in
        gamoakveq'na
        published
        "A letter that we sent to Maka, she published that letter in the newspaper"

The identical *rom*-clauses in prenominal relatives behave differently; they cannot contain a name coreferent with a c-commanding pronoun, resulting in

Principle C violation. The contrast between (36) and (37) clearly indicates that RC in Georgian correlatives does not move from prenominal relatives.

(37) *iman_k [[mak'as_k rom (*c'erili*) misc'eret] *is*   *c'erili*]   gazetši
3sg.E Maka.D   that letter.N 2pl.wrote Dem letter.N newspaper.in
gamoakveq'na
published
"*She_k published the letter that we wrote to Maka_k"

Given this major asymmetry between Hindi and Georgian, we expect that locality requirements should not hold between RC and coNP in Georgian correlatives. If RCs do not move from the matrix clause, coNP and RC can be separated by islands, unlike Hindi. The evidence presented in the next section is more nuanced: correlatives with headed RC do not show island violations, while headless RCs are island-sensitive.

8.3.2. Island Effects in Correlatives

Evidence from reconstruction points to the high origin of RCs in Georgian correlatives. As the relation between RC and coNP does not result from movement, we expect Georgian correlatives to be insensitive to island constraints. However, the prediction is partially borne out: RCs with overt internal head are not island-sensitive, but RCs with silent internal heads are. But as both RC types resist reconstruction, I contend that it is the coNP that must covertly move out of the matrix in correlatives with silent-headed RC in order to license it as a referential nominal.

In (38a), RC is associated with coNP embedded in the postnominal relative clause. In other words, the two parts of the correlative are subject to complex-NP island constraint. (Cf. also Foley 2020:96-99). However, the headed RC in (38b) is not sensitive to the island and can be linked to the deeply embedded coNP, unlike headless RC which obeys the island constraint.

(38) a. *[tkven rom gest'umrat], me ert masc'avlebels vicnob
you   that 2pl.visited I   one teacher.ACC   know
[romelic   *im*   *ekims*   kartuls   asc'avlis]
which.N.rel Dem   doctor.D Georgian.ACC   teaches
"A/the person that visited you, I know one teacher who teaches Georgian to that doctor"

   b. (?)[tkven rom *ekimi*   gest'umrat], me ert   masc'avlebels vicnob
you   that doctor.N 2pl.visited I   one teacher.ACC know
[romelic   *im*   *ekims*   kartuls   asc'avlis]
which.N.rel Dem   doctor.D Georgian.ACC teaches
"A/the doctor that visited you, I know one teacher that teaches Georgian to that doctor"

The internally headed RC in (38b) behaves like a free (or hanging) topic, rather than as a moved case-marked island-sensitive DP topic. In (39a), the topic is moved and conserves the dative case assigned by the embedded verb. The resulting sentence is ruled out, and can't be saved by the insertion of a resumptive 3rd person pronoun inside the relative. On the other hand, in (39b), the topic marked with nominative case is directly adjoined to TP and can be coreferent to the pronoun deep in the island.

(39) a. *im   ekims*$_k$, me ert   masc'avlebels vicnob [romelic t_k/imas$_k$
        Dem doctor.D I   one teacher.ACC   know which.N.rem 3sg.D
        kartuls   asc'avlis]
        Georgian.ACC teaches

   b. *is   ekimi*$_k$, me ert   masc'avlebels vicnob [romelis   imas$_k$
        Dem doctor.N I   one teacher.ACC   know which.N.rel 3sg.D
        kartuls   asc'avlis
        Georgian.ACC teaches
        "That doctor, I know one teacher that teaches Georgian to her"

Why can't headless RCs survive as free topics? Why is it island-sensitive in (38a), even when there is evidence from reconstruction that it does not undergo movement? If RC in (38a) does not move, which element moves and violates the island constraint? Izvorski (1996) argues that in Bulgarian, where reconstruction evidence indicates against movement of RCs from the matrix clause, it is the coNP that overtly moves to the edge of the matrix clause. I propose that coNP undergoes the same type of movement covertly in Georgian correlatives with headless RCs. This movement of coNP is mandatory, as it is the only way to provide the local external nominal licenser for RC, which is a DP relative with silent internal head.

I argued in Section 8.2.3.1 that relatives internally headed by silent head can only appear in contexts that provide a strictly local external nominal licenser. In short answers and in lists, the local licenser is the immediately available discourse prominent nominal antecedent. In prenominal relatives, the local licenser is the adjacent demonstrative phrase. In correlatives, the local licenser is also the demonstrative phrase, which abstractly moves out of the matrix clause and adjoins to RC. This is the reason why island effects are detected in correlatives where RC contains an internal silent head, but not in correlatives where RC involves an overt internal head. In the latter, the overt internal head raises at LF and provides the necessary support for the null functional nominal shell of the relative. The derivations in (40) summarize LF-licensing of internally headed RCs in Georgian correlatives.

(40) a. LF-licensing of RC in (2):
       [$_{DP}$D[NP[$_{CP}$....*rom*....NP.]] [$_{TP}$...coNP....]

    b. LF-licensing of RC in (3):
       coNP[$_{DP}$D[$_{CP}$....*rom*....THING/PERSON...][$_{TP}$coNP][$_{TP}$.....coNP...]

8.4. Conclusion

The aim of this work is to show that Georgian correlatives are not construed by a special relativisation strategy. I argue that both parts of Georgian correlatives—RC and coNP—are nominal expressions. The RC is an internally headed relative with an overt or a silent internal head in CP embedded under D. The coNP is a demonstrative DP that resumes the internally headed relative in the left periphery.

Correlatives are built from the same ingredients as prenominal relatives in Georgian: left-hand internally headed relative and demonstrative phrase. However, correlatives do not result from movement of the internally headed relative from prenominal relatives. Rather, RC is adjoined to the matrix clause in correlatives, and to the demonstrative phrase in prenominal relatives.

Internally headed relatives must undergo head-externalisation at LF in order to function as bona fide referential expressions. (Cole 1987 a.o). When the internal head is overt, its LF-externalisation is sufficient to interpret the internally headed relative as a referential expression (40a). However, the silent internal head is too deficient to do the same, and another external coreferential nominal is required for licensing. In correlatives, this licenser is the coNP that raises at LF above RC with silent head (40b). This movement is responsible for island effects in correlatives with headless RC.

The present analysis provides support to the uniformity approach to correlativisation. Specifically, it confirms the theory of correlatives advanced by Cinque (2009, 2020), whereby correlatives represent structures with a peripheral relative clause and a matrix coreferent demonstrative phrase, and as such fall under left-dislocation structures. Lipták (2012) qualifies RCs in correlatives as *new aboutness topics*. They appear in the left periphery as to "lift the burden off" the sentence internal content by placing new information into a separate discourse and phonological unit.

Georgian is a language where all four universally attested relativisation strategies appear to be at work. However, this study reveals that only two manners of relative clause construal are employed in the language: overt head-raising in postnominal relatives and covert head-raising in internally headed relatives. The other two strategies, prenominal and correlative, are respectively derived by adjoining an internally headed relative to a demonstrative phrase or to the main clause.

References

Basilico, David. 1996. "Head Position and Internally Headed Relative Clauses." *Language* 72(3): 498–532.

Belyaev, Oleg, and Dag Haug. 2020. "The genesis and typology of correlatives." *Language* 96(4): 874-907.

Bhatt, Rajesh. 2003. "Locality in Correlatives." *Natural Language and Linguistic Theory* 21: 485-541.

Boeder, Winfried. 2005. "The South Caucasian languages." *Lingua*, 115(1–2): 5–89

Borer, Hagit. 2005. *In Name Only. Structuring Sense*, Volume I. Oxford: Oxford University Press.

Borise, Lena. 2020. "Tone and intonation in the languages of the Caucasus." In: *Handbook of the Languages of the Caucasus*, In M. Polinsky (ed.). Oxford: Oxford University Press.

Chomsky, Noam. 1965. *Aspects of the theory of syntax*. Cambridge, MA: MIT Press.

Cinque, Guglielmo. 2009. "Five Notes on Correlatives." In R. Mohanty and M. Menon (eds.) *Universals and Variation. Proceedings of Glow in Asia VII* 2009. 1-20. Hyderabad: EFL University Press.

—. 2020. *The Syntax of Relative Clauses: A Unified Analysis*. Cambridge: Cambridge University Press.

Cole, Peter. 1987. "The Structure of Internally Headed Relative Clauses." *Natural Language and Linguistic Theory* 5: 277-302.

Culy, Christopher. 1990. *The Syntax and Semantics of Internally Headed Relative Clauses*. Doctoral dissertation, Stanford University.

Foley, Steven. 2013. *The Syntax of Georgian Relative Clauses*. Senior Thesis, NYU

—. 2020. *Case, agreement, and sentence processing in Georgian*. Doctoral dissertation, University of California Santa Cruz.

Dayal, Vaneeta. 1996. *Locality in WH quantification: Questions and Relative Clauses in Hindi*. Studies in Linguistics and Philosophy, Kluwer Academic Publishers.

Downing, Bruce T. 1973. "Correlative relative clauses in universal grammar." *Minnesota Working Papers in Linguistics and Philosophy of Language* 2: 1-17.

Elbourne, Paul. 2013. *Definite descriptions*. Vol. 1. Oxford University Press.

Grosu, Alex, and Landman, Fred. 1998. "Strange Relatives of the Third Kind." *Natural Language Semantics* 6: 125-170.

Harris, Alice. 1993. "Changes in Relativization Strategies: Georgian and Language Universals." In C. Paris (ed.), *Caucasologie et mythologie compare*. 391-403. Paris: Peeters.

—. 1994. "On the History of Relative Clauses in Georgian." In H. I. Aronson (ed.), *Non-Slavic Languages of the USSR: Papers from the Fourth Conference*. 130-142. Columbus, Ohio: Slavica Publishers.

Hewitt, Georges. 1995. *Georgian. A Structural Reference Grammar*. London Oriental and African Library, vol. 2. Amsterdam: Benjamins.

Izvorski, Roumyana (Pancheva). 1996. "The syntax and semantics of correlative proforms." NELS 26: 133-147.

Kayne, Richard. 1994. *The Antisymmetry of Syntax*. Cambridge, MA: MIT Press.

—. 2005. *Movement and Silence.* Oxford Studies in Comparative Syntax Oxford University Press.

—. 2010. "Why isn't *this* a complementizer?" In R. Kayne (ed.), *Comparisons and contrasts,* 190–227. Oxford: Oxford University Press.

Keenan, Edward. 1985. "Relative Clauses." In T. Shopen (ed.), *Language Typology and Syntactic Description.* Vol.II. *Complex Constructions.* Cambridge: Cambridge University Press, 141-170.

Lipták, Anikó, ed. 2009. *Correlatives Cross-Linguistically.* Amsterdam: Benjamins.

Lipták, Anikó. 2012. "Correlative topicalization." *Acta Linguistica Hungarica* 59(3): 245-302.

Mahajan, Anoop. 2000. "Relative Asymmetries and Hindi Correlatives." In A. Alexiadou, P.Law, A.Meinunger, C.Wilder (eds.), *The Syntax of Relative Clauses.* 201-229. Amsterdam: Benjamins.

Nash, Léa. 1995. *Portée argumentale et marquage casuel dans les langues SOV et dans les langues ergatives: L'exemple du géorgien.* Doctoral dissertation, Université Paris 8.

—. 2002. "Topics in Georgian syntax. Correlative constructions in Georgian." Handout from MIT seminar.

—. 2020. "Structural source of person split." *Linguistic Variation: Structure and Interpretation,* In L. Franco and P. Lorusso. (eds.), 453-50. Berlin : de Gruyter Mouton.

Sauerland, Uli. 1998. *The meaning of chains.* Doctoral dissertation. MIT.

Skopeteas, Stavros, Caroline Féry, and Rusudan Asatiani. 2009. "Word order and intonation in Georgian." *Lingua* 119: 102–127.

Skopeteas, Stavros, and Gisbert Fanselow. 2009. "Effects of givenness and constraints on free word order." In M.Zimmerman and C.Féry, (eds.), *Information Structure from different perspectives.* Oxford University Press, Oxford.

—. 2010. "Focus in Georgian and the expression of contrast." *Lingua,* 120(6): 1370-1391.

Srivastav, Veneeta (Dayal). 1991. "The syntax and semantics of correlatives." *Natural Language and Linguistic Theory* 9: 637-686.

Shlonsky, Ur. 1992. "Resumptive pronouns as a last resort." *Linguistic Inquiry* 23(3): 443-468.

Vergnaud, Jean-Roger. 1974. *French Relative Clauses.* Doctoral dissertation, MIT.

Vries, Mark de. 2002. *The Syntax of Relativization.* Doctoral dissertation, University of Amsterdam.

Williamson, Janice. 1987. "An indefiniteness restriction for relative clauses in Lakhota." In E.Reuland and A.ter Meulen, (eds.), *The Representation of (In)definiteness.* 168–190. MIT Press, Cambridge, MA.

Georgian Sign Language

Chapter 9

Non-Manual Arguments in Georgian Sign Language (GESL)

Tamar Makharoblidze

Ilia State University, Georgia

Ekaterine Nanitashvili

Ilia State University, Georgia;
Georg-August University of Göttingen, Germany

Abstract

This chapter presents a brief overview of Georgian Sign Language (GESL) and its argument structure. GESL is an understudied natural language of the Georgian Deaf and Hard of Hearing community. Research of any unexplored sign language is an indispensable resource for linguists especially when this sign language deploys such interesting features as GESL. The presented article discusses the properties of argument structure and argument marking in GESL. Moreover, it provides the theoretical approach that non-manuals, namely eye-gazing, could be integrated into the system of argument structure and it might be considered as a facial kinetic representation of a verbal person.

Keywords: Georgian Sign Language, GESL, Argument Structure, Eye gaze, Non-manuals, Verbal person

***

9.1. Introduction

Sign language linguistics is a quite young area of linguistic research. Although, it has a relatively long history in comparison to the Georgian Sign Language (GESL) linguistics, which has only been studied in recent years. However, the results of the research conducted on GESL are noteworthy and the recent analyses have laid a solid foundation for the evolution of the GESL linguistics. The polypersonal agreement structure of spoken Georgian verbs is worldwide appreciated among linguists, but the structures of verbs and their non-manual arguments in GESL have not been extensively studied yet. GESL reveals many features that are different from spoken Georgian and are at the same time not typical for Russian Sign Language (RSL) either, though there are some grammatical and lexical properties that are influenced by RSL.

The paper aims to present a brief overview of the GESL argument structure and the authors' approach to its non-manual elements. It is organized as follows: background information is provided in the next section of the paper, followed by a brief discussion of argument structure in GESL and our theoretical approach to non-manual arguments. The paper ends with the conclusion and the bibliography.

9.2. Background Information

GESL is a natural language of the Georgian Deaf and Hard of Hearing community. Since Georgia was the part of Soviet Union, Georgian deaf people alongside the signers from the other Soviet countries used the united sign language that was based on RSL. Predictably, the influence of RSL on GESL is noticeable. However, these effects are mainly revealed on the lexical level. Although linguistic research on GESL has only been conducted in the past few years, significant features have already been explored (Makharoblidze 2012; Makharoblidze 2015; Makharoblidze, Pfau 2018; Makharoblidze 2019; etc.). On the basis of this research, we could presume that GESL possesses more noteworthy linguistic properties and the promising results of future research could be an incredible resource for linguists.

The first boarding schools for deaf and hard-of-hearing children in Georgia were founded in the 1960s. The majority of the students were the children of hearing parents and those schools were the place where they acquired their basic communicative skills. Besides the school, the deaf community had an association – the Union of the Deaf of Georgia. The government provided social services and financial aid to the deaf community, there were special manufacturing enterprises, where deaf people were employed, various sporting activities were held for community members and etc. Thus, deaf people had the possibility to communicate, which developed a feeling of unity among deaf signers and evolved the local sign language.

The development of sign languages in post-soviet countries took different directions after the dissolution of the USSR. While exploring any sign language, the fact that it might be influenced by the surrounding spoken languages should be taken into account. However, the evolution of GESL has never been documented and researched. Thus, the discussion might be based on the current factual information. Nowadays, there are several educational and cultural projects for the Georgian Deaf community, any information and/or social service is available in GESL. More and more deaf signers attend vocational courses in order to obtain practical knowledge, although the school program lacks a systemic approach and competence and unfortunately, a pre-school program is not available for deaf children. Though Georgian Deaf organization faces a lot of challenges, it is a unified community and the integrity and the close relationship between its members stimulates the development of GESL. In fact, nowadays we are able to research this understudied sign language and at the same time to witness and to take part in its standardization process.

9.3. GESL Argument Structure

The ability to mark argument structure is one of the fundamental properties of human languages (Meir 2003), so it is not surprising that argument structure is such an extensively researched topic in sign language linguistics as well. Argument structure is the basic syntactic-semantic frame which is formed by the predicate and its arguments. Generally, the number of arguments is defined by the lexical semantics of a predicate as it gives theta-roles to its arguments. This is the principle of Theta-criterion (Chomsky 1981) that each argument bears only one theta role and each theta role is assigned to only one argument. This is the general principle and it is considered to be the same in sign languages. However, sign languages differ in their semantic, syntactic and morphological properties, so they acquire different mechanisms to form the argument structure. The common properties sign languages utilize to mark argument structures are agreement, word order, the use of classifier constructions, pronouns, etc.

Agreement is possibly the most extensively researched topic in sign language linguistics. It is usually marked by the modification of the direction of movement and/ or the orientation of the hand as the movement starts at the location associated with the subject and ends at the location associated with the object (Meir 2002). Many linguists agree on Padden's (Padden 1998) classification of plain, agreeing (inflection) and spatial verbs, whereas plain verbs are the verbs that have phonologically fixed forms that cannot be modified to express agreement. Some sign languages, namely German Sign Language (DGS), use auxiliaries to overtly express agreement with plain verbs (Steinbach and Pfau 2007, Steinbach 2011). The existence of auxiliaries has not been detected in GESL, but the existence of manual markers (as verbal morphemes) for indirect object has been confirmed (Makharoblidze 2015). In addition to manually marked agreement, some sign languages can express agreement non-manually by means of head tilt towards the locus associated with the subject and eye gaze towards the locus associated with the object (Bahan 1996). The non-manual agreement between a verb and its subject was first described by Shepard-Kegl (Shepard-Kegl 1985). A similar phenomenon was later described for Italian Sign Language (Pizzuto 1986). Non-manual marker that occurs only in combination with agreeing verbs and manual agreement marker was also described in Austrian Sign Language (ÖGS) (Krebs et al. 2020). Hansen (2007) discusses the syntactic function of gaze in German Sign Language (DGS) and claims that "gaze in sign languages display regularities in use that are analogues to the ergative marking in ergative vocal languages" (Hansen 2007). Nordlund (2019) also discusses gaze while describes several strategies for defocusing the agent in Finnish Sign Language (FinSL).

Grammatical relations between arguments could also be marked by word order. Though word order has been studied in other sign languages (Fischer 1975, Padden 1983, Legeland et al. 2018, Kimmelman 2018, etc.), nowadays, the analysis of GESL word order still needs further research. However, we can assume that the word order in GESL has a less crucial role in the process of argument marking. That could be explained by the existence of different markers, which allows the GESL word order to be extremely flexible. On the basis of the previous research, several types of Indirect Object markers have been distinguished (Makharoblidze 2016): the neutral form of indirect object marker (IOM-Neutral), the indirect object marker with some kind of beneficial meaning (IOM-Respect) and the marker with the opposite meaning (IOM-Disrespect).

Figure 9.1. Indirect Object Marker IOM-Neutral

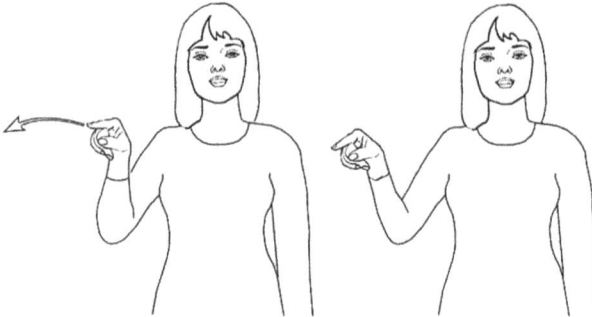

Figure 9.2. Two versions of Indirect Object Marker IOM-Respect

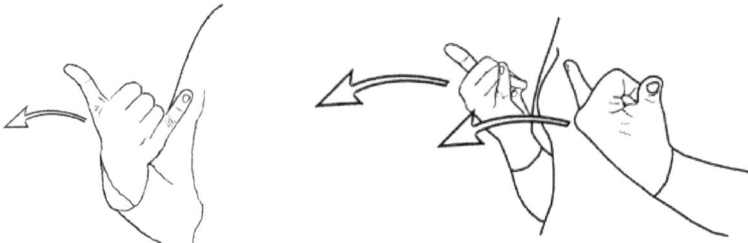

It is noteworthy that the same kind of beneficiary argument is described for RSL (Kimmelman 2018). However, unlike RSL, the indirect object marker with the meaning of disrespect is also attested in GESL.

Figure 9.3. Indirect Object marker IOM-Disrespect

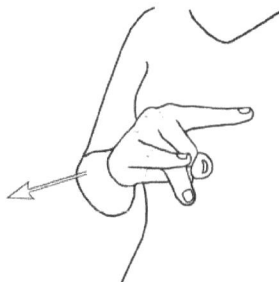

The grammaticalization processes of these markers are discussed in the "Indirect Object Markers in Georgian Sign Language" (Makharoblidze 2016).

9.4. Theoretical Implication

As pointed out previously, some sign languages use non-manual elements to mark agreement. Linguists are not in agreement with regard to non-manual agreement even in the frame of the same sign language. As for American Sign Language (ASL), Bahan et al. (2000) argues that eye gaze agreement can occur with all types of verbs, even with intransitive ones, while Thompson et al. (2006) claim that eye gaze agreement occurs only with the manually agreed verbs. However, we have turned our attention to the fact that non-manual elements are admitted to be the grammatical elements. Thus, it is reasonable to discuss the non-manual element as the part of the argument system. The non-manual element can be expressed by:

1. Head tilt,
2. Facial expression and mimic,
3. Eye gaze, and
4. Eye gaze in combination with some other non-manual elements.

Alongside the elicitation materials, we used five-hour length natural narratives that was filmed for the previous project. The male and female signers of different age and different generations of Georgian native signers were our sources, and all of them signed "Informed Consents" on the basis of which they granted us the right to use the data for different scientific reasons. Use of non-manual elements we detected in the filmed natural discourse, was once again checked and confirmed during the elicitation process with our Deaf informant.

In general, eye gaze seems to be the most leading element among non-manual arguments in GESL, and it mostly appears in combination with head tilt and facial expression. Below we neglect head tilt and facial expression as independent markers for GESL argument structure, since they never appear without eye gaze, and we will talk about eye gaze only. Grammatical activities of non-manual elements are different across sign languages. GESL is a manual dominant sign language and non-manual elements are not very active in GESL. However, these elements might be grammaticalized and have some grammatical functions. Thus, we argue that this non-manual element might be discussed as a non-manual argument in GESL. It usually occurs in the role of object argument, but it might have a function of subject as well. It can appear together with a manual pronoun or a nominal and independently as well.

Figure 9.4. INDEX$_3$+GAZE$_3$ SAY – (S)he says

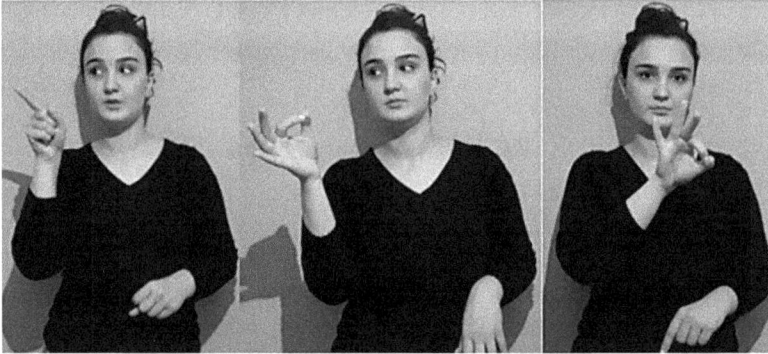

Figure 9.5. INDEX$_3$+GAZE$_3$ SAY – (Somebody) said to him/her

In Figure 9.4., eye gaze appears as an additional element and the main grammatical role for subject is expressed manually. The same case is in Figure 9.5., where the object is conveyed by the combination of the pronoun and eye gaze. Eye gaze could independently perform the function of pronoun (Makharoblidze 2012). In this case, the direction of eye gaze is different for the first, the second and the third person pronouns. Pronouns are usually considered to be deictic. These non-manual pronouns – eye-gaze arguments are also deictic pronouns that use the direction of gaze to differentiate between the first, the second and the third person pronouns. Though the eye gaze argument is mostly a pronominal element, it could appear with the nominal constituent as well.

Figure 9.6. BOY INDEX₃+GAZE₃ LOVE GIRL – The boy loves the girl

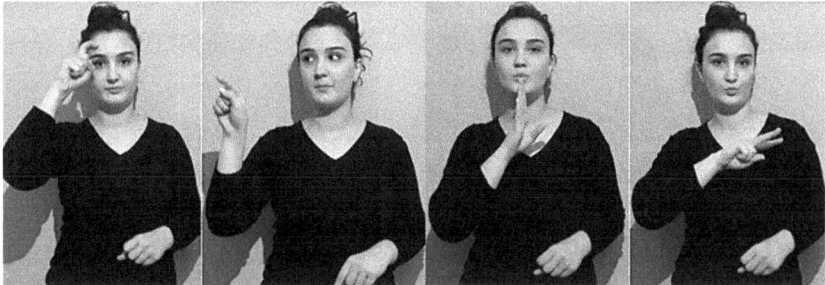

There are three possible appearances of eye gaze argument:

1. Verb is followed by eye gaze argument

$$\text{GIRL LOVE} \overline{\text{gaze}}$$

2. Eye gaze argument is followed by verb

$$\text{GIRL}\overline{\text{gaze}} \quad \text{LOVE}$$

3. Eye gaze argument coincides with a verb

$$\text{GIRL}\;\overline{\text{LOVE}}^{\text{gaze}}$$

When this eye gaze argument is incorporated in the verbal form, it is neither nominal, nor pronominal element, since it is already the morphemic element of a verb as a synergic form, and just like the verbal kinetics eye gaze can make verbs incorporated. The term incorporation is usually defined as "A complex verb formed by the syntactic combination of a verb with a noun (noun incorporation) or another verb; in sign languages often used for the combination of a verb and a classifier or of a noun and a numeral (numeral incorporation)" (Quer et al. 2017, 811). As eye gaze is incorporated in the verb stem, this polymorphic form of a verb and eye gaze can be defined as an incorporated combination of two different elements that conveys verb valency. This can happen only when eye gaze is used independently and when it coincides with the verbal kinetics. Although the eye gaze argument is the syntactic member of a sentence in all of these cases, only the third position is the case of incorporation when it is incorporated into the verbal form.

The examples of independent eye gaze arguments:

Figure 9.7. DO GAZE$_3$ – (S)he does[1]

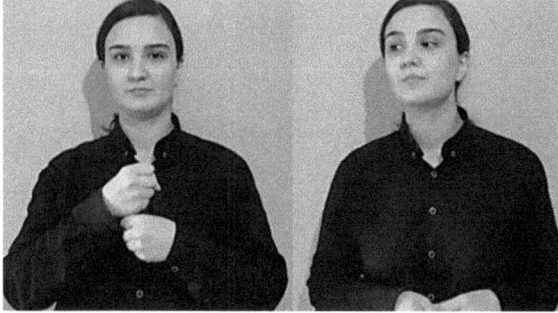

Figure 9.8. MOTHER GAZE$_3$ WRITE – Mother writes to him/her

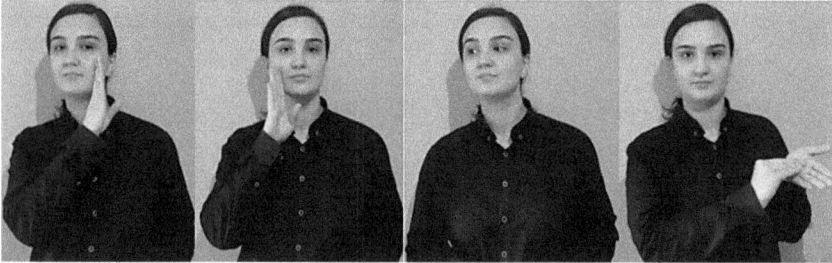

Figure 9.9. BOY LOVE+GAZE$_3$ – The boy loves her

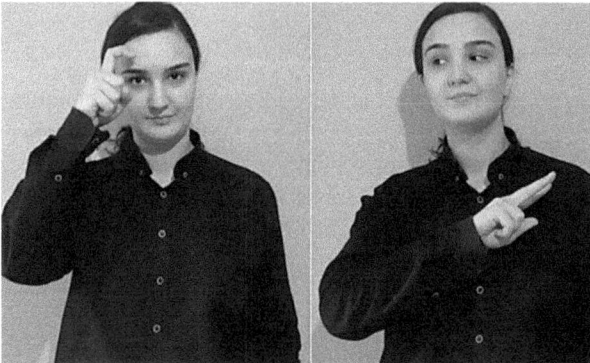

Figure 9.7. shows the example of the first position for eye gaze when following the verb, while the Figure 9.8. we have the second position when eye-gaze

---

[1] GAZE$_3$ is the third person pronoun

precedes the verb. Figure 9.9. shows the last third position, and here we have the fact of incorporation, when eye gaze coincides with the verb.

   Thus, the eye gaze argument might be considered as a non-manual, facial kinetic marker that unlike the manually displayed arguments, could be incorporated into the morphology of a verb. Its use depends on the pragmatic context of the discourse. This non-manual element is usually used in an active communication and it could never be found in asymmetrical conversations. Sometimes the use of non-manual argument obtains additional meaning. Bahan (1996) describes the use of upward eye gaze with the ASL verb DREAM and hypotheses that eye gaze may show the agreement with an implicit argument that is not realized in ASL, unlike English sentences where this argument can be realized: He dreamed a dream (Bahan 1996). The upward eye gaze can be used in GESL, but when the signer uses upward eye gaze argument in GESL, it could denote the higher social status of the mentioned person. Eye gaze is also used to mention someone whose appearance in the communicative act is less desirable or if someone or something needs to be less noticeable. Thus, the use of eye gaze arguments can also have different pragmatic connotations. Besides elicitation, we have used data that was gathered previously for another project and contained natural narratives and we had an opportunity to observe how the signers used eye gaze as an argument in natural discourse. However, it requires further investigation and detailed research in order to reveal different pragmatic connotations.

9.5. Conclusion

In general, abundant use of non-manual elements is not the case for GESL. However, some non-manual elements in GESL obtain grammatical function and as we have already discussed, eye gaze is the most important non-manual verbal argument in GESL. Eye gaze argument can appear even in plain verbs (including body-anchored verbs) and with synergetic forms it makes a verb inflected. This topic needs further scrutiny.

Acknowledgement

We would like thank our Deaf friend – Lamara (Leke) Japoshvili for her help.

References

Bahan, Benjamin. 1996. "Non-manual realization of agreement in American Sign Language." PhD dissertation, Boston University.
Bahan, Benjamin., Judy Kegl, Robert G. Lee, Dawn MacLaughlin, and Carol Neidle. 2000. "The licensing of null arguments in American Sign Language." *Linguistic Inquiry* 31(1). 1–27.

Chomsky, Noam. 1981. *Lectures on government and binding*. Dordrecht: Foris Publications.

Fischer, Susan. 1975. "Influences on word order change in American Sign Language." In C.N. Li (ed.), *Word order and word order change*, 1–25. Austin, TX: University of Texas Press.

Hansen, Martje. 2007. "Warum braucht die Deutsche Gebärdensprache kein Passiv? Verfahren der Markierung semantischer Rollen in der DGS:" [Why can German Sign Language (DGS) do without a passive construction? Ways of marking semantic roles in DGS] *Sign Language and Linguistics*, Volume 10, Issue 2, Jan 2007, p. 213 – 222.

Kimmelman, Vadim. 2018. "Basic argument structure in Russian Sign Language." *Glossa: A journal of general linguistics* 3(1): 116. 1–39, DOI: https://doi.org/10.53 34/gjgl.494

Krebs, Julia., Ronnie B. Wilbur, and Dietmar Roehm. 2020. "Distributional properties of an agreement marker in Austrian Sign Language (ÖGS)." *Linguistics* 58:4.

Legeland, Iris, Katharina Hartmann, and Roland Pfau. 2018. "Word order asymmetries in NGT coordination: The impact of Information Structure." *Formal and Experimental Advances in Sign Language Theory* 2. 56-67. [doi.org/10.31009/FEAST.i2.05].

Makharoblidze, Tamar. 2012. *Georgian Sign Language*. Tbilisi.

—. 2015. "Indirect Object Markers in Georgian Sign Language." *Sign Language and Linguistics*, 18(2), John Benjamins Publishing Company, 238-250 DOI: https://doi.org/10.1075/sll.18.2.03mak.

—. 2019. "On GESL verb." CODFREURCOR *Etudes interdisciplinaires en Sciences humaines EISH*. Vol. 6; Editions Université d'Etat Ilia, Tbilissi, Géorgie. ISBN 1987-8753 pp.50-81.

Makharoblidze, Tamar, and Roland Pfau. 2018. "A negation-tense interaction in Georgian Sign Language." *Sign Language and Linguistics*, Volume 21, 137-151 https://doi.org/10.1075/sll.00013.mak.

Meir, Irit. 2002. "A cross-modality perspective on verb agreement." *Natural Language and Linguistic Theory* 20. 413–450.

—. 2003. "Grammaticalization and Modality: the Emergence of a Case-Marked Pronoun in Israeli Sign Language." *Linguistics* 39, 109-140. Cambridge University Press.

Nordlund, Sanna. 2019. "Agent defocusing in two-participant clauses in Finnish Sign Language." *Glossa: a journal of general linguistics* 4:1.

Padden, Carol A. 1998. "The ASL lexicon." *Sign Language and Linguistics* 1(1). 39–60.

—. 1983. "Interaction of morphology and syntax in American Sign Language." University of California, San Diego PhD dissertation [published 1988, New York: Garland Press].

Pizzuto, Elena. 1986. "The verb system of Italian Sign Language." In B. T. Tervoort (Ed.), Signs of Life. *Proceedings of the Second European Congress on Sign Language Research*, 17-31. Amsterdam: University of Amsterdam.

Quer, Josep, Carlo Cecchetto, Caterina Donati, Carlo Geraci, Meltem Kelepir, Roland Pfau, and Markus Steinbach. 2017. *SignGram Blueprint: A Guide to Sign Language Grammar Writing*. Berlin, Boston: de Gruyter Mouton. Retrieved from https://www.degruyter.com/view/product/467598.

Shepard-Kegl, Judy. 1985. "Locative relations in ASL word formation, syntax and discourse." MIT PhD dissertation.

Steinbach, Marcus. 2011. "What do agreement auxiliaries reveal about the grammar of sign language agreement?" *Theoretical Linguistics* 37–3/4, 209–221.

Steinbach, Marcus, and Roland Pfau. 2007. "Grammaticalization of auxiliaries in sign languages." In Perniss, P., R. Pfau and M. Steinbach (eds.), *Visible variation: Cross-linguistic studies on sign language structure*. Berlin: de Gruyter Mouton, 303-339.

Thompson, Robin, Karen Emmorey, and Robert Kluender. 2006. "The relationship between eye gaze and verb agreement in American Sign Language: an eye-tracking study." *Natural Language and Linguistic Theory* 24. 571–604.

Miscellaneous: Ethnology, Education, History and Religion

Chapter 10

Interview with Khevisberi Pilip'e Baghiauri

Kevin Tuite

Université de Montréal

Paata Bukhrashvili

Ilia State University, Georgia

Romanoz Dolidze

Tbilisi State University

Abstract

Alongside the varieties of folk Christianity practiced to the present day in rural Georgia, a distinct religious system, with its own specialized practitioners and network of sacred sites, survives in the highland districts of Northeast Georgia. The continued existence of Northeast Georgian vernacular religion is threatened, however, by such factors as the demographic decline of the highland population, the hegemonic position of the Georgian Orthodox Church, and, in some localities, attempts to (re)create a Caucasus "paganism" on the basis of ethnographic publications and idealized notions of the Georgian past. We present here an interview, recorded in 2000, with the late Pilip'e Baghiauri, one of the last khevisberis (shrine priests) to have been formed in the traditional manner, through oral transmission of ritual knowledge and an agonistic and costly call to service. In the interview, Baghiauri described how he received his vocation, several ritual practices and beliefs, and some aspects of traditional highland Georgian social organization.

Keywords: Georgian vernacular religion, Pshavi, xevisberi (shrine priest), vocation, ritual

***

10.1. Introduction

Until he passed away in early 2019, Pilip'e Baghiauri was the *tav-khevisberi* (chief priest) of the shrine of St George in Gogolaurta Commune, in the northeast Georgian province of Pshavi. Pilip'e came from a long line of shrine priests, including his father and predecessor Betsina Baghiauri. We first met him in 1997, and over the years he became our principal source on the vernacular religion of northeastern Georgian highlands. It is important to note at the outset that the religious system described here is to be distinguished from the varieties of folk Christianity practiced throughout Georgia, especially in rural areas. Rather than being orally-transmitted fragments of Orthodox Christian practice, carried out by local residents in the absence of ordained clergymen, the rituals, invocations and sacrifices performed by Pilip'e Baghiauri and his fellow khevisberis in Pshavi, and their counterparts in the adjoining province of Khevsureti, are informed by a complex belief system of beliefs and doctrines that some have labelled — and not without justification — as Georgian paganism.[1]

Figure 10.1. Pilip'e Baghiauri speaking to Dolidze [R] and Tuite [back to camera]. Bukhrashvili's son Oto holds the tape recorder. Photo by P. Bukhrashvili

Pilip'e Baghiauri was one of the handful of traditional ritual specialists in the highland districts of Pshavi and Khevsureti who received their call to service in Soviet times, when the practice of vernacular religion was still discouraged by the authorities, and the necessary knowledge was transmitted orally, by observation and memorization. For all of his immense knowledge of ritual

---

[1] For descriptions of the vernacular religious system of the northeastern Georgian highlands, see Bardavelidze 1957, 1974; Charachidzé 1968; K'ik'nadze 1996; Tuite and Bukhrashvili 1999, 2002; Tuite 1996, 2004, 2011, 2016.

texts, practices and norms, Pilip'e was refreshingly down-to-earth, unassuming and a pleasure to be around. Along with a handful of other old-time khevisberis, he possessed what Georgians refer to as *madli* — grace, virtue, or perhaps charisma in something like its older sense. The vocation of khevisberi was never freely chosen — Pilip'e and others of his generation described their struggles against the will of their divine patrons, and the heavy cost they paid for their stubbornness — and there was no material recompense for the burdensome responsibilities that they assumed once in office. By North American standards Pilip'e lived in poverty, and yet he considered himself the richest man alive. And we consider ourselves all the richer for having known him.

Figure 10.2. Baghiauri riding toward Lasharis Jvari. Photo by K.Tuite

The conversations translated here took place on 24-25 June 2000. The first occurred at the interviewers' campsite on the bank of the Matur-Khevi river, close to its intersection with the Aragvi, not far from Gogolaurta. The second took place the following day atop Lasharis Gori, close to the powerful shrine of Lasharis-Jvari. The interview was conducted (in Georgian) by P'aat'a Bukhrashvili (PB), Romanoz Dolidze (RD), and Kevin Tuite (KT); Tuite translated the text into English and added explanatory notes. The original recording is in the archives of the International Caucasological Research Institute (*K'avk'asiologiis saertašoriso sametsniero-k'vleviti sazogadoebrivi inst'it'ut'i*), an independent, non-profit organization headquartered in Tbilisi. Further information, and publications by the members of the institute are available at the sites <www.caucasology.com> and < www.philologie.com>. The authors wish to express their thanks to the Social Sciences and Humanities Research Council of Canada, for its continued support of their research on religious festivals in post-Soviet Georgia.

10.2. The Vocation of the Khevisberi

Pilip'e Baghiauri describes how he became aware of his vocation to succeed his father as khevisberi:

I was a bit arrogant in those days, and gave no thought to [the possibility that] I would become khevisberi. I paid no attention to such things. It was my father then [who served as shrine priest], and when I went to the shrine (*khat'i*),[2] it was to party, and I gave it no thought. I disliked the khevisberi's duties. It is a special matter, you are always busy — and then, fifteen years earlier, no add ten years to that, twenty-five years ago, a man called me, he was priest along with my father, his assistant, and [he said]: "I saw this dream, and, son, be careful of yourself." I laughed. Then there were oracles (*kadagebi*)[3] among us, and they informed us [of this]. [I said]: "What are you saying? How could I do this [i.e. serve as khevisberi]?" Then, I became frightened, I would become startled, I was falling out of bed. Ask my mother how many times she grabbed onto me. I was seeing apparitions. I said: I must not go insane. Now, in 1989, one of my children died, and before a year went by, I had not yet held the anniversary banquet (*c'listavi*),[4] my wife followed [in death]. I was troubled. People knew what happened and they would say to me: "You made this child die, you will destroy your family."[5] I went to a fortune-teller, what we call a 'reader' [*mk'itxavi*].

---

[2] The expression *khat'i* (literally, "icon") is polysemous in highland Georgian usage, covering the senses of (1) a divine image, (2) a shrine or sanctuary, and (3) the supernatural being in whose honor the shrine has been constructed. The word *jvari* "cross" has a similar range of meanings, especially in Khevsureti. The "partying" Pilip'e refers to is the consumption of alcohol and food, dancing and singing, that accompany the annual festivals at the communal *khat'i*.

[3] In earlier times, certain individuals, usually men, had the special vocation of communicating messages from supernatural beings (Mindadze 1987). On such occasions, they would go into a trance-like state and speak with the voice of the khat'i. Most of these oracles were also khevisberis, but this was not always the case. The last kadagi died in the late 1980's, in Khevsureti.

[4] In Georgia, as in other Orthodox Christian countries, memorial banquets are held on the fortieth day after death (*ormoci*), and on the one-year anniversary (*c'listavi*). The former marks the departure of the soul from the earth to the afterlife, as in the Biblical account of Jesus' ascension to heaven forty days after his resurrection, and the latter banquet ends the period of official mourning.

[5] The vocation of a khevisberi characteristically begins with a struggle, rather than immediate acceptance by the candidate. All Pshav and Khevsur priests that I have interviewed (e.g. Tuite 2011), and those whose calls to service are described in the Georgian ethnographic literature (e.g. Mindadze 1981), explicitly mention their resistance to the initial call, their unwillingness to assume the heavy responsibilities of the khevisberi's office. Refusal of the vocation invariably brings the anger of the khat'i upon the

KT: *Was the reader a woman or a man?*

She was a woman, she lived in Tianeti.[6] She said to me: "Why don't you go up? Offer yourself to it [the khat'i] (*tavi daude*); or else worse things will happen to you." She told me directly, like that, she did not light a candle, or anything. [She said] "I know what you are embarking upon." She did not know me personally. Well, so it was, I offered myself to this matter, I anointed my hands and shoulder (*xel-mxari vinatle*), and now I only lack the ninth bull-sacrifice (*mozveri*).[7] So, it was with so much distress, well, my family … they blamed me, as though you destroyed the family. In short, I suffered enormously, I suffered. Now it has stopped. But now, if I get mixed up, or if I do not observe the rules, the norms, (*c'esi, rigi*), do what tradition demands, or if I slip up in an invocation, then I see a dream, it is either my father, or some man in white, who appears to me on such occasions.

PB: *What do you mean by 'slip up in an invocation'?*

Well now, this word, it must come to you. It has nothing to do with learning by memorization, even though so many things are written in books, as much as you want. You must get to it [the right words] during the invocation, somehow. Well, let us say, there are many kinds of sacrifices brought up to the mountain: *gasamq'vano* (for the initiation of boys),[8] *samešvlo* (to ask for special aid), there

---

candidate, and often upon his family as well. Some individuals fell gravely ill or suffered from mental disturbances, others lost family members to death, which they interpreted as the penalty imposed by the divinity for their obstinacy. (One elderly khevisberi told me that the deaths of several of his brothers at the front during World War II were occasioned by his continued refusal to heed the call to service of his commune's khat'i).

[6] Tianeti is a district to the south and east of Pshavi, settled over the centuries by numerous families of highland origin.

[7] The new khevisberi must promise to offer nine sacrificed bulls (*mozveri*) to the shrine. Since few highland peasant families can afford such an enormous expenditure of livestock at one time, the sacrifices take place over several years. Upon assuming his duties, he is anointed by the chief khevisberi with the blood of a sacrificed animal. At Gogolaurta, where we saw this ritual performed, the blood came from a ram, which was held off the ground while its throat was cut by the chief khevisberi. The blood was collected in a glass which also contained some wine. The chief khevisberi dipped his finger in the blood-wine mixture, and made cross-shaped marks on the new khevisberi's chest, hands and forehead.

[8] The presentation (*gaq'vana*) of boys at the shrine is accompanied by the offering of a bull, or sometimes the two-stage sacrifice of a ram, whose blood is used to anoint the bull, with whose blood in turn the boy is anointed (with a sign of the cross on the forehead) by the khevisberi. At Gogolaurta, the boys in addition are made to circumambulate a special "boys' initiation tower" (*c'ulis gasarevi k'ošk'i*) atop Kmodis Gori. After the

are a thousand different kinds. Each has its own invocation, and the main invocation, when the candle is held up to the sacrifice, this is special ... You cannot mix it up, you really must arrive at it, like a memorized poem, but in a different manner.

PB: *In other words, the invocation comes by itself?*

It comes by itself (*tavisit modis*). For example, here is something that is real: Under no circumstances will a khevisberi pass something on to you by communicating that such a thing is somewhere, that a cup is hidden away somewhere.[9] There is something about shrines, such that you yourself must see [the object], it [the khat'i] will compel you (*migabidzgos*). In reality, may God be my witness, my father was khevisberi, but I had no idea that this office would be handed on to me in such a fashion. Many things happen this way ... however I may not talk about certain things.

PB: *Does everything therefore depend on intuitions? That is, does some kind of 'spiritual eye' awaken in you at the wish of the khat'i?*

Even if you are a new khevisberi, it [the khat'i] will teach you the prayers, the chief invocation, whom to commemorate when you light the candles. You will see something in a dream, you will understand something by intellect (*gonit*). That is how this matter is, when you are careful out of fear of the khat'i, you are very careful out of concern for your children and grandchildren, that you do not make a mistake.[10] It might be because you fear it [the khat'i] that you see something through memory, through intellect.

---

presentation, the boys are considered "vassals" (*q'mani*) of their commune's patron divinity (St George, in the case of Gogolaurta). A separate ceremony is held for the presentation of girls and in-marrying women, which does not involve a blood sacrifice. See the descriptions of these rituals at one Pshav commune in Tuite and Bukhrashvili 1999.

[9] Some time before this, Baghiauri consecrated another man as 'treasurer' (*megandzure*) of the Gogolaurta shrine complex. The treasurer is responsible for the various cups, chalices, icons, crosses and other valuables which have been offered to the khat'i over the centuries, most of which are hidden in undisclosed locations to protect them from theft. To our astonishment, Baghiauri said that he has no intention of telling the new treasurer where these items are kept. The khat'i itself will tell him, in a dream, where its possessions are, should it ever be necessary to bring them out.

[10] As in the case of resistance to the call to service, it is believed that the khat'i will exact harsh penalties for errors in ritual performance, even if unintentional, and that these penalties may fall on the family as well as the khevisberi himself.

PB: *This is the fear of God.*

May He be blessed! I have seen nothing, but many things have appeared to me … But what I know I will pass on to the next generation. What is, is, it exists in reality. We should not say, "It doesn't exist." Do not take anything, do not remove anything; they fight mightily against that.[11] If you do not want to, do not bring anything there [to the khat'i], and do not pray. This is what I know from experience.

10.3. Traditional Beliefs and Practices

KT: *If a person is struck by lightning, or falls in the river, or drowns in the sea, is any special ritual performed, such as the offering of a sacrifice, or the killing of a goat? For instance, if lightning kills a man, what happens in that case?*

In general, a sort of angel pursues each person, one that has been driven out by God, a devil (*ešmak'i*), what we call an 'evil angel' (*avi angelozi*). In general, it is best, when this one pursues somebody, to drive it away from the person's soul with a goat, that is, you cut off a goat's head and you throw its head backward over your shoulder (*xeluk'uyma*). No name is laid on this goat-kid [i.e. the sacrifice is not dedicated to anyone], nor is its meat mixed with anything.[12]

KT: *The meat cannot be eaten?*

You can eat it as such (*č'amit č'am*), but they call that 'on the account of the fortieth' (*ormocis angarišze*). You have to drive it [the evil angel] away before the fortieth [day after death]; the person's soul goes to paradise on the fortieth day.[13] Until then it wanders nearby and precisely for this reason you have to drive this evil angel away from it. For this purpose a goat-kid (*cik'ani*) is necessary.

---

[11] This seems to be an injunction against stealing objects from the shrine, which will incur the wrath of the khat'i.

[12] The conventional animal sacrifice to a khat'i in Pshavi or Khevsureti is either a bull or a sheep. Domestic poultry and pigs are regarded as impure, are never sacrificed, and a khevisberi may not eat their meat. Goats, especially goat kids (*cik'ani*), are offered to supernatural beings of ambiguous nature, those which are capable of causing harm unless propitiated or neutralized. The class of spirits which receive goat sacrifices include the 'evil angels' described here, the prophet Elijah (because his lightning bolts can cause death), and the various female auxiliaries of clan or commune divinities. For more on the complementary relation between masculine divinities and ambiguous, mostly non-masculine supernaturals, see Tuite 2004.

[13] See note 4 above.

When a person is dying, he or she has a guardian (*q'arauli*). God forfend —
for example, when someone is dying, don't you stand guard [i.e. keep them
company], don't you remain at their side? But when there is no one — either
lightning strikes them, or they fall in the water, they fall off a cliff, that is, they
die alone, or as we say in Pshavi, they have 'died without anyone' (*uk'acod
mamk'vdar*). In such a case it is necessary to slaughter a goat-kid at the very
place where it happened [where the victim died]. You perform the deed [the
sacrifice], you drive away the evil angel. They throw the goat-kid's head, and
they perform the deed, they drive away this misfortune. Over there, a man fell
[to his death], there where the cross is by the khat'i. It should be on this side of
the river; it is not allowed close to the khat'i. This is where the goat-kid was
sacrificed. That is the kind of rules we have, we mountaineers, Pshavs.

KT: *When they kill the goat-kid, do they leave it on the spot?*

No, they throw the head there.

RD: *Is it necessary to throw the head in the river?*

No, you swing it around in a circle three times, and you throw it away.[14] You say
[addressing the demon]: "You are separated from this affair, evil angel, go where
the head is." This is how we do it. I have performed this deed.

KT: *Do you perform the ritual for someone killed by lightning?*

A single ritual is performed, when a person dies without another person nearby,
that is, without a guardian. This deed liberates everything.

---

[14] The figure of a thrice-repeated counterclockwise circular movement is of particular
importance in highland Georgian religious symbolism, as it serves to mark major life-
stage transitions. Newly-initiated boys perform a triple counterclockwise circumambulation
of the pyramid-shaped initiation tower at Gogolaurta, led by the khevisberi. During their
initiation, girls and in-marrying women turn three times in place while the khevisberi
twirls a round *kada* bread over their heads, likewise three times in a counterclockwise
direction. In the traditional Pshav marriage ceremony, the bride circled her hearth chain
three times to take leave of her father's clan, then performed the same act upon arrival in
her husband's home, to signal her entry into the latter's household. In the context of the
ritual described here, the triple circle made with the goat's head apparently serves to
liberate the drowning victim's soul from the demons holding it at the spot where death
occurred, so that it can complete its trajectory into the 'land of souls' (*suleti*).

KT: *Does one celebrate Eliaoba [the feastday of the prophet Elijah], or is there a sanctuary to Elijah in Pshavi?*[15] *I heard there is one in Khevsureti. There are quite a few in western Georgia.*

We observe Eliaoba here, we have a special khat'i to him up high [on the mountain]. But there are no longer many in Pshavi. We sacrifice a goat-kid at Eliaoba. Of course, you could also kill a lamb, or sacrifice another animal as a petition (*samxvec'ro*), but the principal sacrifice which we would kill as an offering to him is a goat-kid. It is for this reason, as has been passed down by our tradition, that God sent Elijah and said to him: "Take care of the people." There is a great history about him. When he created lightning, fire and everything; just for this reason we sacrifice to him: "Keep the lightning away [from us]," that sort of thing …

KT: *Hail, for example, is that also sent down by Elijah?*

Elijah — is lightning, is accompanied by lightning. He struck the clouds together, suddenly he created lightning, and then people could not understand what this lightning was, and they were dying. I know this from tradition (*gadmocemit*), but whether it is a fact, I do not know. This is how we recall the story of lightning, and of hail too. There is an angel, an angel sent from God.[16] In the invocation we commemorate him: "Glorious force, living K'vira (*k'virao cxovelo*)" — we commemorate the shrine (*khat'i*), then honorable K'vira, that is, K'vira was the first helper to whom people made a resting place (*daesvenebina*, i.e., constructed a shrine in his honor).[17] The people were all

---

[15] The Old Testament prophet Elijah, who called down lightning from heaven to destroy his adversaries [2 Kings 1: 9-14], and who was taken to heaven in a chariot of fire [2 Kings 2: 11-12], has taken on the attributes of a lightning and storm god in the folk religions of many regions of Europe, including the North and South Caucasus (Ivanov 1991; Tuite 2004).

[16] In Baghiauri's usage, the term 'angel' (*angelozi*) is essentially synonymous with *xvtisšvili* ('child of God'), an expression used by many Pshavs and Khevsurs to denote the class of divinities subordinate to God the Creator (*dambadebeli*). Some of the 'angels' or 'children of God' — the various St. Georges and Archangels, and the divinized ogre-slaying heroes K'op'ala and Iaxsar — have the attributes of feudal nobility, in that they rule over and protect the highland communes in exchange for sacrifices and services rendered by the human 'vassals' (*q'mani*) who dwell in their fiefdom (Bardavelidze 1957: 24-29; Tuite 2002).

[17] K'vira or K'viria is the divine intermediary between God and the other 'angels' or 'children of God'. He is said to have his tent (*k'aravi*) pitched in the court of God (*γvtis k'ari*). Two possible sources have been identified for his name, and both might have contributed to some extent: (1) the name of St. Cyricus/Quiricus, whose cult is especially popular in Svaneti; and (2) *K'vira-cxoveli* "Living Sunday", the Georgian Orthodox feast celebrated on the Sunday after Easter. The homophony of K'vira and the Georgian word

working. Then God sent his son, Jesus [to find out] "what are the people lacking?," then this angel, K'vira — he sent this angel, [saying] "help the people." He came down on a Saturday at midday, this is our tradition, as they recall, he [K'vira] set up a tent; that is why we say [in invocations] "O K'vira the tent-dweller" (*k'virao k'araviano*). He set up his tent at midday, called the people and said that "God has sent me, so, come here," — at midday, he [God] sent K'vira and said [to the people]: "From here to here you are free, you will have a day off from work (*ukmi*)." He gave the people one day each week.

PB: *How does sworn brotherhood (dzmadnapicoba) take place, what sort of ritual is there? What have you heard with regard to this?*

I have not only heard about it, I myself have sworn brothers. Among us, in Pshavi, it happens like this: those who love each other, respect each other, or who meet and like each other for their manly virtues (*važk'acoba*), at that time they take a silver coin — it must be of silver,[18] you should know — then they drop it into a drinking cup, then first one of them stands up, says a blessing, then takes an oath of brotherhood: "Your mother is my mother, your father [is] my father." Sometimes the words are a bit different, but they become like true children of the same parents (*dedmamišvilebi*). "My brother is your brother ..." and so it goes. Now the cup is given to the second person, he also says a blessing. The little finger of each person is cut. The little finger (*nek'a*) is the highest finger, it is only responsible for good things. The little finger is cut, a drop of blood is dripped into the cup, three drops, little drops, and this is accompanied by a prayer. They take it [the cup] and first one drinks half, then the other. They embrace each other, kiss each other and they become true brothers. From this time onward they are related like blood siblings. In this way, I am related to them ...

PB: *What drink is used?*

Vodka (*araq'i*) or wine. It must be pure (*supta*). In Pshavi, for example, vodka is usual.

PB: *If it takes place during a shrine festival (khat'oba), can it be done with beer?*

With beer, or with wine, it is not important; the main thing is that you swear as true brothers, and that you be true [to your oath], that you observe this

---

for "Sunday" and "week" (*k'vira*) is likely to underlie the just-so story crediting him with the institution of one day of rest each week.

[18] In another variant of this ritual, known as the 'eating of oath-silver' (*pic-vercxlis č'ama*), the two men scrape a bit of metal from the blades of their daggers into the drinking vessel.

obligation as if it were your own brother. It is often performed by those who do not have brothers and sisters; they choose a friend, a comrade, someone who is close to them, who becomes their brother.

PB: *Can something similar happen between a woman and a man?*

Yes, it does, although much more rarely. Usually this happens as I just said, between men.

KT: *How about between people of different ethnicity, for example, between Georgians and Chechens?*

It has nothing to do with nationality, it does not matter if one is English, or American, or whatever. It could be with whomever you want, as long as it is genuine. But you must observe [its conditions]. If someone doesn't understand and doesn't know, but if you do know everything, you may take the oath and observe the rules, the rules that exist between sisters and brothers, between brothers.

10.4. Admitting New Members Into the Commune

KT: *Now I would like to know how one accepted new people into the commune (temi), families coming from other provinces or communes, who moved into your territory and requested asylum.*

That was a somewhat complicated affair. Earlier land was scarce, take Pshavi for example … Here the people worked tiny plots of land, many people came to us here. Here, where the C'oc'k'olaurebi are, the Baghiaurebi have immigrated.[19] It is still written somewhere, it is handed down in a book. Here is how it happened: For instance, if someone caused disruption in the commune, or did not get along, they would be driven out from there. This also happened in Pshavi. Those who were driven out went to another commune. This is how it was among us here, when they would come here. We Gogolaurebi, we had three people of that kind … This was not a matter decided only by the commune. The commune received them, but took them to the khat'i; when they brought them to the khat'i, they made them swear an oath, what we call a *samani* — they either planted a stone,[20] or made some other kind of offering, on which their

---

[19] The C'oc'k'olaurebi are the principal clan of the commune of Muko, which is adjacent to Gogolaurta. Vaxt'ang C'oc'k'olauri, the khevisberi at Muko, is one of the younger priests now in service (when we first met him in the 1990s, he was under forty years of age).

[20] Traditionally, solemn oaths made before the shrine were marked by the planting of large stones (*samani*) in the ground in the shrine precincts. In standard Georgian, the word *samani* denotes a boundary-marking stone.

name was inscribed, and then this was the custom: they set up three cups, they lit candles, and that man brought an animal for sacrifice. The khevisberi took the three cups and prayed: "We, the clan (*gvari*), the commune, accept this man. Should this person betray us," — he poured out the cup — "thus may it be for him. If he is a brother to us, if he has our confidence, then may we acknowledge him to be a participant (*monac'ile*) in our khat'i, and to be the khat'i's vassal (*q'ma*)." Then the commune granted him [and his family], as a regular segment (*ganaq'ari*) of the clan, some small plots of land. This one carved off a little, that one carved off a little [i.e. each resident gave a bit of land to the new member], and they settled this man here. This was the custom.

KT: *Is marriage prohibited between women and men of the same clan or commune?*

It is not possible, that sort of thing will never happen.[21] In earlier times, they would gather at Lasharis-Jvari, and they expelled (*mohk'vetdnen*) such people: they would not let them in their homes, nor anywhere else. Or else they had means, such as the court of justice (*sasamartlo*).

KT: *Couldn't they split the clan or commune?*

The clan would split (*iq'reboda*). For example, here in Gogolaurta, we have several segmented clans (*ganaq'ari gvarebi*), but now with different family names. For instance, there were once three brothers named Kubrashvili, the black plague killed two of them — it seems that they committed an offense before the khat'i or something of the sort. A fortune-teller, 'reader' or khevisberi — I don't know exactly — said [to the surviving brother]: "Leave this place!" He settled over there. Now the Kubrashvilebi are an entire village, where I live now, in Bulachauri. There was once a man called Kubria, and the clan was named after him. Then the clan was renamed, and they now have a new family name. Take Ilo, for example, he is a Jabanashvili [descended from the Jabanashvili clan], but registered (with the family name) Pxoveli, they changed his name.[22]

---

[21] The Georgian highlanders, like all indigenous peoples of the Caucasus — with the exception of the Daghestanians — observe strict exogamy. Marriage between individuals known to be related is prohibited, or can only be permitted if the clan to which the young couple belongs officially divides into two new lineages (in a ceremony known as *gvaris gaq'ra* 'splitting the clan'), so that marriage becomes an exogamic one. On Pshav-Khevsur exogamy and kinship reckoning, see Tuite 2000.

[22] The late Ilo Pxoveli of Chinti was a well-known local poet. The family names of the Georgian mountaineers were officially registered by the Tsarist administration in the late nineteenth century. Some last names were based on clan or lineage names, others on the individual's village of origin or profession. Not uncommonly, brothers were registered with different last names.

When a clan was divided, [they said]: "go … live separately." They would give you your portion of everything, they settled you somewhere else.

KT: *Is marriage possible between different clans?*

Of course. For example, I am a vassal of the khat'i of Gogolaurta; this person is [the vassal] of Khoshara [commune upriver from Gogolaurta]. If my children have no relation [to them] that could be traced through female ancestors (*deidašviloba-mamidašviloba*),[23] it is permitted, with pleasure, let them marry and celebrate a wedding.

KT: *Who lives in the Gogolaurta commune now? Is there only that one village up there, by the shrine, where you live?*

In fact, the Gogolaurebi — at the head of the road, where Davit Gelashvili [and his family] are, they are true Gogolauris. On the other side where the Lomiashvilebi live, these have moved in, they are Mamiaurebi, and are vassals of Uk'ana-Pshavi. That is where they are from, from Uk'ana-Pshavi.[24]

RD: *Those who live across from Muko, do they belong to Gogolauri?*

One of them is a Gogolauri, P'avle Gelashvili. The Beridzes are likewise Gogolaurebi. But the territory belongs to Muko, from across the ravine down to the river.

RD: *How far does the territory of Muko go in that direction, up toward Gogolaurta?*

There nearby, where the village is, it follows the ridge overlooking it.[25]

RD: *As you go up to your house, it goes about that far?*

Where my house is, it passes close by, there where there is a small hill, it cuts across it, it's a very small place.

---

[23] With the passage of time, genealogical relation through male relatives is more easily remembered than that through female ancestors, who, in these virilocal societies, usually leave their natal village to live in that of their in-laws, and whose children assume the clan identity of their fathers.

[24] Uk'ana-Pshavi, situated along the upper reaches of the Pshavis Aragvi, is one of the more remotely situated communes. In recent decades, many families from less-accessible villages have moved downriver to be closer to the main roads.

[25] The next day, Baghiauri told us that he takes a particular interest in the ancient frontiers of the Pshav communes and the parcels of land that belonged to the shrine, or that were considered off-limits to ordinary use. These traditional divisions of the territory were of course not recognized during the Soviet period.

KT: *How many people are in Muko commune now?*

There is just the one family C'oc'k'olaurebi that lives here. Also one of the children split off, Vaxt'angi [the khevisberi of Muko commune] no longer lives there. There are just two families, the rest moved away.

10.5. Pilip'e Lights a Candle and Makes an Invocation

PB (points to the candle): *The candle must be …*

A real one, of beeswax.[26]

Figure 10.3. Men making beeswax candles at Lasharis-Jvari. Photo by P. Bukhrashvili

PB: *And not one from the church? It has to be one of yours?*

It must be made from beeswax. It will not accept other kinds, our *khat'i*, praised be its truth. There [i.e., in lowland Georgia], among the Orthodox priests

---

[26] Four types of offerings can be presented to the khat'i: (1) sacrificial animals (bulls and sheep), (2) alcoholic beverages, (3) bread, and (4) beeswax candles, or more precisely, bee products. As Baghiauri insisted in this dialogue, it is the material of which the candle is made that has significance, not the fact that it burns and emits light. At Matura in 2001, we noted that the two khevisberis in service there brought a bottle of water mixed with honey to the shrine. In response to our questions, they explained that honey is an acceptable substitute for wine or vodka, because it is produced by bees, and therefore 'pure' (*supta*).

(*samɣvdeloebaši*), you can light whatever you want. They have a thousand different types of candles, some of them made from unclean ingredients (*bindzuri minarevebi*), which would not be permitted before the khat'i. I will not light them, you can light them if you want, and make your petition, but such candles are improper. If you were to buy one lump of beeswax (*pič'a*), it would be enough. When you go up to the khat'i, you can make [candles] directly from the wax.[27]

PB: *Does it have to be made by my own hands?*

It is best if it is by your own hands. Whether or not you accept candles from there [the lowlands], according to Christian laws, is the [Orthodox] priests' affair. But among us, I am telling you the truth, I know for sure, I saw a dream that the khat'ebi would throw them [church candles] away, they wouldn't accept them.

Figure 10.4. Damast'e Shrine. Photo by K. Tuite

---

[27] One common sight at shrine festivals is the production of handmade candles to be offered to the khat'i. Lumps of beeswax are held over a fire until soft. As one man holds a taut string about three or four feet long, another spreads the softened wax over the string, rubbing it between his two hands until it covers the length of the string evenly. It is then cut into candles of about one span length (*mt'k'aveli*), the distance from the thumb to the tip of the little finger of a spread hand [see photo above].

[Invocation] May he be well, may the great Angel of St. George of Matur-Khevi grant you mercy, may the Creator of Damast'e (*damast'urma gamčenelma*)[28] multiply your young generation, may he always go before [you] and greet you and your children with happiness here! Let this be my prayer, may the mercy of the angels be [upon you]. Rejoice, multiply, be well and may your travels always be good and safe. Beside this I will add: Victory (*gaumarjos*) to the sanctuaries that are in our [land of] Georgia: those of Pshavi, of Khevsureti, of Mountain Tusheti. May the praise be theirs, and may they be merciful to our Georgian nation. Let there be peace in our Georgia, let there be happiness, let there be hope for our young people. What power there is that comes from God, that is sent by the angels for the aid of mortals (*xorcielta*), may it help them and assist them. May we see a united Georgia, may we see peace, may we have such a leader, that will bring matters to a peaceful resolution.[29]

This now is the second toast: to you men and those like you in our little corner, our little Georgia. May such people grow up clever, upright and good. May they promote [the cause of] peace. May we lend each other a hand (*šegvec'q'vas xeli*) in love, in mutual understanding. May we raise such a future generation, so that they will love each other, and not have a hostile outlook. Let there be peace, may God look down from above, the angels and the martyrs. Victory to you, may you be well!

......

---

[28] These are the two shrines at either end of the Matur-Khevi valley. The khat'i of the Archangel is the principal shrine of the Matura commune, located outside of a hamlet near the head of the valley. The powerful weather shrine of Damast'e or Damast'uri [see photo] overlooks the confluence of the Matur-Khevi and Aragvi rivers. It received offerings from all Pshav communes on the Sunday before Lent, and in times of drought or excessive rain.

[29] Almost all of the verbs used in the text of this invocation are in the pluperfect conjunctive, a verb paradigm that is rarely used in modern Georgian except in toasts, wishes and the like. Baghiauri formed the pluperfect conjunctive of relative intransitive verbs by postposing the optative of the copula, a non-standard usage characteristic of some Georgian dialects (*gv-q'ol-iq'os* "may we have him"; *h-q'var-eb-iq'os* "may they love [each other]"; cp. standard Georgian *gv-q'ol-od-es, h-q'var-eb-od-es*).

Figure 10.5. P. Baghiauri at Lasharis-Jvari. Photo by K. Tuite

As khevisberi you must behave in exemplary manner, and then you must give a push to (*ubidzgo*) the future generation: so that you, son, grandson, may follow me in this way. This honor, these precepts (*darigeba*), this law (*c'esi*) — if we are to become impure (*uc'mindurebi*), how could we instruct others? We have this obligation.

10.6. At Lasharis-Jvari

The next day the khevisberi and the interviewers went upriver to the central Pshav shrine of Lasharis-Jvari, accompanied by the writer Irak'li Gogolauri and several construction workers.[30] The occasion was a very special one: Gogolauri had raised money and resources for the restoration of several ruined buildings within the precincts of Lasharis-Jvari, beginning with the rebuilding of the salude (beer-storage cabin), to be followed by work on the ancient sadarbazo (meeting-place) where the chief priests of the Pshav communes formerly met to discuss issues of importance to the highland community. Before beginning work, Irak'li Gogolauri and the men who were to participate in the project brought a lamb to Baghiauri to be sacrificed to the shrine's patron divinity Lashara, to ask his blessing and appease him should anyone unwittingly incur his displeasure while working in the proximity of his sanctuary. Lashara, whose name derives from the thirteenth-century Georgian monarch Giorgi IV Lasha, the son of

---

[30] The late Irak'li Gogolauri of Magharos-k'ari was a highly-regarded author and poet.

Queen Tamar, is the most powerful among the divine overlords of the Pshav communes. An eighteenth-century document mentions eleven communes, all of which were inhabited until recently, but according to local tradition there were once twelve or even fifteen groups of villages under the protection of Lashara. During the great mid-summer festival of Seroba or Saghmurtoba, members of all the Pshav communes gathered at Lasharis-Jvari on the Monday following P'et're-P'avloba, the feast of the apostles Peter and Paul (29 June O.S. = 12 July N.S.). The following day, they would visit the shrine of Tamar-Ghele, named after Queen Tamar, situated in a nearby river valley.

Our conversation took place on the slope of Lasharis Gori, overlooking the main candle-altar and sacrifice grounds of the Lasharis-Jvari complex. Some of the men are holding lumps of beeswax with their knives over the fire, to soften it for making candles. Pilip'e Baghiauri points to the various spots on the hillside where the communes used to gather on feastdays.

Each commune that came here sat in its own area (*sajare*). Here is where the Gogolaurebi dug out their area. The Gogolaurebi used to say that at the shrine festival (*khat'oba*), their banner (*droša*) was the first to arrive at Lasharis-Jvari, and the Gogolaurebi represented the largest portion (*c'ili*, i.e. were the most numerous). Gara Turmanauli was one of ours, and they built him the dwelling closest to the khat'i.[31] At gatherings each commune has its place, and each one knows where its place is. They have dug out, levelled off their places, just for them. Everyone comes to Lasharoba, and they gather there. Here in the middle was the beer-storage cabin (*salude*). The Gogolaurebi must have been the smartest, because they set up their place closest to the *salude*.

When the Turmanaulebi came, history does not recall. No one remembers when the Gogolaurta came, that is, they are the *unjni*, the aboriginal ones, among us. The word *unjni* means 'old.'[32] The *unjni q'mani* (original vassals of the khat'i) are to be distinguished from the *q'urum q'mani*. The *q'urum q'mani* are those who immigrated, who entered by oath. They are called 'entered-by-oath *q'urum* vassals' (*šemopicult q'urum q'mani*). These are secondary; those who are primary, they are called *unjni q'mani*. It is a big difference.[33]

There was one khevisberi, but as judge (*mosamartle*) there would be just one from among the fifteen communes, who would be a khevisberi, who could decide matters of justice. He was considered the elder. So that there would be

[31] Gara Turmanauli was a legendary shrine priest, reputed to have been a great warrior and livestock raider. Several legends about Gara are reprinted in K'ik'nadze (2011, 402-412).

[32] In medieval Georgian *unji* means 'treasure', as in the derived form *sa-unj-e* 'treasure trove'.

[33] Bardavelidze (1957, 35) deemed the *unjni q'mani* tantamount to an incipient 'aristocracy', as they were the group from which most community leaders were drawn.

no mistakes in anything. For instance, Gara Turmanauli was a Gogolauri, he was a khevisberi, he was the most intelligent, and here (at Lasharis-Jvari) he officiated. Then there was a man from Axadi,[34] and so on. The primary khevisberi, who performed, took care of matters, was chosen by him [Lasharis-Jvari], the khat'i himself chose him. He was the cleverest in the commune, the most worthy, the most honorable. Then the court of justice (*sasamartlo*) took place, when they expelled people from here. They call it expulsion (*mok'veta*) when they exclude someone, be it a woman or a man. Here the court of justice was held, it sat here, matters were settled. And here was the meeting hall (*darbazi*), where they arrived at decisions, the council of the communes (*temta sabč'o*) — we are finally going to rebuild the meeting hall.

Come here, I will tell you something. You know Lela Buc'ashvili. She had dedicated a five-year-old bull (*mozveri*) as an offering. The woman led it here. Like it or not, she had seen a dream, her children came to her, [saying]: "You must sacrifice it," so she tells me. "I saw you in the dream" [she says], it [the dream] came once, twice, three times. We came down, Ioseb [K'och'lishvili, the khevisberi of Udzilaurt commune] and the others were drinking and didn't accompany the woman. I brought Davit Gelashvili and some others and we came here. They said, "let's slaughter it down here [on the riverbank], we won't be able to get this one up there" [presumably the beast seemed too heavy to walk up the narrow path to the summit of Lasharis Gori, where the shrine is]. I told them, "What do you mean we can't lead it up there, that is the custom!" [They said], "then bring the candles and we'll light them down here." This bull was resisting, we were 9 or 10 men, it's bellowing, the whole unfortunate business. We arrived there, I lit the candle, I put my hand on it, I went in front, it came up here. When we got up here, [they said], "we won't be able to overturn it onto its side."[35] We stood up and tied it up with a thick rope. As I touched the dagger to it, it broke [the rope] and got away, the rope was frayed. I fell back, then I went back to the bull. It followed me, then it knelt down, on its own, right here, where the blood is to go down.[36] This is where it must be sacrificed, for the offering of blood, the sacrifice is to be killed by this spot. People witnessed it.

---

[34] The commune of Axadi, now uninhabited, was located further upstream along the opposite bank of the Aragvi.

[35] Before the bull's throat is cut, it is forced to lay on its side. This is usually done by running a rope around its front, then hind legs, and then pulling until the beast keels over.

[36] Animals sacrificed at Lasharis-Jvari are slaughtered next to a shallow rectangular pit, into which their blood is made to flow.

References

Bardavelidze, Vera. 1957. *The oldest religious beliefs and ritual graphic art of the Georgian tribes*. Tbilisi: Mecniereba. [In Russian].

—. 1974. *Traditional cultic monuments of the East Georgian mountain districts*. Vol I: Pshavi. Tbilisi. Metsniereba. [In Georgian].

Charachidzé, Georges. 1968. *Le système religieux de la Géorgie païenne: analyse structurale d'une civilisation*. Paris: Maspero.

Ivanov, Vjacheslav Vs. 1991. Ilija. *Mify narodov mira*, S. A. Tokarev (ed.), vol. I: 505-6. Moscow: Sovetskaja enciklopedia.

K'ik'nadze, Zurab. 1996. Ge*orgian mythology, I. The shrine and the community*. Kutaisi: Gelati Academy of Sciences. [In Georgian].

—. 2011. *Shrine-foundation myths. Religious-mythological traditions of the East Georgian highlands*. Tbilisi: Ilia State University Press. [In Georgian].

Mindadze, Nunu. 1981. "The institution of (divine) selection and psycho-nervous illnesses in Pshavi." *Materials for ethnography of Georgia* XXI: 146-152. [In Georgian].

—. 1987. The question of the institution of the *kadagi* (oracle) in the East Georgian highlands. *Materials for ethnography of Georgia* XXIII: 174-180. [In Georgian].

Tuite, Kevin. 1996. Highland Georgian paganism — archaism or innovation? *Annual of the Society for the Study of Caucasia* #7, pp 79-91.

—. 2000. "'Anti-marriage' in ancient Georgian society." *Anthropological Linguistics* 42 #1: 37-60.

—. 2002. "Real and imagined feudalism in highland Georgia." *Amirani* #7: 25-43.

—. 2004. "Lightning, sacrifice and possession in the traditional religions of the Caucasus." *Anthropos* 99: 143-159 (Part I), 481-497 (Part II).

—. 2011. "Xevsur shrine invocations: iconicity, intertextuality and agonism." *Folia Caucasica: Festschrift für Jost Gippert zum 55. Geburtstag*. Manana Tandaschwili and Zakaria Pourtskhvanidze (eds), Logos Publishing, Frankfurt/Tbilisi; 197-221.

—. 2016. "The political symbolism of the mid-summer festival in Pshavi (Northeast Georgian highlands), then and now." *Kaukasiologie heute. Festschrift für Heinz Fähnrich zum 70. Geburtstag*. Herausgegeben von Natia Reineck und Ute Rieger. Buchverlag König; 365-390.

Tuite, Kevin, and Paata Bukhrashvili. 1999. "Binarität und Komplementarität in Nordostgeorgien. Die Vorstellung von Jungen und Mädchen am Iaqsari-Heiligtum." *Georgica* #22: 59-72. (French version published in *Amirani* #3: 41-55 (2000), available on-line at <http://www.caucasology.com/amirani.htm>).

—. 2002. Central Caucasian religious systems and social ideology in the post-Soviet period. *Amirani* #7; 2002; 7-24.

Chapter 11

Georgian Language in Education

Tamari Lomtadze

Akaki Tsereteli State University, Kutaisi, Georgia

Manana Mikadze

Akaki Tsereteli State University, Kutaisi, Georgia

Abstract

This article outlines some debates and issues in the field of Applied linguistics. In particular, the Georgian language is discussed in the education of Soviet Georgia and after the restoration of independence, in accordance with the current legislation and real practices in Georgia. Theories and methods from sociolinguistics, survey method, quantitative and qualitative analysis method, statistical method is used in the research. The urgency of the issue is determined by the fact that for the normal functioning of the state, the official language must be known by all socially and economically active residents and it should be used in communications with the state institutions. After the restoration of independence, principal changes have taken place, which has brought forward the necessity for Georgians and for non-Georgians to become aware of their new roles and opportunities in a democratic national state. A part of Georgia's citizens has not adapted to Georgian culture and Georgian language environment and do not feel a connection to the state of Georgia. A representative of a minority had always known native and the official language. After the restoration of independence, the number of Georgian language speakers has grown, but the proficiency of Georgian is still not adequate, since the language of the minority is known by a larger part of minority population than that speaking the official language, especially in the Kvemo Kartli and Samtskhe- Javakheti regions. The solution to the problem lies in the proper planning and implementation of language education policies.

Keywords: Education Language policy, Georgian state language, Georgian language of education, Georgian language acquisition.

***

11.1. Introduction

Linguistic integration problems of Georgian society must be solved on several levels, corresponding to the international standards of the collective rights of minorities and the linguistic rights of an individual.

Georgia is a multi-lingual (multi-ethnic) country. According to the census held in 2014 total population of Georgia is about 4 million. Ethnic Georgians constitute 86.8 % of the population. The other groups in total - 13. 2%. That is why in the education system Georgian language has always been used as the main language, except in the nineteenth and early twentieth centuries, when Russian was the state language in Georgia and Georgian was banned from teaching even at primary schools. After the restoration of Georgia's independence, this problem was solved in 1918, as the Georgian language gained constitutional status and became the official language of the country. At the same time, the language of instruction was Georgian in schools and in the first Georgian University, founded in 1918. Although Russia again occupied Georgia in 1921 and it became part of the Soviet Union, Georgian language was quite firmly represented in education (Gogolashvili, 2013). However, from the middle of the twentieth century, the introduction of the Russificationist policy in the Soviet Union began with the harassment of Georgian language in education. This was especially factual of the Autonomous Republics of Georgia and other regions populated by non-Georgians. In particular, Kvemo Kartli and Samtskhe-Javakheti, where the ethnic Azerbaijan and Armenian populations are in the majority. Georgian, as the state language in Soviet Georgia, had to compete with Russian, as well as Armenian and Azerbaijani in the mentioned regions.

After the restoration of Georgia's independence (1991), when the full functioning of Georgian in education began, difficult economic-political-social conditions and the lack of language policy in education again posed difficulties for the Georgian language in education.

The situation is unknown, especially in the occupied autonomous republics, where the legislation of Georgia does not apply, as well as in the regions inhabited by ethnic minorities. The situation in the latter is complicated by the fact that geographically these territories are located on the border of Armenia and Azerbaijan. Both are peripheral areas where the population is engaged in agricultural activities and the vast majority of them do not consider as an important issue.

In our work, we will try to show how the language policy of education contributes to the establishment of Georgian as a state language in Georgia.

11.2. Scholarship

While the developed countries of the world have made significant progress through theoretical or methodological studies of the education language policy in preserving and prosperous functioning of state or minority languages (Kloss, 1977; Rubin, 1977; Fishman, 1979; Hornberger, 1988; Ruiz, 1984; Cooper, 1989), Georgia was a Soviet country where the language policy of education planned only in Kremlin was allowed. Therefore, no researches have been conducted in this direction. During this period, the language policy of education in America and Western Worlds had become one of the central and key issues of the language policy, whose detailed and purposeful research was so diversified and refined that it created a new stage in the history of language policy.

In this regard, especially important is Spolski's conception of Educational Linguistics. In his introductory textbook on the subject (Spolsky, 1978), educational linguistics (a term borrowed from educational psychology and educational sociology) is offered a model derived from theories of language, learning (psychology), language learning (psycholinguistics), and language use (sociolinguistics), all directed toward second language pedagogy. In an entry of The International Encyclopedia of Education (1985), Spolsky describes educational linguistics as a branch of applied linguistics, further specifying the following subfields: language education policy and planning; first and second language acquisition and teaching, reading, literacy, and composition; mother tongue and bilingual education, minority and immigrant education, and language testing. For Spolsky, language education integrates "the situation in which it takes place and the communicative competence of the learners who are to be educated" (1985, 3095). Spolsky (1999) defines "the task of educational linguistics" as "knowledge from the many and varied branches of the scientific study of language that may be relevant to formal or informal education."

Later, when the language policy issues of micro-level education were also addressed, Georgia was already an independent country (See Martin-Jones, 2011; Chimburtane, 2011; Bonacina, 2010; Cincotta-Segl, 2009; Hult, 2010; Pan, 2011; Yitzhaki, 2010; Fitzsimmons-Doolan, 2009). However, facing such difficult economic, political or social difficulties, he took only the first steps in this direction. The Bilingual Educational Journal was launched in 2010, followed by the Tempus (European Commission) International Journal of Multilingual Education.

The result of the lack of theoretical, methodological or practical research is the fact that the acquisition, use and spread of the state Georgian language in education is still facing challenges.

11.3. For the Terms

The main Terms are: "Language in education" and "Language Educational Policy." The latter is used by Garcia and Menkel, but differ in the way that language education policy focuses more on the facto politics (Garcia and Menken, 2010).

Jonson adopts the term educational language policy to describe the official and unofficial policies that are created across multiple layers and institutional contexts (from national organizations to classrooms) that impact language use in classrooms and schools. Educational language policies are interpreted, appropriated, and instantiated in potentially creative and unpredictable ways that rely on the implementational and ideological spaces unique to the classroom, school, and community. Such policies can, but don't necessarily, impact language education (i. e. the teaching of languages) as they can also impact the language used in content classrooms (e.g. science, history, art). Educational language policies have historically been used to eradicate, subjugate, and marginalize minority and indigenous languages and their users and are, therefore, instruments of power that influence access to educational and economic resources. They have also been used to develop, maintain, and promote indigenous and minority languages, especially in additive bilingual education programs. At every level of educational language policy, and throughout the educational language policy process, there are different and potentially divergent ideologies about language and language education that are unique to the discursive processes within that level/layer/institution (Johnson, 2013).

11.4. Georgian Language in Education in the Soviet Georgia

From the Russification policy in Soviet Georgia, Georgian as a language of education experienced some difficulties. This fact also had a precondition: from the nineteenth century until 1918, the state language in Georgia in fact was Russian.

Getting an education in the Georgian language was forbidden, including in primary education. Georgia gained independence in 1918 and it was written in the constitution that the state language is Georgian. Georgian started functioning as the language of education again. The first Georgian university was opened in Tbilisi in the same year. Georgian was also declared to be the language of higher education. Accordingly, the articles published by the University and the Academy of Sciences were published mainly in Georgian language until the middle of the twentieth century (Gogolashvili, 2013).

Georgian retained its constitutional status even after the loss of its independence under the Constitution of the Soviet Georgia. Although Georgia was a part of the USSR, Russificationist policy began to take hold in the 1950s. The Union

Ministry of Education took into account the language situation in the region and, in cooperation with common Union programs, established guidelines and recommendations for regional tasks to facilitate the Russian-speaking population (Tabidze, 2005). Accordingly, in Georgia the language of communication between different ethnic groups was Russian as well.

From this period, like other republics of the Soviet Union, the number of Russian schools in Georgia increased. Russian classes were also increasing and it was taught at a high level in non-Russian schools. Such kind of schools in Georgia were Georgian, Azerbaijani, Armenian, Abkhazian and Ossetian. However, the status of Russian was not officially a native language, a foreign language, or even a second language. It was evaluated at different levels: second mother tongue, interlanguage, union language, super-dominant language (Gogolashvili, 2013). In 1941, "Circular Russian Teaching at Non-Russian Schools" was published. In the same year, Chistakov's methodological manual was published, which was the methodological standard for teaching a second language in the USSR. The selection of a Russian language teacher as a second language teacher was discussed separately. Preference was given to some Russian (monolingual) teachers. There were special teacher training programs and institutions (Lewis, 1972). In 1961, the Union Council of Ministers established proportions for the teaching of foreign languages. Such approaches were designed to study Russian at a high level.

In the Soviet Georgia there were: 1) Georgian schools, where the language of education was Georgian, Russian started from the second grade, two hours a week, a foreign language was added from the fifth grade, and Russian and a foreign language were taught at the same hourly rate. 2) Russian schools, where the language of education was Russian, foreign language and Georgian started from the fifth grade, 3) Abkhazian schools, in which Abkhazian was taught in primary classes, and from the fifth-grade subject were taught in Russian and a foreign language was added, 4) Ossetian schools were similar to Abkhazian. 5) Azerbaijani schools, where Azerbaijani was taught, added Russian from the second grade, and Foreign language and Georgian from the fifth grade. 6) Armenian schools, where teaching process was held in Armenian, added Russian from the second grade, and Foreign language and Georgian from the fifth grade.

Georgian was studied and mastered at a high level by Georgian school pupils, while in the other schools the study of Georgian was only fictitious and Georgian lessons were almost non-existent. Thus, the majority of the non-Georgian populations in the Soviet Georgia either did not know Georgian at all, or spoke Georgian only at a very low level. They did not know to read and write even at a low level (according to self-esteem).

The Number of Russian kindergartens was growing similarly. As for the higher educational institutions, there was no Russian higher educational institution there, but the number of Russian-speaking sectors at all higher educational institutions was increasing.

In 1978 the Kremlin wanted Georgia to adopt a new constitution, according to which the state language in the Soviet Republic of Georgia would be Russian. Georgian people resisted this intention and the Georgian language retained its constitutional status. In response, the Georgian education system focused on strengthening Georgian and adopted several resolutions that helped to strengthen the Georgian language in the education system. In particular: on April 10, 1979, a resolution was adopted in order to improve teaching Georgian language and literature in Georgian schools. On September 27, 1983, the Council of Ministers of the Republic adopted a resolution. As a result of the above-mentioned resolution, the Georgian language course became compulsory for all higher educational institutions of Georgia, at all faculties and all specialties for one or two semesters. Care for the Georgian language was even reflected in the culture of the Georgian speech.

Thus, planning the existed language education in the Soviet Georgia, on the one hand contributed to the study and spread of the Russian language, as well as in Georgian schools also in the schools and kindergartens of the ethnic minority. It was the source of communication among different ethnic groups. At the same time, ethnic minorities had the opportunity to receive education in their own language, but the function of the Georgian language as the official language of the state was not taken into account and it was not taught at non-Georgian schools. That's why the Georgian language was not established in the regions inhabited by ethnic minorities, where they were the majority.

From the 1950s onwards, Russian became more and more popular in a high society, knowledge of the Russian language was crucial for the career advancement, and many Georgian parents preferred their children to be educated in Russian. At the same time, the teachers of Georgian language and literature, as well as the teachers of history of Georgia tried to increase patriotic feelings in the pupils and students, with the help of which they strengthened the role of the Georgian language in a real-world practice.

11.5. Georgian Language in Education After the Restoration of Independence

After Georgia declared independence (1991), the creation of a new educational system was a logical step to ensure and promote successful integration processes of the Georgian society.

During the ruling of President Gamsakhurdia (1991-1993), the ideological propaganda contributed to the prosperity of the Georgian language - the Russian-language schools lost their contingent and even children from mixed families and other ethnic groups mostly left Russian schools and went the Georgian ones. The number of the Russian schools was considerably decreased and the Georgian became the dominant language for government officials, mass media and education. However, this was a result of the expression of the public will and not the result of a top-down language policy, as neither legislative changes were made to the language policy of the education during this period, nor any attempts to complete new textbooks, especially for minority schools. However, from this time on, the necessity of learning Georgian became obvious to them, because both the educational, public and private sectors demanded knowledge of the Georgian language.

Although the number of people speaking Georgian has increased in cities and towns, sociological and statistical studies that comprise data on Georgian and other Language proficiency revealed that in some regions, there are still many people who do not know Georgian, especially in Kvemo Kartli and Samtskhe-Javakheti regions. The Georgian language proficiency is influenced by the age, sex, education, place of residence and ethnicity of the population.

On August 24 1995, a new constitution of independent Georgia was adopted. According to Article 8 "Georgian is a state language of Georgia; In Abkhazia Abkhaz as well." It is true that Georgian and Abkhazian had constitutional rights, but during this period, Georgian law no longer applied to the Autonomous Republics of Abkhazia or the Autonomous Republics of Ossetia, these territories were occupied.

Article 6 of the 1994 Constitution for the de facto independent Abkhazia states: "The official language of the Republic of Abkhazia shall be the Abkhazian language," Russian being also recognized as a language of State and free use of other minority languages being guaranteed." The situation is similar in Ossetia. In fact, no language planning could be extended to these two autonomies adopted by Georgia. Before the conflict of the 1990s, the Abkhazian language was widely used at schools and universities. It has been taught at Tbilisi State University since 1924. Even today Abkhazian students take entrance examinations at Georgian universities in their native language. Ossetian language is taught in more than fifty schools in Georgia. Ossetian language has been taught at Tbilisi State University since 1918.

Changes started after 2003, when the post-Rose Revolution government, which followed the path of European integration, set one of the directions for the development of a national concept of tolerance and integration. This, concept, which has been implemented mainly since 2009, includes promoting the rise of the state language knowledge among national minorities.

According to the law on 'General Education' adopted on April 8, 2005, language issues in the field of education are mainly regulated by Article 4 of this law: "At general education institutions Georgian is the language of instruction and in the Autonomous Republic of Abkhazia – Georgian or Abkhazian." According to the third paragraph of the same Article, 'Citizens of Georgia, for whom Georgian is not a native language have the right to receive a full general education in their mother tongue, in accordance with the national curriculum and law.' In cases provided by international treaties and agreements of Georgia, in a general educational institution, it is possible to teach in a foreign language, but in this case, teaching the state language is also compulsory; and in the Autonomous Republic of Abkhazia – both state languages.

It seemed that the situation should have improved in terms of strengthening the role of Georgian language in education, but in reality, this did not happen. On the contrary, the teaching of the Georgian language was weakened. Georgian was removed from Georgian language faculties and specialties, English was taught at all levels of education, and Russian was removed as a compulsory subject. As for non-Georgian language schools, Georgian as a state language was limited to 5 hours per week (Gogolashvili, 2013).

It was necessary to create a system of education that would secure a level playing field in the education and labor market to the graduates of all schools. The need to develop Georgia as a country with a consolidated society was an important argument for increasing the proportion of the Georgian language.

Georgian language planning in education was particularly important for the two regions of Georgia where the ethnic minority represented the majority of the population. These were Kvemo Kartli and Samtskhe-Javakheti. Azeris are the majority in 2 districts of Kvemo (lower) kartli, especially Marneuli Municipality, where Azeris predominate with 83%, then comes Dmanisi (67%) Armenians constitute the majority in two districts of Samtskhe-Javakheti: Akhalkalaki (94%) and Ninotsminda (96%). There are also big Armenian communities in Tsalka (Kvemo Kartli, 55%). Despite numerous plans and events, we have not yet achieved the desired result in terms of learning the Georgian language. It is to overcome these challenges in 2015, the Parliament passed the bill of the state language and in 2017 the Department of the State Language was established, which works on the issues of functioning, protecting and developing Georgian as a state language.

According to Article 38 of the Constitution of Georgia, citizens of Georgia will be equal in social, economic, cultural and political life regardless of their national, ethnic, religious or linguistic belonging. In accordance with universally recognized principles and rules of international law, they will have the right to be developed independently, without any discrimination and interference in the culture, to use their mother tongue in private and in public.

The constitution of Georgia defines the rights of ethnic minorities in Chapter 4, Article 129: The free social-economic and cultural development of any ethnic minority of the Republic of Georgia cannot be limited/prevented, especially their education in their native language and self-governance of cultural and national affairs. Everyone has the right to write, publish and speak in his/her native language.

11.6. Georgian Language in Kindergarten Education with Ethnic Minorities

According to the statistics, the total number of kindergartens is 1259 in Georgia. It should be noted that the ethnic minorities of Georgia are not provided with the opportunity to learn the state language at any level of education.

Inequality has already emerged within the early age and pre-school education system in terms of equal opportunities and equality in education, which is caused by the lack of knowledge of the Georgian language. The root of the problem lies in the lack of bilingual teachers and teaching resources, although there are other factors as well. The kindergartens do not meet the goals of the strategies announced by the state, do not provide pupils with the Georgian language competencies and, do not lay the first grain for national integration. Consequently, a large proportion of children do not have the necessary readiness and social skills even at the elementary level of school.

Most of the kindergartens in the mentioned regions are monolingual and the Georgian language is not taught in the kindergartens at all. There are kindergartens where the contingent of children is entirely composed of ethnic minorities, however, the kindergartens operate entirely in Georgian.

Several projects have been implemented to promote the study of the Georgian Language in pre-school education institutions. For example, "we learn through playing – an interactive game for multilingual education (2005-2007). The children who took part in the project and continued their education in non-Georgian language schools already had Georgian language bases. In 2008-2009, the Ministry of Education and Science started developing a model of pre-school multilingual education "Promoting Georgian language learning at the pre-school level in non-Georgian-speaking regions." However, because of the lack of Georgian language teachers and teaching resources, the problem has not been resolved so far.

11.7. Georgian Language in Ethnic Minority Schools

According to the third paragraph of Article 4 and the first paragraph of Article 7 of the Law of Georgia on General Education, all citizens of Georgia have the right to receive general education in the state or mother tongue. However, other regulations of the same law make it compulsory to teach Georgian language and literature in non-Georgian schools, as well as to teach Georgian history, geography and other social sciences in Georgian (Article 5, 1, Georgian Law on General Education)

Although the Georgian government has initiated legislative changes since 2004, till 2006, non-Georgian schools used the curricula/study programs of Russia, Armenia or Azerbaijan. Accordingly, textbooks, guidebooks and other study materials were also brought from these countries. They had a program in Georgian language and Literature specially designed for ethnic minorities in the soviet Period.

There are Armenian, Azerbaijani and Russian language schools and sectors next to Georgian language schools in Georgia. Today there are 2309 schools. Among them are different types of public (2086) and private (223) schools in Georgia, where about 609 000 pupils study.

The number of non-Georgian language schools in Georgia is 10.22% of the total number of public schools. Besides 213 public schools, there are 77 Non-Georgian language sectors in Georgia. The number of pupils in these schools is about 8% of the total number of Georgia public school pupils (Tabatadze, Gorgadze, 2015).

As we have mentioned, in the towns or villages of Kvemo Kartli and Samtskhe-Jabakheti where the ethnic minority represents the majority of the population, the competence to speak Georgian was very low. Therefore, in 2006 a new program, "Learn and Teach Georgian," was launched in the regions with non-Georgian majorities. This program can play a significant role:

1) There were not enough Georgian teachers in these regions. MA students who went there as teachers were funded by the state for their graduate training and were paid more salaries than usual. These benefits partially helped to solve the staff problem.

2) The internet was almost completely out of the usage in these regions. The young educators/teachers made their students start using the Internet. Georgian-language Internet resources helped them to improve their linguistic competence.

3) Most importantly, new types of textbooks based on all four linguistic components (Writing, Reading, Listening and Speaking) were developed specifically for schools.

4) The Teachers' Professional Development Assistance and Assistant-Teacher Support Program was launched. These exams are to be taken in Georgian. Instead, certified teachers receive double salaries, which increases their motivation. This leads to the improvement of the level of competence in Georgian among the teachers of various subjects,

which can well serve as a prerequisite for the transition to bilingual education in the future.

In the Soviet epoch, there was a guidebook of Georgian grammar compiled by Gachechiladze for non-Georgian language schools. As a matter of fact, it was a practical grammar textbook that did not include writing, reading, listening and speaking skills, nor did it contain passages from literature. However, even if there had been a sophisticated textbook, no one was going to study Georgian, since in Soviet Georgia, Russian was regarded as a prestigious language. It was this guide that was used in the early years of the restoration of independence.

In order to improve the quality of Georgian language teaching in non-Georgian public schools, a textbook - Georgian for a second Language, entitled "Tavtavi," was published in 2005 by Nino Sharashenidze and Nana Shavtvaladze. Two additional level manuals were published in 2009. It should be noted that "Tavtavi" is the first textbook of Georgian as a second language and its creation was a step forward, as it included all four competencies: writing, reading, listening and speaking. In 2013, the 11th level textbook "Georgian as a second language: (Students book) was published by Manana Melikidze and Tinatin Tseradze.

In 2006-2008, a project was implemented by the Swiss organization CIMERA, within the framework of which twelve non-Georgian public-school teachers were trained. It seemed that the project was successful, but these approaches were still not implemented because of the low level of knowledge of the Georgian language among the teachers. At the same time, teachers in ethnic minority schools are very old and as they do not have teachers in all subjects, often one teacher teaches several subjects and there is a lack of teaching materials. As a result, 25% of the students who pass the final exam of the school are Azerbaijani and Armenian students. In recent years, due to the lack of teachers, ethnic minority schools in the villages are often closed and children go to Georgian schools, which is also a big obstacle for them, because their parents do not know Georgian. They mostly listen to TV and radio in their native language.

Georgian Language program was launched in Non-Georgian language schools of Georgia in 2010, that aimed to promote the state language while preserving the linguistic and cultural identity of ethnic minorities. The Georgian language program aimed to implement the following tasks: to promote the study of the state language for national minorities, to improve access to textbooks for students in non-Georgian speaking sectors; to develop and implement special linguistic programs for the adult population in ethnically populated regions; to increase the access to higher education.

The problem of the textbooks and the staff is still unresolved. Teachers play an important role in conducting and adapting top-down language policies, applying them in a specific practice. Since 2010, within the framework of the program "Georgian Language Teacher Training for non-Georgian language Schools" 250 Georgian Language teachers at Non-Georgian language schools have been retrained for the project "Promoting the Teaching of Georgian as a second Language in Non-Georgian Language Schools." According to the report of 2015 by the Center for Civic Integration and Interethnic Relations 58.6% of teachers employed in ethnic minority areas are over 50 years old, 16.5% are under 35 years old, and 30% are retired. " Teachers working in ethnic minority schools is a particularly vulnerable group. Most of them do not speak Georgian properly and are not part of the processes planned for raising the qualification of teachers in the state. Ethnic minority schools also have higher age limits and are less likely to replace old staff with new ones" (Tabatadze, Gorgadze, 2015).

Representatives of ethnic minorities consistently acknowledge the insufficient number of Georgian language lessons and the problems with the textbooks. Considering the densely populated areas of ethnic minorities, the borders with the Republic of Azerbaijan and Armenia, their agricultural activities and the nearly total non-Georgian environment, it became clear that bilingual education was essential in ethnic minority areas. Despite existing numerous theoretical and methodological manuals and research in bilingual education and models, as we have mentioned above, it was still difficult to develop bilingual teaching in Georgia. The main problem was caused by improperly and inefficiently planned bilingual textbooks that hindered the level of children's Georgian language knowledge instead of improving it. In 2013 the Ministry of Education acknowledged that these books were not appropriate, although the state has not taken any further steps. Today there is a new curriculum for 2018-2024 years, but as the translation and delivery of the books to the non-Georgian schools is incapable, the old bilingual books that were considered to be irrelevant are still used (Shalvashvili, 2020).

In summary, it can be said that despite the numerous activities, the problem of learning, mastering and using the state language is still a problem for both regions. Many young people are already motivated to be actively involved in the country's integration process and are well aware of the fact that learning the Georgian language is vital. Such motivated students learn Georgian most effectively in schools and later in higher education. However, the turning point in the study of the Georgian language starts after the enrollment in a higher education institution. The school fails to provide the relevant Georgian competence until now.

11.8. High Education

According to statistics, there are 19 state (95,535 students) and 43 (53,268 students) private higher education institutions in Georgia today.

According to the Law of Georgia on General Education, the language of education in all higher institutions is Georgian language (Article 4, paragraph 1, Law of Georgia on General Education). However, in cases provided by international treaties and agreements, it is also possible to teach in a foreign language (Article 4, paragraph 1, Law of Georgia on General Education).

The role of the state language in higher education is crucial. This is confirmed by studies in other countries. For example, Latvian sociolinguists strongly insist on protection of Latvian in higher education and research because it has a great impact on the quality of language in general (terminology, academic writing, popular scientific literature) as well as on the language use and teaching/lerning ideologies and practices in all the hierarchically subordinated education system (Druviete and Veisbergs, 2017, 222). A similar approach is needed in Georgia.

As local government and public sector employees did not know Georgian, and the new legislation required them to have an appropriate level of Georgian language knowledge, in 2004 the Zurab Zhvania School of Public Administration was established. School offers training courses for civil servants. The handbook, aiming to develop all four competencies, contained specific exercises from literature, history and culture.

Since 2009, the state has launched the 1+4 program, which turned out to be a step forward. However, this program could not solve the problem completely. In particular, the members of ethnic minorities have the right to take a higher education exam in their mother tongue, to take an intensive Georgian language course for a year, and then they are automatically transferred to the faculty initially selected, where the language of instruction is Georgian. There are about 1000 students a year, but as the statistics show, a large number of them (about 80%) drop out of the university in the middle of their studies, because they have neither general education nor Georgian competence. However, as a result of the program, much more non-Georgian-speaking youth was given the opportunity to learn Georgian. Textbooks to study different levels of Georgian language were also developed and published for them (authors: Shavtvaladze, Sharashenidze, Gochitashvili, Gabunia and etc…). The problem was also caused by the fact that there was no unified mechanism for language testing standards till 2020.

11.9. Conclusions

Any citizen, actively involved in the country's integration process, should speak the state language. In Soviet Georgia, where Russian was unofficially used alongside the constitutionally recognized Georgian language, non-Georgian ethnic minorities did not face the necessity to learn the Georgian language. Therefore, the study of the Georgian language in preschools, schools and universities was fictious. The situation changed after the restoration of independence, when new laws required all Georgian citizens to use Georgian language in private or public schools and higher education institutions. They were obliged, but as there still exists some program problems, the lack of textbooks and teachers, many laws are not implemented. Language policy in education still needs an effective reform. This, among other problems, concerns the planning of Georgian as a state language. The reforms that Georgia has undertaken in recent years in order to modernize the education system and bring it in line with the European standards aimed at more effective language planning as well as for pre-school also for school and higher education systems. However, the development of the curricula for pre-school, primary and secondary education, the development of textbooks and teaching methods were not easy, and unfortunately the issue of studying Georgian has not been properly resolved so far. A one-year program at university is often insufficient, as a large number of students abandon their studies because of the poor language proficiency. The only solution is a well-planned bilingual school education, that intends to learn the state Georgian language and to preserve minority languages. In recent times, despite many difficulties, success is readily apparent, which can be explained by the improvement of Georgian language knowledge in the younger generation. The improvement of the teaching process of the Georgian language will enable the ethnic minorities to be actively involved in the political, social and economic life of the country. Thus, to respect, protect and develop Georgian as a state language is the duty of every citizen.

References:

Amirjanova, Shalala. 2019. "Azerbaijanis in Georgia: The Difficulties of Getting Good Education and Perspective Job." *Jam News*, https://jam-news.net/ge/

Bonacina, Fabrizia. 2010. "A Conversation Analitic Approach to Practical Language Policies: The example of an induction classroom for newly-arrived immigrant children in France." Ph.D. thesis, The University of Edinburgh.

Cincotta-Segl, Angela. 2009. 2011. "Language/ing in education: Policy discourse, classroom talk and ethnic identities in the Lao PDR." In P. Sercombe and R. Tupas (eds.) *Languages, Identities and Education in Southeast Asia*, Basingstoke and New York: Palgrave Macmillan.

Cooper, Robert. L. 1989. *Language Planning and Social Change*. Cambridge University Press.

Druviete, Ina. and Veisbergs, Andrejs. 2017. *The Latvian Language in the 21ˢᵗ Century. Latvia and Latvians*. Riga: Academy of Sciences.

Dumbadze, Lela. 2018. "Non-Georgian Schools will not get new Textbooks." *Batumelebi*, 08.08.2018. https://batumelebi.netgazeti.ge/news/150732/

Fishman, Joshua. A.1979. "Bilingual education, language planning and English." *English World-Wide* 1(1): 11-241.

Fitzsimmons-Doolan, Shannon. 2009. "Is public discourse about language policy really public discourse about immigration? A corpus-based study." *Language Policy 8:* 377-402.

Garcia, Ofelia. and Menken, Kate. 2010. "Stirring the onion: Educators and the dynamics of language education policies (looking ahead)." In K. Menken and O. Garcia (eds.) *Negotiating Language Policies in Schools: Educutors as Policymakers*, pp. 249-261. London and New York: Routledge.

Gogolashvili, Giorgi. 2009. *Georgian Literary Language (History and Present Sittuation)*, Tbilisi: Meridiani publishers.

Hornberger, Nancy. H. 1988. *Bilingual Education and language Maintenance*. Dordrecht: Foris Publications.

Hult, Francis. M. 2010. "Swedish television as a mechanism for language planning and policy." *Language Problems and Language Planning* 34 (2: 158-181).

Johnson, David Cassels. 2013. *Language policy*. Washington State University, Palgrave Macmillan.

Kloss, Heinz. 1998. *The American Bilingual Tradition*. Washington, DC: Center for Applied Linguistics.

Lewis, Glyn. 1972. *Multilingualism in the soviet Union, Aspects of linguage policy and its implementation*. Hague and Paris: Mouton.

Martin-Jones, M. 2011. *Languages, texts, and literacy practices: An ethnographic lens on bilingual vocational education in Wales. In T. McCarty (ed.) Ethnography and Language Policy*, pp. 231-253. London and New York: Routledge.

Mekhuzla, Salome and Eidin Roshe. 2009. *Education Reform and Ethnic Minorities*. Published in 2009. https://www.files.ethz.ch/isn/106681/working_paper_46_geo.pdf

Pan, Lin. 2011. *English Language ideologies in the Chinese foreign Language education policies: A world-system perspective*. Language Policy 10: 245-263.

Rubin, Jay. 1977. "Bilingual education and language planning." In B. Spolsky and R.I. Cooper (eds.) *Frontiers of Bilingual Education. Rowley*, MA: Newbury House Publishers.

Ruiz, Richard. 1984. *Orientations in language planning*. NABE journal 8(2):15-34.

Shalvashvili, Mariam. 2020. "Deficiencies of Education Policy and Non-Georgian Ethnic Groups." Center for Social Justice. April 29, 2020. https://socialjustice.org.ge/ka/products/ganatlebis-politikis-sisusteebi-da-arakartulenovani-jgufebi

Spolsky, Bernand. 1978. *Educational Linguistics: An Introduction. Rowley*, MA: Newbury House.

—. 1985. "Educational linguistics." In T. Husén and T. N. Postlethwaite (eds.), *International Encyclopedia of Education* (pp. 3095–3100). Oxford: Pergamon.

Tabatadze, Shalva. and Gorgadze, Natia. 2015. *Ensuring equal opportunities for ethnic minority school teschers for professional development and career growth.* Tbilisi: Un Women.

Tabatadze, Salva and Natia Giorgadze. 2015. *Equality of the Teachers of Etnic Minorities for their Professional and Career Development.* Tbilisi, June, 2015. https://cciir.ge/images/pdf/axali%20dokumenti.pdf

Tabidze, Manana. 2005. *Problems of the Georgian Language and its Functioning Factors in Georgia.* Tbilisi: Kartuli Ena publisher.

Yitzhaki, Dafna. 2010. *The discourse of Arabic Language policies in Israel: Insights from focus groups.* Israel: Language Policy.

Chapter 12

The State and Religion in Georgia in the Historical Perspective

Giuli Alasania

University of Georgia, Georgia

Abstract

The article offers an insight into issues like the interference of the church in the political life; the role of the church and Georgian monasteries – strongholds of Christianity in Georgia and abroad - in the spread of education and awareness of the Georgian literature, language and culture, the unification of the country, maintaining the territorial integrity, strengthening the western orientation of the country; the strengthening and support of the Church by secular authorities; the Church and the State competing for influence and power occasionally resulting in confrontation; attempts of rulers to separate secular and ecclesiastical domains; the autocephaly of the Georgian Church and potential problems stemming from the special privileges granted to the Georgian Orthodox Church considering the complex multi-religious composition of the country, the Soviet past, and the politically, ethnically and culturally diverse architecture of the neighbourhood. The sensitive issue of the asymmetrical approach to different religious denominations, their rights and legal statuses are also brought to the fore. The main goal on the national agenda after proclaiming independence - creating a nation-state based on the concept of citizenship and equality before the law is in a certain conflict with the state approach to the Georgian Orthodox Church, whose special role in the history of Georgia is recognized by the Constitution. The imbalance among different denominations, among which the GOC is the leader, is efficiently used by external as well as domestic forces as leverage to achieve political goals (e. g., to shape the political orientation during elections; to set the agenda vis-à-vis the neighbouring states, etc.).

Keywords: The Church, the State, Concordat, Georgia, Christianity, religious equality, monasteries, the clergy, state religion, Catholicos, autocephaly, religious diversity, religious pluralism, Georgian Orthodox Church, church property, tolerance, co-existence

***

12.1. Historical Perspective. The Spread of Christianity

The spread of Christianity in Georgia started in the first century A.D. Ecclesiastical tradition connects the preaching of Christianity in Georgia with Andrew the First-Called, apostles Simeon the Cananite, Matthias and Bartholomew. According to sources, Andrew the First-Called was in Georgia three times, Matthias died in Gonio (south-west of Georgia) and was buried there, while Simeon the Cananite died in Abkhazia and was buried in Nikopsia, Nova Mikhailovka to the north-west of Tuapse. Later, his remains were reburied in Anakopia, presently located in New Athos.

The advent of Christianity was met with developed state traditions in Georgia. The cultural and religious diversity of the country, as well as the peaceful coexistence of various idols point to a high level of tolerance. Sources have not reported any persecution of Christianity by Georgian authorities in Georgia, unlike Rome and some other neighbouring countries. In the years of Caesar Diocletian in Rome (284-305), during the final persecution of Christians, the Roman army commander George of Cappadocia was martyred, and canonized as a saint. After the execution of women for devotion to Christianity by King Trdat of Armenia, Nino, saved by the will of God, came to Kartli, where she preached Christianity for several years without any pressure and persecution. The early spread of Christianity in Georgia is confirmed by Christian burials of the second and third centuries and the remains of a church in Nastagisi, dating back to the third century, as well as the churches of Bichvinta and Nokalakevi built in the fourth century.

In the fourth century (326), Christianity was proclaimed as the state religion in Kartli (eastern Georgia); later in the same year - in Egrisi (Lazica - western Georgia). This decision made by Georgian authorities for Georgia, situated at the crossroads between the West and the East, implied political orientation towards the West, while two strong superpowers, Rome and Sassanid Persia, were competing for world domination. The decision made in favour of Christianity is linked to King Mirian's name. It was he to whom Byzantine Emperor Constantine sent priests, deacons and stonemasons, led by Bishop John, as well as a fragment of the cross, a piece of footboard and nails, on and by which the Lord was crucified. Successive Georgian kings have contributed to the maintenance or the return of these sacred relics.

12.2. State Support of Christianity. The Special Role of King Vakhtang (Fifth-Sixth cc.)

In the wake of the cultural-political expansion of Sassanid Persia, the political choice made in favour of the West turned Christianity into a powerful tool of consolidating the nation and saving the country. Georgian authorities were doing their best to strengthen Christianity, which was under constant threat from various tribes. Kings, appointed bishops and catholics built and renovated churches and monasteries and bestowed lands on them. During Mirian's reign, the Lower Church, the same as Svetitskhoveli (the Life-Giving Pillar), and the Upper Church, or the Samtavro Church (the Church of Principal), were built (Antelava and Shoshiashvili, 1996). After Mobidan, who was secretly writing "wrong books," Michael (Antelava and Shoshiashvili, 1996), a "true priest" (Chalcedonian) sent from Byzantium, was appointed the Archbishop of Kartli in order to eliminate the spread of Zoroastrianism in Kartli. He, in turn, set fire to the "heretic books" written by Mazdean Mobidan. According to Georgian chronicler Juansher, Vakhtang was "growing up and learning from Michael the Bishop all the commandments of the Lord, and in his early days, he whole-heartedly loved Christ the most of all kings" (Antelava and Shoshiashvili, 1996). King Vakhtang was a dedicated defender of Christianity and fiercely fought against representatives of various denominations: "He threw Binqaran the tempter into prison... destroyed and exiled all the followers of Zoroastrianism beyond Kartli." Vakhtang Gorgasali implemented a church reform to strengthen the Western orientation. In order to reconcile Monophysites and Dyophysites, he joined the "Henotikon" (Act of Union) issued by Emperor Zeno in Byzantium and gained the right to appoint Catholicos Peter from Constantinople, to lead the church in Kartli, while the insulted and disobedient Michael, dismissed by Vakhtang, was banished to Constantinople. This meant giving autocephaly to the Kartli Church. At the request of the King of Kartli, Caesar and the Patriarch of Constantinople addressed the Patriarch of Antioch, who appointed Peter as the Catholicos of Kartli. According to "History of Kartli," Vakhtang established twelve new dioceses, and built many churches. The building of monasteries is linked to his name as well.

King Pharsman of Kartli, who arrived in Byzantium in 535, asked Byzantine Caesar Justinian for the permission to enthrone the Catholicos who was elected in Kartli (Beradze and Sanadze, 2003). From now on, the Church of Kartli was also granted the right to hold congregations and to deal with its problems in its own country. The autocephaly of the Church of Kartli acquired by Vakhtang Gorgasali was recognized by VI World Assembly of Constantinople in 681. The Catholicos of Kartli, Ioane, left for Antioch to attend the local assembly, which approved the resolution of the World Assembly (The History of Georgia 2003, 110). However, that was a long process. In the fourth decade of the eighth century, the Church of Kartli sent representatives to Antioch to settle the matter of the autocephaly of the Church of Kartli. The Antiochian patriarch once again canonized the Georgian Bishop's right to sanctify the Catholicos of Kartli. Until the ninth century, the Church of Kartli got the chrism from Jerusalem. In the ninth century, the Patriarch of Jerusalem gave the Church of Kartli the right to prepare chrism in Georgia.

Sources indicate that without the participation of the King, no significant steps were taken for the Church of Georgia and no problems were resolved. After proclaiming the independence of the Church of Georgia, a solid foundation and more opportunities for cooperation between ecclesiastical and secular authorities emerged.

12.3. The Role of the Church in Maintaining Statehood

In its turn, the Church did its best for the country's political power; it fought to revive the "hidden," "buried" language, spread the Georgian language and established it in religious service. From the life of the Assyrian fathers, it seems that they gave special importance to the Georgian language. As a result of the reformation of the Catholicos of Kartli Cyrion, religious service in the Georgian language was restored in Gugark-Tsurtavi (the sixth-seventh centuries).

Most scholars link the introduction of the Georgian script to the advent of Christianity. The clergy translated or created the first original writing samples: multipliers, lectionaries, hagiographic monuments. The clergy was thinking and writing about the future of the country a lot. It is believed that Catholicos Arsen used the source of the sixth century AD in "The Life of Abibos of Nekresi" while writing that during the Persian occupation St. Abibos predicted that the Persian domination would not last long and that Georgia would soon be liberated by the Greeks (Dzveli Kartuli Hagiograpiuli Dzeglebi, 1967).

The function of the Church was broadly expanded at the expense of the weakening of the secular authority. At that time, the Catholicos also acted as a statesman.

The situation was similar at the end of the sixth century. Guaram, sent from Byzantium to rule Kartli, was not recognized by Persia, which, according to sources, could not rule "Entire Kartli," move beyond Mtskheta and "replace Eristavis" in their entities" (Antelava and Shoshiashvili, 1996, 187). Later, his son Stephanos was allowed to sit in Tbilisi as a compromise: "He ruled all over Kartli, and he sat in Tpilisi and he was the subject of Persians" (Antelava and Shoshiashvili, 1996, 188, 189). It seems that his compromise with Persia explains the different attitudes of Georgian sources towards him personally. On the one hand, the Georgian sources refer to him as "Great Stephanos, the brother of Demetre," who "created the Jvari Church," (Moktsevai Kartlisai, 95.) and, on the other hand, he is "a man of arrogance and wickedness," "fearless of God" ("Stephanos was an unbeliever and fearless of God, not a worshiper of God, he did not contribute to the religion and to the churches") (Antelava and Shoshiashvili, 1996, 188). According to the same source, he did not participate in the construction of the Jvari Monastery. At the end of the sixth century, in 599, after the division of Kartli by Byzantium and Persia according to the truce of 591, the Catholicos of Kartli Cyrion, in accordance with the previous rules, was appointed as the Catholicos of Georgia, Gugars and Megrelians. According to the "Book of Epistles," Z. Aleksidze believes that the Catholicos of Kartli "Cyron" (599-614 / 16) appeared to be an amazingly strong and tough person. He quickly subordinated the entire Kartli (both secular and ecclesiastical authorities) to the will of the Catholicos and began implementing a consistent domestic and foreign religious-political agenda" (Aleksidze, 1968, 269). At the same time, he allegedly managed to dismiss a leader unwanted by him - Stephanos I.

M. Chkhartishvili has a different opinion about this issue. According to her interpretation of the sources, **his (Catholicos')** interference in secular affairs seems quite natural in the absence of a supreme secular national authority in Kartli. For her, the evidence of "Conversion of Kartli," in which Stephanos appears on the throne of Kartli in the 20s-30s of the seventh century, is acceptable (Chkhartishvili; Tskhovreba da Moqalaqoba Ts'midisa Serapion Zarzmelisa 1994, 41).

12.4. Relations Between Secular and Ecclesiastical Authorities in the Middle Ages

Significant references are preserved in one of the monuments of ancient Georgian literature in terms of the relationship between religious and secular authorities at that time. According to St. Shio Mghvimeli's collection of wonders, "Miracle Eighth," Stephanos was furious that the Catholicos had received more honour than him in Shiomghvime, saying the following: "I am sitting on the throne of the kings" (Abuladze, 1955, 203-205) In his opinion, his sitting on the throne of the kings was enough to prevent the hosts from exalting the Catholicos, when he was there. However, according to the same work, the clergy's view on the matter is different. According to the father superior of the monastery, ecclesiastical authority is above secular for the clergy. Scholars rightly point to the confrontation between the secular and ecclesiastical authorities of Georgia, which seems to have been relevant throughout the Middle Ages. However, this has never been extreme. On the contrary, secular and ecclesiastical authorities complemented each other and made a significant contribution to the development of the community. In the reference, it is emphasized that the ecclesiastical authority is above the secular, not in general, but only among the clergy. One can see a certain division of functions and the absence of political ambition on the part of the Church. According to V. Jobadze, the referred novel "demonstrates that we are not dealing with religious disputes between the Erismtavari and the clergyman, but rather with their rivalry for the leadership position, which is natural during the termination of the supreme secular authority in Kartli." C. Dundua shares the same opinion. Citing "Miracle Eighth," he sees the appearance of Stephanos' disbelief as the result of a confrontation between Kartli's secular and ecclesiastical authorities (Chkhartishvili, 1994). Enraged Stephanos took back the lands donated to the monastery by the royal family, returned them later and donated new ones. However, this is not a proof of his weakness. According to Juansher, it is true that "Stephanos did not dare to assume the title of the king by fear of the Persians and Greeks, but was considered the Head of Eristavis." When "Samuel the Catholicos died," Stephanos "appointed Bartholomew as the Catholicos" (Antelava and Shoshiashvili, 1996, 188) M. Chkhartishvili draws a parallel between Stephanos and Vakhtang Gorgasali, who also "appointed" the Catholicos, unlike, for example, Guaram, during whose rule the Catholicos "was appointed" (Chkhartishvili, 1994) by passing him.

This situation essentially repeats itself throughout history. But in each case, the strength of personality becomes important in terms of the balance of power. For example, we may recall the years of Grigol of Khandzta (eighth-nineth cc.) when confrontation re-emerged under certain circumstances. Here, the clergy and secular authorities have different views of their rights as well. According to the king, "You must first obey the ruler" (Kartuli P'roza, 1982, 253). But this time, the clergy are bolder than any other secular authority, even the king, and rely on relevant arguments for this: "Great King, you are the ruler of the earth, and Christ is that of the heaven and the earth and the underworld: you are the king of these relatives, and Christ – of all the born; you are the king of these times, and Christ is the eternal ruler, where everything remains unchanged, timeless, boundless, endless. He is the Lord of angels and men and you should listen to his words, who stated that no one can obey two lords ...." (Georgian Prose, 253). The kings are sometimes forced to agree to this opinion: "[Ashot] Curopalate (eighth-nineth cc.) said, "Your words are true," which is followed by the author's comment: "the king, strong in body, was defeated by the men strong in spirit" (Georgian Prose, 291). In some cases, they did not agree (in the case of Ashot Curopalate's son Bagrat), in other cases, they were forced to consider the Church as an ally, which was successfully implementing the project of uniting Georgia and developing a formula: "The country in which liturgy and all prayers are performed in Georgian is considered to be Kartli." It is noteworthy that Ephrem, an apprentice of Grigol of Khandzta, obtained the right of the church to prepare chrism in Kartli (Georgian Prose, 279). Grigol of Khandzta was the nephew of the wife of Nerses II - a ruler of Kartli. He was brought up at the King's court and received a good education. Later, he moved to Ashot Curopalate, and with the help of the latter and his successors, launched extensive monastic construction activities.

In order to reinforce the Bagrationi dynasty, Georgian Christian ideology developed the idea of "the divine origin" of the king's authority and royal ancestry and provided appropriate justification. Grigol of Khandzta addresses Ashot Curopalate with the following words: "The King, the Son of Prophet

David and anointed by the Lord!" (Georgian Prose, 253.) Georgian kings David the Builder, Tamar, Demetre the Devoted (twelfth-thirteenth cc.) were canonized as saints, and Tamar was declared the fourth member of the Trinity. All of this served to strengthen the state.

12.5. Religious Unification of Georgia

In the second half of the ninth century, the leaders of the "Kingdom of Abkhazia" extricated the Church of Western Georgia, whose centers were the Autocephalous Archdiocese of Nikopsia and Sebastopolis and the Metropolitan of Phasis, from Constantinople's subordination and united with the Abkhazian Catholicos. Later, the archdioceses of Sebastopolis and Nikopsia were abolished and their observance moved directly to the Abkhazian Catholicos. The center of the Catholicosate became Bichvinta St. Mary Cathedral. At the end of the tenth century, when the kings of Abkhazia joined Inner Kartli, two autocephalous catholicosates appeared within the framework of the "Kingdom of Abkhazia:" Kartli's – with the center in Mtskheta and Abkhazia's – with the center in Bichvinta (Pitiunt). According to their decision, the Church of Georgia was to be united, and the abolishment of the old eparchies and establishment of the new ones served this purpose. The temples of Chkondidi (Martvili), Mokvi, Bedia and Kutaisi were established, the episcopal cathedrals of Petra and Rhodopolis were annulled and abolished (Beradze and Sanadze, 2003; Alasaniam, 2006). These churches were built by the kings of Abkhazia: George II (tenth c.), Leon II, Bagrat III. The capital city of the Kingdom of Abkhazia was moved to Kutaisi. With rare exceptions, the kings of United Georgia were crowned by Kutateli (bishop of Kutaisi) as well. Political unification was preceded by ecclesiastic unification. The Western Georgian Church joined the Eastern Georgian Church, which also meant liturgy in Georgian.

Kakheti was ruled by chorbishops. Kakheti governors Dachi, Samuel Donauri, Gabriel Donauri, Fadla I, Kvirike I, Fadla II, Kvirike II and David held the title. Scholars point to the ecclesiastical origin of the chorbishop Institute (Japaridze, 2014). In the first half of the tenth century, thanks to Queen Dinara, Orthodoxy prevailed in Hereti, facilitating its political integration into the rest of Georgia. The church was a unifying force in the years of the fragmentation of Georgia. For example, Kakheti, which was a politically independent kingdom, was not independent ecclesiastically.

The existence of the Khevisberi Institute and deacons in the mountains also meant the merging of secular and clerical authorities to better manage society (the deacon served as an icon servant in the mountains, while Khevisberi combined civil and spiritual power) (Kartuli Etnologiuri Leksik'oni, 2009).

12.6. Georgian Religious Centers Abroad and their Role

From the earliest years of Christianity, Georgians were active not only in Georgia but also in various parts of the Christian world and they contributed significantly to the development of Georgian, as well as world culture. The Georgian clergy were especially aspiring to the Holy Land, where they established a closer bond with the World Church. The first Georgian monasteries were established abroad in Egypt and Palestine. There is a legend that the first Christian king, Mirian (fourth century), chose the location of the Cross Monastery while being a pilgrim in Jerusalem.

For centuries Georgian monasteries abroad were renowned for their literary and theological-philosophical traditions: St. Saba's Church near Jerusalem (where the so-called "Sabatsminda" version of the Georgian translation of Biblical books was performed in the eighth-ninth centuries, and the oldest Georgian edition of the typikon was created), Palavra, the Monastery of the Cross of Jerusalem, monasteries established near Antioch or in the Asia Minor. The monasteries of Athos (tenth century) and Petritsoni (Bachkovo - the eleventh century) became well-known among western Georgian religious centers.

One of the goals of the Georgian monks working abroad was to serve the Georgian culture and the Georgian language. On the one hand, cloisters founded by them were the strongholds of Christianity and a part of a larger world; on the other hand, they were indivisible from Georgia, a sort of smaller Georgia that always had tight bonds with the motherland. Historical sources name up to 100 large and small Georgian monasteries in Georgia and abroad. Almost every Georgian religious center abroad had a church (branch) in Tbilisi. Everyday prayers delivered by the monks in Palestine in the ninth and tenth centuries clearly show close links between the Georgian centers abroad and their motherland as well as the main destination of those prayers. "Let's pray to God, for peace in Kartli, the keeping of borders, calming down the kings and rulers, repelling the enemies, releasing the captives, the passing away of the plague, the steadiness of Christianity... Oh, Christ, forgive all brothers, and all Christians, and most of all, the Georgians" (Alasania 2010, 20).

In turn, Georgian kings saw the importance of these hubs and cared about their preservation and strengthening. Similar findings contained in the sources refer to the activities of Georgian kings David the Builder, King Tamar (twelfth-thirteenth cc.), King David VIII (thirteenth-fourteenth cc.), the King of Western Georgia Constantine (fourteenth c.) - the son of David Narin, George the Brilliant (fourteenth c.), Levan II Dadiani (seventeenth c.) and others. The historian of David the Builder writes:

> Lavras and parishes and monasteries not only in their kingdoms but also
> in Greece, the Holy Mountain, and Borgaleti, next Assyria and Cyprus, the

Black Mountain in Palestine, the grave of our Lord Jesus Christ, and the inhabitants of Jerusalem that were located far from his (David the Builder's) kingdom were also donated. He built a monastery on the Mount of Sinai, where Moses and Elijah saw God, gave out a lot of gold, and ecclesiastical books and embellished the servants of holiness with gold. (Antelava and Shoshiashvili, 1996, 270)

12.7. The Immunity and Strengthening of the Church

During his stay in Jerusalem in 1178-1184, Nikoloz Gulaberidze "redeemed" the vineyard of the Cross Monastery and contributed a lot to the monastery (Metreveli, 1962; Papuashvili, 1979). In 1187 Jerusalem was taken over by Muslims, and King Tamar sent an embassy to Salah ad-Din (Saladin) with a special order to return their sacred sites to Georgians, followed by the immunity of Georgian tabernacles and the inviolability of the Georgians living there (Papuashvili, 1979). Similar to David's chronicler, Tamar's chronicler informs us: "Not only was the kindness inside the Kingdom, but for every Christian," "She sent the trustworthy and the entrusted so "Starting with Alexandria with all of Luby (Libya) Mount of Sinai," and sent regards to their private churches, monasteries and Christians. Not to mention Jerusalem, where she sent to all the churches chalice and bowls, and holy headwear and innumerable gold for the nuns and poor people (Kaukhchishvili 1959, 141).

By the beginning of the eleventh century, the Church was a powerful feudal organization, the owner of land and property struggling for tax immunity.

The kings themselves contributed to the strengthening of the church and the clergy. As a proof of the above, the majority of scholars quote the so-called document of the time of Bagrat III or Bagrat IV (tenth-eleventh cc.). An excerpt from Bagrat Curopalate's Law Book, reads: "If the King gets angry at the bishop fairly or unfairly, the imprisonment will not happen, for the bishop is the second king and an affirmation of the law of the Christians, and if the king has to deal with the Holy law, he will have mercy on him accordingly" or "If a priest, or a king's nun, or a bishop sins, which means that they sin against the religion and against the church, they can't be captured by anyone" (Dolidze 1963, 464-465).

During the reign of Bagrat III, the church was granted immunity, as reported in the document issued by Melchizedek Catholicos (1031/33). The document reads: "And the villages which formerly belonged to this holy capital were open and available. And I spoke to my mentor Bagrat Curopalate, and made them immune and gifted them immunity. And the profit that could be made from the holy capital: sheep, horses, and wine as supplementary and whatever was ripped off by Emir Ali and I relieved the Holy Catholic Church" (Enukidze,

Silogava, Shoshiashvili 1984, 27; Berdzenishvili 1967, 244-245; Lortkipanidze, 1979, 169). Bagrat is Bagrat III (Georgian king - 978-1014) and Ali – Emir of Tbilisi. Immunity was granted to the Church in 1011-1014.

12.8. Church in Disarray and the Intervention of the State

Under Bagrat IV (1027-1072), the king's personal intervention in church affairs became necessary, since, at that time, the church was in disarray. High church positions were in the hands of feudal aristocracy and positions were sold. To restore order in the church, the King of Georgia invited Giorgi Mtatsmindeli, who worked at the Iviron Monastery on Mount Athos. He worked tirelessly for four years to establish order in the church. For this purpose, first of all, he rejected the "estate principle" of promotion in ecclesiastical hierarchy and established the tradition of personal selection (Lortkipanidze, 170). When King Bagrat IV lost both Ani and Tbilisi, he decided to fight against the disobedient *eristavis* and convened the first church council. The congregation also had to consider the religious dispute between Armenians and Georgians. The representative of the king, the Royal chancellor, was present at the ecclesiastical meeting of the Armenian-Georgian clergy: "There was a Royal chancellor by the name of Euthymius," according to the source. The Armenian monks attending the meeting were negotiating with king Bagrat on the liberation of Ani from Byzantines (Beradze and Sanadze, 130, 133).

12.9. David the Builder's Epoch. The Intervention of the State in Ecclesiastical Affairs

During the years of David the Builder, the issue of relations between the church and the state was even more pressing. The king began to conduct domestic policy by resolving ecclesiastical affairs, since at that time "holy churches, houses of God were occupied by bandits", who were "teaching everybody dependence on them, disbelief instead of belief in God," "dishonest and disgraceful people with properties rather than dignity occupied most of the episcopates as bandits and appointed similar priests and chorbishops" (History of Kartli, 250). Monasteries rose against the king. In 1104, David convened an ecclesiastical council that was held simultaneously in Ruisi and Urbnisi. "the record" of the council was found to be so significant that it was also included in the "Great Nomocanon (Dogmatikon)." At the beginning of the document, it is said: "the Legal Code of the holy council assembled by the order of our King David, the king of the Abkhaz, Kartvels, Rans and Kakhs" (Javakhishvili 1982, 53; Zhordania 1897, 56). Sources confirm that not only "bishops loving God, honest priests and worthy deacons, nuns loving God and the isolated and hermits" participated in the meeting, but the wider audience as well. "Numerous nations," including David's aunt Martha - a queen from Byzantium, listened to the discussions of the most important issues for Georgia. As the historian of David points out, there were also Ioane - the Catholicos-Patriarch who prepared the council, and George – *mtsignobartuhkutsesi* who was a monk - royal chancellor known as a distinguished figure "of this holy congregation," (Zhordania 1897, 69) who was formerly regarded as the king's father and the first vizir of the state, the Catholicos of Abkhazia - Eustatius the monk and Arseny - the monk (the congregation secretary). In an agreement with the king, these people were engaged in church and public affairs. The Ruisi-Urbnisi council explicitly defined and restricted the rights of the church, dismissed the bishops who opposed the king, and appointed faithful people instead. The Ruisi-Urbnisi congregation once again reconciled the Georgian church rules with the laws of the World Orthodox Church, according to the "Minor Nomocanon" translated by Ekvtime Mtatsmindeli and "Great Nomocanon" translated by Arsen Iqaltoeli. The Armenian Monophysites, who were considered "heretics" at that time, were especially criticized at the Ruisi-Urbnisi council, as the issue of joining northern Armenia and converting Armenians to Orthodoxy was on the agenda.

Earlier, for this purpose, David the Builder invited Georgian clergymen, including Catholicos-Patriarch Ioane, Arsen Iqaltoeli, and other Georgian and Armenian theologians to his kingdom. However, he could not achieve this goal. For this very reason, a similar council was held in 1205 by King Tamar, and in 1205 and 1207 by Zakaria Mkhargrdzeli, who wanted to bring Armenian church rules closer to Georgian church rules and convened Armenian church congregations. The Code of the Ruisi-Urbnisi council is enclosed with the king's praise, whom the author of the document addresses" (Zhordania, 69).

After the Ruisi-Urbnisi council, the king's donations to the church increased, churches and monasteries were actively upgraded and the church received tax immunity. But it was David the Builder who united the positions of the royal chancellor (mtsignobartuhkutsesi) and the Chkondideli (bishop of Chkondidi in western Georgia), and in fact, the king gained the right to interfere in the internal affairs of the church. The royal chancellor was set to rule the court - *saajo kari* - the court of justice. In addition, there was a Catholicosate court, which the minority obeyed. On the other hand, the Church was actively involved in discussing state affairs, and four clergymen attended the hall: two catholicos of Georgia, the Head of the Church and the Chkondideli - royal chancellor (Lominadze 1979, 654). The clergy were involved in drafting and issuing important legal documents. For example, in the introduction to the law issued by prince Vakhtang (the future Vakhtang VI – eighteenth century), it is clearly emphasized, "Whoever sees and hears, no one should think we would do anything by ourselves alone, but with the help and confirmation of the high priest and our brother - Archbishop and prince Domenti, as well as Archbishop Gregory - the son of Aragvi Eristavi and other metropolitan bishops…" (Dolidze, 478).

12.10. Church Immunity Issues in George III's Reign

During the reign of George III (the twelfth century), the immunity of the church was abolished and after the suppression of the Orbeli uprising (1177), the church congratulated the king on his victory and it requested immunity again. It seems that under the circumstances, the king had to agree to the request. "We have not created the church for the glorification of gods or the protection of our kings, or for the spiritual salvation from suffering but rather for the liberation of our kingdom from unfair taxes and the salvation and liberation of the poor." (King George's certificate of 1177 to the Church of Georgia) (The Corps of Georgian Historical Documents, 1984, 72). According to the same certificate, the king was reminded of the church's problems when "Monks and bishops, the western and eastern population (Imerni and Amerni), the Catholicos, priests and hermits were gathered from all over the kingdom and they also told us of the hardship of the church and the deterioration of legal cases" (The Corps of Georgian Historical Documents 1984, 72; Dolidze 1963, 24; Lortkipanidze, 294).

12.11. Conflict Between Secular and Ecclesiastic Authorities in Queen Tamar's Reign

In the beginning of Queen Tamar's reign, an influential person Catholicos Michael, who also seized the position of Chkondideli - Royal Chancellor, together with his supporters opposed and confronted the young king. After suppressing Qutlu Arslan's rebellion, the king tried to restrict Michael's power and for that, the ecclesiastical council was convened. In spite of the fact that Michael did not attend the council, Tamar's desire to remove him from the position of Catholicos was not implemented. However, at that time, many unworthy bishops were dismissed.

12.12. Peripeteia During the Mongol Rule – Granting Tax Immunity to the Church Followed by Reclaiming Church Property

In the middle of the thirteenth century, when Georgia was under Mongol control, the church found itself in a relatively better condition. In addition to being granted tax immunity from the king of Georgia, it was granted the same privilege from Mongols. But due to the overall difficult socio-economic circumstances, the Georgian king was forced to resort to extreme measure and allowed the nobles to reclaim lands donated to the churches at different times. Such an initiative was considered as "the disintegration of churches, episcopates and monasteries." The Georgian church opposed the government's decision; at first, by cursing the recipient of the land from the government and then called for a council. David VII, the king of Georgia was forced to agree to convene a council which took place in approximately 1263. The participants of the council reprimanded the king for protecting those damned by the church when he did not have the right to interfere with such a matter. They reminded the king that earlier "those, who were cursed for some reason or deed were condemned by him as well; they were deprived of land and were not allowed to join the army." The participants of the council remembered the fact that in spite of many hardships earlier "none of those wishing the property of the churches of the country and its dismantlement, ever dared to bring up such a reason." "If any of the lords or nobles or courtiers or peasants were given a certificate from your dynasty, they would not hide it and if someone had it, why did not they show whom the village of the church was given to; besides, it had to be mentioned that it was you who had issued this certificate and bestowed upon them" (Javakhishvili, 353-372). The leaders of the church mentioned the fact that "the Holy Law is primary for the kings too." However, at the same time, in order to retain lands, they gave up tax immunity and were prepared to pay taxes. "We will compensate the taxes that the churches owe, and we will not back down either" and "We will serve you in accordance with our strength and ability" (Corpus of Georgian Documents, 172-174). Despite huge resistance, the clergy could not achieve the desirable result and could not make the king roll back his decision. Once again, the king's power was demonstrated. The only issue on which the church leaders prevailed over the King's wishes was the immediate execution of Basil Chkondideli-Ujarmeli, who was sentenced to death by the king for a completely different reason, based on trumped-up charges. The Georgian clergy was generally obedient and loyal to the king. In turn, the king, as a rule, cared for the Church, strengthened it and built new churches.

To an extent, George Brilliant's "Dzeglisdeba" (Code) separates secular and ecclesiastical fields. It is written in the preface: "ecclesiastical and church cases, no matter what the dispute is about: murderers, the profaners of the church, wife abandoners, kidnappers of innocent men and other legal cases," are subject to the ecclesiastical court (Dolidze, 402).

12.13. The Military Power of the Church

Alexander I, who ruled the country after the devastating Tamerlane attacks, became especially famous for building and restoring churches and monasteries. There is one noteworthy element with reference to the Georgian church preserved in the document given to Catholicos Basil by King Alexander – the supreme leader got one special advantage: to have his own army, which participated in battles under its own commander. According to Ivane Javakhishvili, it is unimaginable that in the reign of David the Builder or Tamar, the Catholicos had a separate commander of his army. Javakhishvili considers it a relatively later event (Javakhishvili, 68). However, it should be noted that the taking of fortress-town Samshvilde took place in 1110 under the leadership of George Chkondideli, who later, together with David the Builder, brought Qipchak warriors from the north to reinforce the Georgian army.

A similar reference to the document of Alexander I is found in a document issued to Rustaveli by the king of Kakheti David in 1772. "Hence, we describe the flag designated for the army which was established by the kings before us and which we agree upon" (Javakhishvili, 69). Every large church and monastery had its own well-trained army which, in case of need, joined the king's banner and together, they fought against the attackers of Georgia (Japaridze, 236).

The Georgian Orthodox church always struggled for the preservation of Christian traditions and not only in Georgia but in the North Caucasus as well; during times of hardship, it strived to preserve families and was against polygamy.

12.14. Attempts to Split the Georgian Orthodox Church in the Fifteenth c.

In February 1438, an ecclesiastical council opened in Ferrara (Italy), and afterwards continued in Florence. The representative of Georgia attending the Ferrara-Florence council was given fifth place after the patriarchates of Constantinople, Antioch, Jerusalem and Alexandria. But the council's resolution about the unification of the Orthodox and Catholics was not signed by the representative of the Georgian Church, who left the council early. The reason being that always and especially at that time, maintaining the independence of the Georgian Church was crucial to the country that was on the brink of political collapse (Makharadze 2005, 80-93).

In the fifteenth century, the integrity of the church was the main target of separatist Georgian governors on the road to independence. In the years of Alexander the First, Ivan Atabeg tried to remove Samtskhe from the Georgian Catholicos-Patriarch and subordinate it to the patriarch of Antioch. After 30 years, Kvarkvare II, who forbade the bishops of Samtskhe to mention the king of Georgia and patriarch during the divine service, confiscated the Vardzia Monastery in Samtskhe and church lands from the Catholicos of Georgia. These undertakings were vain since bishops of Meskheti were forced to promise: "Neither to let in the foreign clergy nor to read their books, nor to listen to their commandment, nor to believe in their faith. Our clergy and deacons must be ordained only in Mtskheta and we must obey your orders" (Beradze and Sanadze, 233-234; Alasania, 24).

During his visit to western Georgia in 1470-74, the patriarch of Jerusalem consecrated the new Catholicos of Abkhazia, Iovakim. This, in fact, meant the independence of the Church of Western Georgia. According to the document issued in the second quarter of the sixteenth century, "the Catholicos rules congregation from Likhi to Kaffa, between the Russian border and Chaneti" (Dolidze, 178).

12.15. Georgia in the Muslim Surroundings

From the sixteenth century, Georgia found itself in the Muslim surrounding. The survival of the nation was linked to Christianity and the kings, above all, set an example of devotion to faith. A list of martyred kings and nobles includes: the king of Kartli Luarsab II (1622), the queen of Kakheti Ketevan (1624), Bidzina Cholokashvili, the lords of Ksani Elizbar and Shalva who were martyred in 1661. In the years of political disintegration, we encounter a deviation from the centuries-old tradition: namely, a confrontation between Rostom - the viceroy (vali) of Kartli sent from Iran who was converted to Islam and Catholicos Evdemon Diasamidze. This confrontation ended with the killing of the latter. Catholicos Evdemon was in the group of Teimuraz's supporters and Rostom's opponents whose purpose was to murder Rostom and put Teimuraz on the throne. But even in the years of Persian domination, the example of George XI illustrates loyalty towards the Georgian church: although he was converted to Islam by force and pretendedly, a cross was found on his chest after his death. In 1774, as a result of persistent attempts, the kings of Kartli and Kakheti regained the right which was taken away from them since 1633, namely, to coronate the king in a Christian manner. Vakhushti Bagrationi emphasized that the sense of unity did not vanish even under the conditions of the decentralization of the country and the church: "If you ask any Georgian, that is Imeri, Meskhi and Her-Kakh, what their origin is, they will reply instantaneously: "Georgian" (Bagrationi 1973, 291) This is the time when faith determined ethnic affiliation, while "Georgian" and "Orthodox" became synonyms.

In the late Middle Ages, the church struggled against slave trade and the spreading of Islam, while kings granted it tax immunity. Appropriate testimony is preserved in the "Iadgari of Bichvinta (Pitiunt)."

"… No one will be able to change this order, neither kings, nor Dadiani-Gurieli, nor Atabeg-Amirspasalar, nor lords or nobles, nor nobility and nor peasants" (Dolidze, 1965, 178). In western Georgia the church forced the princes of Imereti and Odishi to promise: "We should not promise Tamar to ruin and devastate Imereti and in case the Tatar army arrives here to ruin Imereti, we should neither come to her, nor lead or believe them." In 1707-1710 the Catholicos made the serfs of Imereti Catholicosate promise that they would not be involved in slave trade. In 1709, nobles Chachua promised the Catholicos that they would not let the buyers of slaves stay on their land (Chkhataraishvili 1973, 483-485).

In 1758, king Solomon of Imereti, king Erekle of Kakheti and king Teimuraz of Kartli signed a treaty of friendship and relationship. December 4-5, 1759, an ecclesiastical council was held in Western Georgia where it was resolved to prohibit slave trade. Secular and ecclesiastical governors of Imereti, Megrelia and Guria promised the king that they would obey while the church exempted from taxes (Chkhataraishvili, 639-640).

12.16. The Treaty of Georgievsk and the Abolition
of the Independence of the Church

It was no accident that under limited statehood, the Treaty of Georgievsk (1783) first of all attacked the Georgian church, thus laying a foundation for the abolition of its independence. The above can be inferred from the following statements of the above-mentioned document: "After unification with Russia and the Russians - our coreligionists, His Excellency wishes that the Catholicos, i. e. the Archbishop occupy the eighth place on the hierarchical scale of Russian bishops after Tobolsk" (Paichadze 1983, 34) This was confirmed and implemented with the decision of the Emperor and Russia's Holy Synod in 1811, after the Russian invasion of Georgia in 1801. At that time, the kingdom of Imereti was ruled by the king jointly with the "council," which included four bishops together with the nobles: 1. Metropolitan Dositheus of Kutaisi, 2. Metropolitan Ekvtime of Gelati, 3. Metropolitan Sophron of Nikortsminda, 4. Archbishop Anton (Gonikishvili 1979, 53). As organizers and leaders of the uprising against Russia in 1818-1820, the first two - metropolitans of Kutaisi and Gelati were captured and exiled to Russia. Metropolitan Dositheus was murdered on his way to the place of exile (Surguladze and Surguladze 1991, 41; Japaridze, 371).

Once the Georgian statehood was abolished, liturgy in the Georgian Orthodox Church was conducted in Russian. The Georgian clergy constantly fought to maintain the Georgian language and in order to retain it in parish schools, taught it free of charge to the poor Georgians who had no opportunity to receive an education. The struggle to restore Georgian statehood and the autocephaly of its church never ceased throughout the nineteenth century.

In a letter of a Georgian noble addressed to the Russian Emperor dated October 11, 1905, one can read: "In order to save the Georgian Orthodox church, it should be free, its traditional legal rule should be restored and the Catholicos with plenipotentiary rights and responsibilities elected by the people should be returned…" (Japaridze, 383).

12.17. Restoration of the Autocephaly of the Georgian Church in the Twentieth C.

The restoration of the autocephaly of the Georgian Church and the returning of the Georgian language to the divine service, as it was the case throughout history, was finally achieved on March 12, 1917. That success facilitated the process of the restoration of the Georgian statehood as well. Catholicos-Patriarch Cyrion (Sadzaglishvili) addressed the Georgian nation with the following words: "It is our church's duty to constantly remind humanity of the name of the Georgia nation. It should contribute to our consolidation and unification" (Japaridze, 390). However, National and religious leadership of Russia tried to hinder bringing to life the "Act of Independence" proclaimed in the Patriarch's temple "Svetitskhoveli" (Vardosanidze 2001, 306). However, by the decision of the Russian provisional government, the autocephaly of the Georgian Church was proclaimed not by territorial, but by ethnic affinity (Phyletism). The other religious institutions had to stay under Russian control. This was not carried out.

12.18. Secularization During the Democratic Republic

In the years of the democratic Republic (1918-21), the Georgian social-democratic government started to implement an order of the time that implied the speeding up of secularization. On July 17, 1920, the ecclesiastical council convened in Tbilisi considered the issues of the separation of the church from the state, the transmission of theological schools to the ministry, the church budget, clergy household and the unification of Mtskheta-Tbilisi eparchies.

12.19. Autocephaly Following the Annexation of Georgia by the Bolsheviks

The annexation of Georgia by the Bolshevik Red Army on February 25, 1921, was followed by the address of Catholicos-Patriarch Ambrosius (Khelaia) who appealed to the "Genoa conference" held in 1922. The leader of the Georgian church informed the world that "Georgia experienced severe despotism and unbearable oppression for 117 years by the Russian bureaucracy. Therefore, when the artificial integrity of the Russian empire was dismantled, the Georgian nation declared independence. Certainly, its former master, the oppressor of small nations, could not reconcile with it, it dispatched the occupation army to the borders of Georgia and on February 25, 1921, in a small unequal battle, put the yoke of slavery on bleeding Georgia for the second time. The Catholicos-patriarch demanded that the Russian occupation army be immediately withdrawn from Georgia. It would allow the Georgian nation to arrange forms of social-political life without outside interference which would be appropriate for its psyche, spirit, morals, customs and national culture (Japaridze, 395-396). His voice was unanswered. The Orthodox patriarchates did not recognize the Georgian Church's autocephaly. It was considered as an integral part of the Russian Church, fully controlled by and subordinated to the government. By 1943 the number of functioning churches was reduced to 15. Activities undertaken by the Georgian Church during WWII in support of the fighting nation had their effect. Owing to the diplomatic talent and relentless work of the Georgian Catholicos-Patriarch Kalistrate Tsintsadze, in 1943 the Russian Church officially recognized the territorial autocephaly announced by the Georgian Orthodox Church already on the 12th of March, 1917. The struggle to reinstate cancelled churches and monasteries and to recover holy relics started. The persecution of the Georgian churches continued after Stalin's death as well. Despite repressions, in 1917-78 the Georgian clergy held 12 ecclesiastical councils.

In 1921-1927 all was done to replace faith by atheism. The Church's property was destroyed, ecclesiastic schools were closed. During the 20-50s more than 1000 churches and monasteries were closed or destroyed, over 1200 clergy – detained, and over 100 – killed (Vardosanidze 2014, 5). All those measures brought to replacing of confrontation by compromise (Saria 2019).

On 23 December 1977, Ilia (Shiolashvili-Ghudushauri), the Metropolitan of Tskhum-Abkhazeti was elected as Catholicos-Patriarch in Tbilisi. In 1988 Moscow permitted the consecration and reopening of closed churches and the restoration process began. On March 3, 1990, the World Ecumenical Patriarch Demetrios in Constantinople issued two documents: one recognized the historical autocephaly and **independent** structure of the Georgian Church, the issue which convoys Georgia along its history (Tkeshelashvili 2012) and the other one recognized the title of the Catholicos-Patriarch of the Georgian Church (Vardosanidze, 81). The Georgian polyphonic chanting was restored in the Georgian Church.

12.20. Freedom of Religion After the Restoration of Independence

Historical justice was once again restored on April 9, 1991, and Georgia regained political independence. The years of aggressive atheism were over. Everyone was given the right to free choice to worship, which is defended by the constitution. Article 9 of the current Constitution of Georgia provides for the complete freedom of belief and religion.

Throughout history, the multi-ethnic nature of Georgia, located at the crossroads of different cultures, traditions, religions, dictated a definite way of life – maximum tolerance for peaceful coexistence. However, the extent of this tolerance was limited for survival considerations. Even in times of political fragmentation and religious diversity, Orthodoxy was not only the dominant religion, but the characteristic that defined the Georgian nation. However, thanks to the wise policy of the Georgian authorities, religious confrontation in medieval Georgia rarely grew into ethnic conflicts. The Georgian kings promoted cultural interaction among the different ethnic and religious groups. Such traditions developed tolerance, prevented ethnic conflicts and promoted cultural diversity always open to novelties and adaptation even in times of conflicts and wars (Alasania 2007, 289-303, 549).

12.21. Current Situation

12.21.1. Asymmetrical Approach to Different Religious Denominations

The situation has changed recently.[1] After proclaiming independence, the main goal on the national agenda of Georgia has been to create a nation-state based on the concept of citizenship. However, enclaves of religious and ethnic minorities in Georgia bordering Armenia, Azerbaijan and Russia especially considering the visa-free regime with all these states, as well as the Georgian Muslim population, irrespective of their compact settlement, in some cases, could be regarded as a threat to a weak state entity. That is the main reason why the requirement of the Georgian Constitution concerning all citizens' equality before the law has not yet been achieved. It is especially true when considered from the perspective of their beliefs and religious rights. The Constitution recognizes the "special role ... in the history of Georgia" of the Georgian Orthodox Church but stipulates that the latter should be independent of the state. The latter tenet is not always implemented. There is a certain recognizable controversy created by the asymmetrical approach to different religious denominations, their rights and legal statuses. The existing concordat is signed only between the State and the Georgian Orthodox Church, effectively leaving out all other denominational churches, de facto assigning one church an exceptional domineering role and placing it in the privileged position. The Constitutional Agreement between the Georgian State and the Apostolic Autocephalous Orthodox Church of Georgia - an agreement defining the relations between the two entities was signed by the President of Georgia Eduard Shevardnadze and the Patriarch of Georgia Ilia II on the 14th of October 2002 at Svetitskhoveli Cathedral in Mtskheta, Georgia.

---

[1] The following information is from "Protection of Religious Minorities. Report on the monitoring of the implementation of human rights strategies and action plans for 2016-2017" – Authors: LGBT persons' rights - Women's Initiatives Supporting Group (WISG), Freedom of Speech - Georgian Young Lawyers' Association (GYLA), Religious minorities - Human Rights Education and Monitoring Center (EMC), USAID, East-West Management Institute; Georgia. International Religious Freedom Report for 2018. United States Departments of State, Bureau of Democracy, Human Rights, and Labor; 2019 Report on International Religious Freedom: Georgia (June 10) – US Embassy in Georgia.

12.22. Concordat Between the Sate and the Georgian Orthodox Church

12.22.1. Asymmetrical Approach in Relation to Other Dominations

The concordat signed between the state and the church:

- confirms the Georgian Orthodox Church's (GOC) ownership of all churches and monasteries on the territory of Georgia; recognizes the special role of the GOC in the history of Georgia and devolves authority over all religious matters to it;

- gives the patriarch legal immunity;

- grants the GOC the exclusive right to staff the military chaplaincy;

- exempts GOC clergymen from military service;

- gives the GOC a unique consultative role in the government, especially in the sphere of education.

The government of Georgia recognizes the legitimacy of the wedding ceremonies performed by the Georgian Orthodox Church, while maintaining that in legal matters government records must be used.

As a partial owner of what was confiscated from the church under the Soviet rule (1921-1991), the State pledges to recompense, at least partially, for the damage.

Under the concordat, the Georgian Orthodox Church was the only officially recognized religious denomination in Georgia.

All other denominations were deprived of these privileges. Thus, they were forced to fight for the same rights. Till today, religious minorities are the subject of growing discrimination, which has increased since Georgia joined the Council of Europe in 1999. This is especially pronounced against non-traditional religions. The violation of law extends the general gap between law and reality, the denial of legal registration, the confiscation of their religious literature, refusal of entry visas, etc.

Although other minorities such as Catholics and Muslims have the freedom to exercise their religion, they can officially register their religious groups only as organizations, and not as churches.

Under the concordat, smaller branches of Eastern Orthodoxy in Georgia, such as the Russian Orthodox Church, were also subject to the jurisdiction of the GOC on the entire territory of the Georgian state.

In 2003, an effort by the Roman Catholic Church to negotiate its own concordat with Georgia failed after the government yielded to pressure from the GOC leadership and public demonstrations said to have been organized by the GOC.

In July 2011, the Georgian parliament enacted legislation allowing religious organizations to register as "legal entities of public law," a status closer to that held by the GOC.

The leadership of the GOC criticized this proposed law and made an unsuccessful effort to influence the parliament not to adopt it.

Prior to this change in 2011, religious groups other than the GOC had only been allowed to register as "noncommercial legal entities of private law," which some churches considered unacceptable and refused to apply for.

The public debate over the new law inter alia also aired concerns that the Armenian Apostolic Church (AAC) would use the new, improved status to renew challenges over the ownership of numerous churches claimed by both the GOC and the AAC.

12.23. Distribution of Religious Denominations in Modern Georgia

The US government estimates the total population of Georgia at 4,9 million (July 2018). According to the 2014 census, GOC members constitute 83,4% of the population, followed by Muslims at 10,7% and members of the Armenian Apostolic Church (AAC) at 2.9%. According to the census, Roman Catholics, Yazidis, Greek Orthodox, Jews, growing numbers of "nontraditional" religious groups such as Baptists, Jehovah's Witnesses, Pentecostals, the International Society of Krishna Consciousness, and individuals who profess no religious preference constitute the remaining 3% of the population.

A small number of mostly ethnic Russians are members of several Orthodox groups not affiliated with the GOC, including the Molokans, Starovers (Old Believers) and Dukhobors (Spirit Wrestlers).

Ethnic Azerbaijanis are predominantly Shia Muslims and form the majority of the populations in the southeastern region of Kvemo-Kartli. Other Muslim groups, including ethnic Georgian Muslims in Adjara and Chechen Kists in the northeast, are predominantly Sunni Moslims. They are also present in Samtskhe-Javakheti. Ethnic Armenians belong primarily to the AAC and constitute the majority of the population in Samtskhe-Javakheti.

12.24. Restitution and Imbalance in the Application of Law

In the public discourse on this subject, some additional criticism was expressed towards the proposed legal instrument: Under the submitted law, Muslim religious associations were not distinguished from each other based on schisms (Shia and Sunni), while Christian religious churches were considered separately. One of the major imbalances in the application of the law is the issue of the equitable restitution of state property to the existing religious denominations. Ownership rights were restored only to the GOC. Starting from 2014, all religious organizations other than GOC, were given the right to use, as opposed to the right to property. This cannot be considered as restitution proper. It is noteworthy that most of the returned property (284 cases in 2016 and 205 in 2017) were related to the Orthodox Christian Church and the Muslim community. For instance, 4 historic buildings of the cult were handed over to non-dominant religious organizations: in 2017, two synagogues in Vani and one synagogue in Sachkhere - to the Jewish Union, and one operational building of cult in Tbilisi – to the Evangelist Lutheran church. There is no separate registry of religious monuments and thus, there is no list of priorities for their restoration. Moreover, despite the existing separation between the State and the Church, the non-religious nature of state education is not always preserved and is frequently violated by interjecting the ecclesiastical curriculum into the secular education system. Over the years, reports - foreign and domestic, refer to examples of indoctrination and proselytism, as well as discrimination against other religious beliefs in the system of public education.

Not all tax benefits legally granted to GOC extend to minority churches.

The government paid compensation to 5 religious groups – the Georgian Orthodox Church, the Muslim community, the Catholic Church, the Armenian Apostolic Church and the Jewish community - for "material and moral damages" they incurred during the Soviet period. In determining the compensation, the government took into account levels of damage and the present conditions of religious groups. Although SARI insists that the payments were of a "partial and symbolic nature."

The media reported that on May 8, by a vote of 96-0, the parliament approved a change to the labor code declaring May 12 a public holiday celebrating Virgin Mary, although, May 12 was already a public holiday, devoted to St. Andrew. In the discussion preceding the parliamentary vote, there were some groundless and totally irrational proposals originating from some Members of Parliament. For example, it was suggested that it was important for Georgia to be officially declared as the domain of Virgin Mary, the statement, which is as illegal as naïve.

The imbalance among different denominations, among which the GOC is the leader, is efficiently used by external as well as domestic forces as a leverage for achieving political goals; in shaping the political orientation during elections, in setting the agenda vis-à-vis the neighbouring states, etc.

In most cases, interference from outside forces is aimed at deepening the confrontation between different denominations and encouraging a split within the state. Unfortunately, despite longstanding traditions of tolerance, this still holds true in Georgia, the country which is rightfully proud of its multicultural, multi-ethnic and multi-religious diversity since ancient times.

References

Abuladze, Ilia. 1955. *Old editions of the books of the life of the Assyrian figures.* Texts by research and dictionary published by Ilia Abuladze. Tbilisi. [In Georgian].

Alasania, Giuli. 2007. "Religious intolerance and ethnic tolerance in Middle Ages (in case of Georgia)." *Historic Collection*, Tbilisi, 289-303, 549.

—. 2006. *Twenty Centuries of Christianity in Georgia.* Tbilisi.

—. 2010. *Twenty Centuries of Christianity in Georgia.* Tbilisi.

Aleksidze, Zaza, ed. 1968. *The Epistle Book.* Armenian Text with Georgian Translation, Research and Commentary by Zaza Aleksidze. Tbilisi. [In Georgian].

Anania Japaridze. 2014. *A Concise History of the Holy Apostolic Church of Georgia,* 236.

Antelava, Ilia, and Nodar Shoshiashvili, eds. 1996. *History of Kartli – The Life of Kartli.* Prepared for publication, with a preface and an explanation of the terms by Ilia Antelava and Nodar Shoshiashvili. Tbilisi. [In Georgian].

Bagrationi, Vakhushti. 1973. *Description of the Kingdom of Georgia, History of Kartli,* IV, Simon Kaukhchishvili. Tbilisi.

Beradze, Tamaz, and Manana Sanadze. 2003. *The History of Georgia.* Tbilisi. [In Georgian].

Berdzenishvili, Nikoloz. 1967. *Issues in the History of Georgia.* IV. Tbilisi.

Chkhartishvili, Mariam. 1994. *Martyrdom and Patience of Saint Eustate Mtskheteli. Life and Citizenship of Saint Serapion Zarzmel.* Tbilisi: Metsniereba. [In Georgian].

Chkhataraishvili, Kakha. 1973. *Church, Essays on the History of Georgia,* IV. Tbilisi.

—. 1973. *Liberation of Western Georgia from Ottoman Domination, Essays on the History of Georgia,* IV. Tbilisi.

Conversion of Kartli. (Revaz Chelishi version), 95. [In Georgian].

Dolidze, Isidore, ed. 1963. *Monuments of Georgian Law.* I. Tbilisi.

—. *Monuments of Old Georgian Hagiographic Literature.* IV. Tbilisi. 1967. [In Georgian].

Enukidze, Tinatin, Valerian Silogava, and Nodar Shoshiashvili, eds. 1984. *Georgian Historical Documents, IX-XIII c.* Tbilisi.

Georgian Prose. 1982. I. Tbilisi. [In Georgian].

Gonikishvili, Mikheil. 1979. *Imereti on the Eve of XVIII-XIX Centuries.* Tbilisi.

Isidore Dolidze, ed., *Monuments of Georgian Law,* I, 402.

Japaridze, Anania. 2014. *A Concise History of the Holy Apostolic Church of Georgia.* Tbilisi.

Javakhishvili, Ivane. 1982. "History of Georgian Law," I, *Thesis,* Vol. VI, 53. Tbilisi.

Kaukhchishvili, Simon. ed. 1959. *History of Kartli,* II. Tbilisi.

Lominadze, Babilina. 1979. *Measures for the Restoration and Settlement of Central Government, Essays on the History of Georgia.* III. Tbilisi.

Lortkipanidze, Marika. 1979. *Foreign and Internal Political Situation of Georgia in XII c. From the 2nd Quarter to the Early 80s, Essays on the History of Georgia,* III. Tbilisi.

Lortkipanidze, Marika. 1979. *The Struggle for the Unification of Georgia (X Century - XI 60s), Essays on the History of Georgia*, III. Tbilisi.

Makharadze, Mirian. 2005. *Georgia-Ottoman Relations in XV Century*. Tbilisi. 80-93.

Metreveli, Elene. 1962. *Materials for the History of the Georgian Colony in Jerusalem*. Tbilisi.

Papuashvili, Tengiz. 1979. *Culture, Essays on the History of Georgia*, III. Tbilisi.

Saria Andria. 2019. "Relation between the State and the Church of Georgia in 1921-1927 years." Doctorate dissertation, Tbilisi.

Surguladze, Akaki, and Paata Surguladze. 1991. *History of Georgia*. Tbilisi.

Tkeshelashvili L. 2012. "The main issuies of the history of the Georgian Church's autocephaly." Doctorate dissertation, Kutaisi.

The Corps of Georgian Historical Documents. I. 1984. Tbilisi.

The Georgian Ethnological dictionary. 2009. Tbilisi. [In Georgian].

The Treaty of Georgievsk: Treaty of 1783 on Russian Entry into Eastern Georgia. 1983. Text prepared for publication. Introduction and notes by Giorgi Paichadze. Tbilisi.

United States Departments of State, Bureau of Democracy, Human Rights, and Labor. *Georgia. International Religious Freedom Report for 2018*.

US Embassy in Georgia. *2019 Report on International Religious Freedom: Georgia (June 10)*.

US Embassy in Georgia. *2019 Report on International Religious Freedom: Georgia (June 10)*.

Vardosanidze, Sergo. 2001. *Orthodox Apostolic Church of Georgia in the 1917-1952-ies*, Tbilisi.

—. 2014. *The Georgian Church in the 50-70-ies of the twentieth century. History unvarnished*. Tbilisi.

—. (n.d). *The Georgian Church on the International Field. – The History Unvarnished*. Tibilisi.

Women's Initiatives Supporting Group (WISG), LGBT persons' rights, et al. *Protection of Religious Minorities. Report on the Monitoring of the Implementation of Human Rights Strategies and Action Plans for 2016-2017*.

Zhordania, Tedo. ed. 1897. *Chronicles*. II. Tbilisi.

About the Authors

Jean Leo Leonard

Jean Léo Léonard (62) is full professor in anthropological linguistics at Montpellier 3 Université (France). He works on general dialectology (including linguistic typology) and the interdisciplinary study of the anthropological context of the typological diversity of languages. Since his dissertation on dialectal variation on the island of Noirmoutier (1991), in the Poitevin-Saintongeais domain, he has developed the "Toulouse" variant of ethnolinguistics (Dinguirard, Séguy, Fossat): an approach to dialectal and geolinguistic variation that is sensitive to the ecology of the interactions and sociolinguistic pressures that languages experience through the fabric of their dialectal networks. His contribution to dialectometry evolved in the context of Complex Systems (with Marco Patriarca and Els Heinsalu, NICPB, Tallinn, Estonia), including cladistics, alongside with Pierre Darlu (Inserm and CNRS). More recently, Jean Léo Léonard used Levenshtein's algorithm for the study of Occitan (THESOC database, with Guylaine Brun-Trigaud and Flore Picard), Mazatec (IUF project and PPC11 operation of the Labex EFL, Paris) and Georgian (IDEX project LaDyCa at Sorbonne University, 2017-18, co-directed with Prof. Tamar Makharoblidze, ILIA State University, Tbilisi). The LaDyCa project (*Language Dynamics in the Caucasus*) explored language dynamics from the standpoint of "Alpine Linguistic and Ethnic Geography," as defined by Johanna Nichols in a seminal paper published in 2004: the multidisciplinary survey of areas of high linguistic diversity layered from highlands to foothills, Lowlands and the sea shore, entailing a complex web of relationships and interactions intertwining languages and communal aggregates (linguistic communities) for centuries in a complex biotope.

Tinatin Margalitadze

Tinatin Margalitadze is Professor of Lexicography at the School of Arts and Sciences of Ilia State University and research director of the Centre for Lexicography and Language Technologies.

Since 1985 one of the compilers, editors, then editor in chief and publisher of the *Comprehensive English-Georgian Dictionary* (14 published volumes; online version – www.dict.ge, comprising 100 000 entries). One of the compilers and editor of *English-Georgian Learner's Dictionary* (30 000 entries https://learners.dict.ge). Editor of *English-Georgian Military Online Dictionary* (10 000 entries http://mil.dict.ge), *English-Georgian Biology Online Dictionary* (23 000 entries http://bio.dict.ge) and *English-Russian-Georgian Technical Online Dictionary* (18 000 entries http://techdict.ge).

Tinatin Margalitadze studied linguistics and English at Iv. Javakhishvili Tbilisi State University (TSU), Georgia. She did her postgraduate studies at the Chair of English Philology of TSU and in 1983 defended her candidate's thesis (PhD). In 1997 as a visiting scholar she spent one term at the Department of Linguistics, Cambridge University, Great Britain. She was an organizer and chair of the XVII EURALEX International Congress (Tbilisi, 2016) and co-organizer of two International Symposia in Lexicography in Batumi (2010 and 2012). Her research interests include: bilingual lexicography (general and specialized); the problem of equivalence in non-related and related languages; universal models of polysemous words; history of Georgian lexicography; parallel corpora; corpus-driven lexicography; machine translation.

Giorgi Meladze

George Meladze – Doctor of Philology, a senior editor of the Centre for Lexicography and Language Technologies of the School of Arts and Sciences at Ilia State University, Tbilisi, Georgia. From 1994 he was one of the compilers of the Comprehensive English-Georgian Dictionary (CEGD) and subsequently, an editor; 14 fascicles of the dictionary have been published so far. In 2010 an online version of the Dictionary, comprising 110,000 entries was uploaded to the Internet (www.dict.ge). He is also one of the compilers of the English-Georgian Learner's Dictionary comprising 30,000 entries (https://learners.dict.ge); English-Georgian Military Online Dictionary (10,000 entries—http://mil.dict.ge); English-Georgian Biology Online Dictionary (23,000 entries—http://bio.dict.ge); and English-Russian-Georgian Technical Online Dictionary (18,000 entries— http://tech.dict.ge); he was also the Editor-in-Chief of the Chrestomathy of Gothic and Anglo-Saxon Written Records (https://germanic.ge/en/got/).

In 1993 George Meladze graduated from the Faculty of the Western European Languages and Literature of Tbilisi State University (TSU). In 2016, in the same university, he defended his doctoral thesis titled "The Issues of Linguistic Equivalence on the Example of the Vocabulary of Germanic Origin (based on the material from English, German, Swedish and other languages" and earned the academic degree of Doctor of Philology (Ph.D.). His scientific interests include: comparative linguistics; lexicography; Germanic languages; the origin of language; digital humanities; parallel corpora; corpus-based lexicography; machine translation.

Nino Sharashenidze

Nino Sharashenidze is an associate professor at Tbilisi State University and has a PhD in Linguistics. She is the author of four monographs, more than 50 scientific articles and several textbooks for both schoolchildren and university students. Her field of study is historical linguistics, morphology, dialectology, semantics, Georgian language teaching methods. She is an expert in teaching Georgian as a second and foreign language and works as a consultant at the Teacher Professional Development Center.

Rusudan Gersamia

Rusudan Gersamia is an associate professor of the School of Arts and Sciences at Ilia State University, a specialist of Kartvelian languages - Megrelian and Laz. She is the author of a few dozen publications and several books. For the last few years, her subject of interest has been the study of the semantics of space and motion. The results are reflected in the monograph *Space and Motion in Language Representation (Analysis of Megrelian and Laz Linguistic Data)* Tbilisi: Ilia State University Press, 2020 – Isabella Kobalava is a co-author.

Ellen Lau

Ellen Lau is Associate Professor in the Department of Linguistics and the Neuroscience and Cognitive Science Program at the University of Maryland, College Park. She serves as the Co-Director of the KIT-Maryland MEG Lab and collaborates with the Maryland Language Science Center at the University of Maryland. She specializes in neurolinguistic investigations of natural languages.

Maria Polinsky

Maria Polinsky is Professor of Linguistics at the University of Maryland, College Park, and Director of the National Heritage Research Center at UCLA. Her main interests are in theoretical syntax, and her research combines theoretical work with in-depth investigation of understudied languages. Another area of her interest is in heritage languages and bilingualism. She is the author of over a hundred scholarly articles and several books including *Deconstructing Ergativity* (2016) and *Heritage Languages and Their Speakers* (2018).

Nancy Clarke

Nancy Clarke is a Senior Conversational Designer at Amazon Web Services in Boston, MA.

Michaela Socolof

Michaela Socolof is a graduate student in Linguistics at McGill University.

Svetlana Berikashvili

Svetlana Berikashvili holds a Ph.D. in Greek Linguistics from the Iv. Javakhishvili Tbilisi State University. Her research interests lie in theoretical syntax, contact linguistics and morphology. She has worked on a less-studied variety of Pontic Greek as spoken by the Pontic-Greek community of Georgia and has published several works on different aspects of Greek and Georgian grammar (including three research monographs). Nowadays, she is engaged in the joint research programme of the Ilia State University and the Georg August University of Göttingen doing research in generative syntax.

Irina Lobzhanidze

Irina Lobzhanidze is Professor of Linguistics at Ilia State University, Georgia, where she is also the Director of the Institute of Linguistic Studies. She received her Ph.D. in Linguistics from Ilia State University, Georgia. She held visiting Georgian studies fellow position at the Oxford School of Global and Area Studies (2019-2020). Her main research interests lie in the areas of morphology and syntax, and their interface. She has worked extensively on developing language processing tools and resources for Georgian and covered topics on Natural Language Processing, particularly, the computational modelling of Georgian Language implemented as a finite-state transducer. She is the Linguistic Coordinator of the Georgian Language Corpus (GLC), a co-author of the Dictionary of Idioms (2014-2017) and the Principal Researcher in the construction of the Wardrops' Collection Online (WCO).

Yidian SHE

Yidian She is a PhD student in Linguistics, working under the supervision of Professor Jean-Léo Léonard at École Doctorale 58, Université Paul Valéry – Montpellier. He holds a master's degree in Linguistics from Sorbonne Université, France. He is interested in the Kartvelian languages and his master's dissertation focused on the interface of deep structure and surface structure in Georgian, Megrelian and Laz. Currently, his doctoral work explores the diasystem of Svan language (Kartvelian) and the ethnolinguistics of Svaneti (Georgia). His other interests include Sinitic tonology and the tone sandhi of Wenzhounese (Sinitic).

Léa Nash

Léa Nash is a Professor of Linguistics at Université Paris 8. Her area of specialization is syntax, with a special interest in Romance, Slavic and South Caucasian languages. She received her PhD in linguistics from Université Paris 8 in 1995. She has published many articles on argument structure, case theory, ergativity, and edited several volumes on intransitive verbs and complex predicates. She is one of the cofounders South Caucasian Chalk Circle Project which aims to create an international research community of scholars working on Kartvelian languages.

Tamar Makharoblidze

Tamar Makharoblidze is a Full professor of the School of Arts and Sciences at Ilia State University. Her areas of interests are: General linguistics, World languages – Kartvelian languages (Georgian), Sign languages - Georgian Sign language, typology, language acquisition. She is an author of a few new linguistic theories, 30 monographs and textbooks, and more than 100 scientific publications. She is a Member of a several scientific organizations and editorial boards for various academic publishing houses worldwide.

Makharoblidze has produced screenplays and stage plays, published books for children, more than 200 documentary films, TV and Radio programs with different worldwide media.

In 2017 she was awarded by Shota Rustaveli National Scientific Foundation as THE BEST SCIENTIST in the field of Kartvelian/Georgian Studies.

Ekaterine Nanitashvili

Ekaterine Nanitashvili is a PhD student at the Carl Friedrich Lehmann-Haupt International Doctoral School in Philology, linguistics funded by Shota Rustaveli National Science Foundation of Georgia and Volkswagen Foundation, the first dual program of the University of Göttingen and Ilia State University, and she is the first doctoral student in the field of SL studies in Georgia. The title of her PhD thesis is "The argument structure in GESL." Nanitashvili actively participates in educational scientific researches and linguistic events.

Kevin Tuite

Kevin Tuite teaches anthropology at the Université de Montréal. He has been conducting ethnological and linguistic fieldwork in Georgia since 1985. Recent publications include *Sacred Places, Emerging Spaces: Pilgrims, Saints and Scholars in the Caucasus* (edited with Tsypylma Darieva and Florian Mühlfried) and *On the origin of Kartvelian version*. His current research interests include a five-year project on vernacular religion in Soviet Georgia (funded by the Social Sciences and Humanities Research Council of Canada), a grammar of the Svan language, and a study of the cult of St. George in the Caucasus.

Paata Bukhrashvili

Paata Bukhrashvili is a full professor of History and a Head of the Laboratory of Visual Anthropology and Local History at Ilia State University. He has received Postdoctoral education as a Volkswagen Foundation Fellow at the Institute for

Oriental Archaeology and Art at the University of Halle-Wittenberg (Germany) with Prof. Dr. Winfried Orthmann between 1998-1999. Research thesis on "The Economic and Cultural Structure of the South Caucasian Population in the Third Millennium B.C."

Romanoz Dolidze

Romanoz Dolidze is an independent scholar based in Tbilisi. He is retired. Dolidze worked at TSU cine-photo laboratory as a documentalist.

Tamari Lomtadze

Tamari Lomtadze is a Professor, Department of Georgian Philology, Akaki Tsereteli State University, Kutaisi, Georgia; Senior Researcher, Arnold Chikobava Institute of Linguistics, Iv. Javakhishvili Tbilisi State University, Tbilisi, Georgia. Tamari Lomtadze is the author of numerous scholarly articles/academic essays, several books/monographs and textbooks. Her research focuses on Judeo-Georgian, Language policy, sociolinguistics and cultural Linguistics. Tamari lomtadze is a member of Association of Jewish Studies (AJS) and European Associations of Jewish Studies (EAJS).

Manana Mikadze

Manana Mikadze is a Doctor of Pedagogical Sciences, a full professor of Kutaisi Akaki Tsereteli State University. She is the author of 8 monographs in the field of methodology, 29 textbooks, and more than 300 scientific articles. Has participated in various scientific forums around the world. She is also a Director of the Foundation for the development of Art and Pedagogical Sciences and is the Editor-in-Chief of the Scientific Peer Reviewed Journal "Language and Culture." Manana Mikadze's scientific interests are: the methodology of teaching Georgian and English, grammar, lexicology; Language of translation, language policy and literature.

Giuli Alasania

Giuli Alasania is a founder and the President of the University of Georgia. She was a professor of the Tbilisi State University since 1990. Alasania was a vice-rector of the IBSU in 2000-2014. As a Doctor of Historic Sciences, she published 142 papers, 12 monographs in the fields of the source studies of history of Georgia and the Caucasus, history of the Middle East, History of Turks and Turkey, relations of Georgians and Turks, history of Georgian culture, national self-determination.

   Alasania has been awarded several prizes.

Index

David the Builder, 259, 260, 262,
263, 266
deictic orientation, 85
deictic pronouns,, 73
deixis, 87
demonstrative, 178, 180, 183, 184,
186, 187, 189, 190, 191, 192,
193, 194, 197, 198
demonstrative phrase, 180, 184,
186, 189, 190, 191, 194, 197, 198
derivation, 122
determiner, 128
diasystemic modelling, 170
direction of motion, 82
dissimilation, 174
DP/pronouns distinction, 131
dynamic principal parts, 169
dynamicity, 76

E

Elijah, 223, 225
Ellis, George, 36
emphatic vowel, 124, 125, 129
ergative, 122, 124, 125, 126, 128,
129, 130, 131, 132, 136, 141,
142, 144, 146
ergative construction, 122
ergative-absolutive languages,
124, 130
ethnic minorities, 238, 242, 245,
246, 247, 248, 249, 250
event-related brain potential, 107,
108, 109, 110, 112, 113, 114,
115, 116, 117, 118
experiencer, 138
exponence paradigm, 163
eye gaze agreement, 207
eye-gazing, 203

F

Fähnrich, Heinz, 41
falling (descending) diphthong,
123
Figure., 77
finite-state morphology, 123
fusion, 75
future, 139

G

genitive, 123, 125, 126, 127, 128,
132, 141, 143
Georgian, 107, 108, 109, 110, 112,
114, 117, 118, 119
Georgian Orthodox Church, 266,
272
Georgian verb template, 156, 158
GESL, 203
Gippert, Jost, 46
Gogolaurta, 218, 219, 221, 222, 224,
227, 228, 229, 234
Gorgasali,Vakhtang, 255, 258
Gorgijanidze, Parsadan, 33
Grigol of Khandzta, 258
Gurian, 150, 163, 166
Gvarjaladze, Isidorè, 41

H

headless, 178, 179, 180, 186, 187,
188, 189, 190, 192, 193, 195,
196, 197, 198
heteroclisis, 173
holistic approach, 164

I

implicational graph, 171
incremental approach, 152
indirect speech marker, 124

Lightning Source UK Ltd.
Milton Keynes UK
UKHW020017051022
409941UK00009B/174/J

9 781648 894756